THE THEMATIC
APPERCEPTION TEST

THE THEMATIC APPERCEPTION TEST

The Theory and Technique of Interpretation

By

SILVAN S. TOMKINS, Ph.D.

*Research Associate, College Entrance
Examination Board;
Visiting Lecturer in Clinical
Psychology, Princeton University
Formerly Lecturer in Clinical Psychology
Harvard Psychological Clinic
Harvard University*

With the Collaboration of
ELIZABETH J. TOMKINS, B.A.

GRUNE & STRATTON

New York and London

Library of Congress Catalog Card No. Med47-3536

First printing, October 1947
Second printing, September 1948
Third printing, May 1950
Fourth printing, November 1952
Fifth printing, October 1955
Sixth printing, October 1959
Seventh printing, May 1962
Eighth printing, July 1965

Printed in U.S.A. (E-W)

To

ROBERT W. WHITE

PREFACE

This is a book about a test which is barely fifteen years old—a promising adolescent emerging from the rites of puberty. The TAT has not yet attained full stature, that is certain, and perhaps this book should have awaited its further development. It is with the hope that the maturation of the test might be accelerated that I venture to publish a series of lectures delivered to a seminar on the diagnosis of personality. Many of the characteristics of lectures will be found in these pages—more questions are asked than answered, hypotheses are illustrated more than proven, much that might have been mentioned briefly is laboriously illustrated, and what might have been elaborated is expressed obliquely. It is a workbook and not a compilation of established doctrine. I have addressed myself to two audiences: those who are completely unfamiliar with the TAT and research psychologists whose interest I hoped to enlist in the exploration of a host of problems—problems of test interpretation which are also of import for the science of which the test is a constituent element. Because of these aims, the psychologist who is long familiar with the technique of interpretation and whose interests are primarily diagnostic may find too much that is well known and too much that is remote from his immediate clinical concern.

There is much that should have been said which has not been said. Evidence is sometimes too slender to support generalization. This is due in part to my ignorance, in part to our collective ignorance. In some measure this was necessitated by the exigencies of publication. Complete documentation would have necessitated an encyclopedia rather than a book. For this reason the reader is asked to take much on faith. It is proper therefore that he be told something of the larger sample on which this work is based. I have analyzed over 300 protocols of individuals of both sexes who ranged in age from 5 to 55 years. Approximately 200 were normal and about 100 were psychoneurotic or presented behavior problems. There are no more than ten psychotic records in this sample; this is the area in which my experience is most seriously limited. More important than the number of records is the care with which one has examined the history of the individual who told the stories. I have frequently compared my interpretations with material gathered by other clinicians who employed a variety of techniques in the study of the same individual. When this was not possible I personally gathered other evidence by interview and clinical and experimental techniques. More specifically, these records were obtained from cooperative studies at the Harvard Psychological Clinic, from a series of records which I analyzed as consultant to the Dartmouth Eye Institute, from a group of young women at a junior college, from industrial consultant work, vocational counseling, diagnostic testing of neurotics, and finally from the records collected by graduate students in the course of their clinical training.

This is the work of one who turned from psychology to the study of philosophy some fifteen years ago when psychology seemed indifferent to the problem of personality. The theory of value seemed to me an inquiry more pertinent to the study of man than did any investigation of either the higher or lower mental processes. It was in the course of postdoctoral work in philosophy that a reading of *Explorations in Personality* by Henry A. Murray and the workers of the Harvard Psychological Clinic renewed my enthusiasm for the science I had found so unrewarding as a graduate student. Under the guidance of Robert W. White I resumed my study of psychology and learned from him the technique of interpretation of the TAT. His friendship sustained the effort of a decade which is reflected in these pages—the effort of a philosopher to acquire the competence of a professional psychologist. His careful and unhurried work provided at once a model and support for one who was temperamentally unsuited to the prevailing climate of the academic scene—the coercive clamor that the tempo of publication be ever accelerated. For these reasons I have dedicated this book to Robert W. White, Director of the Harvard Psychological Clinic.

My greatest single indebtedness is to my wife, Elizabeth Tomkins, who collaborated with me. Chapters VI, VII, VIII, and IX are as much her work as mine. She analyzed mountains of protocols, battled against my obscurities and infelicities of expression and rewrote large sections of the manuscript. These labors are gratefully acknowledged by her name on the title page.

My debt to Henry A. Murray is great. It was his work which turned me back to the study of psychology. In his seminars I have learned much of what I know of personality. His TAT workshops provided the stimulation for many of the ideas in this work which are original. Though much of what I have said diverges in varying degrees from his doctrine, the intellectual ferment created by his genius provided the conditions necessary for creative effort. His work with the TAT opened vistas of the possibilities inherent in projective techniques which none of the workers of the Harvard Psychological Clinic will forget.

Any book is necessarily a social undertaking into which one's colleagues are inevitably drawn. My debts are many. To my friend Sheldon J. Korchin I owe thanks for heroic efforts in coping with my obscurantism, which he reminded me is a privilege reserved for philosophers. Chapter V owes any clarity that it may possess to the careful criticism of Eugenia Hanfmann, Robert W. White, and Eli Robins. Chapter I is better than it might have been for the incisive critique of Leo Postman. I called upon the experience of

Morris Stein in connection with Chapters VIII and X. To Thelma G. Alper
and her husband, Abraham Alper, I acknowledge an indebtedness for their
extremely generous expenditure of time and energy when my own energy was
at its lowest ebb. I am grateful to Mrs. Korchin for her assistance in reading
proof. Mrs. Hahn prepared the index—for which I want to thank her again—
since this is the second time she has volunteered her good services. To Mrs.
Brecher I owe the typing of this manuscript, and to her husband, Melvin
Brecher, I am grateful for countless assists in the birth process. To Henry
Stratton I should like to express my gratitude for his infinite tolerance in
bearing with delays in the preparation of this manuscript which tried his
patience and mine.

S. S. T.

April 1947
Cambridge, Massachusetts

CONTENTS

PAGE

PREFACE vii

CHAPTER

   I. History and Development of the Thematic Apperception Test..   1

  II. The Technique of Administration 21

 III. The Scoring Scheme 26

 IV. Introduction to the Technique of Interpretation 42

   V. Level Analysis 55

 VI. Diagnosis of Personality: The Region of the Family 109

VII. Diagnosis of Personality: The Region of Love, Sex, and Marital
      Relationships 153

VIII. Diagnosis of Personality: The Region of Social Relationships... 201

 IX. Diagnosis of Personality: Work and Vocational Setting 234

  X. Diagnosis and Psychotherapy 266

REFERENCES 287

INDEX 293

Chapter I

HISTORY AND DEVELOPMENT OF THE THEMATIC APPERCEPTION TEST

A. Precursors of the Thematic Apperception Test *

Sensation and perception, long the concern of philosophy, claimed the exclusive energies of the infant science, experimental psychology, for the first two decades of its neonatal existence. In the closing decades of the nineteenth century, however, more complex and higher mental processes were brought under experimental scrutiny. Memory, attention, reaction, and feelings were yielding to experimental control.

It was in 1879 that the first free-association experiment was performed. Francis Galton (33) was the experimenter; his subject, himself. Prophetic were his findings that associations which recurred several times, over a four month period, could be traced largely to his boyhood and youth, and associations which occurred only once stemmed from more recent experience. The diagnostic power of this method did not escape Galton. "It would be very instructive to print the actual records at length, made by many experimenters . . . but it would be too absurd to print one's own singly. They lay bare the foundations of a man's thoughts with more vividness and truth than he would probably care to publish to the world." But he pursued this no further. The study of individual differences in imagery proved more congenial to Galton.

By the turn of the century, experimental psychology was invading the "highest" mental process. The issue was an experimental psychology of thought. This was for some time experimental psychology's highest reach.

It was the educator who first turned the psychologist's attention to more complex problems. Binet's scale for measuring general intelligence was in part an outgrowth of his work as a member of a commission appointed in 1904 by the French Minister of Public Instruction. It was the commission's assignment to make recommendations for the instruction of feeble-minded children in the public schools of Paris. A year later, in July 1905, the school authorities of Breslau asked Ebbinghaus (26), among others, to investigate the fatigue effects of the continuous five-hour session in the schools of that city. In the course of this investigation Ebbinghaus developed what he called "a real test of intelligence . . . a simple, easily applied device for testing those intellectual abilities that are fundamentally important and significant both in the school and in life."

* This survey of the history of the Thematic Apperception Test systematically excludes precursors of other projective techniques. Several reviews of the history of the Rorschach and other projective techniques have appeared elsewhere.

The stimuli requisite for the study of personality came in large part from the mental hospital. The mental testing movement was too narrowly conceived. Its scope was defined by educators and psychologists alike, primarily in terms of intellectual function. As a consequence the study of personality fell to the psychiatrist, expert primarily in the biological sciences. His was the responsibility for applying a nonexistent science of personality. The psychologist was both unwilling and unable to provide either a theoretical or experimental foundation for psychopathology.

In such a climate of psychological opinion it was inevitable that techniques and findings full of promise for the study of personality would remain unnoticed, to be rediscovered when the science was ready. This was the case with Brittain's (17) paper, "A Study of Imagination," which appeared in 1907 in *The Pedagogical Seminary*. He presented a series of nine pictures to a group of boys and girls ranging in age from 13 to 20 years and asked them to write stories suggested by the pictures presented. The stories were analyzed according to their use of names of persons or animals, their use of the first person, use of details of the pictures, their imaginative quality, their unity, length, explanatory power, and their use of religious, moral, and social elements. Significant sex differences were found. Girls' stories revealed more religious, moral, and social elements, more interest in clothes and the preparation of food; boys were more interested in the consumption of food. The stories told by the girls were full of pity, sadness, and the fear of being left alone. Brittain considered this "almost a neurotic tendency" caused by a society which blocked normal social and physical activity for girls. He concluded that the correspondence of a particular kind of physical activity, affective life, and imaginal activity suggested some causal relationship. He envisioned the possibility that these three aspects of life were mutually interactive.

One year later there appeared a similar study by Libby (52), who investigated the relation between the imagination and the feelings of school children. He found that the stories of younger children were "objective," those of the older children more "subjective," and that the significant difference occurred between the thirteenth and fourteenth year. Libby's interests in this study were developmental. He thought he had proved that the imagination of pupils in high school was not poorer than that of grade school pupils.

A variant of the story technique was reported by Clark (19) at the ninth International Congress of Psychoanalysts in 1925. He used what he called the "phantasy method" for the psychoanalysis of narcissistic patients who were incapable of developing a transference neurosis. He requested his patients to imagine themselves as infants and to report the feelings and attitudes which very young infants might have. He found that by this indirect method he was able to evoke material permeated with the emotional feelings of infantile life which enabled him to cure patients otherwise inaccessible to psychoanalytic therapy.

Brittain's original technique remained unexploited for twenty-five years. It was rediscovered by the psychiatrist Schwartz (92), working at the Clinic for Juvenile Research in Detroit. In the overcrowded conditions of the juvenile court clinic he did not have sufficient time to develop the rapport requisite for psychiatric interviewing. As an aid in initiating the interview of delinquent children he developed the Social Situation Picture Test. This consisted of eight pictures representing situations most frequently encountered in the histories of delinquents. The subject was first asked to describe what he saw, then to tell what the boy in the picture was thinking. On the basis of the subject's responses, the examiner then questioned the subject further, following up every "lead" suggested by the child's answers. The child was then asked to tell what *he* would think and do if he were the boy in the picture. The test was never widely used by psychologists, perhaps because of the limited scope of the pictures but more probably because standardization was made difficult by the serial questioning in which the nature of each successive question depended on the child's response to the previous question.

B. The Thematic Apperception Test

The first publication on the Thematic Apperception Test by Morgan and Murray (62) appeared in 1935. The test, they said, was based on the well known fact that an individual confronted with an ambiguous social situation and required to interpret it was likely to reveal his own personality in this process. While interpreting the objective situation the individual was apt to be less defensive, less aware of the scrutiny of the examiner, and consequently more likely to reveal much of his own inner life. At first, subjects were instructed to interpret the action in each picture and to make a plausible guess as to the preceding events and the final outcome. Only through experience was it learned that much more was revealed if the subject was asked to create a dramatic story.

Three years later, in *Explorations in Personality* (63), the preliminary Thematic Apperception Test * results were integrated with the general theory of personality developed by Murray and the workers at the Harvard Psychological Clinic.

Since 1938 the scope of inquiry has expanded, the pace of research quickened. The TAT was employed in the study of a wide variety of psychopathological syndromes: hysteria, anxiety hysteria, and obsessive-compulsive neurosis (2), schizophrenic psychosis (6, 12, 37, 71, 78), head injury (73), psychopathic delinquency (49), stuttering (75), and mental deficiency (86, 88,

---

* Hereinafter referred to as TAT.

89). The TAT has proven a useful instrument in the exploration of such diverse areas as child development (83), social attitudes and sentiments (14), assessment of military personnel (39, 67) and, most recently, culture and personality (40, 68).

C. PROBLEMS OF RELIABILITY

There is a twofold problem in connection with the reliability of the TAT. First, to what extent do independent analysts agree with each other in their interpretations of the same TAT protocols? Second, what is the degree of similarity between TAT protocols of a given subject in successive administrations of the test? Let us consider first the reliability of TAT interpretation.

I. INTERPRETER RELIABILITY

The extent to which independent interpreters of TAT protocols agree with each other will depend somewhat on the nature of the protocol being interpreted, the training and competence of the interpreter, and the conceptual scheme employed in interpretation. As a consequence, the reliability coefficients of correlation reported by various investigators are themselves variable, ranging from coefficients of $+0.30$ to $+0.96$.

Sanford (84), employing the quantitative need-press analysis on the TAT's of children, reported a rank-order correlation of $+0.57$ for need ratings and $+0.54$ for press ratings by 4 judges rating the protocols of 10 subjects. Mayman and Kutner (58) have reported high contingency coefficients for ratings of both formal and content characteristics of stories. (The coefficients of correlation were not reported in their preliminary note.) Mayman, in his review of Slutz's paper, reports the latter to have found good agreement between interpretations made independently by two examiners. Slutz (94) in her published abstract does not cite correlation coefficients.

Combs (23) reported a reliability study on the ratings made by 4 judges on 10 protocols. The mean percentage of agreement between 3 of the judges and Combs was 60 per cent. Six months after his original analysis he reanalyzed 100 TAT stories as a check on the reliability of his own ratings. The mean percentage of agreement with his own original ratings was 68.8 per cent. Both of these results seemed disappointingly low to Combs.

Harrison and Rotter (39) independently analyzed the protocols of 70 subjects given five pictures in group administration. On the basis of these TAT stories, they rated candidates for Armored Officer Candidate School at Fort Knox on emotional maturity and stability. They employed a three-point scale and also a five-point scale. On the shorter scale, complete agreement was reached in 64 per cent of the ratings, partial agreement in 30 per cent and complete disagreement in 6 per cent. The contingency coefficient for the three-point scale, when corrected for broad categories by the method of Garrett, was $+0.73$. For the five-point scale, complete agreement was found in 43 per cent of the cases; complete disagreement, in no case. Considering all ratings, with agreement arbitrarily defined as a disparity of one point or less, and disagreement as a disparity greater than one, there was an essential concurrence in 74 per cent of the ratings and disagreement in 26 per cent. The corrected contingency coefficient for the five-point scale was $+0.77$.

Clark (21) reported tetrachoric correlations on the agreement of two sets of ratings on one story from 50 subjects. All tetrachoric correlations were $+0.90$ or above for the following categories: effect of the environment on the organism, reaction of the organism to the environment, adequacy of the principal character, and the nature of the endings. But on the rating of "needs" expressed in the story the correlation dropped to $+0.30$. Clark gives one example of the type of disagreement responsible for this drop in inter-interpreter reliability. In a story dealing with a man's wish to get married, Clark rated the wish as indicating two needs, affection and sensory gratification (sex), whereas her co-worker rated it simply as a need for affection. This is in part a matter of clarity of definition of the scoring categories.

This type of unreliability typically disappears in cooperative research when co-workers have the opportunity of discussing the rationale of their ratings. Thus, in TAT workshops, it is common for the reliability of ratings to be very low at the beginning but to increase to respectable magnitude with practice. The exact degree of consensus is a function of the competence of the group and the time they spend in thrashing out their differences. At the Harvard Psychological Clinic some investigators have been able to achieve interinterpreter reliabilities as high as $+0.95$. But this hard-won group achievement will remain an essentially local phenomenon until TAT investigators agree on some mutually acceptable conceptual scheme for rating stories. At the moment each investigator is a law unto himself. Fruitful comparison of research findings is all but impossible without some degree of standardization. But it is not easy to assess the advantages of early standardization against the possible yield of the creative ferment of a longer period of free experimentation.

The reliabilities reported above range from $+0.30$ to $+0.96$. Since these reliabilities are a function of using diverse scoring schemes, of diverse case material, of judges of varying ability and acquaintance with the scoring schemes, it is not surprising to find that the reported rater reliabilities are so variable. Reliability in the rating of material as complex as TAT protocols will not come easily. It will be an achievement requiring the active cooperation of psychologists on a nation-wide basis.

So much for interpreter reliability. Let us turn now to the problem of repeat reliability—the degree of similarity between the TAT protocols of a given subject in successive administrations of the test. The degree of repeat reliability must necessarily depend on the basic stability of the personality and its fluctuations as a function of time. The more stable the personality the more we should expect repetitions of the test to yield similar protocols. If the personality is less stable we should expect repetitions of the test to reflect this fact in a lower degree of repeat reliability. In part the degree of repeat reliability also depends on the magnitude of the temporal interval between successive administrations of the test. If we were to administer the TAT to an individual at the age of 6 and again at the age of 30, we should certainly expect to find greater difference between the two protocols than if the test had been repeated one month after the first administration. Differences between successive administrations of the test may then be expected either if the individual is changing rapidly or if the change is slower but the test is repeated after a long period of time. Finally, we might well expect a decrease in repeat reliability if experimentally induced changes are introduced between successive administrations of the TAT.

a) *As a Function of Time Between Successive Administrations*

In a study by the writer (99), 45 young women ranging in age from 18 to 20 years were given the TAT by group administration. Three groups of 15 members each were then chosen at random from the group of 45. The first group of 15 was given the test two months later; the second group, six months later; and the third group, ten months later. These stories were then rated according to Murray's quantitative need-press scheme. The ratings between the first administration and successive administrations were then intercorrelated. The reliability coefficients for the group given the test two months later was +0.80; for the second group, in which there had been a six month interval between repeated administration, the reliability coefficient fell to +0.60, and for the third group, after a ten month interval, to +0.50. The difference between repetition at two months and at ten months is clearly significant. Between two and six months and between six and ten months the differences are less reliable. It is clear, however, that as we increase the time between successive administrations the repeat reliability of the TAT declines. This however is a general group trend and need not be true of any particular individual. If the personality of the individual is extremely stable, the temporal interval between repeated administrations may make little or no difference. Let us examine the influence of this factor on repeat reliability.

b) *As a Function of the Stability of the Personality*

We shall compare the repeat reliability of three sets of data from individuals whose personalities differed in their stability. First, a group of rapidly developing adolescents, second a neurotic whose personality underwent spontaneous reconstruction, and third a neurotic of a particularly stable personality structure.

1. *Personality of low rigidity.* Childhood and adolescence represent the period of maximal plasticity of the individual—the organism is never again so malleable. We should therefore expect successive administrations of the TAT during this period to yield the lowest repeat reliability. This is in fact the case. Sanford (84) reported an average repeat reliability of +0.46 of the needs expressed by children and adolescents who had been given the TAT at yearly intervals over a three year period.

2. *Personality of moderate rigidity.* In the study of Joseph Kidd reported by White (104), the TAT was administered when Kidd was 19 and again when he was 22. This period was witness to a spontaneous process of reconstruction of his disorganized personality. Although psychoneurotic, his personality was not particularly rigid. Consequently we might have anticipated marked changes when the TAT was repeated three years later. This was the case. In the earlier test there were three main themes: the longing for lost love, the transformation of cruelty and greed by the sympathetic interest of an older man, and a theme of sadism and masochism. In the second set of stories the first two themes had virtually disappeared. This probably reflected Kidd's working through the grief occasioned by an unhappy love affair and the improvement in his relation with his father, with less need for regeneration and a greater tolerance of himself. There was also more open expression of the aggressive and acquisitive wishes from which he had previously been rescued by the older man. This represents a modification of the remaining theme. White does not report the coefficient of reliability between these two administrations. Although there are continuities between these two sets of stories, it is evident that the repeat reliability is not high, though perhaps higher than the correlation of +0.46 reported for adolescents. It is clear that the changes in the personality after a three year period have been reflected in the second TAT and thereby reduce its repeat reliability. Let us consider now a personality of marked rigidity.

3. *Personality of marked rigidity.* In a study by the writer (98), a psychoneurotic subject, "Z," 18 years old, was presented five days a week with a different picture and asked to write a story about it. This was continued for a period of ten months. These were pictures other than those included in the TAT set and were used in order to assess the influence of the nature of the picture on the repeat reliability of the TAT. In addition the complete

set (30) of TAT pictures was administered three times, at intervals of three months. The third administration was immediately followed by a fourth administration when the subject was under the influence of alcohol. Moreover, the subject's dreams were recorded over the ten month period and the results of approximately seventy-five hours of additional testing and experimentation were available. In general, the main themes that appeared in the first 30 stories given at the beginning of the. investigation were repeated in the second, third, and fourth administrations of the TAT, as well as in the stories written daily. During a two week period of euphoria the subject was presented with very pleasantly toned pictures in an attempt to modify his typically unhappy stories, but despite this change of both pictures and mood the stories remained the same. The writer submitted half of all the stories to one rater and the other half to another rater. This procedure yielded a correlation coefficient of +0.91 between approximately 200 stories rated by one interpreter and 200 stories rated by another interpreter. It was clear that the constancy of these stories, despite differences in pictures, time of administration, mode of administration (spoken and written), condition of the subject (normal, euphoric, intoxicated, fatigued, etc.) was a function of the unusual rigidity of this particular person. This rigidity was the consequence of Z's neurosis, which we will discuss at greater length in another chapter.

Thus we have seen that for rapidly developing adolescents the repeat reliability of the TAT is approximately +0.46. In the case of a psychoneurotic who underwent a spontaneous process of reconstruction during a three year period there was a relatively low repeat reliability, but when the personality is extremely stable the TAT will reflect such stability in a repeat reliability as high as a coefficient of correlation of +0.91, in the case of stories told over a period of ten months.

c) *As a Function of Experimentally Induced Changes*

If the TAT were sensitive to transitory fluctuations in the feelings and moods of the individual we would expect these fluctuations to further reduce the repeat reliability of the test. This problem is most easily studied by introducing experimentally induced changes between successive administrations of the TAT.

Bellak (9) administered the TAT before and after sharp criticism of his subjects' stories. He found, following this insult, a statistically significant increase in the amount of aggression expressed in the stories.

Rodnick and Klebanoff (76) administered a modified TAT to the best and most poorly adjusted members of an NYA camp, before and after experimentally induced frustration. The more poorly adjusted group showed, as a result of this frustration, a distinct decrease in themes of superiority, an increase of aggression, and a decrease of themes concerned with "emotional states." The better adjusted group showed an increase in the themes dealing with "emotional states" and no decrease in themes of superiority of the central characters in the stories.

Thus we see that changes in the momentary situation of the individual being tested a second time may reduce the repeat reliability of the TAT. This is clearly the consequence of experimentally induced stress preceding the second administration of the TAT.

We have examined the twofold problem of interpreter and repeat reliability. We have seen that the reported interinterpreter reliability coefficients ranged from $+0.30$ to $+0.96$. We assumed that this variability was a function of using diverse scoring schemes, diverse case material, and of interpreters of varying ability and acquaintance with the scoring schemes.

Repeat reliability was seen to depend in part on the time that elapsed between successive administrations, in part on the stability of the personality being tested, and also on the stability of the individual's environment.

D. PROBLEMS OF VALIDITY

Inasmuch as the TAT is designed to reveal the wishes, expectations, hopes, and fears which underlie overt behavior, the problem of validating the test results is peculiarly difficult. Such impalpable material as hopes and fears frequently cannot be directly observed in overt behavior and have to be inferred from their effects on behavior.

There are however, several avenues of approach open for the study of the validity of the TAT. First, we may compare the TAT with other material, such as past history or dreams, and determine the extent to which these find faithful reflection in the TAT protocol. Second, we may compare this technique with the findings of other techniques administered to the same subjects. The TAT may be compared with the findings of other projective techniques, such as the Rorschach; it may be compared with psychoanalytic study of the same individuals; or it may be compared with the intensive case study which employs a wide variety of techniques converging on the same individual. Third, we may assess TAT results on groups or individuals whose characteristics are well known, and determine the extent to which these characteristics are faithfully reflected in the TAT. Fourth, validity may be assessed by the TAT's success in exploration and prediction on the frontier of scientific inquiry. Fifth, its validity must be considered in the light of its interaction with other data and other techniques. More generally, we must consider the relationship of the TAT to the stage of development of the science of which it is a constituent part. Let us turn then to a discussion of these diverse aspects of the problem of validity.

1. COMPARISON OF TAT WITH OTHER MATERIAL

Inasmuch as fragments of the individual's past history, his present overt behavior, as well as covert fears and wishes, are all reflected in the mosaic of his TAT stories, we must compare the latter with material from other sources. Let us consider, first, past history material as it is revealed in written autobiography and interview.

a) *Autobiographical and Interview Past History Material*

It must be admitted that any attempt to reconstruct the past history of the individual, whether it be on the basis of written autobiography or interview, is itself open to question. Whatever the validity of such an attempt, it is worth while to compare such data with the TAT. We may thereby emerge with a rough estimate of the degree to which the TAT reveals at least some of the individual's actual past history.

Murray (66) has reported that the subject, in responding to the pictures, draws upon four major fields for his plots: books and movies, actual events occurring to friends or to family members, experiences in the subject's own life, and the subject's conscious and unconscious phantasies.

Markmann (55) studied the relationship between three TAT pictures * and the past history of 40 individuals who told stories to these pictures. The past history had been determined through a combination of autobiography and interview. She discovered that the past history was more faithfully reflected in some pictures than others. Stories to picture 1 most frequently reflected the individual's actual past history. She further showed that the story was more likely to be a true portrait of the individual's past history, if certain themes were expressed. Thus all those who expressed aggression either toward their parents or toward the violin, in stories told to the first picture, were in fact aggressive in their childhood. But stories told to the same picture, which were concerned with a benefactor through whose help the child was enabled to succeed, were less valid. In 1 out of 3 cases this was found to have no basis in the past history of the individual who told such a story. It was not the case, however, that an aggressive story told to any picture meant that the individual had been aggressive. There is much work to be done following up these leads of Markmann's exploratory study. It is clear that certain past history data is reflected in the TAT. The conditions under which this happens need further exploration.

Combs (23) has investigated the extent to which TAT stories were based on personal experience as this was recorded in autobiographies. He assumed that the autobiography represented a valid, if somewhat selected, description

* Picture 1, the boy and the violin; picture 6 BM, young man and elderly woman; picture 7 BM, young man and older man.

of the individual's experience. He found that approximately 30 per cent of the TAT stories contained significant material drawn from the subject's own life experiences as revealed by their autobiographies. This is said by Combs to be a conservative estimate, inasmuch as he was comparing "situations" and not attitudes or feelings in either TAT or autobiography. In terms of his criterion he found that picture 2, showing an adolescent with a book in her hand, encouraged the most transfer of personal experience. He attributed this to the fact that the girl seems to be a student, which seemed to Combs to confirm the finding of Symonds (95) that the best results are obtained with pictures containing characters with which the subject can most readily identify himself in terms of age, status, and general similarity. Combs found that picture 11, the dragon in the chasm, gave the least frequent situational identification. Combs and Symonds are in all probability correct. But it must be remembered that if the TAT were too heavily weighted with pictures which elicited ready identification with the figures in the picture, much of the specific value of the test would be sacrificed. Thus Renaud (74) found responses to picture 11 of critical importance in differentiating head injury cases and psychoneurotics. This happened primarily because the scene was so remote from everyday life that it permitted the expression of impulses which were equally remote from the individual's overt behavior. The rationale of these bizarre pictures will be considered in a later chapter.

It is clear, then, that at least 30 per cent of the TAT stories contain significant material from the individual's own life experience and that in the case of stories told to particular pictures, principally 1 and 2, this percentage may increase sharply. Further, within such stories, particular themes are more likely than others to represent past history material.

b) *Dreams*

If the TAT elaborates wishes which may never appear directly in overt behavior, we should expect some of these phantasies to be found in the individual's dreams. The dream, there is reason to believe, is the medium par excellence for the expression of wishes and fears ordinarily subject to some degree of inhibition in overt behavior.

Sarason (87) compared the TAT stories with the dreams of the same individual. His subjects were 34 mental defectives. In general, dream material and stories were similar, even though all the major themes of the stories were not found in the dreams. In no case, however were the data from these two sources at complete variance. He felt that the similarity was sufficient to have demonstrated the validity of the test interpretations.

In the intensive study of a single subject by the writer (98), which was mentioned previously, many of the major themes of the TAT appeared as manifest content of the subject's dreams but again, as in Sarason's study, not all the themes of the TAT appeared in the dreams.

Thus we have found that sources as disparate as the past history and dream life of the individual find representation in the imaginative productions of the TAT. The TAT reflects but a fragment of his past history but more of his wishes than appear in his dreams.

2. COMPARISON OF THE TAT WITH OTHER TECHNIQUES

In attempting to validate the TAT, investigators have compared its findings with other projective techniques, with psychoanalytic studies and with intensive case studies of the individual employing a variety of techniques.

a) *Other Projective Techniques*

Harrison (38) has compared the TAT with Rorschach findings. He reports substantial overlap between the results obtained with the two techniques. Henry (40) also reported close agreement between TAT and Rorschach findings on Navaho children. These results are in general in agreement with the writer's own experience. There is, however, a type of discrepancy, which I have noticed from time to time, that calls for more investigation. This is seen in the case of the individual who gives very few movement responses in his Rorschach record but who gives TAT stories suggestive of a very rich inner life. It is possible that for certain individuals one medium of expression is much preferred to the other, inasmuch as the writer has also seen cases in which there are many movement responses in the Rorschach record but very meager imaginative productions in the TAT protocol.

b) *Psychoanalysis*

Murray and Morgan (62) reported on a patient whose TAT stories showed all the chief trends which five months of psychoanalysis were able to reveal. To date this represents the only attempt at such validation. A systematic investigation by Bellak, who administered the TAT to individuals about to undergo psychoanalysis and planned to repeat the administration of the TAT after the termination of their psychoanalysis, was interrupted by World War II. This technique of validation is open to the criticism that one unvalidated method is being used to validate an equally unvalidated method. Much depends on the validity of psychoanalytic interpretation if we are to employ it as an instrument of validating the TAT. In addition, differences in interpretation among psychoanalysts further complicate the use of psychoanalytic findings as a technique of validation.

c) *Intensive Individual Case Study—the Case of "Z"*

In the intensive case study of Z by the writer, seventy-five hours of interviews, tests and experimental procedures disclosed no material inconsistent with his TAT protocol. It has been the writer's experience that the intensive case study usually reveals much that is not found in the TAT and the latter contains material not revealed by the case study. There is of course much overlap. But more important than the overlap between TAT and other techniques is the interaction between them. The TAT usually throws new light on the other material and the latter may clarify the meaning of the TAT. Horn (42) demonstrated that such *interaction* exceeds the *sum* which *both* contribute to diagnosis when TAT and case material are used as independent techniques. This has also been the experience reported by Henry in his study of the Navaho and Hopi.

3. COMPARISON OF TAT RESULTS WITH GROUPS OF KNOWN DIFFERENCES

One of the most widely employed techniques of validation consists in administering an unvalidated technique to groups whose characteristics are already well known. If the results are in agreement with previous knowledge, evidence for the validity of the technique is considerably strengthened. This may be done in one of two ways. First, it may be done "blind" in an attempt at postdiction. The experimenter may analyze the TAT results without knowledge of the characteristics of the subjects and then compare his results with previously established findings in an attempt to discover similarities between the TAT and other data. The former method is the more convincing, although it suffers the disadvantages of error in interpretation of the TAT. There may in fact be evidence of similarity which the interpreter overlooked in "blind" analysis, but which might have been discovered had he known the characteristics of the tested group and been sensitized to these characteristics as he interpreted the TAT. Perhaps the best validation procedure would be the utilization of both methods—first "blind" analysis and then a re-examination of the protocols in the light of further knowledge of the characteristics of the tested group.

a) *Postdiction of Groups of Known Differences*

Harrison, in conjunction with a qualitative study by Rotter (39), undertook a quantitative investigation of the validity of the TAT. The subjects were 40 patients at the Worcester State Hospital. Following his administration and analysis of the test protocols, Harrison wrote a thumbnail personality sketch of each patient. These sketches included a description of characteristic traits, biographical facts, attitudes, level of intelligence, and personal problems and conflicts. The correctness of these items were then checked by an assistant against the hospital records.   Eighty-two and five tenths per cent of the inferences made were correct.   The correlation between guessed and actual I.Q.'s was $+0.78$.   Inferences as to diagnostic classification were 75 per cent correct.   There were no significant differences between the proportion of correct inferences that he made concerning biographical items and personality or intellectual items.   In another experiment by Harrison (37) an additional control was introduced.   The test was administered by another person in order to eliminate the cues from face-to-face contact with the patients.   He then did a completely blind analysis.   With this procedure the percentage of correct inferences fell from 82 to 74 per cent, a statistically insignificant difference. But it would be surprising if face-to-face contact with the subject had not contributed somewhat to the write-up of the personality sketch.   Although the difference is statistically insignificant in this experiment, if the experiment were replicated it is the writer's guess that this small difference would continue to result from the employment of these two procedures.

Murray and Stein (67) rated leadership ability in officer condidates in ROTC on the basis of the TAT.   These ratings correlated $+0.65$ with independent judgements of these same men made by their officers.

An impressive demonstration of the diagnostic power of the TAT was Henry's (40) blind analysis of the stories of Navaho and Hopi Indians.   These reports were read by anthropologists who were familiar with the Navaho and Hopi cultures.   In the opinion of these independent experts, the analysis based on TAT stories alone agreed essentially with all known facts available on the two cultures.   In addition, Henry compared his interpretations with material already published on the Hopi and Navaho.   The congruence of field anthropological studies and TAT findings is striking.   As previously mentioned, Rorschach findings on the Navaho were also compared with TAT results and disclosed substantial agreement.   This comparison substantiated many of the psychological variables measured by the TAT which could not be validated by customary anthropological data.   These findings revealed important psychological changes in children of Navaho society at different age levels at which cultural restraining forces exerted their influence.   Henry concluded that the data were of sufficiently high validity to have justified the use of the TAT in the research on Indian education and recommended its further use in the study of culture and personality.

Let us consider next those investigations in which the interpreter utilized the knowledge which was available on the group he was testing.

b) *Comparison with Groups of Known Differences*

Several investigators have analyzed the TAT with full knowledge of the known characteristics of the groups they have tested in an effort to determine the extent to which these characteristics were reflected in the TAT protocols.

Richardson (75) found the TAT relatively useless for eliciting differences between stutterers and nonstutterers, though other tests did reveal significant differences between these two groups.

Balken and Masserman (2) were able, by means of an analysis of the language of the protocols (the actual words used by the patients), to demonstrate statistically significant differences between patients diagnosed as conversion hysteria, anxiety hysteria, and obsessive-compulsive neurosis. They caution us, however, that their cases were relatively "pure" examples in which the dynamisms underlying these categories were particularly clear. For the more typical "mixed" cases it is less certain that the TAT or any other technique could yield such differential diagnosis.

Renaud (74) found significant differences between the TAT's of psychoneurotics, brain disease cases, and head injury cases. The nature of some of these differences will be discussed in a later chapter.

We see then that the TAT has to some extent been validated by both types of comparison with groups of known differences. Less seems to depend on the "blindness" of the analysis than on the nature of the groups studied. Thus Harrison's completely blind analysis of psychotics was correct in 74 per cent of the cases, whereas Richardson, with all knowledge available to him, was unable to differentiate between the TAT's of stutterers and nonstutterers. To what extent another investigator might have discovered differences we cannot say, inasmuch as the attempt has not been repeated. At our present stage of relative ignorance of TAT interpretation it is necessarily the case that these varying estimates of the test's validity are conservative. Further knowledge of the test will probably improve the validity of the inferences we can make from the TAT.

A further problem in the use of this technique of validation is that which we raised in connection with the use of psychoanalytic findings. To what extent are the "known findings" themselves valid? The ratings of leadership by ROTC officers may or may not be valid. One of the lessons of the war experience was the uncertain validity of the judgements of army personnel which were used to validate psychological tests. Consider also the validity of hospital diagnosis on the basis of Kraeplinian categories. These admittedly leave something to be desired. Anthropological studies are also somewhat less than certain as a basis for validating other techniques, and, as we have seen, on certain aspects described by the TAT anthropological evidence was mute, so that the TAT had then to be compared with Rorschach findings. With Renaud's study we are on more solid ground; head injury, brain disease, and psychoneuroses are capable of relatively certain differentiation. Least controversial of the "known differences" is that between stutterers and nonstutterers; however, the test proved least valid in differentiating these groups. Inasmuch as other techniques did reveal differences between stutterers and nonstutterers, it would be important to replicate this experiment in order to determine whether these results are peculiar to Richardson's sample, and further, if these two groups can *not* be differentiated by the TAT, to determine *why* this is so. Negative evidence has, in the history of science, not infrequently provided the opportunity for crucial investigation.

4. THE TAT AS AN INSTRUMENT OF EXPLORATION AND PREDICTION

Impressive as postdiction may be, the acid test of any technique is its usefulness in exploration and successful prediction on the frontier of science. If and when, by use of the TAT, we are enabled to make significant contributions to the science of which it is a constituent part, the test will have established its validity beyond question.

To date such attempts are conspicuous by their absence. It is the conviction of this writer that the TAT provides data of sufficient import and scope to justify a coordinated program of research on a nation-wide scale. The TAT is peculiarly sensitive in eliciting material which the individual ordinarily guards zealously from public scrutiny. Since this is the source of much of what we call mental disease it would be most rewarding if several thousand records of psychopathological syndromes of every variety were available for analysis. Such an enterprise would necessarily involve the energies of many individuals for many years. But the possible fruit of such labor might be a reclassification of mental diseases which yielded truly homogenous entities. Once in possession of such knowledge the pace of significant research could be rapidly accelerated. Our position without such knowledge is not unlike that of a medical scientist who intended to study organic disease armed only with the knowledge that some diseases were characterized by subnormal temperatures, others by higher temperatures, and still others by unusually high temperatures, although most diseases seemed "mixed." This is perhaps a caricature of our position. But if evidence is needed to underline the urgency of this problem, let the reader spend an afternoon perusing the official dossier on any patient sent from one mental hospital to the next to come to rest finally in a state mental hospital. One typically finds a series of assorted diagnoses from each institution based on five to four decisions of an earnest but puzzled staff. Among these diagnoses will be many labeling the patient "mixed type" or with a more definite label qualified by many "trends" of other syndromes. This condition must of necessity continue until our classification of mental diseases allows less ambiguous diagnosis.

5. INTERACTION OF THE TAT WITH OTHER DATA AND OTHER TECHNIQUES

In the preceding sections we have examined the validity of the TAT as if the test were an isolated technique of investigation and to some extent as if its validity were a static characteristic of the test itself. Both of these assumptions are to some extent untenable. Let us consider the latter assumption first.

We cannot meaningfully inquire whether the TAT is a valid test, but we *may* ask whether inferences based on TAT stories are true. Similarly, we do not usually ask whether the experimental method is a valid method, but we do ask whether inferences based on the experimental method are likely to be true. There can be no guarantee that the inferences drawn from either the TAT or experimental data will necessarily be true. The history of science is witness to the frequency with which even the best experimental data have led to inferences which later proved to be false. It is even more certain that the data provided by the TAT have in the past, and will again in the future, prompt investigators to draw inferences which are untrue. But the value of a method, be it the experimental method or the procedure employed in the TAT, does not necessarily rise and fall with each success or failure in interpretation.

If the validity of our inferences is not guaranteed by the precision of our methods, on what does it depend? The meaning of any data stems ultimately from the fabric of interconnected propositions we call science and proximately from the hypothesis which we would relate to the already established system of accepted propositions. Any particular fact may become "crucial" only in the context of a hypothesis related to the larger matrix of previously established laws. Within such a context, the new fact both receives its significance and contributes to the further unification of its particular science. A collection of facts may all be "true," but such truth yields neither control nor prediction of any import. Facts provide the raw material, but not the mortar for the edifice of science. They are again crucial when the superstructure of this edifice must be tested.

What consequences does this excursion into the philosophy of science entail for the problem of the validity of the TAT? Simply that the validity of inferences drawn from this test or any other test is limited by the stage of development of the science of psychology. No method, however precise, can lift a science by its bootstraps. Were we today in possession of a psychologic periodic table, the validity of inferences from the TAT or any other technique would be greatly increased by the general accruement of knowledge of personality dynamics. But in the infancy of its development, the science is capable only of halting, uncertain, and frequently invalid inferences—whatever the method employed. The experimental method, it can not be denied, is an impeccable method, but its application to personality study does not immediately yield a full-blown science of personality free of invalid propositions. It is always much less difficult to devise techniques for answering questions than to know what questions to put to Nature. In the TAT the writer has found answers to many questions, but only after he was able to ask the questions. We do not believe that the future of the TAT depends on the refinement of clinical intuition. Both TAT interpretation and clinical intuition itself can be no better than the general stage of development of the science permits.

If validity is not a static characteristic of the TAT itself, we should not then treat the test as an isolated technique of investigation. Most of the studies cited in the preceding sections have examined the validity of the test as an independent instrument. "Blind" analysis may be impressive, but the value of a technique need not depend on its potency in splendid isolation from other techniques and other data. Let us consider one empirical study which presents us, in microcosm, with a paradigm of how increments in validity may accrue to inferences based on TAT stories. White (102) studied the extent to which hypnotic susceptibility might be correctly inferred from the TAT stories told to card 13 by hypnotic subjects. The TAT stories when first analyzed yielded a correlation of only $+0.34$ with hypnotic susceptibility. Predictions based on autobiographical and interview material were slightly better, the correlation being $+0.40$. When both sources of information were used the prediction improved to the extent of a correlation of $+0.59$. This increment was a function of combining different data and techniques. But White found he could improve the validity of inferences based on TAT stories alone through further study of the relationships between the stories and hypnotic susceptibility. He found that the 7 most hypnotizable subjects all stated explicitly in their stories that the hypnosis was a success, but the remaining 8 made this point incidental, merely implied it, expressed repugnance for hypnosis or explicitly declared it a failure. When this subsequently discovered relationship was used as a criterion, the correlation rose to $+0.56$, which was almost as high as the correlation of $+0.59$ when the original criterion plus autobiographical and interview material had been used as the basis of prediction. White then employed the new criterion plus autobiographical and interview material, and the prediction on this basis rose to $+0.75$. This is a striking demonstration, first, of the accrument of validity to inferences based on the TAT when this material is illuminated by other material, and second, of the accruement of validity to inferences based on the TAT alone after further study of the relations between stories and the storyteller's hypnotic susceptibility.

The latter suggests a more frontal attack on the problem of the validity of the TAT. Although we may be limited by the primitive state of our science, White's experiment shows us that we can improve the validity of our inferences by examining more carefully the relationships between the stories and the personalities of the subjects who tell them. We have barely scratched the surface of such inquiry. This reorientation would involve a strategic retreat. We would, for some time, have to relinquish our attempt to prove that the test was valid and turn our attention to the problem of why it was either valid or invalid. Frequently more can be learned from invalid test results than from valid inferences. In the technique of the questionnaire, for example, it is well known that subjects frequently rate themselves with a minimum of self insight. If we were to infer from these self ratings that the individual has presented us with a faithful portrait of his own personality, we might be mistaken as frequently as we were correct. But if we were to relinquish, temporarily, our aspiration to employ the questionnaire as a completely adequate basis for valid inference and study the conditions under which the individual is likely to rate himself accurately and the conditions under which he will deceive himself or others, then ultimately we might make important contributions to the science of personality and at the same time be enabled to employ the questionnaire method with greater assurance. Similarly with the TAT, if more attention is given to its signal failures and the conditions under which inferences are grossly in error as well as the conditions under which inferences are valid, we may ultimately contribute not only to the greater usefulness of the TAT but, more important, to an understanding of the dynamics of personality.

SUMMARY

In our examination of the precursors of the TAT we saw that experimental psychology in the nineteenth century was more concerned with an examination of the lower and higher mental processes of the person than in the study of the person himself. It was the educator who first turned the psychologist's attention to more complex problems. But the mental testing movement was so narrowly conceived that it fell to the psychiatrist, expert primarily in the biological sciences, to apply and develop a nonexistent science of personality. We also observed that in such a climate of psychological opinion, techniques and findings full of promise for the study of personality remained unnoticed, to be rediscovered some twenty-five years later when the science was ready.

The first publication on the Thematic Apperception Test by Morgan and Murray appeared in 1935. Since that time the scope of inquiry has expanded, the pace of research quickened. The TAT has proven useful in diverse fields of inquiry.

We examined the twofold problem of interpreter and repeat reliability. Reported interinterpreter reliability coefficients ranged from $+0.30$ to $+0.96$. We assumed that this variability was a function of using diverse case material, diverse scoring schemes, and of interpreters of varying ability and acquaintance with the scoring schemes. Repeat reliability was seen to depend in part on the time which elapsed between successive administrations, in part on the stability of the personality being tested and also on the stability of the individual's environment.

We next examined the problem of validity. We found that sources as disparate as the past history and dream life of the individual found representation in the imaginative productions of the TAT. We saw further that comparison of the TAT with other techniques, such as the Rorschach, psychoanalytic, and the intensive case study, revealed considerable overlap and no evidence of inconsistency in findings. Comparing the TAT results on groups of known differences, we found evidence of substantial agreement, whether the analysis was done "blind" or with prior knowledge of characteristics of the tested groups. Only in the case of stutterers did the TAT fail to reveal differences from the TAT's of nonstutterers. It was suggested that this experiment be replicated.

Attempts to use the TAT as an instrument of exploration and prediction were seen to be conspicuous by their absence. It was suggested that such exploration might profitably be directed toward the problem of the reclassification of mental diseases.

Finally we examined the interaction of the TAT with other data and other techniques. We maintained that validity was a characteristic of inferences based on the TAT rather than a characteristic of the test itself. We maintained that the validity of such inferences was as dependent on the maturity of the science as on the adequacy of the method. We showed in an examination of an experiment that validity could be increased either by the accruement of data from other sources or from further study of the test itself. We suggested a strategic retreat involving a temporary abandonment of clinical application of the test in favor of a study of the conditions under which valid and invalid inferences might be drawn from the protocol.

CHAPTER II

THE TECHNIQUE OF ADMINISTRATION

DESCRIPTION OF TEST MATERIAL

The test consists of 29 pictures and one blank card. Cards 1, 2, 4, 5, 10, 11, 14, 15, 16, 19, and 20, are used for both sexes and all ages. For cards 3, 6, 7, 8, 9, 17, and 18, there are alternate forms marked "BM" for boys and older males, and "GF" for girls and older females. Card 12 has three forms marked "M" for males over 14, "F" for females over 14 and "BG" for boys and girls under 14. Card 13 also has three forms marked "MF" for males and females over 14, "B" for young boys and "G" for young girls. Thus there are four sets of twenty cards suitable either for men or women, boys or girls. The present series of pictures is the third revision of the first set distributed by the Harvard Psychological Clinic in 1936. Each set is divided into two series of ten pictures. The pictures of the second set were purposely chosen for their unusual and bizarre quality.

ADMINISTRATION

The subject, depending on his preference, may be seated in a chair or stretched out on a couch, either facing the experimenter or with his back to him. Murray (65) and Rotter (79) suggest that his back be to the experimenter; Rapaport (71) prefers the person to sit up facing him. Rotter admits that some subjects dislike having the examiner behind them. In the experience of this writer, there are subjects who prefer the couch, others become anxious and refuse to lie down, and some reluctantly lie down but keep one foot on the floor to reassure themselves. Some individuals required to sit facing the examiner avoid his eyes and look into space, while subjects who prefer the face-to-face position will turn their heads around to achieve this if they are required to sit with their back to the examiner.

INSTRUCTIONS

The instructions, in one of the following forms, are read slowly to the subject. Form A * (suitable for adolescents and for adults of average intelligence and sophistication):

This is a test of imagination, one form of intelligence. I am going to show you some pictures, one at a time, and your task will be to make up as dramatic a story as you can for each. Tell what has led up to the event shown in the

* Reprinted by permission of the Harvard University Press.

21

picture, describe what is happening at the moment, what the characters are feeling and thinking; and then give the outcome. Speak your thoughts as they come to your mind. Do you understand? Here is the first picture.

Form B (suitable for children, for adults of little education or intelligence, and for psychotics):

This is a storytelling test. I have some pictures here that I'm going to show you, and for each picture I want you to make up a story. Tell what has happened before and what is happening now. Say what the people are feeling and thinking and how it will come out. You can make up any kind of story you please. Do you understand? Well, then, here is the first picture.

These are the instructions used by Murray, with the exception that any reference to the time available to the subject has been omitted from these instructions, since in our experience, brief stories cannot be lengthened, and stories which run over five minutes are sometimes too valuable to cut short. The exact words of these instructions may, as Murray suggests, be altered to suit the subject. In using the test with young children, the writer has achieved best results by turning the test into a game. If the intent is therapeutic and the child still avoids certain topics, it is possible to lure him into these regions by alternating the telling of stories between therapist and child. The therapist can then make up a story close to the child's problem and hesitate in telling it. The child, impatient either to get on with the game, or to outdo the therapist, will often volunteer to fill in the gaps.

After finishing the first story, it is recommended by Murray that the subject be commended and then reminded of the instructions; and that the examiner say very little for the rest of the hour except to inform him whether he is ahead or behind schedule, encourage him from time to time, and prompt him briefly if he has omitted some crucial detail. Rapaport, perhaps because he tests more difficult subjects, namely, psychotics, is more insistent that individuals who refuse in one way or another comply with the instructions. The writer has not personally administered TAT's to psychotics, but, in his experience with seriously disturbed neurotics, refusal ·to comply can be changed neither by insistence nor entreaty. Resistance in the testing situation yields, if at all, only in a completely permissive atmosphere. Attempts by the examiner to elicit material which the neurotic is unable or unwilling to give usually result in more resistance and even greater impoverishment of material. Consider one aspect of compliance: the instructions ask that the subject speak his thoughts as they come into his mind. Lasaga (50), through the use of the inquiry, investigated the rejected ideas which first occurred to the subject on seeing a picture but which were not used in making up the stories. In some cases, the story proved to be a variant of the rejected idea or another aspect of the same idea. In other cases no light was shed on the patient's personality by the rejected ideas. In general, however, Lasaga found that the rejected ideas taken together usually reflect the same preoccupations which the stories themselves revealed.

Rapport with the subject is of critical importance. The writer has, on occasion, repeated the procedure with patients after a better relationship has been achieved and obtained revealing protocols even though the first attempt had been very disappointing. Murray recommends that the subject be praised for his efforts in order to stimulate his imagination. In general, we have found this to be advisable though individuals vary somewhat in the kind of approbation needed for their best effort. If some knowledge of the individual's basic needs is available before testing, this should govern the attitude which the examiner manifests toward the subject. Some subjects need respect; others sympathy and support, for their creative efforts. There are also subjects who respond best to a press of dominance from the examiner, but others, under such prodding, respond with negativism or complete withdrawal from the whole situation. If the subject is suffering acute anxiety or any other acute disturbance, testing is contraindicated since the stories will reflect only his specific preoccupation, giving so little elaboration that the dynamics of the state can not be inferred. In the case of a Marine, for example, who had returned from combat to find that his wife was in love with another man, every TAT story was nothing more than a description of one person who "was worried" and "wondered how everything was going to turn out."

Ordinarily, at least one day should intervene between the first and second sessions, unless the stories are so short that the entire set of twenty may be finished within an hour. Generally, no testing session should exceed one hour. In certain cases, as many as three one hour sessions may be required to complete the series. The instructions for the second session are modified as follows:
Form A:

> The procedure today is the same as before, only this time you can give freer rein to your imagination. Your first ten stories were excellent, but you confined yourself pretty much to the facts of everyday life. Now I would like to see what you can do when you disregard the commonplace realities and let your imagination have its way, as in a myth, fairy story, or allegory. Here is picture no. 1

Form B:

> Today I am going to show you some more pictures. It will be easier for you this time because the pictures I have here are much better, more interesting. You told me some fine stories the other day. Now I want to see whether you can make up a few more. Make them even more exciting than you did last time if you can—like a dream or fairy tale. Here is the first picture.

Card 16, the blank card, is accompanied by a special instruction. The examiner says, "See what you can see on this blank card. Imagine some picture there and describe it to me in detail." If the subject does not succeed in doing this, the examiner says, "Close your eyes and picture something." After the subject has given a full description of his imagery, the examiner says, "Now tell me a story about it." This modification of instructions is a type of "testing of limits." Many subjects will not comply; they may or may not be aware that they are not complying. But those who accept the instructions frequently tap remote recesses of their imagination which otherwise might not be reached.

INQUIRY

In this part of the procedure we suggest that the examiner follow up leads based on the hypotheses he has formulated in analyzing the stories. This may be done by direct question, free association, or by presenting the subject with special cards designed to evoke further phantasies on critical areas. Such a recommendation involves postponing the inquiry until the stories have been analyzed. Inquiry after each story, as suggested by Rapaport, will too frequently arouse suspicion and resistance. Many subjects interpret such frequent inquiry either as an indication that they are not satisfying the examiner, with a consequent decrease in productivity, or as an unwelcome limitation on their freedom.

Murray recommends that inquiry be made into the sources of various stories. This is sometimes useful in identifying autobiographical material if it is not already available. Rapaport uses the inquiry, among other things, to discover whether lack of perceptual clarity represents pathological perceptual distortion. This would be most important in the case of psychotic patients and sometimes with psychoneurotics. In the inquiry, unclear verbalization as well as any lack of clarity in the meaning of the story should be investigated.

RECORDING

Recording of the stories and the inquiry is best done either by a stenographer in another room, with transmission through a concealed microphone, or by wire, disk or tape recording devices. In our experience the presence of a microphone does not disturb most subjects, but there are some for whom it is better to use a concealed microphone. Writing down the exact words of the subject is all but impossible without proficiency in shorthand and the imaginal productivity of a facile subject may be seriously impaired if he has to be slowed down to the speed with which the examiner can write. If recording is impracticable, we prefer that the subject write his own protocol in ink. In this way, many slips of the tongue which might otherwise be lost appear in the material; they can only be crossed out, not erased. Preliminary research by the writer indicates that, in general, there are no significant differences between stories written and spoken, although there are individual subjects who are more productive in one medium than another.

A Criterion of Effectiveness

One criterion of effectiveness of technique of administration is the length of the stories. The average length of stories spoken by adults is three hundred words. The average for 10 year old children is one hundred and fifty words. According to Rapaport, the average story in the clinical situation is about one hundred words. Murray suggests that "stories from a sane adult averaging less than 140 words per story indicate lack of rapport and cooperation, lack of self-involvement. As a rule they are not worth scoring." This has to be qualified somewhat in terms of Henry's (40) experience with protocols from the Navaho and Hopi indians. The average story consisted of a few brief sentences, but the interpretations were nevertheless illuminating.

Group administration of the test is practicable but systematic differences between results of group administration and individual administration have yet to be investigated.

CHAPTER III

THE SCORING SCHEME

METHODOLOGICAL PROBLEMS

In view of the complexity and scope of the material of TAT protocols, the dimensions of interpretation cannot differ in any appreciable degree from those necessary for personality analysis in general. A language of interpretation adequate for *all* TAT protocols will, we venture, also be adequate for any type of personality analysis. Such a language is still to be achieved. What we will offer towards such a conceptual scheme can, in view of the stage of development of our science, be but a short step in that direction.

More important than these suggestions for analysis is an understanding of the requirements which any such attempt must satisfy. In general, the variables of analysis must allow us to discover functional relationships of an ever increasing scope. The power of a set of variables might be described as an inverse relationship between the mass of empirical data and the mass of relating concepts. If we were to use for our analysis the language of the protocol itself, the possibility of generalization would be minimal. It is, moreover, essential that we employ variables which result in something more than taxonomic classifications. Description is the beginning but not the end of scientific inquiry, in which our highest aspiration has ever been the discovery of causal relationships.

Criteria for inclusion and exclusion of concepts in such inquiry ultimately rest on the power of the complete *set* of variables rather than the power of any variable in isolation. Thus, in physical science, the concepts of mass and velocity taken independently might have yielded little; but mass, velocity, and a derivative of velocity, namely, acceleration, proved to be dimensions which allowed the discovery of general causal relationships.

Perhaps the most important option we have in the selection of a set of categories for our purposes is the degree of generality and specificity of the concepts we employ. Consider first the dangers inherent in concepts of a high degree of generality. One such set of concepts is that employed by Murray in his general language for personality and TAT analysis—his language of needs and press. Although the use of this language frequently yields incisive analysis of TAT protocol, there are nonetheless instances in which this language blurs specific aspects of a class of phenomena. Thus Renaud (74) reported, in connection with a study of head-injury cases and psychoneurotics, that he could find no significant difference between these groups with respect to any need or press described by Murray or Sanford. He did, however, find that the length of the stories about picture 11 told by head-injury cases significantly exceeded that of the length of stories told by psychoneurotics.* On the basis of this difference in length, Renaud examined more closely the differences between the two sets of stories to this picture. He found that the stories of the head-injury cases were distinguished by a theme of the cataclysmic convergence of two opposing forces, of a last-ditch stand where the situation is either one of overpowering or being overpowered by aggressive force. He found the endings to this struggle varied; sometimes the hero killed the monster; in others the hero was killed by the monster. This is indeed press and need aggression according to the Murray-Sanford scoring scheme, but the summated score for the whole protocol has masked the significant difference which is elicited only in response to a remote other-world picture. We shall discuss this finding at some length in Chapter V, where we shall attempt to show that the degree of "remoteness" under which certain wishes are expressed is an index of the depth of repression. The general need "aggression" does not distinguish these cases from psychoneurotic cases, but aggression qualified by the particular circumstances under which it may be expressed does. This is reflected in the differences in response to this single picture. Renaud's findings underline the danger of atomistic quantification and summing of responses according to concepts of too great generality. But the use of the Murray scoring scheme *did* elicit significant differences between head injury and brain disease cases on the one hand, and between psychoneurotics and brain disease groups. We see then, in the case of a single investigation, at once both the strength and weakness of the same conceptual scheme.

If it is possible to miss the critical, finer differentiations through the use of concepts which are too general, it is also possible that the same concept, too general in one instance, will be too specific in another context. Thus, in a study by the writer of an individual who was given the TAT before and during hypnosis, there was no statistically significant rise in the strength of either the need aggression or rejection, but if both of these needs were added together, the increase from the normal to hypnotic state *was* statistically significant. In other words, the needs rejection and aggression scored according to Murray's definitions were too specific to reveal the significant differences in this case. For this individual rejection was in fact another way of expressing aggression.

If then, the same concept may in one case have precisely the degree of specificity required, in another case be too general, and in still another context be too specific, how shall we select our original dimensions of analysis?

* Picture 11 shows a road skirting a deep chasm between high cliffs. On the road in the distance are obscure figures. Protruding from the rocky wall on one side is the long head and neck of a dragon.

Our decision rests in part on the generality of our purpose. If our intent were to study the differences between normals and abnormals, we would probably have to use concepts of a higher order of generality than if we tried to delineate the differences between psychotics and neurotics. If, however, we wished to distinguish obsessive-compulsive neurotics from hysterics, we would probably need more specific categories; and even more highly differentiated catgories would be needed if our aim were to separate obsessive from compulsive neurotics. This is so because the data itself may vary in degree of generality or specificity. But, in general, when the TAT is used as an exploratory instrument, we do not know exactly what to look for. If we prejudge the categories of analysis, we may commit serious errors. What check then have we on the adequacy of our selection of categories of analysis? It is our conviction that the logic of the individual's phantasy itself must be our ultimate criterion. Consider the following hypothetical examples. Let us suppose that in the stories of A we find the following sequences: (1) the hero injures another person—outcome, the hero is unhappy; (2) the hero is angry with someone—outcome, the hero is unhappy. In the stories of B (1) the hero injures another person—outcome, the hero is unhappy; (2) the hero is angry with someone—outcome, the hero gets over it and is happy. In the stories of C (1) the hero, helped by his gang, injures another person— outcome, the hero is happy; (2) the hero injures another person—outcome, the hero is unhappy. By using the individual's own phantasies, we are enabled to discover those differences in specificity and generality which "make a difference." For A, B, and C, we would have to employ different types of categories in the analysis of the aggressive need if we were to catch the causal relationships in these examples. In A's case, the concept "aggression" would be adequate, since the manifestation of any kind of aggression, whether felt covertly or overtly expressed, results in the same state of unhappiness. But in B's case, we would have to distinguish aggression according to the psychological level on which it was expressed. By using this type of differentiation, we can show that the expression of overt aggression is one thing, as judged by one outcome, but that the feeling of anger means something else, since the consequences are different and depend on whether the feeling of anger is covertly or overtly expressed. In C's case, aggression would have to be specified by the context in which it was expressed; aggression expressed as a member of a group has a different meaning from aggression for which the individual assumes complete responsibility. This is but a sample of the different degrees of differentiation of "needs" in personality organization. But, though the varieties are great, the logic of the individual's stories do provide the clues necessary for the determination of those categories most adequate for the analysis of his protocol. We should employ those concepts which yield the greatest degree of unification of the individual protocol. To the extent to which differences in the stories themselves can be explained, we have succeeded. Thus, had we used the concept "need aggression" in case C, we would have left unexplained the reason why the need aggression sometimes resulted in a good outcome, sometimes in a bad outcome. There are records which are recalcitrant to such analysis; but, in our experience, the principles of unification, if undiscovered, are testament more to the failure of the analysis than the poverty of the material. Not infrequently, this writer has all but given up the interpretation of a protocol, only to find the explanation some time later when the analysis was resumed. In the present state of our knowledge, an individual protocol may demand the same type of arduous exploration necessary for any frontier inquiry in science. It may be argued that the expenditure of such effort on a single case is unprofitable. It is the writer's conviction, however, that this attempt to extract lawfulness from the productions of the individual will ultimately yield uniformities of a broader scope.

The Scoring Scheme

Our solution to the problem of the set of concepts most likely to yield significant functional relationships from TAT stories is necessarily a tentative one. By its use we have been able to uncover relationships which otherwise escaped our attention. It must be admitted, however, that it suffers many of the inadequacies of other contemporary attempts in this direction. Its rationale consists in tapping *varying levels of abstraction* in the hope that significant aspects of diverse types of protocols will be detected by the use of concepts which range from a level of broad generality to a high degree of differentiation.

In the writers' scoring scheme, each story is scored according to four main categories: vectors, levels, conditions, and qualifiers.

Vectors

By *vectors* we mean the psychological direction characteristic of behavior, striving, wishes, cathexes, or feelings. We do not, in attributing direction, distinguish whether the behavior is a "need" or simply an act which is instrumental to a "need." As we have differentiated them, they are not so general as the vectors employed either by Lewin (51) or Horney (43), or as specific as the needs differentiated by Murray (62).* Ten vectors are distinguished, their general meaning signified by a preposition. These vectors may have as their objects other persons, the self, social institutions, physical objects, ideas; in short, any object of any human interest.

---

* The writer has borrowed much from Murray, dedifferentiating his system of needs and press, and further differentiating other aspects of his conceptual scheme which it seemed useful to expand.

I. Vector "on"—to depend upon objects.
Examples: to seek or ask for help, admiration, recognition or in any way depend upon any object. To depend on the self, institutions, ideas, intuitions, etc.

II. Vector "from"—to acquire positive valences from objects.
Examples: to earn or acquire money, possessions, to learn, to win love, to seduce, to eat, to learn from experience, etc.

III. Vector "toward"—to approach or enjoy objects of positive valence.
Examples: to make friends, to make love, to experience esthetic enjoyment, to aspire to something, to love one's self, to sympathize or empathize with, etc.

IV. Vector "with"—to share experience with objects of positive valence.
Examples: to play with, to have sexual experience with, to laugh with, to share intimacies, to work together, to commune with nature, to commune with self, etc.

V. Vector "for"—to bestow positive valence upon objects.
Examples: to help another person, to repair objects, to create objects, to help the self, etc.

VI. Vector "over"—to govern objects.
Examples: to dominate persons or situations, to overcome barriers, to continue or change a state, to drive an automobile, to control the self, etc.

VII. Vector "under"—to be governed by objects of negative valence.
Examples: to comply, to surrender, to be superstitious of dreaded objects, to comply with an unwelcome super-ego or ego-ideal, etc.

VIII. Vector "by"—to be governed by objects of positive valence.
Examples: to identify with a loved object, to be governed by lucky charms, to conform to an accepted super-ego or ego-ideal, etc.

IX. Vector "away from"—to avoid or escape or leave objects.
Examples: to leave home, to avoid dangers, to escape harm, to avoid threats to pride, to suppress feelings, to forget unpleasant experiences, etc.

X. Vector "against"—to attack objects.
Examples: to break the law, rebel, aggress upon others, to reject, to ridicule, to destroy, to criticize the self, or commit suicide.

LEVELS

By *level* we mean the plane of psychological function involved in the story. We have differentiated the following levels:

I. Object description
Example: the scene is a farmhouse.

II. Events
Example: it is his birthday.

III. Behavior
Example: he plowed the field.

IV. Perception
Example: he looked at the field.

V. Attention
Example: he listened for the sound.

  VI. Interest
      Example: he was curious.
 VII. Intention
      Example: he planned to do it.
VIII. Sentiment
      Example: he was in favor of religion.
  IX. Thought
      Example: he pondered over the problem.
   X. Expectation
      Example: he thought it would rain.
  XI. Wish
      Example: he wanted to do it.
 XII. Feeling, Mood
      Example: he was angry.
               he was depressed.
XIII. Physical sensations
      Example: his arm hurt.
 XIV. Memory
      Example: he remembered his childhood.
  XV. Daydreams
      Example: he imagined himself as a great violinist.
 XVI. Nightdreams
      Example: he had a nightmare.
XVII. Special states
      Example: he was intoxicated.

These levels may or may not have objects. Thus, the protocol may simply
state: "This boy is daydreaming" or it may continue and tell what the daydream is about.

Conditions

By *conditions,* we mean any psychological, social, or physical state which
is not itself behavior, striving, or wish. For example, if the hero has lost his
parents, this is a "given," and is not his striving. Similarly, if the hero thinks
he lacks ability, this is a condition with which he must cope, but, itself, is not
his wish or striving. Inner states and feelings may also have this condition
quality. The hero may be unhappy or in a state of depression (these would
also, by our definition, be classified as conditions, since they are not in themselves strivings or wishes). A condition may, however, be the *object* of a
striving, as in the case of the hero who wishes to be happy or talented. We
have distinguished the following conditions:

  I. States with negative valence.
     A. Lack
        Examples: to lack ability, skill, interest, feeling, knowledge, energy,
        control, persistence, courage, health, senses, success, love objects, sex
        objects, friends, advice, help, attention, sympathy, loyalty, parents, group

membership, stimulation, money, possessions, free space, time, congenial environment, etc.

B. Loss

Examples: same object as under lack.

C. Excess

Examples: same objects as under lack but negatively cathected—the hero is thought to have too many friends, too much money, too much ability, too much success, etc., for his own "good."

D. Danger

Examples: threats of lack, loss or excess, physical injury, drowning, fire, wild animals, etc.

E. Structuration

Examples: situations which are too well defined or not sufficiently defined, too unchanging, or too unstable.

F. Inner states

Examples: depression, anxiety, guilt, shame, uncertainty, conflict, disenchantment, etc.

II. States with positive or neutral valence.

A. Abundance

Examples: same objects as under lack, except that these are possessed in abundance.

B. Gratuities

Examples: same objects as under abundance except that the individual is the passive recipient of valuable objects.

C. Moderation

Examples: same objects as under abundance, except that conditions are neither lacking nor abundant, but are sufficient.

D. Security

Examples: states free of any threat of danger, lack, loss, or excess.

E. Structuration

Examples: situations well defined, undefined, unchanging or unstable. These situations may be identical with those under negative states, but the hero finds them to his liking or accepts them.

F. Inner states

Examples: optimism, happiness, confidence, certainty, etc.

QUALIFIERS

By *qualifiers* we mean more specific aspects of either vectors, levels, or conditions. We distinguish the following qualifiers:

I. Temporal characteristics: A. When does it happen? B. What is its duration?

A. Past, present, or future.

Immediate, distance, or remote.

Examples: He loved her. He loves her. He will love her. He met her yesterday. He met her some months ago. He met her long, long ago.

B. Transitory, medium duration, enduring.

Examples: He loved her and left her. They knew each other for some time. He loved her all his life.

II. Contingency—how certain is it?
    A. Possible, probable, certain, improbable, uncertain.
        Examples: He might do it. He will probably do it. He will do it. He will probably not do it. He doesn't know whether he will do it.
III. Intensity—what is its strength?
    A. Slight, medium, strong.
        Examples: He likes her. He loves her. He is desperately in love with her.
IV. Negation—any type of denial. This may be signified by parentheses around that which is denied.
        Examples: He didn't want to do it. It didn't happen. He did not have what he wanted.
        The statement, "He was not daydreaming," would be represented: (daydreaming).
V. Subsidiation—any means-end relationship. This may be signified by the letter S following the behavior which is directed toward some end.
        Example: He made money in order to help his friends. (Vector "from" S Vector "for.")
VI. Causality—any causal relationship. This may be signified by the letter C following the cause.
        Example: His ability enabled him to succeed. Condition, Abundance— C Condition, Abundance.

In the use of this scheme, any variable may have any other variable as its object or it may have no object. Thus a vector may have as its object another vector, level, or condition, or any other object. Similarly, a level or condition may have any object.

Objects of Vectors

Consider the possible objects of the vector "away from." An individual may wish to escape others or himself. He may wish to escape certain conditions, such as lack of money, a dull environment, or inner conflict. Or he may wish to escape certain levels, such as remembering, daydreaming, wishing, planning, acting, and so on. Or the object of this vector may be another vector, so that he wishes to escape helping or hurting someone (vector "away from," vector "for" or vector "against"). Or the vector may have no object, as in the statement, "He went away."

Objects of Levels

Levels may or may not have objects. If the protocol says, "The man is daydreaming," there may be no object of the level indicated in the story. Consider the level of thought. The object may be a vector, as in the statement, "He is thinking of leaving" (level—thought; object—vector "away from"). The object may be a condition, as in the statement, "He is thinking of the death of his friend" (level—thinking; object—condition—loss). Or the object may be another level, as in the statement, "He is thinking about his decision" (level—thinking; object—level—intention). The object of a level may be another person. Thus in the statement, "He is thinking about his mother" the object of the level is "his mother." The object of the level may be the behavior of another person toward the hero, as in the statement, "He is thinking she will leave him," the object of the level is a person ("she") and the object of this person is the vector "away from," and the object of this vector is himself (level—thinking; object—she; object—vector "away from"; object—him). But a level may also have the characteristic of a qualifier, as in the statement, "He chopped wood," the level is behavior, which is a qualifier of vector "over"; object—wood.

OBJECTS OF CONDITIONS

Conditions may or may not have objects. Thus, in the statement, "He felt there was something lacking," the object of the condition of lack may not be specified. But the condition may have as its object a vector, as in the statement, "He lacked self control," the object of the condition "lack" is the vector "over," object self. The condition may have as its object a level, as in the statement, "He lost his memory," the object of the condition "loss" is the level "memory." Or the condition may have another condition as its object, as in the statement, "He lost his confidence," the object of the condition "loss" is the condition "abundance."

A SCORING SAMPLE

Let us consider the scoring of the following story:

> The small boy hates to play his violin and his mother has made him practice because she hopes that some day he'll be a great musician. He gets so angry that he breaks the violin and then is sorry because he knows he'll get whipped— and sure enough, he does 'cause it was a genuine Stradivarius.

It is convenient in scoring a story to employ a large scoring sheet divided by ruled lines to allow space for every character and object mentioned in the story plus space for vectors, levels, conditions, and qualifiers. In this story there are two characters and one object. Three lines would be required for these, and four more lines for the scoring categories.

Before scoring the story it is convenient to rewrite it so that temporal and functional relationships appear more clearly. We would rewrite the previous story as follows:

> Because she hopes that he'll be a great musician some day.
> His mother has made him practice.
> The small boy hates to play his violin.

He gets so angry that
He breaks the violin.
And because he knows he'll get whipped
Then is sorry.
'Cause it was a genuine Stradivarius.
Sure enough he does.

This type of rewriting does some violence to the actual organization of the story and would obscure a study of its formal characteristics, but it is useful in exposing the story's dynamics.

Let us turn now to the scoring of the rearranged story. Inasmuch as any category under which a sentence may be classified involves some distortion of its literal meaning, it is our practice to include with the categorization the exact words of the protocol on which the assignment of category has been based. This is done so that in the event the particular protocol calls for the employment of concepts of a level of generality different from that used in this particular scoring scheme, this new abstraction may be made more easily by inspection of the relation of the protocol to the assigned category.

We shall illustrate the technique of scoring of this story, line by line. We shall first illustrate the general appearance of the scoring sheet followed by a running commentary on the rationale of the scoring. Let us examine the scoring sheet for the first sentence, "Because she hopes that he'll be a great musician someday."

	1	2	3	4
1. Violin				
2. Mother	Subject "she"			
3. Son		Object "that he'll"		
4. Vectors				
5. Levels	Wish "hopes"		Event "be a great musician"	
6. Conditions			Abundance	
7. Qualifiers	Temporal immediate past Contingency certain Intensity medium		Temporal distant future "someday" Contingency certain	C "because she hopes"

In column 1, row 2, we have written "subject," since it is the mother who is hoping her son will be a great musician. In row 5, the level is "wish," because "she hopes." In row 7, the temporal qualifier is "immediate past," because her wish slightly precedes the main action of the story, although its object is in the future. The contingency is certain, since there is no qualification to the activity of hoping. The protocol does not say "she might hope." The intensity is rated medium, since it does not appear unusually strong or weak.

In column 2, row 3, we have written "object" because it is the mother's son who is the object of her hopes.

In column 3, row 5, we have written "event," since, "being a great musician" makes no mention of behavior. In row 6 we have written "abundance," since being a "great" musician implies more than moderate achievement. In row 7, the temporal characteristic is "distant future," since it is hoped for "someday." But although it is put into the distant future, the contingency is certain, since the hope is that he "be" a great musician, not that he "might be" one.

In column 4, row 7, we have written "C," indicating that because of the preceding conditions, what follows is a result.

Let us analyze the next line of our rearranged story: "His mother has made him practice." This would be scored as follows:

	1	2	3
1. Violin			
2. Mother	Subject "his mother"		
3. Son		Object "him"	
4. Vectors	Over "made him"		From "practice"
5. Levels	Behavior		Behavior
6. Conditions			
7. Qualifiers	Temporal immediate past "has made" Contingency certain Intensity medium		Temporal present

Column 1, row 2, the mother is still the subject. In row 4, the vector is "over," since the mother "made" him practice. In row 5, the level is behavior, since the mother actually forces the child to do this. In row 7, the temporal qualifier is "immediate past," since it slightly precedes the present situation as described in the remainder of the story. The contingency is certain, since it has actually occurred. The intensity is medium.

In column 2, row 3, the object is the son, who is made to practice.

In column 3, row 4, the vector is "from," since the son has been forced to practice. Implicit is the vector "under," since this represents being governed by negatively cathected objects, but we do not score this, since the sentence tells us only that the mother forced him to practice—his compliance is not mentioned directly. In row 5, the level is "behavior" since he has been made to do something. In row 7, the temporal qualifier is "present."

Let us next analyze the sentence, "The small boy hates to play his violin."

	1	2	3
1. Violin			Object "play his violin"
2. Mother			
3. Son	Subject "the small boy"		
4. Vectors	Against "hates"	From "to play"	
5. Levels	Feeling	Behavior	
6. Conditions			
7. Qualifiers	Temporal present Contingency certain Intensity medium	Temporal present	

In column 1, row 3, the subject is the son. In row 4, the vector is "against," since he "hates" to play his violin. In row 5, the level is "feeling," since it is a feeling of hatred rather than overt aggressive behavior. In row 7, the temporal qualifier is present, since his hatred is described as a consequence of the immediate past coercion by his mother. The contingency is "certain," and the intensity would be considered "medium," since it is only later that this feeling grows more intense.

In column 2, row 4, the vector is "from," since the object of his hatred is not the violin, but the playing of it. In row 5, the level is clearly behavioral. In row 7, the temporal qualifier is still the present.

In column 3, row 1, the object of the vector "from" is the violin which is what he must play. The object of the feeling of hatred is the vector "from—playing" and the object of the vector "from" is the object "violin."

Let us turn next to the sentence, "He gets so angry that."

	1	2
1. Violin		
2. Mother		
3. Son	Subject "He"	
4. Vectors	Against "gets so angry"	
5. Levels	Feeling	
6. Conditions		
7. Qualifiers	Temporal present Contingency certain Intensity strong	C "that"

In column 1, row 3, the subject is still the son. In row 4 the vector is "against," since he "gets so angry." In row 5, the level is still that of feeling. In row 7, the temporal qualifier is still the extended present, the contingency is certain and the intensity has increased to strong, since he says "so" angry.

In column 2, row 7, the qualifier is causality, since he says "that," implying that what follows is a consequence of his growing anger.

Let us analyze next the line, "He breaks the violin."

	1	2
1. Violin		Object "breaks the violin"
2. Mother		
3. Son	Subject "he"	
4. Vectors	Against "breaks the violin"	
5. Levels	Behavior	

	1	2
6. Conditions		
7. Qualifiers	Temporal present Contingency certain Intensity medium	

In column 1, row 3, the subject is still the son. In row 4, the vector is "against" because he breaks the violin and, for the same reason, on row 5 the level is now behavior. On row 7, the temporal qualifier is still the extended present, the contingency remains certain, but the intensity of the behavior is rated as medium, since there is no reference to the intensity of the behavior, although there had been mention of intense feelings of anger. If there had been elaboration of his destructive behavior, with mention of breaking it into little pieces, etc., it would have been rated strong in intensity. In column 2, row 1, the object of this destruction is the violin.

Let us analyze next the line, "And because he knows he'll get whipped."

	1	2	3
1. Violin			
2. Mother			
3. Son	Subject "he"	Subject "he'll"	
4. Vectors		Under "get whipped"	
5. Levels	Expectation "knows"	Behavior	
6. Conditions			
7. Qualifiers	Temporal present Contingency certain	Temporal immediate future Contingency certain	C "because . . . then"

In column 1, row 3, the subject continues to be the son. In row 5, the level is expectation, since he "knows" and expects to get whipped. In row 7, the temporal qualifier is still the extended present, the contingency certain.

In column 2, row 3, the subject of the expectation is himself. In row 4, the vector is "under," since he allows himself to be governed by a negatively cathected object. In row 5, the level is behavioral, since he knows he will behave submissively. In row 7, the temporal qualifier is the immediate future, indicated by the word "he'll," and the contingency is certain, since he does not say he'll probably get whipped.

In column 3, row 7, the qualifier is causality, since he says "because he knows . . . then."

The next line to be analyzed is "then is sorry."

	1	2
1. Violin		
2. Mother		
3. Son	Subject	
4. Vectors		
5. Levels		Feeling "is sorry"
6. Conditions		Negative inner state
7. Qualifiers	Temporal immediate future "then"	Temporal immediate future Intensity medium

In column 1, row 3, the subject remains the son. In row 7, the temporal qualifier is the immediate future, indicated by the word "then."

In column 2, row 5, the level is feeling—"is sorry," which is a negative inner state, marked on row 6. On row 7, the temporal qualifier is the immediate future, and the intensity is medium.

The next sentence to be analyzed is, " 'Cause it was a genuine Stradivarius."

	1	2
1. Violin	Subject "it"	
2. Mother		
3. Son		
4. Vectors		
5. Levels	Object description "was a genuine Stradivarius"	
6. Conditions	Abundance "genuine"	
7. Qualifiers		C "'cause it was"

In column 1, row 1, the subject is the violin. On row 5, the level is "object description." In row 6, the condition is abundance, since the violin is characterized as a valuable one. In column 2, row 7, the qualifier is causality, since the value of the violin is the reason for what follows, " 'Cause it was a genuine Stradivarius."

The final line to be analyzed is, "Sure enough he does."

1

1. Violin

2. Mother

3. Son   Subject
                  "he"

4. Vectors   Under
                  "does"

5. Levels   Behavior

6. Conditions

7. Qualifiers   Temporal
              immediate future
              Contingency certain
              "sure enough he does"

In column 1, row 3, the subject is still the son. In row 4, the vector is "under," since he submits to a whipping, and, by the same token, the level, on row 5, is behavioral. On row 7, the temporal qualifier is the immediate future, and the contingency is certain—"sure enough he does."

This sample of the application of the scoring scheme may well discourage the reader from ever attempting to score the TAT. The busy clinician will certainly doubt the practicability of such time-consuming microscopic analysis. But we would nonetheless argue its usefulness. One or more perusals of a protocol may reward the experienced interpreter and yield significant and accurate diagnoses of personality. But, in the writer's experience, it is no less frequent a phenomenon that repeated perusals of a single protocol may yield little of significance and less of certainty. In such cases, continued effort sometimes rewards the labors of the interpreter; and one may be astonished at the simplicity of the functional relationships which had somehow escaped scrutiny for so long. In our experience, however, systematic analysis, though laborious and time-consuming, may be less time-consuming and more effective than endless perusal of a protocol recalcitrant to intuition. After completing such a microscopic analysis, rapid breakdowns may be made on the stories. One may consider outcomes, inner states such as anxiety, vectors such as aggression, and determine relatively quickly what are the specific patterns of conditions which produce, or result from, these variables. This cannot be done so easily by inspection of the protocol, since a single sentence may contain "hidden" variables which may be explicitly recognized only after careful analysis of the elements of the story.

We would also argue its usefulness as an instrument of training. Refined discrimination, whether it be in microscopy, crime detection, or music appreciation, is necessarily a hard-won achievement. Befoie one may abstract general relationships of scope and power, the elements entering into these relationships must be differentiated.

But perhaps the most important consideration is the necessity at this time for some consensus of meaning on the part of those utilizing this test. Such consensus cannot be put off indefinitely if the test is to be useful. It is the writer's hope that the suggested conceptual scheme may be a step in this direction.*

SUMMARY

We have examined some of the requirements which any scoring scheme for the TAT must satisfy. Most important, we held, was the requirement that the set of dimensions employed enable us to discover functional relationships of an ever increasing scope. The first option concerned the degree of generality or specificity of concepts to be used. We saw that a concept which was useful in one protocol might be too general for another protocol and yet too specific in still another one. We suggested that the ultimate criterion in the initial selection of concepts was the logic of the individual protocol—that we should employ concepts of that degree of generality or specificity which matched the level of the protocol we were analyzing. Since differentiations which are crucial in one case make no difference in another, our suggested scoring scheme was based on the rationale of tapping as wide a range of levels of generality as possible. Thus, by the use of qualifiers, concepts which may be too general for many protocols are made more specific through further qualification. Flexibility and economy of language were sought by assigning variables a twofold function, that of subject or object, so that any variable might be either the subject or object of any other variable. We differentiated four general classes of variables. Vectors were defined as the psychological directions characteristic of behavior, striving, wishes, cathexes or feelings. Level referred to the plane of psychological function involved in the story. Conditions were defined as those "given" states, psychological, social, or physical, which are not behavior, striving, or wish. Qualifiers were defined as the more specific aspects of vectors, levels, or conditions.

* The writer has not however systematically employed the language of this scoring scheme in the text, since he believes that the utilization of the TAT should not be inextricably linked with any particular language of analysis. Implicit in many of the techniques of analysis presented in this text, however, are the concepts employed in this scoring scheme. The writer has striven to translate these concepts into common English wherever possible.

Chapter IV

INTRODUCTION TO THE TECHNIQUE OF INTERPRETATION

After identification and scoring of the variables of each story is completed we are at the threshold of interpretation. "Interpretation" has, in psychoanalytic doctrine, lost some of its pristine meaning. Interpretation is an activity common to all science. Unless it is our assumption that the interpretation of psychological data necessitates principles of inference peculiar to psychology, we must adopt the methodology common to all inductive and deductive science. It is our purpose in this chapter to demonstrate the applicability of long-accepted canons of inference to picture-provoked phantasy. Let us consider first the method of agreement of John Stuart Mill (60).

A. Method of Agreement

Let us consider the relationship between the following stories.*

1. This boy has just been given a violin and he's delighted with it. He wants to become a great violinst. He is encouraged by his parents. He works hard and eventually he becomes a great violinst.

2. This boy is very unhappy because he has no friends. His parents encourage him to make friends. He still has no friends until one day a new boy moves into the neighborhood. The new boy asks him to play with him and eventually they become good friends.

These two stories may be analyzed according to Mill's method of agreement, "If two or more instances of the phenomenon under investigation have only one circumstance in common, the circumstance in which alone all the instances agree is the cause, or effect of the given phenomenon." Let the given phenomenon be the successful outcome. In every condition which precedes the outcome, the encouragement by the parents is the only common condition. Thus, in 1 he has been given a violin; in 2 he lacks friends. In 1 he is happy; in 2 unhappy. In 1 the region is work and achievement; in 2 it is the social region. In 1 he works hard; in 2 he is passive in the face of social isolation. In 1 the means to eventual success and happiness is through hard work; in 2 it is through a gratuitous event for which he has

---

* The stories have been edited in this chapter, for didactic purposes. The number of the picture to which stories have been told has been omitted throughout, partly because many of the stories have been told to pictures not included in the present set of TAT cards but primarily because the principal techniques of interpretation employed in this book are not based on the relationship between the picture and the story.

not worked. The outcome—the gratification of the original wish—may be said to be the effect of the encouragement of his parents, since this alone is what the two instances have in common. This type of analysis is particularly illuminating in this case because in neither story is the encouragement of the parents causally related by the storyteller to the final outcome. The individual may not, in his imaginative productions, know, or clearly tell us what is cause and what is effect.

B. Method of Difference

Consider now the relationship between these stories.

1. This is someone who has just lost a person very dear to him. He is in the depths of despair. Life has lost all meaning for him and he doesn't want to go on living. But then he meets a woman who understands the way he feels and gradually he forgets his sorrow and he finds again that there is meaning in life.

2. This is the picture of a man who is mourning someone who was very close to him. Nothing seems to matter very much to him since her death. He sees no more point in living. Death comes as a welcome relief from his misery.

The relationship between these stories illustrates Mill's method of difference. "If an instance in which the phenomenon under investigation occurs, and an instance in which it does not occur, have every circumstance in common, save one, that one occurring only in the former, the circumstance in which alone the two instances differ is the effect, or cause, or an indispensable part of the cause of the phenomenon." Thus, in 1 and 2, there is the loss of a love object, and a consequent depression. But in 1 there is the intervention of a new love object who understands him; and the outcome is regeneration. In 2, there is no new love object, and the outcome is a continuation of the depression to its end in death. Thus, we may say that recovery from depression is the effect of the intervention of another love object.

C. Joint Method of Agreement and Difference

Let us reconsider now the protocol of the first case, adding two more stories from the same protocol.

1. This boy has just been given a violin, and he's delighted with it. He wants to become a great violinist. He is encouraged by his parents. He works hard and eventually he becomes a great violinist.

2. This boy is very unhappy because he has no friends. His parents encourage him to make friends. He still has no friends until one day a new boy moves into the neighborhood. The new boy asks him to play with him and eventually they become good friends.

1'. He has just been given a raise. He wants more than anything to become the head of the firm, and he works very, very hard, but somehow he never makes the grade.

2'. This fellow is very unhappy because he doesn't have any girl friends. He mopes and mopes. One night when he is feeling very lonely a girl picks him up and after that he sees quite a lot of her. But eventually she leaves him and he is lonely again.

This set of stories may be analyzed according to Mill's joint method of agreement and difference. "If two or more instances in which the phenomenon occurs have only one circumstance in common, while two or more instances in which it does not occur have nothing in common save the absence of that circumstance, the circumstance in which alone the two sets of instances differ is the effect or the cause or an indispensable part of the cause, of the phenomenon." Since one can never be certain that either the method of agreement or difference is being perfectly applied, the joint method strengthens the evidence. It must be rememberd that there are always similarities and differences between stories which may be unrecognized by the interpreter.

Here 1 and 1' are similar and 2 and 2' are similar, but not exactly alike. Thus, in 1 and 1', the age of the hero is different; in 2 the region is social, whereas in 2' it is the love region which is described. Otherwise, however, the fit is very close. In both 1 and 1' the hero is given something; the hero aspires to great achievement and works hard for it. The difference is primarily in the success of the outcome and the absence of parental encouragement in 1'. In 2 and 2', both heroes are unhappy because of the lack of cathected objects—both are rescued by more active individuals and this leads to friendship. The difference, again, is primarily in the success of the outcome and the absence of parental encouragement in 2'. The evidence for the necessity of parental support if the hero is to achieve his ends is thereby strengthened. Just as we can never be certain in experimental work that all factors have been controlled, we rarely find in TAT protocols the homogeneity of conditions which would allow unambiguous interpretation of differences between stories. For this reason the joint method is to be preferred wherever it is possible to employ it.

D. METHOD OF CONCOMITANT VARIATION

Frequently, stories do not involve the complete presence or absence of certain effects or causes but, rather, variations in degree. This is the case in the following stories.

1. He has had a hard time of it. He has never had much money, and has always had to work hard. He manages to make a living, but he is not a great success.

2. This is a fellow who has struggled all his life. He has never had the money he wanted, but he worked very hard. When others took vacations, he would work all the harder. After years of backbreaking effort, he became a millionaire.

Here we may employ Mill's method of concomitant variation. "Whatever phenomenon varies in any manner whenever another phenomenon varies in some particular manner, is either a cause or an effect of that phenomenon, or is connected with it through some fact of causation." In 1 and 2, we find that the degree of success varies concomitantly with the degree of effort, all other factors being equal. These stories do not reveal what are the causes of this difference in effort, but the relationship between effort and success is clear. The harder he works, the more successful he is.

E. Two Factors, Both Necessary and Sufficient Causes

These methods of Mill take us part of the way. Mill's "phenomenon" is, in psychological matters, rarely a single factor, and the cause of an effect usually involves gestalten. Let us, then, expand the inquiry to cope with causes or effects which involve at least two factors.

Let us consider the relationship between these four stories.

1. This man is in a state of indecision. He is wondering what he should do in his business. His father advises him what he should do. He works hard and becomes a success.

2. He is wondering what to do. His father gives him advice and shows him how to run his business. He comes down to his store and helps out, but the business flops.

3. He is in a quandry. He doesn't know what to do with his business. His father says, "I told you you'd never make a go of it." He works hard to save it, but he goes bankrupt.

4. This man is facing bankruptcy, and his father is berating him for his stupidity. He becomes more and more depressed, and his business goes downhill steadily till it fails.

In these stories we have an example of the case in which two factors are both necessary and sufficient causes of the phenomenon "success." Where, in 1 there is *both* advice from the father and hard work by the hero, the hero becomes a success. But, in 2, the hero is both instructed and helped by the father. There is no mention, however, of the hero's efforts, and the outcome is failure. In 3, he works hard, but he is criticized rather than advised, and the business fails. In 4, there is again criticism which depresses the hero to such an extent that he does not try to save the business, and the outcome is again failure. It appears that neither the father's advice, nor the son's hard work is sufficient to guarantee a successful outcome if one is present and the other absent. When the father's advice is followed by actual help and intervention in his son's enterprise, there is no mention that the son works. It would seem that advice is necessary, but it must not go beyond advice or the son's initiative will be stifled. The son's hard work alone will not guarantee success; presumably his efforts must be guided to some extent, or the effort is in vain.

Let us generalize this type of analysis and call paternal advice x and the hero's own work y. If we are to assert that both x and y are necessary and sufficient causes of phenomenon P, it is necessary to show that, when x and y appear, P is a consequence and that when only x appears, as in 2, P does not appear and when only y appears, as in 3, P does not appear and, when neither x nor y appears, as in 4, P does not appear. In other words, for both x and y to be necessary and sufficient causes, the phenomenon must appear as a consequent only if x *and* y appear. This type of relationship is of critical importance in the diagnosis of personality for therapeutic or guidance purposes. In the treatment of anxiety or depression we not infrequently find that the pathological reaction is incited or sustained by a combination of factors, neither of which occurring separately is pathogenic. Using this knowledge, if we can reduce either factor the reaction may be controlled. Similarly, an anxiety state may be sustained by the absence of two or more factors. Therapy of such conditions calls for the introduction of a combination of factors and if we were to employ only one factor at a time the condition would not yield. Thus, in a case similar to that above, TAT analysis revealed that success depended on paternal advice which did not stifle initiative. Wherever this advice was extended to the point of assuming some of the individual's responsibilities, the patient experienced anxiety. Wherever this individual worked without such advice, there was also anxiety. In his past history, the only period free of anxiety occurred when he was working for a paternalistic scientist on a government project. The latter helped him but allowed him considerable initiative in the solution of his problems. On leaving this environment, this individual developed acute anxiety attacks. Rapport in the diagnostic and therapeutic situation hung on a delicate balance between a directive and nondirective attitude on the part of the therapist. If the therapist veered too much in one direction or the other, it precipitated acute anxiety. The therapist was able to reduce substantially the patient's anxiety by maintaining the attitude which the TAT indicated was necessary for the patient's adequate functioning. Eventually he was again willing to continue the career which he had relinquished under the pressure of his anxiety attacks.

Similar problems arise in marital relationships. Individuals who need both support and respect may experience acute frustration in marriage if either element is missing from the relationship. The same joint needs will be found characteristic of some individuals in the work setting. Others are able to split the satisfaction of these two needs, requiring support from their wives and respect from their business associates. This type of analysis of TAT protocols yields insight into the precise pattern of conditions necessary for adequate functioning in a variety of regions.

Though asserting that two factors are both necessary and sufficient conditions for a phenomenon, we have not specified the exact relationship between these two factors. It is a synergistic relationship, so that success depends neither on hard work nor on advice but on the pattern of hard work which is guided. It cannot represent a chain of causal connections where, for example, advice leads to hard work which in turn produces success. The case in which there is *hard work without success,* i.e., story 3, precludes the possibility that advice alone is sufficient cause for hard work, since the hero works without advice. It also precludes the possibility that hard work is sufficient cause of success, since hard work results here in failure.

F. Either of Two Factors but Not Both as Sufficient Cause

Let us consider another type of causal relationship, exemplified in the stories which follow.

1. This fellow is having a fight with the girl. They have been in love for years and now he is telling her that he no longer loves her and that they are through. He leaves her and feels better than he has in years.

2. These are two lovers. They are very deeply in love, and they are sharing the intimacy which only those who have lived together for so long are capable of. These are the moments they both live for.

3. This man is in a great conflict. He has been in love with this woman for a long time, but there is something about her which he can't stand. They were to be married, but he cannot bring himself to marry her or let her go. They go on for years this way. He wonders why he can't be happy with her or without her.

4. This fellow is lonely and miserable. He is in a strange town and is on the prowl. But all the women have escorts and he goes back to his hotel room more miserable than ever.

Here we see the instance in which one or the other of two factors is a sufficient cause of a phenomenon, but not both together. This individual tells us that he will be happy if he rejects a love object, or accepts a love object, but that he will be unhappy if he both accepts and rejects a love object, or has no love objects. Generalizing these relationships, let us call love x and rejection y. To assert that either x or y is a sufficient condition of P, but not both x and y together, we must show that, when x appears, the resultant is P;

when y appears, the resultant is P; when x and y appear, P does not appear; and that P does not appear under any other circumstances than x or y. In 1, y, rejection of the love object, produces P, a happy outcome. In 2, x, the acceptance of the love object, produces P, a happy outcome. In 3, the simultaneous acceptance x and rejection y of the love object does not produce P, a happy outcome. In the absence of either x, the acceptance of a love object, or y, the rejection of a love object, in story 4, the quest of a love object does not produce a happy outcome.

In this type of relationship, the simultaneous operation of two factors detracts from the efficacy characteristic of each independent factor. In contrast to the relationship in which both factors are necessary and sufficient, here each factor does stand in a means-end relationship to the resultant phenomenon. It is not a means-end chain between x, y, and P, but either x or y may be a means to the same end (P). In these stories, the hero can be happy whether he loves or hates, but he cannot be happy if he has no object to love *or* hate or if he both loves and hates the same object.

The paralyzing consequences of two antithetical forces need no underlining. But the implications of this type of relationship are broader than the problem of psychological conflict and ambivalence. Thus, in the work region, let us suppose that x is a skeptical attitude on the part of the individual's employer and that y represents work of a difficult nature. There are protocols in which an individual may be challenged sufficiently by either the difficulty of the work or by the skeptical attitude of his employer to work well and achieve success. But the combination of difficult work and a skeptical attitude on the part of the employer may produce passivity rather than counteractive effort. The TAT thus affords us, through this type of analysis, an insight into the frustrations which elicit the best energies of the individual and a delineation of the specific conditions under which the load may become too great. The same technique of analysis may be used to determine the degree of rejection which spurs a person to win a love object, and the concatenation of barriers which produces withdrawal. Again, by this technique we may analyze the general type of threat which produces heroic struggle and the cumulative dangers which result in abject surrender.

G. Either or Both of Two Factors as Sufficient Cause

Another type of causal relationship is exemplified in the following stories:

1. The older man has just given the younger man a pep talk. The young man goes to work with new enthusiasm. He does his work so well that he gets a raise.

2. This man has a problem. The other fellow shows him what he knows and he is such an apt student that before long he is given more responsibility.

3. He seems unhappy and discouraged. Then somebody comes along and asks him what the trouble is. He tries to make him feel better, and shows him what he's been doing wrong. In no time at all he does feel better, and he sees that all he needed was a little know-how, and he can do it as well if not better than the next fellow.

4. This guy is in a mess. He's only been working a few days and he doesn't know exactly what to do, and his foreman is always bawling him out, and yelling at him to keep working. He does keep working, but at the end of the week when he gets his pay check there is a slip in it telling him that his services are no longer required.

In these stories we have an example of the case in which *either or both* of two factors is a sufficient cause of the phenomenon "success." Thus in 1, encouragement leads to success. In 2 instruction results in success. In 3 both encouragement and instruction produce success. But in 4, neither encouragement nor instruction is offered, and the outcome is failure. Generalizing, let x represent encouragement and y represent instruction. If we are to assert that either x or y, or both, is a sufficient cause of phenomenon P, we would have to show that P appeared when x appeared or when y appeared or when x and y appeared but did not appear if neither x nor y appeared. These stories satisfy these criteria; a successful outcome follows either encouragement or instruction or both. When neither encouragement nor instruction appears, the outcome is unsuccessful.

In this type of relationship, x and y are, as above, means to the same end, but they do not interfere with each other in the production of this end. They may result in precisely the same phenomenon or their action together may be synergistic. Thus encouragement and instruction may result in precisely the same degree of productivity, or in a greater degree than if either were present alone. In the examples above, there was no synergistic interaction. This type of analysis is of diagnostic importance in vocational guidance when it is important to know whether an individual requires *both* instruction and encouragement; or one *or* the other but *not both;* or *one* or the *other or both.*

H. MULTIFACTOR ANALYSIS

We have examined some of the techniques for analyzing two factors as cause or effect. Let us turn now to the problem of multifactor analysis. We have seen that what appears to be a cause and effect relationship within any single story may in the light of other stories prove to be something quite different. It is clear that we cannot interpret any single story without considering other stories which involve related factors.

Let us consider a hypothetical story in which a hero who has worked hard all his life loses his job, becomes pessimistic and commits suicide. We shall attempt to show that this single story provides no basis whatever for interpretation, that it can be interpreted only on the basis of the concomitant variation of the elements of this story with related elements in other stories. We will now examine the varieties of meanings which may be expressed by this story, as an example of the interpretation of any story.

1. THE STORY AS AN EXPRESSION OF THE INDIVIDUAL'S VALUES

The story may be an expression of the individual's values. Suppose that our hypothetical story meant that work was the individual's central value. If this were the case we would find that in other stories which mentioned threats to other values—disruption of love, family or social relationships—the hero was not seriously disturbed but that the hero was seriously disturbed in any story in which his work was threatened.

On the other hand, suppose that both work and love were the individual's central values. If this were so, stories involving threats to either of these values would be disturbing; threats to any other value, however, would be less serious.

2. THE STORY AS AN EXPRESSION OF THREAT

The story may express threats with which the individual is concerned. Thus our story might mean that the individual was peculiarly sensitive and vulnerable to the threat of loss. If this were the case there would be other stories in which there were losses of many kinds which also resulted in pessimism and suicide—losses of love objects, friends, parents or physical objects. In stories in which he suffered no loss, the hero would be optimistic and the outcome happy.

Or this story might be an example of a general fear of any kind of frustration rather than fear of the specific threat of loss. If this were the case we would find other stories expressing a variety of frustrations of many values, all leading to pessimism and suicide. Stories in which the hero suffered no frustration would end more happily.

Or the story may be expressing the individual's differential reaction to one type of threat. Thus it might mean that he can tolerate any state of lack, but not a state of loss. If this were the case there would be other stories involving losses of all types which resulted in pessimism and suicide, but in stories where the hero *lacked* the same objects, he would overcome the deficit.

Or the story might express the individual's differential reaction to losses of varying magnitude. If this were the case there would be other stories in which losses of less serious magnitude resulted in less serious disturbance. The hero in this story loses his job and commits suicide; in another story he might lose a week's pay through illness, be distressed, but not commit suicide.

Or he might in one story lose his wife's affection and commit suicide and in another lose the affection of a girl friend and be distressed but not commit suicide.

3. THE STORY AS AN EXPRESSION OF INVARIANCE

Any story may express an invariant characteristic of the individual which is reflected in invariant repetitions of some element throughout the stories.

Thus this story might mean that the individual expects to be unsuccessful in whatever he does. If this were the case we would find that all his stories, whatever the nature of the wish or striving, involve failure.

It might, however signify that he expects to be unsuccessful only in his work. If this were the case we would find that all other stories involving work end in failure but whenever any other striving is involved the hero is successful.

Or the story might be an expression of the individual's general pessimism rather than his expectation of failure. If such were the case, all heroes would be pessimistic whether they succeed or fail and whether the theme of the story is concerned with work or another region.

If the story signified that the hero is pessimistic only with respect to work, all other stories involving work would describe a pessimistic hero, but the hero would be optimistic in stories involving other regions.

The story might indicate a basic self destructive wish. If this were the case all other stories would involve a hero who ultimately destroyed himself.

But if this story meant that the hero had such wishes only in connection with his work, there would be other stories in which work leads to suicide but no suicide in any other type of story.

4. THE STORY AS AN EXPRESSION OF NECESSARY CONDITIONS

Any story may be an expression of the conditions necessary for any element within the story. Thus this story might be an expression of the conditions necessary for the hero's success or failure in work. If this were the case other stories in which the hero worked hard all his life would also end in failure, but there would be stories of heroes who did not lose their jobs and in these we would find some preceding condition other than hard work. Such heroes might, for example, have worked for employers who were interested in them.

The story might also be an expression of the conditions that cause the individual to become pessimistic. If this were the case there would be other stories in which the loss of his job made the hero pessimistic and stories in which the hero was prevented—by his wife's sympathy, for example—from becoming pessimistic over the loss of his job.

Finally, the story may define the conditions which would incite the individual to commit suicide. If this were the case the hero would take his life in situations similar in any way to this one, but he would not commit suicide if conditions were different in any way—if, for example, he did not lose his job or if he were not pessimistic following such loss, or if someone encouraged him after he had become pessimistic. An examination óf the conditions which did *not* lead to suicide in other stories would enable us to determine which of the conditions in this story *did* lead to suicide—whether it was the loss of his job or the pessimism which followed this. If the loss of his job were responsible for his suicide there would be other stories in which the hero, having lost his job, commits suicide. If, however, it was pessimism that caused him to take his life, he would not commit suicide in other stories in which pessimism did not follow the loss of his job.

We have attempted to demonstrate the varieties of interpretation possible in *any* single story and the technique of analysis used to discover the specific meaning which may be inherent in the story. Such analysis necessarily involves a consideration of the total protocol and, as we shall illustrate in a later chapter, may involve information which must be sought outside the TAT.

Summary

We have examined seven techniques commonly employed in the interpretation of any type of scientific data. We have suggested that the interpretation of TAT stories may employ canons of inference long accepted by other sciences. These were seen to be "models" to which empirical data might be fitted with varying degrees of error. Since the presence of unrecognized factors is an inherent characteristic of empirical inquiry, the employment of these methods cannot guarantee valid inferences, but will reduce some of the error which might otherwise enter into our interpretations.

As applied to TAT stories, Mill's method of agreement require two stories in which a common effect is preceded by only one other common condition. This common condition is then the cause of the common effect. In our examples we chose common outcomes as effects, but any element in the story may be analyzed in the same manner. According to the method of difference, two stories must be similar in every respect but one; this difference is then the cause of the difference in outcome. In the joint method of agreement and difference, both methods are employed and the evidence is thereby strengthened. There must be two stories with only one common condition leading to the same effect and two sets of stories in which each set of two is similar in every respect but one and with differences in outcomes which are the result of the dissimilar causes. In the method of concomitant variation, differences in degree of an effect are related to concomitant variation in differences in degree of the causal condition.

Inasmuch as most psychological phenomena involve a pattern of factors as cause and effect, we expanded the inquiry to cope with at least two factors. Where two factors are both necessary and sufficient causes it is necessary to show that the effect must follow only if both factors appear. If either one, or neither, is present, the effect cannot appear. When either of two factors, but not both, is a sufficient cause of an effect, it must be shown that the effect follows when either factor appears, but that it does not follow if neither factor appears and if both factors appear. Finally, where either, or both, of two factors is a sufficient cause, it must be shown that the effect follows the appearance of either factor, or both together, but does not follow if neither factor appears.

Finally, we considered the problems of multifactor analysis. We saw that the interpretation of any story involves an analysis of concomitant variation of related elements in other stories. We found that any story might be an expression of the individual's values, or the threats which beset him, or characteristics of the individual which are invariant, or the conditions necessary for any element within the story.

CHAPTER V

LEVEL ANALYSIS

The determination of the relationship between story and storyteller is the keystone of interpretation. This relationship can never be less complex than the one between phantasy and the larger matrix of the personality. Considering the nature of the imaginative productions called for by the TAT, it may be even more complex. The individual is asked for something more than his fleeting, diffuse, private phantasies. He is called upon to interpret the behavior, feelings, and expectations of individuals represented pictorially. It is for this reason that the storyteller in his interpretation of the lives of these characters may expose fragments of his own past history, his contemporary behavior, and his future expectations and aspirations. He may reveal his public behavior, those facets shared only with intimates, and private feelings guarded from any public scrutiny as well as wishes whose existence has been somehow guarded from even the individual's own awareness. We will address ourselves in this chapter to the unraveling of these diverse strands from the fabric of TAT protocol.

A. The Relationship Between Overt and Covert Needs

An individual may have wishes which he does not translate into overt behavior; this is one of the salient characteristics of any socialized human being. There is considerable evidence for the assumption that such wishes are frequently attributed to the heroes of the individual's TAT stories. One of the most systematic explorations of this area occurs in Sanford's (84) study of school children. He examined the relationship between needs as they are expressed in the TAT and as they are expressed in overt behavior. The average correlation was $+0.11$, from which he concluded that we cannot assume that a need which appears in TAT stories will be manifested in the behavior of that individual. He found evidence that certain needs most commonly inhibited by the children appeared most frequently in their TAT's. Thus there was a correlation of about -0.30 between TAT expression and overt expression of the following needs: acquisition, aggression, autonomy, harm avoidance, sex, and succorance. He also found needs which were of low intensity in the TAT but high in overt behavior. These needs were: understanding, order, counteraction, blame avoidance, deference, construction and sentience. Finally there were needs showing high intensity in both the TAT and overt behavior: achievement, nurturance, affiliation, dominance and cognizance. The explanation offered for the presence in the TAT of antisocial needs which did not appear in overt behavior was that cultural prohibition or internal conflict prevented the overt gratification of these needs and thereby increased their intensity on the level of phantasy. Needs found to be low in the TAT but high in overt behavior proved to be socially acceptable needs whose expression was not only permitted but encouraged and which consequently left little residual tension to stimulate phantasy. To explain needs which appeared high in both the TAT and overt behavior it was assumed that these were encouraged by our culture but given insufficient opportunity for satisfaction, either through circumstances or because the individual lacked ability to satisfy them. To account further for the similarity between phantasy and behavior, two additional hypotheses were suggested. First, that needs in conflict with either social or personal ideals would appear both in phantasy and behavior if the need were strong and self control weak. Second, that needs socially acceptable if expressed in one way and socially unacceptable if otherwise expressed might be high in both phantasy and behavior but expressed more primitively in phantasy than in behavior. Evidence for the second hypothesis was found in a correlation of about +0.30 between the need sex as it appeared in the TAT and the needs affiliation, nurturance, and deference as these appeared in overt behavior.

These hypotheses concerning the relationship between needs in phantasy and those expressed in overt behavior are not contradicted by any contemporary knowledge in the field of personality. Why, then, do the intercorrelations offered in support of these hypotheses typically average about +0.30? It is our opinion that the dynamic relationships postulated by Sanford are valid hypotheses of the relation between covert needs and overt behavior and perhaps between phantasy and behavior. But we do not believe that the quantitative scoring of needs in TAT protocols provides us with an accurate estimate of the strength of either phantasy or covert needs. We have presented evidence in Chapter I that at least 30 per cent of the TAT reflects the past history of the individual, that in general every level of psychological function finds representation within the stories. Repressed and suppressed, covert and overt needs, the past, the present and the future—all these are woven into the imaginative productions of the TAT. For this reason we cannot assume that correlations between needs expressed in the TAT and needs expressed in behavior represent correlations between covert and overt needs, or even between phantasy and behavior. The TAT represents more than the individual's private phantasies.

The relationship between overt and covert needs can frequently be found *within* the TAT stories themselves if attention is given to the levels and qualifiers portrayed in the story. Scoring according to either the Murray-Sanford needs or our vectors does not differentiate the level of psychological function or specific qualifications of such a function. Both Murray and Sanford score one qualifier—that of the intensity of the need or press—but differences in level or contingency or temporal dimension are not scored. The statement, "He achieved what he had worked for," and the statement, "He wanted to work and achieve great success," are both rated need achievement, and the only qualification of this rating would be the degree of intensity of the need. The fact that one represents actual work and achieved success and that the other represents these same needs on the level of wish is not indicated in the scoring of a need, except insofar as there are differences in intensity. In the interest of flexibility and economy of language it is desirable that needs or vectors be scored without reference to levels or other qualifications. But if we are to understand the relationship between covert needs and overt behavior these differences must somewhere be included in the scoring of the protocols. The qualifiers of contingency and temporal characteristics are no less important for this purpose. It is one thing for the hero to say, "He will probably achieve success," but another to say, "Ten years later he did achieve success." Although both events are placed into the future, the latter indicates a greater degree of confidence. Again, the statement, "He will achieve success," means something other than the statement, "He was successful in the past." The first might be the statement of an individual looking hopefully into the future, the other the longing for a return to a golden age. Needs and press, vectors and conditions, without further specification of level and other qualifiers cannot yield important functional relationships either within the TAT or between TAT and the personality of the story-teller. The first step toward an understanding of the level of psychological function represented in TAT protocol is an analysis of the degree of variance of the levels employed in each protocol.

B. Degree of Variance of Level

We sometimes find that a protocol may be invariant with respect to the level on which the stories proceed. Stress may produce invariance of level in an entire protocol. An example is that of the Marine who discovered that his wife had been unfaithful to him while he had been overseas. In his TAT every one of his heroes "worried and wondered how everything was going to turn out". The content of this worry and wondering was not specified nor was there interaction between the characters of his stories. This invariance of the level of feeling and expectation was a representation of the constriction of his functioning and the hypertrophy of these two levels induced by his unhappiness.

If the testing situation itself significantly raises the level of anxiety, a not uncommon sequel is invariance of stories on the level of object description:

"The violin looks like a Stradivarius," "This woman is middle aged," "This is a farm scene and they are farmers and she is a student with a book." These are typical of the "stories" such individuals tell, commenting "I don't get much out of that."

Occasionally one finds protocols which employ only the behavioral level. "This boy is playing the violin. When he finishes he goes out and plays ball, and then he comes and eats supper." "The farmer is plowing the field and the woman helps him. The girl is going to school and when she gets back she will do the washing." Such individuals, we have found, are extraverted to such an extent that their behavior is imbedded in the external world and they are free to a great extent of endopsychic barriers which might interfere with the spontaneous expression of their wishes. Wish and behavior are one and the same for these individuals. They are aware of a wish only as it is reflected in their behavior, in the manner in which one who is gardening does not differentiate between himself and hoe. Although the hoe is the instrument of the person, the individual, if there are no obstacles to his activity, experiences only the "hoe activity" as an undifferentiated whole.

Other individuals may be so deeply engrossed in their inner life that instead of assimilating their inner life to the external world they assimilate the world to their inner life. If this is the case we may find an invariance of the level of feeling or thought or memory throughout the protocols. Commerce with the external world on the behavioral level is evaluated in terms of its effects on this inner life. Thus in the following story the violin becomes a part of the hero's inner life.

> A youth at dreams. Into many lives come moments which are extremely enlightening. Those may be the times of daydreams, or they may be the beginnings of a reality. A young lad sat as in a sleep over his best of friends in a mechanical way. It was as if his best friend were giving a support for his dreams. Those friends are generally the ones which become a part of one's own being. As this child sat over his violin in a dream, he saw his future in a sort of way. He dreamed of his playing before the last thrones of the world; he dreamed that he was the creator of a new world in music. From that Saturday morning dream came a great man. Today Dr. X has made his life shape around his friend over which he visioned his future. He is only one of many men of vision who took time out to dream.

Or the inner life of feeling may assume proportions which completely remove the individual from interaction with the external world. Stories in such cases employ the level of feeling or mood throughout as in the following example:

> This is the picture of a man who is very depressed. Nothing seems to matter any more—what's the use. He has the feeling there is nothing inside of him— no feelings—nothing. It was better before when he felt miserable.

There are protocols which portray one or two levels exclusively. But this is rare. *In such cases, as we have seen, the level which is invariant is a literal representation of the predominant level on which that individual functions.*

C. Relative Frequency of Levels

Most individuals, however, operate on many levels. They behave. Events happen. They perceive, attend to, and take interest in the world about them. They have plans. They are governed in part by expectations and by their sentiments and wishes. They have feelings and physical sensations. They remember and they have daydreams and night dreams. But there are important differences in the relative time and energy devoted by different individuals to these levels. A very rough index of these differences may be achieved from the relative frequency of appearance of each level in the protocol. This type of analysis is particularly valuable in the comparison of cultural differences. For example the TAT stories given by Navaho children are characterized by a predominance of behavior and event, with relatively little elaboration of personal feelings, memories, daydreams, and so on. Further evidence of the usefulness of such a technique of analysis may be found in a consideration of the data presented in Kutash's (49) study of the TAT's of psychopathic defective criminals. These individuals, suffering restraint of behavior because of their imprisonment, might be expected to employ the levels of object description, feeling, and wish more frequently than the level of behavior in their stories. Examination of his findings confirms this expectation. The category of highest frequency was separation anxiety, the next most frequent category was description, and third was the category ambition—a *wish* to achieve something in the future. The responses next in frequency were conflicts and guilt feelings. These results are also illuminating in connection with the discrepancy between TAT findings and overt behavior. Stories involving the wish to achieve great things and thereby to make people happy are indeed discrepant with the behavior but not with the total personality of these individuals. They do *wish to* achieve much and to redeem themselves in the eyes of society. These wishes are expressed in their stories. There is, however, no less discrepancy between their wishes and their actual behavior than between the TAT and their behavior.

D. Cause-Effect Relations of Levels

Although a comparison of the relative frequency of a variety of levels may yield a general picture of the level economy of the individual, much more specific analysis is required to evaluate the meaning of different levels as they are attributed to the heroes of the TAT stories. The level attributed to the hero may be characteristic of the personality of his creator if it is invariant throughout the stories. But since this is relatively infrequent we must employ another technique. A level may vary from story to story for two quite different reasons: It may be either the cause or the effect of some condition which varies. Let us consider the following two stories told by a young man.

> This looks like a fellow looking out of the window, just dreaming. He's dreaming of the day when he'll be head man at his office. They're beautiful thoughts and ten years later we find him at the same window dreaming the same beautiful thoughts. He's still a clerk.

> He's a tired, but very happy man. Today he realized the goal of years of hard work. It wasn't easy, slaving hours when all the others had gone home at five o'clock, but it was worth it.

We are told in effect that daydreaming results in failure, and hard work leads to success. This was the protocol of an extremely industrious young man whose actual behavior is illustrated by the second story. The first story represents his ideology and his belief that if he *were* to relax his efforts and give himself over to daydreaming he would certainly fail. Differences in level here are causes or conditions; the important variable is the success which he feels can be accomplished only through work on the behavioral level. The hero who daydreams is *not* a projection of either the behavior or the wish of the storyteller, but a reflection of a *belief* about the *consequences* of the level of daydreaming. It is for this reason that an analysis of the relative frequency of various levels must be interpreted with caution. It may by no means indicate that the individual daydreams as much as he works if, as in this protocol, each appears with the same frequency.

Let us now consider the case in which a variation in level appears as the effect of preceding conditions. The following two stories are illustrative.

> He's a very hard-working young man. He's brought some work home from the office to do. He's interested in it and in no time at all he finishes it and goes to bed.

> He's got some kind of a problem—probably ran up against something that was too much for him. Let's say he was working on something and he ran up against a tough problem. Finally he loses interest in it and begins to think of other things. And let's round it off by his daydreaming of being the smartest man in his line of work.

We are told that when the hero is interested in his work and there are no serious barriers to the solution of his problem he is a hard worker and finishes his job. But when insurmountable difficulties arise he takes refuge in daydreams of glory. In this case the variations of level do *not* tell us that he is half worker and half daydreamer. It is rather a projection of the *conditions* which allow the individual to work, or which inhibit work and force him to the level of daydream. Whether in actual fact this individual works hard or daydreams cannot be determined by a comparison of these stories. We can predict the conditions under which he will and will not be able to carry his work through to a successful completion but we would have to inquire further, either in the TAT or other sources, to determine the relative frequency of these levels of function in the life of the individual.

The analysis of the levels of psychological function should employ the techniques outlined in the preceding chapter. The meaning of the appearance of any level in a story must be evaluated in terms of the concomitant variation of other elements in the stories. As we have seen, its introduction may signify that the particular level is a resultant of specific conditions, and that when these conditions are different, the resultant level changes. Or the specific level may signify that it is the specific condition of a certain sequel, and that if the hero's level of function were to change, the sequelae would be different.

E. Sequence Analysis of Levels

Having determined the relative frequency of levels and the causal relations between levels and other dimensions of the stories, we may now turn to another technique of analysis. This consists in a systematic examination of the *sequence* of levels.

1. SEQUELAE OF THE LEVEL OF WISH

Let us consider first the sequence of levels which may follow the expression of a wish. The wish may be followed by a change to the level of thinking and then by the level of behavior. Generally such sequences signify a deliberative conjunctive personality for whom the expression of any wish necessarily involves an intermediate step in thinking, as in the following story.

> Well, it looks as though the violin is broken and he feels sad about it because he likes to play. Uh . . . he's about eight years old and he wants to be a violinist. His family can't afford to get him another one. He's probably thinking about how he can earn some money to get it repaired. He gets a job delivering newspapers and gets the violin repaired and takes up his studies again. Because of his interest he becomes a success.

The wish may be followed by thinking but without further translation into behavior. This sequence signifies an overemphasis on the deliberative phase of activity, so that action is paralyzed by excessive planning.

> This little boy is an only child. He has great ambitions, but he knows it won't be easy. He'll have to learn how to read music and then he'll have to learn to play scales, and then he'll have to work very hard and practice 10 hours a day, but he thinks he can do it and he figures out how many years it will take him to accomplish all of this, and we see him here figuring it all out.

A similar sequence is that of wish-thinking-daydream. This sequence differs from the preceding one in that the overelaboration of the level of thinking does not paralyze action, but rather short-circuits the wish through the level of daydream.

> The little boy wants to be a violinist and he goes about it very methodically. He figures on asking his parents if he can take violin lessons, and if they say yes he plans on getting the best teacher they can afford, and as he thinks of all of this he sees himself on the stage at Carnegie Hall with thousands of people spellbound at the greatest violinist of the age.

In another common sequence, the wish is followed by daydreaming and this followed by behavior. In these cases the means-end cognizance is less important to the individual than the vision of the future goal which inspires him to translate the wish into appropriate behavior. This sequence of levels is represented in the following story.

> The girl is daydreaming. She wants to become a great artist, the kind that people admire. She is a very smart girl and she wants to make a name or reputation for herself so she studies diligently and develops into a renowned person.

But the sequence wish-daydream may also be followed by an expectation of an event rather than by behavior. In the following story the boy wishes he could play the violin; this leads to a daydream which leads to the expectation that he will someday *be* a violinist; the latter is an event and the object of the expectation. Daydreams in this case create sufficient certainty to require no behavior on the part of the hero.

> This boy wishes more than anything that he might be able to play the violin like his father. He dreams of the day when he'll be old enough. He's certain that when he does get older he will be a great violinist like his father.

The wish may however lead to a daydream which becomes an end in itself, preceded by no thinking and with neither behavior nor the expectation of behavior or event following the daydream. There is in such a case even less value to the daydream as an instrument for evoking behavior. In the preceding two stories the daydreams served the function of either inspiring work, or at the least, creating confidence in a future event, but here it merely has the effect of short-circuiting the wish. The following is an example of such a sequence.

> This kid is daydreaming about being a great violinist. He's always wanted to be a violinist, and here he sits staring at the violin imagining how wonderful it would be. He's so lost in reverie and completely absorbed that he forgets about everything else.

Another variety of passivity following a wish is the sequence wish-day-dream-event, in which the event is the result of the behavior of another person. This represents either the story of an individual who has in fact received an abundance of gratuities without effort on his part or a wish fulfillment phantasy. The following story was told by an individual who had received many gratuities in his childhood:

> The little boy has been wishing he might have a violin. Wouldn't it be wonderful, he thought, to have my own violin like father has. One day as he was dreaming about this his father marches in and says look what I've got for you, and sure enough it's a violin.

The wish may be followed by an event without elaboration on the level of daydream. The event may gratify or frustrate the satisfaction of the wish, but, in either case, the individual is pictured as the passive object of external forces. The following two stories provide examples of this sequence.

> This young kid wishes he could be violinist. But his parents don't have much money and that's that. He never becomes one.

> The young boy pictured here is staring enraptured at the violin he's just gotten. He's wanted a violin for a long time and had about given up hope, but his parents at last bought him one.

The wish followed immediately by behavior is a curiously rare sequence. This is probably because the extraverted individual who is imbedded in the external world is less aware of the existence of wishes as separate entities. The following story is representative of this sequence.

> This boy is tired of playing the violin, he'd rather be playing ball anyway, so he puts down the violin and goes out and plays ball with the kid next door.

The wish may be followed by neither daydream, intention, nor behavior, but stand alone, ungratified. Such a story is not uncommonly told by an individual whose wishes, by their very nature, seem impossible of gratification.

> This is a very peculiar child. He has always wanted to play his mother's violin. Otherwise he's a perfectly normal child. We see him here looking at his mother's violin, wishing he could play it.

The wish may be followed by a counter wish and then behavior. The behavior may be directed toward fulfilling either the former or latter wish. If the first wish leads to an inhibiting wish, and the behavior expresses the inhibiting wish, this signifies an individual who yields to the forces of inhibition. But if the behavior represents the original wish, it is an indication of an impulsive personality, but somewhat less impulsive than if the counter wish had not been mentioned. The following two stories are representative of these sequences.

Johnny wants to get out and play—still he should practice. Doesn't he want to be a great violinist? After a while he will pick up the violin and practice.

This chap is in a fix. Today is the first day of spring, and there's a swell game going on just outside his house. It isn't that he doesn't like to practice the violin, he does, but he likes to play baseball too, especially today. He plays baseball and has a wonderful time. He forgets all about his violin till he hears his mother calling him into the house for supper, and then he remembers, and he feels a little bad because the next day his music teacher is coming and he hasn't yet memorized the piece he was supposed to.

2. INSTIGATORS OF THE LEVEL OF WISH

We have thus far considered common sequences of levels which are sequelae to the level of wish. We will now consider the levels which *precede* and instigate the level of wish.

A wish may be instigated or reactivated by events. Protocols characterized by such relationships signify an individual whose inner life is essentially reactive to outer stimuli of an impersonal nature. In the following story the rumor of an event reactivates a wish the hero has always possessed.

Ah—here's our circus performer—a very agile tumbler, a gymnast. He's climbing up so he can look out, hmm, he sees something I can't figure. It's at a circus, though that straight line back there doesn't look like a circus. And it's while they're setting up the show. Oh, yes. He's heard the rumor that the elephants have broken loose and he always wanted to see what would happen if the elephants broke loose. He had been a gym teacher up to a few months ago, before he joined the circus. And he gets a big kick out of this. And now he's running up the rope to see if the elephants are really loose. And sure enough they are. There's a couple running downtown—not fast or doing any damage—just loping slowly, ambling along. The women faint and the men cheer (laughs) and it's a big excitement in this middle sized town—till the trainer comes along.

Wishes may also be activated or reactivated by memory. Individuals who suffer grief, shame, or anxiety may tell such stories. One of the salient characteristics of such inner states is their peculiar sensitivity to rearousal through memory. In our experience the sequence memory-wish has usually signified serious disturbance of the inner life of the individual telling the story. In the following story the hero's wish for the days of slavery is reactivated by the memory of his ex-master.

This picture takes place in the 1880's. Shown here is an ex-slave praying at the tomb of his master. Every year this man performs this act on the anniversary of the night his ex-master was killed during the fight following the Civil War. This Negro longs again for the days of slavery although all his younger friends laugh at him.

The wish may be activated by physical sensations. This is particularly characteristic of children and adolescents, who are apt to be governed to a great extent by their bodily states. In the following story told by an adolescent girl, the combination of fatigue and hunger activates the wish to return home.

Somebody's going to have a child, I see. Or is that just the picture? Well, this girl's family was illiterate and she was quite a bright person and wanted to go to school. So when they moved over here from Jugoslavia—they look like they came from Jugoslavia—she immediately registered in school. However, with the Mother nagging that she should stay at home, she didn't do as well as she should. She could have done better. Finally, the nagging got so bad she decided to leave. Oh, she got about fifty or sixty miles from the house, realized she was very tired and hungry, started to wish she hadn't left. Meantime her parents were frantic. Both were feeling sorry for the other one—parents for the child and the child for the parents—and both decided to give in to each other. Now, how to finish? After a week or so, kid starving, the child returned home due to a policeman's kindness and her excellent memory. She knew how to get home but was scared. She finished up school and married a rising lawyer. Moral: Go to school and don't let your parents interfere with you.

A common activator of any wish is an expectation. This may be the individual's own expectation, that of another person, or both. In the following story, the wish to make a success of playing the violin is intensified by the hero's thought of how much his mother counted on his success, and the expectation of his mother's disappointment should he fail. In this case the content of his own expectation is his mother's wish.

Why must I practice so hard? and so long? and every day? And yet I love Mother so. I must make a success of this violin playing. Oh I must! Mother is counting on it; it's everything to her; if I fail and can't become very famous as . . . well the Great Jonny Jerome Mrs. Albert Jerome's Jonny Jerome . . . that would be better still, I certainly will deserve the booby prize. Then Mother can dress up and feel very proud and forget her failure. Mother, gosh, she must have been very pretty. Somehow they didn't see how talented she was . . . or maybe her voice was too small . . . it sounds so pretty here in the apartment but maybe it didn't sound like that in the big opera houses; maybe that's why she wasn't a success. I've got to work hard, real hard, terribly hard so she will be pleased. Tommy and Bud just don't understand why I'm so gone on this fiddle and catgut. It's Mother—when some extra special sound comes out she is so happy. Gee, I want an awful lot of extra special sounds to come 'cause she seems to even have Dad with her in this room—here on earth, not really but just pretend . . . This A string doesn't sound quite true—there she is . . . tum . . . tum . . . tee . . . tum, there it was right that time, but maybe I'd better do that scale once more; then I can go on to that new one. Gosh, I'm getting sleepy. Now, Jonny Jerome, are you going to sleep when you have another hour to practice? Here goes tum . . . tee . . . tum. This is the last time for the scale D E F G A, then I can go on to the new one . . . tum . . . tee . . . tum. I can't . . . go . . . to . . . t' . . . sleep . . . slee . . . slee. *The following is an excerpt from a local newspaper printed some 10 years later:* "A young, blond, and handsome chap, known to this town's other young and handsome chaps as 'Jonny' and to the 'olsters' as 'Mrs Albert Jerome's son who plays the violin so well' has been claimed by both 'chaps' and 'olsters' as the GREAT JEROME. Last evening he strummed and plucked those strings as no other seventeen year old since Paganini has ever dared. If we are not mistaken we see a brilliant future for this violinist. Mrs. Albert Jerome may well be proud of such a son."

Not uncommon is the activation of a wish by a special state, such as intoxication. The presence of a special state as instigator generally signifies that the wish is under some inhibition in the normal state, and some de-inhibiting force is required to activate it.

These two are lovers. They have known each other for a long time. Up to this point they have had a very platonic relationship, but tonight they are both feeling pretty high after a couple of highballs, and they are both suddenly seized with a passion neither of them had ever felt before. We see them here afterwards. She is naked, and he is sobering up and wondering what ever came over him. They will both feel upset for some time to come, and it will be a long time before they see each other again.

Wishes may be activated through the perception of human objects in the external world. This generally signifies an individual whose inner life is governed in large part by the presence of other human beings. In the following story the perception of a beautiful woman activates the wish for intimacy.

This is a man standing under a street light, just hanging around. As he stands there the most beautiful woman he thought he had ever seen in his life walked by. He felt himself suddenly moved deeply—he must see her, talk to her, touch her—but how? He followed her till she went into an apartment building and he hesitated. He could not follow her. But he could and did wait evening after evening outside her apartment to catch a glimpse of her, and eventually he talked to her and then they became more and more intimate till one day he asked her to marry him. They were married and it was only then that she told him that she had felt exactly the same way that he did that first night, and had hoped he would follow her.

Wishes may be activated by the behavior of others, rather than by their presence. This sequence is typical of individuals whose wishes are essentially reactive to the behavior of others. In the following story the individual's sex wishes are incited by the seductive behavior of a woman:

The woman in bed is naked. The man was a boarder in the same house. He had never been interested in women, but she was always leaving her door open, and exposing herself half naked to him. Tonight she was more forward, and came into his room in negligee. As she touched him he suddenly felt he wanted her and they slept together. Now he is full of remorse.

Finally, wishes may be activated through the medium of moods or feelings. This may signify an individual whose inner life exerts massive pressure and is more self regulative than reactive to outer stimuli. In the following story the mood of bitterness and despair activates the wish for self destruction.

This man is at the end of his rope. His life was full of bitterness and black despair. He curses the destiny that brought him to such degradation. He broods and broods, till one day he feels he would rather die than live on like this. But though he wants to be free, he cannot bring himself to take his own life.

We have thus far considered single instigators of wishes. Usually, a sequence of levels responsible for the evocation of a wish involves complex chains of determinants. Let us examine one such example. In the following story the initial level is behavior—the young man leaves home—the level then changes to event—he is surrounded by the darkness of the night. This, and the light coming from homes, leads him to the level of thinking—he considers these happy homes. The level of thinking changes to the level of mood— he is lonely and depressed—and this mood leads to the wish to be back home with his family. Thus the sequence is behavior-event-thinking-mood-wish.

This young man has left home in an effort to make his way in another part of the world. At the point of this picture he's standing outside, surrounded by the darkness of the night which is spotted here and there with the warm light of what he considers happy homes. He is lonely and somewhat depressed and wishes that he were back home now with his family. In the near future this feeling will not be as frequent and when it does come will not burden him to the extreme it does this first time he is feeling it. He will become a man of the world with little regard for sentiment in other people although always very sentimental himself.

In the preceding examples we have considered the sequence of levels preceding and following a particular level, that of wish. The same type of analysis may be applied to any other level. We may analyze the sequence of levels which precede and follow events, behavior, intentions, thoughts, moods, and feelings. Documentation of each of these varieties of analysis would require encyclopedic treatment beyond the scope of this book, but the logic of this type of analysis is clear. We examine the protocol with respect to sequence of levels, disregarding the content of the level. By means of this type of analysis patterns of such level-sequences may be extracted which might otherwise escape attention because they may be embedded in a variety of heterogeneous strivings and conditions. Interpretation of these sequences is governed by the logic of all interpretation. We cannot assume that a sequence literally represents something typical of the storyteller unless that sequence is invariant. If it is not invariant we must examine the conditions under which the sequences may vary to determine the meaning of the variability. Thus we might examine the effect of any single level on the sequence of levels which follows. Let us suppose that the typical level sequence of a conjunctive deliberate individual is that of wish-intention-thinking-behavior, in which the hero implements his wish by planning to do something, then considers the various steps to be taken, and finally does it. We might then examine the influence of any other level preceding the wish, to determine whether any particular level changes this typical sequence. We might discover that if the level of wish is preceded by mood or feeling, let us say depression or anxiety, the sequence changes to a less deliberative one in which the wish leads immediately to impulsive behavior, or to a more deliberate sequence in which the wish leads to excessive planning and conflicting expectations which paralyze behavior.

F. Analysis of Awareness

We have thus far addressed ourselves to the problem of the relationship between the various levels of psychological function as they are reflected in the TAT. Another problem is the degree to which the individual *is aware* of his own wishes or behavior. It is not uncommon for individuals to be unaware of the determinants of their feelings. An individual may be anxious or depressed and be unaware either of why he feels so, or even what the object of the anxiety or depression may be. Less frequently an individual may be anxious or depressed and not "know" it, then suddenly realize that he has had these feelings during the day and been only dimly aware of them. The extent of awareness of behavior may be similarly limited. Such awareness of the nature of overt behavior may be limited to an awareness of single concrete fragments of behavior. The patterning of behavioral sequences may entirely escape the attention of the individual. The contemporary determinants of such patterns are even more elusive, and the relationship of these to their genetic precursors is the achievement of only the most reflective individuals.

Determination of the degree and scope of awareness of the storyteller, as this is revealed in his TAT stories, is a relatively simple procedure. In our experience the storyteller cannot attribute such awareness to his heroes unless he possesses an equivalent degree of awareness of his own wishes and behavior. When stories are told without causal or motivational connections woven into the fabric of the story, this typically reflects a similar lack of awareness in the personality of the storyteller.

Consider the individual who tells a story of a hero who has been devoted to his mother all his life and who because of this regrets very much that he must leave home. The hero finds no happiness in his work away from home because he misses his mother, and consequently becomes more and more depressed, finally deciding that the only remedy is to return home. We may be certain that the individual telling such a story possesses an equivalent degree of awareness of the genetic determinants of his own depression and inability to work.

Suppose, however, that the story told of a hero who feels lonely and depressed, and because of this can find no happiness in his work, becomes more and more depressed about it and decides, as a result, to go home. Such an individual is unlikely to be aware of the genetic determinants of his loneliness, and consequently is incapable of attributing them to his hero.

Let us suppose, on the other hand, that the story told of a hero who finds no happiness in his work and decides as a result to return home. In this case the individual is unaware that his unhappiness in work may be the result of loneliness, even though he returns home because he does not enjoy his work.

Or the story might have told of a hero who is vaguely unhappy and who returns home, with no motivation attributed either to the unhappiness or the return home. In this series of examples, such an individual would have least awareness of the context of his own motives.

There are many fine gradations possible in the extent and scope of awareness. Thus, in the first story, less awareness of the functional relationships might have resulted in a story about a hero who has been devoted to his mother all his life *and* who leaves home with regrets *and* who finds no happiness in his work *and* who becomes more and more depressed *and* finally returns home. All the motivational connections in this story have been omitted; instead, there is a series of only partially related events and feelings. Such a story would be told by an individual less aware of his own motivation and the larger matrix in which it is embedded than the individual capable of telling the first story.

One typically finds in the TAT stories of patients who have received psychotherapy attribution to their heroes of complex patterns of motivation. Psychotherapy is of course not the only road to such insight. In the following series of stories, we present "insightful" stories from 3 individuals who have been psychoanalyzed, and 3 whose stories were told without benefit of prior therapeutic intervention.

In this story, told by a young woman who had renounced her tomboy wishes with regret, we are given insight into the dynamics of this change.

She's sitting in a room looking out of a window and she's watching her brothers and their friends outside playing baseball. It's spring. She's very proud of her brothers but she's also wishing she were a boy and could play with them too. She's about fifteen years old. What happens to her is, she reverts from her tomboy wishes and aspirations and becomes extremely feminine in a couple of years. She sort of realizes she can't be a boy, subconsciously, and she decides that, if she can't, at least she wants them to notice her some way or other, and she does it by becoming very popular so that all her brothers' friends take her out.

In the following story by an adult, we are told of the motives underlying his adolescent interest in boxing lessons. Again, this represents a page from the past history of the individual.

Here is a picture of a young man participating in a gym class. The young man was probably underdeveloped as a young child and consequently was subject for the taunts of his fellow youths for his inability to play or participate in the more strenuous games. With a feeling of inferiority he made up his mind that he would take every means at his disposal to develop himself. Entering into gym classes he worked hard and in time did develop the bulging muscles and the stamina that seemed so necessary to win the respect of his fellow youths. Here in this picture he is winning the rope-climbing event and, from the expression on his face, a great deal of satisfaction.

In the next story told by a middle-aged woman there is realization, at one point, that the material is autobiographical, but despite this the logic of her motivation is pursued to the end.

Oh she is a nasty little bitch really. She's made him so angry he's trying to get away. She is turning on everything she has got to keep him. She hates to lose control of the situation. She has been spoiled all her life. She can't stand to be rejected by anyone. This sounds autobiographical. She can be successfully sweet and charming—her charm is disarming—that is an awkward way to put it. She is the kind most people can't know well. She's got such a skillful technique. . That kind of person is dangerous—the greater the charm, the greater the viciousness underneath.

In the story which follows the individual correctly diagnoses the relationship between his paranoid ideas and parental indoctrination:

This chap is a paranoid. Feels wherever he goes someone's about to follow, choke or seize him. Can't get the idea out of his mind. Unable to sleep at night because he thinks someone is under the bed. Wherever he goes he has this terrible sensation of being followed. He finally ends up in an institution where his obsession is located but had progressed so far that it is impossible to eliminate it. He ends up hopelessly nuts. His mother was oversolicitous of his behavior. As a youngster she told him when he walked on the street that wherever he went there were eyes at every window which were criticizing his behavior. Therefore he must always behave right or he would bring dishonor to his family. You can say that again too. The last is a personal experience. I used to be afraid to move out of the house when I was seven or eight because of the eyes that were supposed to be watching.

The young woman who told the next story describes accurately her technique of coping with her feelings of aggression.

That hideous woman at the back is this woman's evil nature which she has long suppressed. This woman wasn't really evil when a child but things went against her. She felt frustrated on every hand. Now however she wants to restore her own mental health by attaching herself to some great and selfless cause. The more she strives in this direction the fainter and fainter grows the woman at the back. Eventually the finer qualities in her are completely reinstated.

And finally the self diagnosis in the case of Joseph Kidd, reported by White (104), as this was revealed in one of his TAT stories.

The story of a youth who throughout life considered himself persecuted and unhappy because of others' attitude toward him. He never quite understood why people did not like him, taking any attitude people had towards him as being one of hate. And thus finally he turned away from outside activities altogether, remaining aloof from people whom he had come to fear, having no friends, living only by himself. He developed an attitude of animosity toward his fellow men and wanted to become a greater success so that he could in this way dominate and as a result satisfy his persecutory complexes. He never realized that perhaps the fault lay in himself. The people's attitude toward him depended on himself, not on other people, but for years he struggled under the impression that the trouble was on the outside, not that anything he would do was wrong; until the day he came to the realization, having met a girl he loved, that the world was right and he was wrong, that all his trouble, unhappiness, general lethargy was a result of his own imagination, and in an attempt to get on a normal footing with the outside world for the sake of this girl, he found it was too late— the little part of his life had come and gone, and that to start out again he would have to revert to a second childhood, and could in no way adjust his feelings of animosity to the outside world, with the final result being that it only led to greater introversion. The more he tried the more secluded became his life until he desperately committed suicide.

Each of these stories represents incisive insights into the nature of the dynamics of the motivation of the individual who told the story. Such attribution to these heroes reflects the genuine awareness these individuals possessed of the dynamics of their own behavior. It is possible for an individual to possess such knowledge and not attribute it to his heroes, but we have not found individuals who attribute more awareness of motivation to their heroes than the awareness they themselves possess of their own motivation.

G. The Problem of Repression

The attribution of complex motivation to the hero of a TAT story may indicate an equivalent degree of awareness on the part of the individual who tells the story. But there are certainly motives important in the determination of behavior which escape the scrutiny of the most self-conscious individual. Exploration of the deeper recesses of the personality calls for a more indirect technique of analysis. It is a relatively simple matter, if one possesses autobiographical and observational data, to determine whether the material of the protocol represents private wishes or overt behavior. Discrepancies between what is known of the individual's daily behavior and the behavior of his heroes provides a simple criterion for distinguishing whether the latter represents overt behavior or covert wish or expectation. We have not elaborated indirect techniques useful in this connection, since knowledge of the individual's actual behavior provides the most certain basis for this differentiation.

The problem of assessing levels of psychological function *within* the covert sphere is more complex and difficult. Although forces within the covert sphere may exert varying degrees of pressure for admittance into consciousness or translation into behavior, behavioral criteria for the measurement of such differences in pressure have not yet been clearly defined.

The TAT, because of its sensitivity in eliciting repressed material, offers a unique opportunity for the investigation of the mechanism of repression. In order to exploit these potentialities fully an excursion into the theory of repression will be necessary. Let us turn our attention first to Freud's treatment of repression.

I. HISTORY OF THE CONCEPT

Freud's theory of repression was based upon the empirical datum of resistance—the temporary blocking of free association. From this phenomenon he inferred that there was a force responsible for this inhibition of the associational process. He found further evidence in such phenomena as slips of the tongue that the wish might be of sufficient strength to break through the repressing force. He further assumed that in neurosis the repressed wish exerted pressure on the door of consciousness sufficient to require continual vigilance lest a break-through be effected. This much was the insight of genius. Whether this mechanism operates universally and, if it does, whether the repressed always "returns" or threatens to return, are questions which have yet to receive a definitive answer. We have not learned much more concerning the nature of this mechanism than Freud originally taught us.

In order to employ the TAT in the diagnosis of the degree of repression it will be necessary to reformulate and extend Freud's theory of repression.

2. A THEORY OF REPRESSION

We shall treat the phenomenon of repression as a special case of the larger problem of the determination of the resultant of psychological forces. Let us consider first the nature of psychological forces and their relation to personality.

a) *Intensity, Extensity, and Pressure*

We shall assume first that any personality has a finite quantum of energy at its disposal. Our second assumption will be the scientific fiction that a personality or psychological system may be treated for analytical purposes as a closed system. This latter is an assumption which many sciences have found useful despite the fact that no single system can really be a "closed" system. Physical systems, for example, are certainly "open" to intervention by human and social systems, but the exclusion of the influence of the latter upon physical systems has simplified the problems of physics and allowed prediction within the science of physics.

If we make both of these assumptions, our next requirement is a unit of energy for this closed system. We shall define psychological energy in terms of units of psychological *pressure* and further asssume that any single wish within the personality may have any pressure, not exceeding the total amount of pressure available to the personality. We shall also assume that because of the finite quantum of pressure units available to the person, the expenditure of pressure units in one area limits the amount of pressure available for other purposes. Thus, if we assume arbitrarily that an individual has 400 units of such pressure available for general expenditure, then if one wish consumes 200 units of pressure, the remainder of his activity would be limited to 200 units of pressure. This might be spread over ten other areas, in which case each area would have a pressure of 20 units, or it might be expended in one other area which would then have a pressure of 200 units or in two other areas, one of which consumed 150 units, the other 50 units and so on.

We shall now assume further that a unit of pressure is the product of two components—intensity and extensity. Thus 10 units of pressure might be the product of a wish with an intensity of 2 units and an extensity of 5 units, or conversely, or the product of a wish with an intensity of 10 units and an extensity of 1 unit or conversely. By intensity we mean the strength of the wish or drive; by extensity we mean its scope or mass. Consider the following example. Individual A wants very much to buy a book. Individual B has an equally intense wish to go to college. Neither A nor B can afford to satisfy his wish. Although the intensity of both wishes may be high, the total pressure of B's wish is much higher because of its higher extensity, since pressure is defined as the product of intensity times extensity. There would be differential sequelae in the case of A's and B's frustration. B would suffer more frustration because of the greater pressure of his wish. Consider further a psychophysiological example. A, due to a vitamin A deficiency, has a specific craving of high intensity for carrots. B, due to a general malnutrition, has a craving of high intensity for any food. Although each individual's wish is of equal intensity, the total pressure of B's wish is greater due to the greater extensity of his need—both psychologically and physiologically.

The pressure of a wish might be equivalent if it were either of high intensity and low extensity, or low intensity and high extensity. For example, the pressure of the specific craving of high intensity for carrots might be equivalent in pressure to a wish to study, of low intensity and high extensity, on the part of a student.

b) *The Relation of Pressure of Conflict to Total Pressure*

Let us now consider the problem of conflict in the light of these distinctions. It follows from our assumptions that as the total pressure of two wishes in conflict increases, the pressure available for the remainder of the system decreases. If two wishes which were in conflict consumed, together, 10 units of pressure in a 400 unit system, the secondary consequences of this conflict for the personality as a whole would not be serious. But as the conflict involved more and more of the total pressure available to the personality, the conflict would become more and more pathogenic. Thus a conflict between viewing one or another moving picture on a particular evening rarely involves pathogenic sequelae—although the intensity of the wishes may be high, their extensity is typically so low that the total pressure of each wish is low, and the combined pressure of both wishes is relatively low. But a conflict between two wishes of high pressure, each wish involving half of the total pressure of the personality, represents civil war within the individual. Similar phenomena may be seen on the somatic level. The focal infection represented in a pimple which has been effectively segregated from interaction with the rest of the body ordinarily permits effective functioning of the organism, but a systemic infection may mobilize the entire energies of the organism in self defense and in so doing leave very little energy for any other purpose—the individual is "sick."

c) *Relation of the Ratio of Conflicting Pressures to Total Pressure*

Whether a conflict will be pathogenic and, more specifically, whether the repressed will "return" is also a function of the relative pressure of the two forces which stand in opposition to each other. It will be our hypothesis that as the repressing force increases in pressure, relative to the repressed force, the possibility of a return of the repressed wish decreases and, further, that this entails a reduction in disturbance to the personality as a whole. Conversely we will assume that as the balance between two forces in opposition approaches equality there will be a greater tendency of the repressed wish to return and an increase in general disturbance to the personality as a whole. Our doctrine is, in this respect, contrary to that contemporary opinion which attributes serious pathogenic potentialities to "deeply" repressed material. We are maintaining in effect that the "deeper" the repression the less pathogenic the conflict. We prefer to speak of the relative pressure of two forces rather than the "depth" of repression, since the former is more susceptible of measurement than the concept of depth. Let us consider next the relation between this ratio and the ratio of the whole conflict to the total pressure.

d) Relation of Ratio of Conflicting Pressures to the Ratio of Combined Pressures of the Conflict to Total Pressure

We have maintained that a conflict may be pathogenic for one of two reasons: either it consumes the entire energies of the system or the opposed pressures are evenly balanced. We must now consider the relationship between these two factors.

If our hypotheses are correct, the most serious conflict would be one in which there were two fairly evenly balanced forces, consuming between them the entire energies of the system. The least serious conflict would be that between two forces of low pressure, in which one of the forces was relatively much higher in pressure than the other, although only a small part of the total pressure of the system was expended by the two of them. As a conflict approached either of these end points, it would be either more or less pathogenic. It would also follow that if one ratio was favorable, the pathogenic potentiality of the other ratio would be reduced. Thus, if the conflict were evenly balanced between two forces, it would be less pathogenic as the total pressure of the conflict decreased. Or if there were a high total pressure of the two forces in conflict, it would be less pathogenic as the disparity in relative pressure between the two forces increased.

Let us examine these hypotheses more closely. It would be generally admitted that a conflict of two forces of relatively low pressure in which one force was of much greater pressure than the other rarely involved pathogenic sequelae. Such a conflict might involve a choice at the end of a meal between two types of desserts, one of which was much more highly cathected than the other.

It is perhaps less obvious that a conflict between two high pressure forces evenly balanced represents the most pathological condition. It has been assumed by psychoanalysis that weakening the forces of repression will permit the neurotic to admit repressed wishes into consciousness, give cathartic expression to their pent-up energy, and eventually enable the individual to integrate these wishes with his adult personality and restore internal peace. But psychoanalytic practice employs such a procedure only in the case of the neuroses. It is contraindicated in prepsychotic conditions. In these conditions psychoanalysis admittedly may precipitate a psychotic state, and if this seems probable analysis is promptly terminated. We would explain this difference in the efficacy of psychoanalytic therapy in neurotic and prepsychotic conditions in the following way. In the case of the neuroses, the combined pressure of the opposed forces is less than the pressure available for the total personality, and the repressing force is relatively stronger than that which is repressed. In the prepsychotic condition the combined pressure of repressing and repressed force represents almost all of the pressure available to the individual, and the opposing forces maintain a more unstable equilibrium. The repressing force is only slightly stronger than the repressed force. If the repressed element is then admitted into consciousness by psychoanalytic intervention which weakens the force of repression, there is civil war within the personality. But in the neuroses there is a condition more akin to that of a revolutionary party which has been driven underground by a frightened democracy. It might be possible for the democratic society to tolerate and assimilate its own revolutionary minority, but not if the revolutionary element represented almost half the country. Originally repression of one of the forces drives it underground, but, as Freud showed us, an incessant guerrila warfare is maintained, and the individual must maintain constant vigilance lest the repressed element break forth again. But the severity of this guerrila warfare is clearly a function of the relative strength of the two forces. In the neuroses the repressed element is a minority party, and for this reason a relatively small army will be sufficient to contain this threat. But in the prepsychotic condition the personality is split in two, and the repressing force is not much more representative of the personality, or much stronger, than the repressed force. Consequently any alteration of the distribution of these forces may precipitate a psychotic episode. The psychoses are characteristically more labile in both inception and remission than the neuroses.

Perhaps the least plausible of our derivations is that concerning the type of conflict in which the repressing force is very much greater than the repressed force. We have been reminded so often of the pathological sequelae of an overly strict super-ego that our hypothesis requires considerable clinical evidence if it is to be seriously entertained. In general we would maintain that an overly strict super-ego can result in symptom formation only if its pressure is matched by a repressed wish of almost equal pressure; that if the pressure of the repressed wish is much less than that of the repressing force, there will not be sufficient counterpressure to produce symptoms. Clinical evidence for this hypothesis will be presented in a later section.

3. THE PROBLEM OF MEASUREMENT OF REPRESSION

Having defined our units of analysis and proposed a set of hypotheses concerning the dynamics of repression, let us now consider the empirical problem of measurement of these forces.

The measurement of the absolute and relative strength of two forces, one of which represses the other, is peculiarly difficult because the nature of the repressed force can be investigated only when the pressure of the repressing force has been reduced to zero. Let us assume that there are a number of individuals who are hostile to their fathers but who are overtly submissive because of fear of their fathers. Suppose then we were to experimentally weaken this fear by giving these individuals equivalent amounts of alcohol. We might find that one individual remained quite submissive in feeling and behavior toward his father, another felt hostile but did not express his hostility, another might express his hostility verbally to his father, and another might murder his father. There are two possible interpretations of this phenomenon: the first is that all of these individuals wished to murder their fathers but the *pressure of their fear varied* and alcohol, which was sufficient to release the inhibitions of one individual, was not enough to free the others. A second and equally plausible interpretation is that the *pressure of their repressed hostility varied*—that the alcohol effectively removed the repressing fear, and the differences in degree of hostility expressed under alcohol faithfully represented the degree of hostility that had been repressed. To determine which of these alternatives was true would involve reducing the strength of the fear to a zero quantity, and then the unfettered behavior would indicate the pressure of the hostility. An estimate of the pressure of the fear could be achieved by measuring the force necessary to reduce the fear to a zero quantity. One of the principal obstacles to such measurement is our ignorance of techniques of reducing the strength of repressing forces to a zero quantity. In our present state of knowledge, quite apart from the problem of manipulating human subjects as scientific guinea pigs, we could never be sure that we had reduced this force to a zero quantity. Unless we were sure we had done this, we could never measure the pressure of the repressed wish; there would always be the possibility that if we weakened the super-ego a bit more something else might appear in overt behavior. Nor could we measure the strength of the super-ego unless we were certain when we had reduced it to a zero quantity, since it is defined by the pressure it exerts against repressed wishes.

a) *The Use of the TAT as an Indicator of Repression*

If these are some of the problems inherent in the experimental investigation of repression, in what way can we utilize the TAT to estimate the pressure of repressing and repressed wishes?

It is our belief that the analysis of the individual's imaginative productions does allow a more satisfactory measure of these forces than we can at present achieve through experimental investigation. We believe this is so because the strength of repressive factors is weakened by allowing the individual to achieve distance between himself and the characters of his stories. If we were to ask the individual to tell us what *he* would do if he were the person in the picture the repressive forces would be alerted and the privacy of inner thoughts guarded. The writer has investigated the effect of changing the instructions in this way and found that subjects either refuse to comply with these instructions or offer meager, impoverished stories or consciously attempt to confuse the examiner.

In addition to the distance which the test itself places between the storyteller and his stories, the nature of the picture contributes distance. The second ten pictures, which are more bizarre and unrealistic, were chosen to increase this distance. Such pictures permit the individual license in telling stories unfettered by realistic considerations. In such a setting the subject can tell "crazy" stories with the feeling that they may be appropriate to the picture. Further, he is encouraged to do this by the change of instructions at the beginning of the second session—that he may give freer rein to his imagination. For these reasons the individual may attribute wishes to his heroes which no amount of alcohol or other experimental manipulation might induce him to express in overt behavior.

But because the force of repression is only weakened and not reduced to a zero quantity, repressed wishes are usually not given completely free expression even under these conditions. These wishes are given somewhat freer expression only in those stories in which the conditions are sufficiently distant from the everyday life of the individual to permit such license. We must therefore employ the technique of comparing the behavior of those heroes who are interacting "normally" with parents or others with those heroes who are represented in a setting psychologically "remote" from normal interaction.

Let us consider some examples. If the TAT of an individual portrayed a son submissive to his father and to every other male figure in all his stories but one, and in this story a hero under the influence of alcohol, and in prehistoric times, destroyed some physical property in a blind rage, we would assume that the pressure of the repressing force was very great. We would assume this since it forbade the expression of any aggression except under the most unusual and remote conditions of this story and then only toward a nonliving object. If the same individual had also given us a story of a hero who attacked the prehistoric monster of card 11, we would have said that the pressure of repression was somewhat less, since it permitted aggression toward living organisms.* If in addition the hero had rescued a princess from this monster, we would suppose that there was somewhat less repression, inasmuch as a *human being* had been introduced as the reason for this aggression. If the individual had portrayed all his heroes submissive in face-to-face relationships but in one story the hero led a revolt against the government, we would assume that the repressing force had been still weaker because it sanctioned aggression against human agencies. If in addition there had been stories of the hero's hatred of policemen, we would assume still less pressure of the repressing force because the impersonality of authority had been concretized in the person of the policeman. Less repression would have permitted some heroes to aggress upon other adult males with whom they had a more personal relationship. Finally, if the individual had also told stories in which the hero behaved submissively towards his father in the face-to-face relationship, but nursed private and unexpressed wishes for revenge, we would assume that the pressure of the repressing fear operated only to prevent the overt expression of the wish but did not prevent awareness of the wish.

It is our assumption that the remoteness of conditions under which anti-social wishes may be expressed is a function of the relative pressure of repressing and repressed forces. As the repressing force increases in pressure relative to the pressure of the repressed force, the conditions under which the latter may be given expression in TAT stories become more and more "remote." As this ratio approaches equality the expression of the repressed force will appear under less and less remote conditions in the stories.

Since we will employ "remoteness" as an index of repression, let us consider in more detail the varieties of remoteness. There is remoteness of object— the wish may be directed toward a parent who is usually the original object of the repressed wish, or toward a parent surrogate, policemen, the law, government, animals, or physical objects. This represents a typical series of increasingly remote objects for the displacement of repressed wishes. There is remoteness of time—the present, the immediate past or future, the remote past or future. There is remoteness of setting—the individual's customary habitat or geographically remote settings, ranging from other countries to other planets. There may be remoteness of level, ranging from behavior to wish, memories, daydreams, nightdreams, and special states. Finally there may be remoteness of conditions ranging from the heroes' everyday conditions

---

* Renaud (74) found that responses to card 11 by head-injury cases were distinguished by the life and death struggle between the hero and the monster, but that aggression expressed in the other stories was neither more nor less intense than in the control groups. This would be consistent with the theory that these individuals harbor intense hostility bound by repressive forces and that the pressure of this hostility is sufficient to call for intrapunitive injury because of guilt.

to states of extreme fatigue, frustration, or anxiety, and so on. A story may be extremely remote in one respect but not in another. For example, normal individuals occasionally murder their parents in their TAT stories. This represents a minimum of remoteness of *object* but some other dimensions will usually be extremely remote—the individual will depict either the parent or the hero as suffering some special condition. The parent may be represented as particularly brutal because he is under the influence of alcohol, or the hero may be particularly frustrated or " queer."

By means of these criteria we may estimate, crudely, differences in remoteness of expression of repressed wishes between one protocol and another. If we were able to measure with any precision the degree of remoteness and the pressure of repressing force and repressed force as these appeared in TAT stories, we would be able to give an empirical value to the functional relationship which we have said obtains between these two forces and the degree of remoteness of expression. Since we lack a scale of measurement with a zero point and equal intervals we will have to await the further refinement of our scaling methods to determine more accurately the dynamics of repression. But we can estimate somewhat crudely whether one force is greater than another and whether one expression of a repressed wish is more remote than another. We will now consider how this may be done, and how we may use such estimates in clinical diagnosis.

It is necessary first to estimate the ratio of the combined press .re of repressing and repressed wish to the total pressure available to the personality. This may be done by totaling the number of stories which refer either to the repressing force or the repressed force and computing the percentage of such stories to the total number of stories.* In our previous example of an Oedipus conflict we might have found that every story involved either a son who was submissive to his father or a hero who expressed aggression under more remote conditions. If this were the case, we would estimate that the combined pressure of repressing and repressed forces was 100 per cent of the total pressure. But if only half of the stories were concerned with this conflict, we would estimate a conflict of medium pressure, or 50 per cent. If only two stories referred to this conflict, we would assume a conflict of low pressure or 10 per cent. This is of course a very crude estimate of the total pressure of the conflict, but we have found it useful clinically in that the more seriously disturbed the individual the more frequently the protocol is weighted with such conflict throughout the stories. Less disturbed individuals have more stories free of this type of conflict.

* This assumes that the set of 20 stories is a representative sample of the total available pressure—an assumption demonstrably untrue in the case of some protocols. To what extent this assumption is generally true requires further empirical investigation.

We must next determine the ratio of repressing to repressed force. We have said before that experimental manipulation of the individual was limited by the fact that we could never be certain whether the force of repression had been reduced to a zero quantity—hence we would be equally uncertain of the extent of the repressed wish. The TAT offers a unique opportunity for estimating the nature and pressure of a wish which has been repressed, if we examine the wish when allowed its freest expression in the TAT. This will generally be found under those conditions which are most remote. It may be argued that we cannot be certain that the forces of repression have been sufficiently reduced in the TAT to allow any more certainty than might be achieved through experimental de-inhibition. Such a criticism might be justified, but there is reason to believe that such uncertainty has been much reduced, because normal individuals do give expression to extremely antisocial wishes in their TAT stories. The same individuals may exhibit none of these wishes either in their everyday behavior or when under the influence of alcohol. The same individuals may be completely unaware that such wishes attributed to their heroes are in any way related to their own personalities.

Since we do not possess an equal interval scale for the measurement of psychological forces, the assignment of numbers to such variables as remoteness and the pressure of repressed and repressing wish cannot be more than a metaphorical venture. Assignment of numbers under such conditions might indicate that one quantity was greater than another but would not indicate precisely how much greater. For this reason these quantities could not be manipulated mathematically. We must therefore await the development of more precise scales of measurement before we can undertake a precise quantitative formulation of the dynamics of repression. If we possessed such measuring techniques the diagnosis of the degree of repression would be a relatively simple matter.

If we cannot measure these variables accurately we may yet attempt crude estimates of their strength. For our purposes four measures are needed: *the degree of remoteness of expression, the pressure of repressing wish, the pressure of repressed wish,* and *the ratio of the combined pressure of repressing wish and repressed wish to total pressure.* The latter ratio may be estimated by the number of stories mentioning either the repressing or repressed wish. This number can then be expressed as a percentage of the total number of stories.

The degree of remoteness may be estimated roughly as very high, high, medium, low, and very low according to criteria previously discussed.

The pressure of the repressed wish may also be estimated on the same scale: very high, high, medium, low, and very low. Since this pressure is the product of the intensity and extensity of the repressed wish, these must first be estimated before pressure can be determined. We must rate the intensity and extensity of the repressed wish as it appears *in each story*—estimate the product of both components and then *add* these separate estimates to achieve a total estimate of the pressure of the repressed wish. Let us suppose that an individual told only one story in which there was expression of an anti-social wish of high intensity and high extensity and that another individual told the same kind of story, but also told 10 other stories in which the same wish was expressed although of lower intensity and lower extensity. The estimate of pressure of the repressed wish in the first case would be low and in the second case high. Although the first individual told a story giving expression to a wish of high intensity and high extensity, the fact that this was the only story of this kind would indicate that its total pressure was lower than the pressure of the wish of the second individual who told an additional 10 stories expressing the same wish—even though the wish was at lower intensity and extensity in *each* of the additional stories.

In order to estimate the pressure of the repressing force, we would employ our hypothesis that remoteness is a function of the ratio of repressing pressure to repressed pressure. Having determined the pressure of the repressed wish and the degree of remoteness, the estimated *product* of these two estimates provides an estimate of the *pressure of the repressing force*. Thus, if remoteness were high and pressure of the repressed wish were high, the estimated pressure of the repressing force would be very high. If remoteness were very high and pressure of the repressed wish medium, the estimated pressure of the repressing wish would be high. We have not attempted quantification of these relationships because measurement is only crudely approximated. But although these suggested operations of estimation leave much to be desired, they may nonetheless yield operationally testable hypotheses, as we shall see in the application of these techniques to case material.

Before turning to the case material, let us consider briefly the problem of identifying the repressed and repressing forces. In general almost any wish may be repressed by any other wish. Usually these wishes are "antisocial," but the definition of what is antisocial varies from culture to culture and from individual to individual within a culture as heterogeneous as ours. The interpreter must, in his assessment of repressed wishes, know the larger cultural pressures and the more particular pressures to which the individual has been subjected. The TAT protocol itself will provide some of the clues in such an assessment: wishes which occasion the hero anxiety, shame, embarrassment, remorse, or guilt or which the hero tries to conceal from others or which lead to his punishment—these are wishes which may in that individual suffer repression.

4. THE CASES OF X, Y, AND Z

We shall now present in some detail 3 cases—X, Y, and Z—to illustrate our hypotheses concerning the nature of repression. Each of the TAT's revealed that aggression against a parent had been repressed by these individuals. In X's case this wish and its control expended much of the available energy, representing a high pressure, medium pressure conflict with low remoteness of expression of aggression. In Y's case the combined pressure of repressing force and aggression was high. The repressing force was of high pressure, but the aggression was of very low pressure, having high intensity but very low extensity. Remoteness of expression of aggression was high. In Z this conflict consumed less energy than in X or Y. It represented a high pressure, low pressure conflict. Remoteness of expression of aggression represented a mid-point between the other cases, being of medium degree. We shall also examine the extent to which each of these individuals was disturbed. X was most seriously disturbed, Y least disturbed, and Z represented a mid-point between the two. Let us consider first the case of X.

a) *The Case of X*

X is a young women who describes her father as a quite refined man with many gifts and a fine personality. She is admittedly much fonder of her father than her mother, but feels sorry for her mother because her life has been a hard one and X feels her mother deserved a better fate. It is evident from her stories that her hostility toward her mother is marked. In the face-to-face situation her heroine feels this hostility, but suppresses it.

> This woman is trying to talk some sense into this girl. She is reading a preceptual passage to her but the girl's mind is far away. She does not want to listen to this woman (her mother) because she associates most of her previous humiliating experiences with her. She wants to get away, to be free. She has mixed feelings of self pity, aggression, and a desire to start out on her own. However she makes an effort and suppresses this mood and listens to what her mother is reading.

On the basis of this story we would expect to find further evidence of aggression directed toward other females and would predict that remote displacement would not be required, since the existence of hostility is freely admitted into the consciousness of the heroine in the face-to-face situation.

In the following story we see the transference of this affect to other women.

> This woman is jealous of the other woman because she has a sweeter disposition, etc., etc., and men seem to prefer *the* company of woman two because she is so gay and charming, even though not one fifth as intelligent

as woman one. "I don't care" says woman one and returns to her book. Little by little the woman becomes absorbed in her book and the petty jealousies, etc., seem to fall off. In fact when she puts the book aside she feels very friendly toward the whole world and even goes out of her way to be good to woman two.

There is a continuation of hostility and jealousy toward other females, and the reasons are similar—she feels that she is inferior to her mother and other women in competition for the attention of men. We are told in addition that she has learned to control this aggression, which she could do no more than suppress in childhood, by turning to books, which enables the petty jealousies to "fall off." In the following story there is the same attempt to manage the aggression born of frustration and feelings of inferiority by immersing herself in something which removes her from her own bitterness.

That hideous woman at the back is this woman's evil nature which she has long suppressed. This woman wasn't really evil when a child but things went against her. She felt frustrated on every hand. Now however she wants to restore her own mental health by attaching herself to some great and selfless cause. The more she strives in this direction the fainter and fainter grows the woman at the back. Eventually the finer qualities in her are completely reinstated.

These are the conditions of her mental health, identification with and dedication to something which will make the aggression grow "fainter and fainter." This mechanism must be distinguished from reaction formation. She does not "pretend" to be more friendly than she really is. In the previous story she "went out of her way" to be friendly towards the woman she hated because she had been able to overcome her aggression through absorption in something which interested her, and this diminished the feelings of inferiority which aroused her aggression. In this story her attachment to a noble cause is the instrument of dissipating the aggression and inferiority at the same time. As a *result* the aggression fades. It can be reduced in intensity and extensity because it is not an end per se but the consequence of her intolerable feeling of humiliation and inferiority. For this reason reading, in one case, and dedication to a selfless cause, in the other, can at once dissipate both the feeling of inferiority and the aggression which results from it.

We are also told, indirectly, how her mental health might be irreparably shattered. If her feelings of inferiority were for any reason to increase beyond a critical point, with no possibility of overcoming them, we might predict that she would be overwhelmed by the aggression which would result from her humiliation. This happens to one of her heroines and the aggression is directed against the original object, the mother.

The woman who is strangling the other woman is crazy. She used to be a pretty girl once but she developed a physical deformity—her hand became swollen and ugly. She was so distressed by this fact that her whole personality changed. She felt nobody cared for her any more. She became morose and suspicious of others even when they were being genuinely nice to her. Little by little this neurotic trend grew till she became positively dangerous. Her mother loved her and wanted to protect her so she would not hear of the girl being sent to the asylum. However in one of her fits the maniac caught her mother by the throat as she was coming down the stairs, and strangled her. The rest of the family rushed in but it was too late. They did not punish her of course but they put her in a mental home.

The presence of an inferiority which cannot be overcome results in a feeling of humiliation and suspicion of the attitude of others toward her, which leads ultimately to an overwhelming "fit" of aggression against her mother.

That the joint problems of inferiority and resultant aggression are the principal concern of this young woman is further indicated by the following three stories.

This woman is pleading with this man to leave his work for a while and relax. She offers herself to him. The man here seems to be hesitating between his duty and his love, but actually he knows which really matters to him. Besides he will soon grow tired of the woman and the temporary pleasure is nothing compared with the rewards of his work. So he fools around with her for a while and then throws her off without a remorse because after all she got what she wanted, and he gave as much as was his to give. The woman takes it badly at first but she recovers and throws herself into her own work with greater determination. She is thrilled to find how well she makes out on her job.

This woman is blissfully happy because she has found someone who returns her affection with equal intensity. The man is here a little amused at her childish clinging because he had thought her so mature and self-contained. She on her part is happy because she can cling to him as much as she likes without fear of his ceasing to respect her on that score; she wants to feel thus protected and cherished always so that she might in turn be a source of strength and faith. A year ago she despaired of ever meeting such a person. Now she laughs because she had doubted her destiny. The two work together and make great contributions to the welfare of humanity. They are a sort of combination of Einstein and Madame Curie.

This woman is afraid that her husband is not fond of her any more. She feels that she has failed to come up to his expectations even though he has not said anything to that effect; he is at present sitting in an armchair, reading a newspaper. She steps into the room and feels frustrated by his absorption in the paper. She tries to break in through his reading with some totally unintelligent remark. As he looks up she feels he despises her because she is so obviously asking for attention. She feels that by her foolish behavior on this and other occasions she has lost his esteem and is mad both at herself and at him. I don't know how such a story would end. She would have to take herself in hand I guess.

In these stories the conditions necessary for her happiness in love and work are presented. She can be happy if she can be dependent without fear of losing self respect or the respect of her lover. Through the secure gratification of this dependency she is enabled to offer something in return, and the couple working together make great contributions to the welfare of humanity. But if the superior male rejects her and makes her feel inferior she will turn to work to escape her misery. She is "thrilled to find how well she makes out on her job" but she does not make "great contributions to the welfare of humanity." Nor is she a "Madame Curie."

This young women suffered acute feelings of inferiority and rage and much of her energy was expended in coping with these feelings, controlling the aggression she felt, repressing its more intense and primitive components. Evidence from the TAT concerning the combined pressure of repressing and repressed wishes is congruent with this fact. Approximately 75 per cent of her stories are concerned either with the repressing force (the wish to be respected and loved) and the repressed wish (the wish to aggress upon those who humiliated her). Approximately 40 per cent of all the stories express the latter wish with varying degrees of intensity, consequently we estimated the pressure of aggression as medium. We have rated the remoteness of expression as low since she is aware of these feelings in the face-to-face situation with her mother, although she suppresses the overt expression of these feelings. She continues to be aware of these feelings throughout the stories, although the most intense aggression is *expressed* under more remote conditions—by a "maniac" in a "fit." We have rated this remoteness as low (but not very low) because of the continuity of the expression of aggression from face-to-face normal conditions and remote conditions. The repressing force was estimated as a force of high (but not very high) pressure—the *product* of low remoteness and medium pressure of the repressed wish (the product of any multiplication is necessarily higher than either multiplier, unless one multiplier has a value of one or less).

According to our previous hypotheses, such a constellation of forces is approximately midway between a neurotic and prepsychotic state, since much but not all of the individual's energies are consumed in conflict (75 per cent). If less energy had been consumed it would have been nearer the neurotic type of conflict. If more energy were expended it would have been nearer the prepsychotic state. Moreover the ratio of repressed to repressing forces, although not equal (high pressure against medium pressure) is sufficiently near equality to provide an unstable equilibrium of forces. In such a case the individual's mental health is capable of being shattered through the intensification of the strength of the repressed force. As in the story told by X, she might lose her sanity if she suffered sufficient increase in her feelings of inferiority to intensify the aggression which results from intolerable humiliation. She might, however, become a "Madame Curie" if she found a man who made her feel both loved and *respected*. Under these conditions she would be capable not only of trust and dependence, but she could in addition offer nurturance to such a man, and together they would make great contributions to the welfare of mankind. This case illustrates very clearly one of the neglected aspects of neurosis—the unstable equilibrium characteristic of certain conflicts. Although her suppressed aggressive wish presents a real problem and might conceivably produce a psychotic state, it is not in and of itself the primary problem. It is a resultant force—the resultant of feeling inferior and unloved by the father surrogate. For this reason the vicissitudes of her love and work can, as they vary from day to day, intensify or completely do away with her feelings of aggression, so that the relationship which we have assumed to exist between the repressing force and the repressed wish is true only under certain specific conditions of frustration. When these are increased or decreased the relationship between repressed aggression and repressing force may change radically. A necessary condition of an unstable equilibrium between two psychological forces is a delicate balance of their respective pressures. If this is the case, an important corollary may be drawn: that such individuals would be most sensitive to therapy which was directive or which attempted manipulation of the patient's environment. Placing such individuals in an environment optimal for their specific needs could reduce conflicts which might otherwise be recalcitrant to therapy and which might under adverse environmental conditions result in serious impairment of their mental health.

b) *The Case of Y*

Y is a young woman, 20 years of age, whose attitudes as they were expressed in interviews were not dissimilar to those of X. Y adores her father, feels much less tenderness toward her mother, although she tries to be fair, "I realize that she's that way and apparently cannot overcome it so I think nothing of it." There are, however, important differences: Y's father reciprocates her feelings, "He is especially friendly towards me and is happy if I am happy." "The respect which my father has for me is very great and to me this is very important because unless I am worthy of his respect we could not be close friends as we are." This latter is reminiscent of X's need to be respected by the idealized father who elicits her respect.

Despite the great similarity of the basic personalities of X and Y, the differences are profound. Y has achieved the relationship which might save X from being overwhelmed by humiliation and rage. Y's worship of her father has not interfered with her plans for marriage. She has transferred to her future husband the adoration which she has felt towards her father and seems destined to achieve a happy marriage.

The TAT stories told by her are what we might have expected. In the following story she tells us again of her adoration of her father.

> Frank's father was a well known violinist and Frank worshiped him. His main ambition in life was to be a great musician, as proficient as his father, but he doubted if anyone else could be so talented. He has had only a very few lessons and sits, pondering over the violin. Frank cannot visualize just how such beautiful music can come from such an instrument and wonders whether he should give the whole idea up or if, after many years, he could attain the goal he wants to set for himself. He concluded that even though he's young he is somewhat like his father and he too can be a musician.

In her second story her somewhat ambivalent but not overly intense feelings toward her mother are delineated.

> Ethel had always gone to a country school and was interested in getting an education. Ethel's mother had very little education but was happy with what she had been accustomed to and could not understand why Ethel must have more than a high school education. Ethel does not like to go against her mother's wishes but tries to explain that many changes are taking place in the world today and that she cannot be satisfied with the insignificant life she had led thus far and she wants to go to school, get an education and see what is really going on in the world.

Finally, the transference of her love from her father to her future husband, as well as her fulfillment in maternity, is expressed in a wish fulfillment phantasy.

> Mary and John had been married just a year ago, before he joined the Navy. He had been home on leave two months ago and was now at sea. Mary loves him deeply and naturally misses him but tries to keep her mind occupied and not to worry about him. On this particular night, however, she's restless and cannot sleep. She tries reading but can think of nothing but Johnny. She walks out in the hall and stands by the window, dreaming of Johnny and the day he'll be back. Mary doesn't feel well the next morning and goes to the Doctor, to learn that she is going to have a baby. After this she is very busy, making preparations for the baby and the time passes very quickly. Johnny gets another leave and is with Mary when the baby is born.

These three stories are typical of the entire protocol and indicate that there is no discrepancy between her overt behavior, publicly expressed attitudes and her private world. She is not an individual divided against herself, or one whose behavior exemplifies any pathogenic mechanism which we could detect. She is entirely free of neurotic symptom formation and anxiety.

Her stories were all like this, with the *one* exception which follows.

As much as Richard disliked it, he was becoming quite accustomed to having his father come home in a drunken condition but ·this· evening when, in addition to being highly inebriated, he was angry and started beating his wife, it was too much for Richard, who was very fond of his mother. Richard tried to control his temper but with no avail. He was certain that his father did no good for his family or anyone and before he realized just what he was doing, he reached for the revolver and shot him. Richard has now decided that even though he must give himself up, it is much better this way than having his mother tortured the way she has been for the past two years.

The murder of parents in TAT stories is an extremely rare phenomenon in "normals." Had we found any evidence of such a wish we would have expected it to be directed against the mother, although there were no indications of hostility of such proportions. That this story could be told by an individual who loves both her father and future husband so deeply, and is apparently so free of ambivalence is very puzzling when one is accustomed to expect all asocial wishes which suffer repression to press toward expression and to produce symptoms if they are not expressed. To the best of our knowledge this story is an isolated fragment in the total picture of an otherwise well adjusted individual. What it represents one can only guess. It is conceivably a residue of accidentally witnessing the primal scene, seeing the father who was distinguished for his kindness and even temper excited and passionate and apparently hurting the mother. But whatever its meaning it is clear that the father is seen to be different from his normal self. He is pictured under the influence of alcohol, and the aggression which he displays is given a finite course—two years. Presumably this represented a change of character in the father. Consonant with our hypothesis that this fragment produces no pressure symptoms is the hero's lack of remorse for this murder.

We have said that Y's conflict was between a force of high pressure and very low pressure and that the remoteness of expression of aggression was high. The combined pressure of the repressing force—adoration of the father and the wish to be like him and be loved by him—and the repressed wish to kill him, is equivalent to that in the case of X—approximately 75 per cent of the stories are devoted to one or the other of these two wishes. But in this case we have rated the pressure of repressed aggression as very low because this aggression appears in only one story. Although its intensity is very high in this story the total estimate of pressure (based on its intensity and extensity throughout the protocol) would be very low, since there is no other evidence of the wish. We would rate the remoteness of expression as high since there is no continuity between the face-to-face normal relationship with the father and the murder of the father under remote conditions. We would have rated it as very high if the hero had instead murdered an animal or an adult other than the father. The pressure of the repressing force we would rate as high— the product of high remoteness and very low pressure (as if we had multiplied a high degree of remoteness by one).

We have said before that a conflict between a high and very low pressure wish should not permit a return of the repressed wish or sequelae which are pathogenic. This hypothesis would appear to be supported by the evidence from this case. The positive love of the father and future husband exerts sufficient pressure to contain this repressed fragment of hostility and at the same time permits the individual no awareness of its presence. It is as remote from the personality as it is isolated within the microcosm of the TAT.

c) *The Case of Z*

Z is a young man of 19 who was studied intensively over a ten month period. He was given four successive administrations of the TAT at three month intervals. He was also presented with other pictures daily. He told over 400 stories during this period.

Not unlike X and Y, Z was also much possessed by the family romance. He had, in many respects, a classical Oedipus conflict. He loved his mother dearly, respected his father and was deferent to him. The TAT revealed aggression toward his father less repressed than in the case of Y, but more repressed than in the case of X.

Let us examine first those stories in which we see the hero in a face-to-face relationship with his father.

> This fellow has had amnesia and they are now taking his measurements. By these measurements they will discover that he is the son of a wealthy man. He goes to live with his father who is a sadist and because of the treatment he runs away, getting another attack.

The son is submissive to the sadistic father and runs away, to suffer another attack of amnesia. In the next story we are told of the enduring consequence of his father's severity.

> These children have been told by their father definitely not to leave the house. Their friends are at the window coaxing them to come out and play. They shake their heads but after a long while sneak out. They are caught and severely punished and this is the way their childhood is spent. When they grow up they become strict disciplinarians, except the boy who will be very gentle, almost effeminate.

The consequence of this severe paternal discipline is that the boy "will be very gentle, almost effeminate." This again is the relationship in the face-

to-face situation. But as the pictures and stories lead into general social relationships and away from the family this picture changes.

> This picture is supposed to represent a person hypnotizing another. This
> person is an older fellow sitting there. He is an insane person. He has
> great illusions about himself. He thinks he can cause the will of another
> to snap into his own will and make him do whatever he wants. This person
> has gone to sleep and pays no attention. This upsets him and he goes back
> to the insane asylum.

The father surrogate is still portrayed as an omnipotent figure but he is
insanely so, and the younger man refuses to comply with his wishes. There
is here no overt aggression or even overt rebelliousness but a passive resistance—
he has "gone to sleep and pays no attention."

As the stories increase in remoteness there is a gradual change in the
hero's reactions.

> This old guy. I hate him. He is the most disgusting individual. He is a
> bourgeois capitalist and he spies on his friends, sees things they don't want
> him to see. His life is not complete unless he observes his friends unaware.
> Such a low individual has been completely summed up. Somebody will
> catch him spying and shoot him through the heart.

In this story the older male adult is a more remote object of displaced
aggression, inasmuch as he is seen as a representative of a *class* of men who
are rejected. The hero's reactions have as a function of this increased distance
changed from passive resistance to a feeling of hatred, but there is still no
overt aggression. The father surrogate is still portrayed as someone who
exercises too much dominance over the lives of others and who "spies on
his friends." Although the hero does not express his hatred, the story ends
with the possibility that "somebody will catch him spying and shoot him
through the heart." This is the first act of overt aggression against a father
surrogate, although it is not the hero's doing.

With more remoteness, there is a change to overt aggression.

> This man has been blinded by tear gas, and is now being led by a friend
> out of a group that is being dispersed by the police. His activities in this
> group were innocent; he now becomes a cop-hater. This may sometime lead
> him to get in an argument with a policeman and strike him. For this there
> would be a jail sentence and further rooting of his dislike for the police.

This story represents one further step away from the father in that the
policeman is not the representative of a class, but the representative of the law
and society at large, and he envisions a possible overt expression of aggression
towards policemen. In addition, the punishment for this act of aggression
will intensify his hatred.

In this story he was "innocent" at the beginning. In the next story he is less innocent.

> The man in the picture is a laborer. He has just been to a labor agitation meeting. Now he is being forceably exited. The result of this is that he will become more antisocial than ever. He will become more stubborn, perhaps run up against the law and go to jail. Anyway you look at it this fellow's life will become less and less satisfactory to society.

Here he becomes "more antisocial than ever" and "more stubborn." The implication is clear that he went to the labor agitation meeting in the first place with antisocial intent. The hero is still portrayed as the victim of persecution. The "law" and "society" are no less sadistic than the father, but we see him turning more and more openly against these paternal surrogates. His role is becoming less and less passive.

The following story represents the underlying wish displaced to the object at greatest remove from the father.

> The man is an instigator of a revolt. Having laid his plans he now has gone home and standing at the window with the room darkened he watches the explosion in a gov't building which is a signal for the revolt to begin. Mingled emotions are experienced by him at this instant, fear for an instant then excitement and joy—trust of his companions.

This is the clearest expression of the underlying wish to get rid of the omnipotent and ubiquitous father. The object is remotely displaced. It is the impersonal force of authority represented by the established government. It is of further interest that this revolt is not punished. It would appear that the cooperation of trusted allies had made a successful holy war of this revolt. But although revolt may call for the cooperation of the oppressed, and although it may be successful against the "government" it is not so successful when the parent surrogate is a less remote and more concrete tyrant.

> An eclipse—colored slaves are unloading a boat. The wife of the foreman is on the bridge looking for the law for the men are bootlegging. The Negroes will take the eclipse as a sign and revolt and kill their master. The wife will run away, the slaves will be caught and sold again—all because of the eclipse.

Here the condition of revolt is the pact of slaves against the master. This is the most open aggression expressed towards the father figure, albeit at some distance, but although there is group responsibility for the act, the whole group is caught and sold again. This aggression is less remotely displaced insofar as the object of aggression is a "master" rather than the more impersonal government.

If these feelings of aggression are as intense as they seem to be we would expect that the sadism embodied in the father's behavior toward the son might well engender sadistic impulses of revenge in the son. We have as yet seen no evidence of a purely sadistic enjoyment on the part of the hero. He has expressed hatred, he has struck a policeman, overthrown the government, and with others killed his master. We would assume that the conditions necessary for the full expression of this sadistic wish would be an extreme degree of remoteness of the displaced object of his aggression. Such is the case in the only story of its kind told to over 400 pictures.

> This man has just set fire to a stable full of horses, but he couldn't resist the temptation to stay around and watch the agony of the animals. While he was doing this a watchman catches him and he is taken to prison.

This is at once the most remotely displaced object of his aggression and the most open expression of the depth of his feeling. The conditions of this story are remote in two senses. First, aggression is expressed towards animals rather than human beings, and second, the objects of his aggression are helpless victims who are incapable of counter aggression. Under these joint conditions of remoteness he can aggress, torture, and enjoy the agony of his victims.

We should expect that any harm which befell the father would in no way be the responsibility of the son. The following story is an example of such a story.

> Bringing home the groceries a father slipped and sprained his ankle. It hurt and so he got into the bath tub and turned on the hot water. This caused increased swelling and the man lost two weeks from work besides much sleep.

The father suffers an "accident," but the son is in no way responsible. Another story of the same variety follows:

> The man's son is leaving on the train after spending a week's furlough with him. This is the last time that the man will see his son. Within a week the man is dead.

The father dies after seeing the son; but the son is by that time far away and is clearly not responsible for his father's death. The death of the father, for no apparent reason, is testament to the remoteness of the death wish from the individual's consciousness.

In order to evaluate the pressure of this repressed wish we will have to consider at some length the other wishes expressed in his protocol. We are fortunate in finding in this individual another important wish which is also repressed. The comparison of two repressed wishes within the same individual will allow us a crucial test of our hypothesis concerning the dynamics of repression.

There is much evidence for a repressed wish for the exclusive and complete possession of his mother. The fusion of the wish for love and sex from his mother has created serious problems. It has been further complicated by a fusion of sex and aggression. In the face-to-face relationship with the father we saw no evidence of any trace of the repressed wish of aggression. In the face-to-face relationship with the mother, there is evidence of his love for his mother in the following rescue thema.

> This woman heard someone in the living room and thinking it was her son and friends she has opened the door to say goodnight before she retires. Instead it turns out to be robbers who turn a gun on her and force her to tell where the valuables are. As they are leaving her son comes in and being an impetuous person attacks them. They shoot him and escape. She immediately goes to aid him. Does he die? No, it's only a severe flesh wound.

This classical thema is apparently close enough to consciousness and of sufficient pressure to be projected into the mother-son relationship rather than toward some more displaced object. Individuals in whom this wish is more repressed express it under more remote conditions, such as a response to card 11 about a prince who rescues the fairy princess from the dragon.

More striking than this manifestation of his wish is the following story in which a fusion of sex and aggression is attributed to the mother:

> The person on the left is the boy's mother. While fondling the boy she all at once bit off part of the boy's ear. After this she became a perfect wreck and had to be separated from the boy, who became very afraid of her. Later she died in an insane asylum.

We are told in effect that "fondling" between mother and son may lead to loss of control, in a fusion of sex and aggression, and this may lead to suicide.

This story, with modifications, is repeated with the brother as the hero, rather than the mother.

> There has just been a murder committed. The man has killed his sister and dazed and stunned stumbles out and stubs his toe. Gangrene sets in and his toe is cut off. Then he is hung.

This story was told to card 13, the picture of a naked woman in bed and a man standing near by. It is important in the interpretation of this story to know that this subject has no sister, but that he considers his mother more of a sister than a mother to him. From material which will be presented later, it is clear that this picture of a naked woman incited the same fusion of sex and aggression which seized the mother above, when she was fondling her son. It is no less dangerous an act for the son than the mother. The consequences are peculiarly severe—he "stubs his toe. Gangrene sets in and his toe is cut off. Then he is hung." It is interesting to compare the punishment suffered by heroes who aggressed upon paternal surrogates and this punishment, which presumably stems from the same source. Aggression against father figures received relatively light punishment—the slaves were caught and sold again for killing their master, the hero was jailed for his antisocial behavior toward the policemen and toward the horses, and when he revolted against the government there was no mention of punishment of any kind. But for the murder of his "sister," no single punishment is severe enough. And the consequence of similar behavior on the part of the mother is insanity.

In another response to the same card in another administration of the test, he told the following story.

> The man is very drunk. In this condition he has gone to see the woman shown here. She has gotten undressed and into bed and is now pretending to pay no attention to him and to be disinterested. He is getting undressed in order to get into bed with her. In the moment shown, he has gained some of his faculties and is at this moment thinking how wrong it is to do the thing he has contemplated. Immediately, however, liquor will cloud his mind and his body will take control. Afterwards, he will probably be very upset about it.

In this response, where the remoteness of the object and condition is increased—he is "very drunk"—he is able to consumate the sexual act. We see a third type of remoteness in this act in that he disclaims responsibility for it—"immediately however liquor will cloud his mind and his body will take control." Concomitant with this increased remoteness, there is a decrease in the severity of punishment. He "will probably be very upset about it," but suffers nothing more severe. This is a page from the subject's past history. Previous to the period of testing he was involved in one such episode, very much under the influence of alcohol, and suffered remorse afterwards.

His heroes are generally tortured by the problem of the control of their sexual impulses and the serious consequences of the loss of such control. A typical example of this conflict appears in the following story.

> The scene is an English churchyard at night about a century ago. The man is a clergyman and he is worshipping at the grave of a woman whom he loved deeply but never revealed his emotion. The struggle between celibacy and his natural desire has ruined his health. Now he is thanking God that the struggle is over and he can sublimate his passion by loving her memory.

It is clear from this story that Z suffers no split in his libido. His sexual and love wishes are directed toward the same object.

In the following story the typical sequel to actual loss of control is given.

> The man while suddenly kissing the girl on the cheek bit her cheek. He apologized profusely. He could [slip?] tell why he had done it. No avail— their acquaintanceship was broken off.

This story was written and the words "could tell why" probably represent a slip of the pencil, again indicating the pressure of the repressed wish and the relative weakness of the repressing force. We see again the fusion of oral aggression with sexuality that was first noted in the story of the mother who bit off part of her son's ear. The consequence of this loss of control is less serious than the loss of control on the part of the mother. The relationship is broken, but there is no insanity following loss of control.

In the following story the same thema is repeated.

> This couple are dancing together. They have been old friends for a long time. Now the man tells the woman that he loves her. He kisses her lightly on the lips. Then she'll tell him that she doesn't love him and not to put her in a position where she'll have to forfeit his friendship by not allowing him to see her.

It is of some interest that where the hero suffers either the disruption of the relationship, or external punishment, there is no guilt or remorse, and conversely, where the hero suffers guilt there is no punishment. But some form of punishment, either exogenous or endogenous, is present in all his love stories.

In the following story there is an interesting denial of sexual wishes.

> The woman has just gone through a harrowing experience. She has come to tell her friend about it but at the memory of it she faints as is shown. That he is not making undesired advances to her is shown by the way he holds her. Of interest is the semicircle near his forehead, which may either be a lock of hair or part of the door, and also the picture which doesn't seem centered or significant in such a large frame.

Notice that the statement "That he is not making undesired advances to her is shown by the way he holds her" creates sufficient anxiety to disrupt his story and lead him to describe small details of the picture. This was a rather typical response to anxiety which was incited by his own stories. We see again that the repressed sexual wish is sufficiently powerful to generate anxiety at the thought of it breaking through. Stories of his repressed aggressive need did not result in such small detail response to anxiety.

Arising from the fact that his love object and his sex object are one and the same person and that his love and sex need have a passionate oral aggressive component, there is such a generalization of these repressed wishes to more remote love and sex objects that he cannot, in his stories, allow any consummation of marriage.

The following story is typical of this inhibition.

> The woman has heard some very sad news—perhaps a person close to her has died. She turns to the man, a close friend, perhaps a lover and seeks consolation. . . . In another way, depending on how the girl's eye interprets

emotion to the observer, the girl might be dancing with the boy. She acts very sophisticated and he seems amused, perhaps at something she'd said. They will be good (not close) friends but won't ever marry.

"Good" friends are typically not "close" friends. In the following story there is further evidence of the repressing force:

> Both these people are married [crossed out] working and they have made it a point to get time off together and go for a bicycle trip during the summer. This has now become almost a tradition and will go on for years. They are friends and never show any warm feelings for each other.

He began the story about a married couple and then penciled over it to make them friends who "never show any warm feelings for each other." Again, good friends are not close friends.

In the following story the same logic determines the nature of the relationship.

> These two people had been in love in their youth but had separated. The woman is a widow and now in their old age they enjoy each other's company calmly and dispassionately.

Where there is mutual passion, the couple is separated, and allowed to reunite only after they are capable of a more calm relationship.

Another example of the same thema is the following.

> These two children play together often. The little girl learns that her family is to move away. She tells the little boy nothing about this but kisses him good-bye. She joins a nunnery when she grows up and doesn't see the boy again until she is very old when she is visiting a dying man in the poor district. He smiles and she follows an impulse to kiss him although she does not recognize him. He begins to get better but then dies suddenly.

Although there is the reunion here of two lovers who still are capable of passion, the man after a brief improvement "dies suddenly."

Or, the couple may be separated by the premature death of one of the lovers.

> When a young boy, Roger Rollins brought his girl, Mary Caudry, to this tree and carved their initials on it. Later in her teens, Mary died and Roger every year makes a pilgrimage to this tree.

The following two stories are typical of a series of similar stories, showing the destiny of those who are brave enough to marry.

> This couple has been traveling on their honeymoon and now they are tired of hotels and are talking about the new house they are going to move into next week. On the morrow he will be called into service and she will go back to her mother—the house sold.

This couple are quite poor but they have decided to stop worrying about it and go to Florida. They have come back from a vacation in Florida, he unable to support his wife in a satisfactory manner, joins the army and she goes back to her folks.

Marriage is typically dissolved shortly after its inception, primarily because the hero is unable to provide for his wife in a satisfactory manner. The hero generally joins the army—he is not drafted. At the time of this testing the draft was not a serious concern of this subject.

Now let us consider the application of our theory of repression to the analysis of the repressed sexual and aggressive wishes. The sexual wish is fused with oral aggression in this record and the consequence of its expression can be compared with the consequences of expressing aggression toward the father.

Of approximately 400 stories about 300, or 75 per cent, deal with the conflict of either sex or aggression so that this individual is under relatively high pressure from both of these wishes. Of these 300 stories, approximately 100 dealt with aggression and approximately 200 with love and sex. Hence we would expect more pressure from the latter conflict than the former, since 50 per cent of the total pressure of the system would be involved with the control of love and sex and 25 per cent with the control of aggression toward the father.

Let us consider next the relative pressure of repressing and repressed wishes. In the case of the aggressive wish we rated its pressure as low, since it does not appear at all in the face-to-face father-son stories and only gradually increases in intensity in the remaining stories. There is clearly less pressure to the aggressive wish in this case than in the case of X, who was rated medium in pressure, but more pressure than in the case of Y, who was rated very low in pressure. Remoteness was rated medium, since there is a gradual increase in the expression of aggression with increasing remoteness. It is clearly not so remote in expression as in the case of Y, who was rated high, and is more remote than in the case of X, who was rated low in remoteness. The product of a low pressure repressed wish and a medium remoteness is a repressing force of high pressure. There is then a high, low ratio between repressing and repressed wish as contrasted with a high, medium ratio for X and a high, very low ratio for Y.

The ratio in the case of the fused love-sex wish resembles the ratio of the aggressive wish in the case of X. The pressure of Z's love-sex wish, however, is higher than that of his aggression, since it appears in the face-to-face situation and has both high intensity and extensity in stories involving love objects other than the mother. The conflicts of the hero concerning the control of sex are equivalent in pressure to those of X in attempting to control aggression. The love-sex wish is also low in remoteness of expression, appearing as a wish to rescue the mother, as an act of aggression toward the sister and as undisguised passion towards love objects at one remove from the mother. Moreover, the mother loses control of herself while fondling her son. The product of the medium pressure of this wish and the low remoteness of expression is a high pressure repressing force. This constellation is roughly equivalent to the aggression in the case of X. In both cases the individuals are chiefly concerned with the *control* of the wish—in one case the aggressive wish, in the other the love-sex wish. But in the case of Z's aggression there is no indication that any hero ever *feels* hostile towards the father in face-to-face relationships—he either runs away or becomes very gentle and effeminate. Whenever a hero struggles with the control of a wish we may be certain the storyteller is repressing the wish with considerable difficulty and that there is a delicate unstable equilibrium between the forces of repression and the repressed wish.

How can we test these derivations? There is a relatively simple method which is available. If we could generally weaken the forces of repression we would be able to test whether a differential effect was produced by this weakening of the forces of repression. We would assume from our estimation of forces that some decrease in the forces of repression should allow Z's love-sex wish freer expression in face-to-face relations in TAT stories than the aggressive wish, since the ratio of the repressive force to the love-sex wish is smaller than the ratio of repressive force to the aggressive wish. In order to test this we administered the TAT to Z while he was under the influence of alcohol. It was our prediction that in this state his stories would become frankly incestuous in theme, but that the aggression towards the father would not appear so openly. Following are two of the stories pertinent to this prediction.

This poor little dope is looking at a violin. He plays—what does he play? Sonata on a G String. And all the kids call it on a G string. It must be by Rachmaninoff. My mother stood right next to Rachmaninoff. She touched him. She went to a concert by him and she stood right beside him. She almost swooned. This poor little dope. No doubt he is taking music lessons. Just the way they've got his hair cut into bangs. Still, he is a plump little chap. No reason why he doesn't play football. Somewhere back in his mind he wants to study, but he doesn't want to be forced to study. The meeting having agreed that he doesn't want to be forced to study, we'll say that he will be a very good violinist, but not a professional. Maybe he will go into engineering as a reaction. Well, the poor little guy has got to be an engineer, but music will be very close to his heart.

This naked woman is the man's sister. I am forced to say that because I have said she is his lover for so long that it becomes trite. She is his sister and she has had what is considered by the rules of modern society an inappropriate relationship with him. What's that? Incest applies to mother and son as well as sister and brother. A broad term. So much more than pure physical love. A soul and a mind. Incest—society shudders at the word. Why? Why? Society has set up barriers. On a certain island it is indecent to be seen eating with a woman. Incest or any other relationship is not considered indecent. So here is this woman in love with her brother, her brother in love with her. So they have this baby. And this other woman, the aunt, is brought up in a Victorian school. She is insulted. She is very angry. In her anger she kills the baby. Through projection of her hate for her nephew-in-law and her niece, she kills the baby. Life is snuffed out. How do perverted relationships differ from normal?

Our predictions have been confirmed. In the first story the Oedipus triangle appears more openly, but the father is cast in the role of Rachmaninoff, the master who is capable of making his mother swoon. The sexual meaning of this music is indicated by a pun "all the kids call it on a G string." The hero in comparison is "this poor little dope" who has had his "hair" cut. The hero is clearly envious of the father's virtuosity, and although oppressed and inferior, thinks there is really no reason why he could not play a more masculine role—"No reason why he doesn't play football." He thinks "he will be a very good violinist, but not a professional," i.e., he will never be able to achieve his father's virtuosity. But then even this is qualified, and in the end he "has got to be an engineer, but music will be very close to his heart." In other words, though aspiring to the father's place, he does not see how he can achieve it. This is a discussion of his feelings towards his father, which had never before appeared so openly. But despite this weakening of the repressive forces against his aggression there is yet no indication here of actual aggression against the father. In the second story the incestuous wish towards the sister is given frank, poignant expression. He does not understand why it is considered inappropriate. The sister-brother relationship is thought to be no different than the mother-son relationship—"Incest applies to mother and son as well as sister and brother. A broad term." He is then reminded of the oral nature of his wish—"On a certain island it is indecent to be seen eating with a woman." But on the same island it is thought that incest, if it does not involve oral wishes, is permissible. But then conscience in the form of a "Victorian" aunt kills the baby that is the fruit of the consummation of their love. The story ends on a pathetic note, "How do perverted relationships differ from normal?" *

* The affect of this individual while telling these stories was intense and massive. It must not be supposed that it was entirely the consequence of alcohol per se. The subject had insisted that the examiner drink with him, and this I did. My intoxication matched that of the subject's. Previous experience with alcohol administered to subjects in a "scientific" manner had convinced the examiner that a large part of the reduction of inhibition resulting from alcohol intoxication was a consequence of the social atmosphere. An experimenter who dispassionately tests and observes the behavior of an individual who has been asked to drink 50 cc. of alcohol will not achieve a reduction of high pressure repressive forces.

If so much appears in the TAT, under the influence of alcohol, one may ask whether the forces of repression are *ever* sufficiently weakened to permit the expression of overt aggression toward the father. We have found no evidence that this ever happens. Dreams over a ten month period revealed phantasies very similar to the TAT stories under alcohol. This would be consistent with the theory that there is some reduction of vigilance in dreams, but that the forces of repression are by no means completely vanquished.

The following two dreams are typical of those recorded daily for ten months.

> I was stripped to the waist when my mother came in. I was glad I hadn't put on my shirt. Mother didn't seem to pay much attention to me. I embraced my mother. The other woman said "so he didn't go overseas." Then I started looking at a pocket sized notebook with a dark green cloth cover and black printing hardly noticeable on it. This had been dropped beside me by a man who came in with my mother. I then realized it was a passport and it was my father's. I looked up and the man was my father whom I hadn't recognized till then.

> My mother and I were cleaning floors. We both had mops. First her mop got tangled in my hair, which caused very little commotion and then my mop got tangled in her hair which upset everyone. I felt very unhappy.

The first dream is not unlike the first TAT story told under alcohol, except that embracing the mother reveals overt expression which was achieved only in the second TAT story told under alcohol. The father is recognized belatedly and is the apparent cause of the mother's indifference to the son. This also repeats the relationship between Rachmaninoff and the son. But as in the TAT story there is no aggression toward the father. In the second dream the sexual significance of hair appears thinly veiled as it did throughout his TAT stories. No one is alarmed by the mother's advances towards the son, but everyone, including the hero, is unhappy when he makes advances towards the mother.

The relationship between these dreams, interpreted on the level of manifest content, and his TAT stories is of considerable theoretical significance. We have seen that his deeply repressed wish to kill his father appears in the TAT displaced to remote objects but that it does not appear in his dreams, insofar as their manifest content is concerned. This would seem to indicate that the censorship which Freud postulated as operating in the dream life is probably correct. There would appear to be some relaxation of vigilance, but the forces of repression have not been completely inhibited. The TAT seems to offer the individual greater distance and more opportunity for the displacement of deeply repressed wishes to very remote objects. That this type of displacement occurs in dreams is also certain but in this case the wish, because of low pressure and higher counterpressure, could not be projected into the manifest content of dreams. The latent content of the dream revealed through association to elements of the dream stands in the same relationship to the manifest content as remote stories to face-to-face normal stories. Thus if we regard such a normal story as if it were a dream and ask the individual to free-associate to it we not infrequently arrive at the content of the more remote stories.

In this case we have found further evidence that the return of the repressed is a function of the total pressure of the conflict and the relative pressure of opposed forces. The sexual conflict was of greater pressure and more evenly balanced than that concerning his aggression towards his father. For both of these reasons he suffered more anxiety from his incestuous wishes than from his aggressive wishes, even though the source of punishment in both cases was the father. His stories also indicate that the punishment for incest or sexual expression in general is much more severe than the punishment for the expression of aggression. The consequence of this difference in strength of repression, for his love life and general social relationships, is noteworthy. Because the incestuous wish is so close to the surface and countered by a relatively high pressure fear there has been a widespread generalization of both the wish and the fear to other possible love objects. Because the aggressive wish is relatively weaker and under greater counterpressure than in the sexual conflict, this wish has not suffered the same degree of generalization to social relationships. Z can be more aggressive to other males than he can be tender or passionate to other females.

We have offered these few cases as illustrations rather than as conclusive evidence. We do not believe that crucial evidence can be presented until these forces can be measured with more precision. We do believe that if the techniques of measurement had been more refined and truly quantitative these cases could have been offered as crucial evidence for our hypotheses. Despite these limitations the methods we have employed have enabled successful prediction of the effect of experimental and environmental pressures in several other cases in which the TAT indicated high pressure forces in unstable equilibrium.

SUMMARY

The determination of the relationship between story and storyteller was the problem to which this chapter addressed itself. We examined first the relationship between overt and covert needs. We maintained that the hypotheses offered by Sanford in this connection were probably correct but that the supporting evidence—correlations between needs as expressed in the TAT and needs expressed in overt behavior—was not so strong as it might have been because the TAT did not permit an accurate estimate of the strength of covert needs. This we said was because repressed and suppressed, covert and overt needs, the past, present and future are all woven into the imaginative productions of the TAT. Since the individual is called upon to interpret the behavior, feelings, and expectations of figures represented pictorially, he reveals something more than his fleeting diffuse private phantàsies.

The relationship between overt and covert need can frequently be found within the TAT stories themselves if attention is given to the levels and qualifiers portrayed in the story. Scoring according to the Murray-Sanford needs does not differentiate the level of psychological function or specific qualifications of such a function.

We saw that only when a protocol is invariant with respect to the level on which the stories proceed may we assume that this level is a literal representation of the predominant level on which that individual functions. An example of such invariance is the individual whose anxiety is reflected in his stories by exclusive reference to the level of feeling and expectation. Anxiety exacerbated by the testing situation itself may produce an invariance of stories on the level of object description. Occasionally one finds protocols which employ only the behavioral level. Such individuals we have found are extraverted to such an extent that their behavior is imbedded in the external world and they are free to a great extent of endopsychic barriers which might interfere with the spontaneous expression of their wishes. Other individuals may be so deeply engrossed in their inner life that instead of assimilating the inner life to the external world they assimilate the world to the inner life. If this is the case we may find an invariance of the level of feeling or thought or memory throughout the protocols. Or the inner life of feeling may assume proportions which completely remove the individual from interaction with the external world. Stories in such cases employ the level of feeling or mood throughout.

But since most individuals operate on many levels, such protocols as those described above are rare. However there are important differences in the relative time and energy devoted by different individuals to these levels. A very rough index of these differences may be achieved from the relative frequency of appearance of each level in the protocol. Illustration of the usefulness of such a technique was the analysis of the TAT's of Navaho children by Henry, who showed the predominance of behavior and event in their protocol and relatively little elaboration of personal feelings, memories and daydreams. The TAT's of psychopathic defective criminals were shown by Kutash to employ the levels of feeling, description, and wish most frequently, which we explained on the basis of their imprisonment and limitation of behavior.

Although frequently useful as a technique of analysis of group data, we said that a much more specific analysis of the different levels was required. This involved an analysis of a level that varied which showed that the variation was either an effect of variation in some preceding condition, or the cause of variation in some consequent condition.

We next considered the sequence analysis of levels. In this type of analysis we disregarded the specific content of the stories and extracted the sequence of levels which either preceded or followed any particular level. We illustrated in some detail the sequelae and levels which preceded one particular level—that of wish. The same type of analysis may be applied to any other level. Typical sequelae of the level of wish were the following: (1) wish-thinking-behavior, signifying a deliberative conjunctive personality for whom the expression of any wish necessarily involved an intermediate step of thinking; (2) wish-thinking, signifying an overemphasis on the deliberative phase of activity, so that action is paralyzed by excessive planning; (3) wish-thinking-daydreaming, signifying a short-circuiting of the wish through the daydream after some reflection on the wish; (4) wish-daydream-behavior, signifying the means-end cognizance to be less important to the individual than the vision of the future goal which inspires him to translate the wish into appropriate behavior; (5) wish-daydream-expectation, signifying that the daydream creates sufficient certainty of the future event to require no behavior on the part of the hero; (6) wish-daydream, signifying an individual whose daydream is neither preceded by thinking nor followed by behavior nor the expectation of a future event, but which simply short-circuits the wish; (7) wish-daydream-event, signifying an individual who has in fact received an abundance of gratuities without effort on his part or a wish-fulfillment phantasy; (8) wish-event, signifying that the individual is the passive object of external forces (the event may gratify or frustrate the satisfaction of the wish); (9) wish-behavior is a curiously rare sequence, probably because the extraverted individual who is imbedded in the external world is less aware of the existence of wishes as separate entities; (10) wish followed by no other level commonly signifies an individual whose wishes by their very nature seem impossible of gratification; (11) wish-counterwish-behavior signifies either a somewhat inhibited or impulsive personality, depending on which wish is expressed in behavior. We next considered the levels which preceded the level of wish: (1) event-wish signifies an individual whose inner life is essentially reactive to outer stimuli of an impersonal nature; (2) memory-wish commonly signifies an individual who suffers grief, guilt, shame, or anxiety—since one of the salient characteristics of such inner states is their peculiar sensitivity to rearousal through memory; (3) physical sensations-wish signify an individual governed to a great extent by bodily states (this is particularly characteristic of children and adolescents); (4) expectation-wish signifies an individual whose inner life is governed either by his own expectations or those of others; (5) special state-wish signifies that the wish is under some inhibition in the normal state and some de-inhibiting force is required to activate it; (6) perception-wish signifies, in the event that this is the perception of human objects, an individual whose inner life is governed by the presence of other human beings; (7) behavior-wish, if this is the behavior of others, signifies an individual whose wishes are essentially reactive to the behavior of others; (8) moods- or feelings-wish signify an individual whose inner life exerts massive pressure and is more self regulative than reactive to outer stimuli.

We also examined a single story to illustrate the more complex sequence of levels usually found in the protocol. The particular sequence was behavior-event-thinking-mood-wish. We saw that these sequences of levels cannot be assumed literally to represent something typical of the storyteller unless that sequence is invariant in the protocol. If it is not invariant we must examine the conditions under which the sequences vary to determine the meaning of the variability.

We next examined the problem of awareness—the degree to which the individual is aware of his own wishes or behavior. We saw that awareness of the nature of overt behavior might be limited to the awareness of single concrete fragments of behavior—that the patterning of behavioral sequences might entirely escape the attention of the individual—that the contemporary determinants of such patterns were even more elusive, and that the relationship of these to their genetic precursors was the achievement of only the most reflective individuals. We said that an individual may possess awareness of his own motivation and not attribute it to his heroes but that we had not found individuals who attributed more awareness of motivation to their heroes than they themselves possessed of their own motivation. One typically finds in the TAT stories of patients who have received psychotherapy attribution of complex patterns of motivation to their heroes, but psychotherapy is not the only road to such insight. We presented 6 "insightful" stories, 3 from individuals who had been psychoanalyzed and 3 whose stories were told without benefit of prior therapeutic intervention.

We examined next the problem of repression. We said that discrepancies between what is known of the individual's daily behavior and the behavior of his heroes provides a simple criterion for distinguishing whether the latter represents overt behavior or covert wish. The problem of assessing levels of psychological function within the covert sphere was seen to be much more complex and difficult. Although forces within the covert sphere may exert varying degrees of pressure for admittance into consciousness or translation into behavior, behavioral criteria for the measurement of such differences in pressure have not yet been clearly defined.

In order to exploit the sensitivity of the TAT in eliciting repressed material, we undertook a revision and extension of Freud's theory of repression.

We assumed first that any personality has a finite quantum of energy at its disposal. Secondly, a personality may be treated for analytical purposes as if it were a closed system. We defined psychological energy in terms of units of psychological pressure and assumed that any single wish within the personality may have any pressure not exceeding the total amount of pressure available to the personality. We also assumed that, because of the finite quantum of pressure units available to the person, the expenditure of pressure units in one area limits the amount of pressure available for other purposes. We further assumed that the unit of pressure is the product of two components —intensity and extensity. By intensity we meant the strength of the wish or drive and by extensity its scope or mass. Thus the pressure of a wish might be equivalent if it were either of high intensity and low extensity or low intensity and high extensity.

It followed from these assumptions that as the total pressure of two wishes in conflict increases the pressure available for the remainder of the system decreases. Thus a conflict between two wishes of low pressure rarely involves pathogenic sequelae, but a conflict between two wishes of high pressure is the condition par excellence for pathology, since if each wish involved almost half of the total pressure of the personality this would be civil war within the individual.

Whether a conflict will be pathogenic, and more specifically, whether the repressed will "return" are also functions of the relative pressure of the two forces which stand in opposition to each other. It was our hypothesis that as the repressing force increases in pressure, relative to the repressed force, the possibility of return of the repressed wish decreases and, further, that this entails a reduction in disturbance to the personality as a whole. Conversely, we assumed that as the balance between the two forces in opposition approached equality there would be a greater tendency of the repressed wish to return and an increase in general disturbance to the personality as a whole. Our doctrine was in this respect contrary to that contemporary opinion which attributes serious pathogenic potentialities to "deeply" repressed material. We maintained in effect that the deeper the repression the less pathogenic the conflict.

If these hypotheses are correct, the most serious conflict would be one in which there were two fairly evenly balanced forces, consuming between them the entire energies of the system. The least serious conflict would be that between two forces of low pressure but in which one of the forces was relatively much higher in pressure than the other, although between them a relatively small part of the total pressure of the system was involved. As a conflict approached either of these end points it would be more or less patho-genic. It would also follow that if one factor was favorable the pathogenic potentiality of the other factor would be reduced.

We next considered the empirical problem of the measurement of these forces. We saw that the measurement of the absolute and relative strength of two forces, one of which represses the other, is peculiarly difficult because the nature of the repressed force can be investigated only when the pressure of the repressing force has been reduced to zero. It was our suggestion that the analysis of the individual's imaginative productions did allow a more satisfactory measure of these forces than we could at present achieve through experimental investigation. We thought this was so because the forces of repression were greatly reduced by allowing the individual to achieve distance between himself and the characters of his stories and by the use of pictures which are either ambiguous, bizarre, or remote. Such pictures permit the individual license in telling stories unfettered by realistic considerations. Further, he is encouraged to do this by the change of instructions at the beginning of the second session—that he may give freer rein to his imagina-tion. For these reasons the individual may attribute wishes to his heroes which no amount of alcohol or other experimental manipulation might induce him to express in overt behavior. But since the force of repression is only weakened and not reduced to a zero quantity, repressed wishes are usually not given completely free expression even under these conditions. We must therefore employ the technique of comparing the behavior of those heroes who are interacting "normally" with parents or others with those heroes who are represented in a setting psychologically "remote" from normal interaction. It was our assumption that the remoteness of conditions under which antisocial wishes might be expressed was a function of the relative pressure of repressing and repressed forces. As the repressing force increases in pressure relative to the pressure of the repressed force, the conditions under which the latter may be given expression in TAT stories become more and more "remote." As this ratio approaches equality the expression of the repressed force will appear under less and less remote conditions in the stories.

We suggested that the ratio of the combined pressure of repressing and repressed wish to the total pressure might be crudely estimated by totaling the number of stories which refer either to the repressing force or the repressed force and computing the percentage of such stories to the total number of stories. In order to determine the pressure of the repressed wish we must rate the intensity and extensity of the repressed wish as it appears in each story—estimate the product of both components and then add these separate estimates to achieve a total estimate of the pressure of the repressed wish. In order to estimate the pressure of the repressing force we would employ our hypothesis that remoteness is a function of the ratio of repressing pressure to repressed pressure. Having estimated the pressure of the repressed wish and the degree of remoteness, the product of these two estimates provides an estimate of the pressure of the repressing force.

We then presented three cases, X, Y, and Z, to illustrate these hypotheses. Each of the TAT's revealed that aggression against a parent had been repressed by these individuals. In the case of X, this wish and its control expended much of the available energy, representing a high pressure–medium pressure conflict with low remoteness of expression of aggression. In the case of Y the combined pressure of repressing force and aggression was high. The repressing force was of high pressure but the aggression was of very low pressure, having high intensity but very low extensity. Remoteness of expression of aggression was high. In the case of Z this conflict consumed less energy than with X or Y. It represented a high pressure–low pressure conflict. Remoteness of expression of aggression represented a mid-point between the other cases, being of medium degree. In accordance with our hypotheses, X was the most seriously disturbed, Y least disturbed, and Z represented a mid-point between these two. We further showed that a special hypothesis in the case of Z was confirmed by experimental evidence. The incestuous wish, we said, was opposed by a relatively weaker force than was the aggressive wish and should therefore appear first if the forces of repression were somewhat weakened. This prediction was confirmed by the stories which he told under the de-inhibiting effect of alcohol.

CHAPTER VI

DIAGNOSIS OF PERSONALITY: THE REGION OF THE FAMILY

Freud's dictum of the importance of the family romance pervades modern psychopathology and personality theory and has so insinuated itself into the contemporary climate of opinion that only today, partly as a result of the war experience, are we beginning to question whether a halt should be called to the now almost unconscious assumption of strict causal relationship between early childhood and adult personality. The TAT provides a valuable technique for assaying, with more precision than we could before, the exact relationships obtaining between the personality of the child as it is formed in the family setting and the adult personality. Our purpose in this chapter, however, is twofold: we shall delineate techniques useful in such assessment and more generally address ourselves to the criteria for determining the relative importance of the family region for the individual personality.

A. Direct References

The protocols may contain direct references to the importance of the family to the individual.

> This is a picture of a mother and son. The father died when the boy was only two and so his mother has been more than a mother. She was both mother and father, and they have always been very close to each other. She means more to him than anything else in the world, and now when he has to leave her to go into the army, he doesn't know how to tell her. But she senses it, and is understanding about it as she has always been about everything. When he comes back from the army she will still be there, and they will go on as if nothing has ever happened.

B. Introduction of Parental Figures

Such direct references are not common. In general more indirect techniques must be employed. One such technique involves an examination of the protocol for the frequency of introduction of parental figures, *where the picture contains none*. Such introduction must however be evaluated further in terms of the specific picture. Thus in picture 1, the boy with the violin, the introduction of a parent is less significant than a similar introduction in a story to the blank card. The possibilities of introducing people or objects into the blank card are endless but the possibilities of such introduction are limited in the former by the fact that the parent is the usual mediator of the child's musical training in the American family. The significance of such introduction, however, must not be overlooked simply because it reflects the cultural setting. Common cultural influences are no less important than individual differences to an understanding of personality.

C. Ambiguous Figures Interpreted as Parental Figures

Another criterion is the interpretation of ambiguous figures as parents. Such pictures as 3BM (the figure huddled against a couch), 10 (two vague figures embracing), 14 (a silhouette of a figure), and 20 (an ambiguous figure standing under a lamp) may be seen as individuals of any age or sex, and when the family is more important than other regions these individuals may be seen as parents.

D. Older Figures Interpreted as Parental Figures

For children, almost any figure that is not a child may be seen as a parent, whereas for early and late adolescents and adults the picture of an older adult presents the option of interpretation as either an older adult or a parent. With the qualifications treated in the discussion of repression, there is a direct relationship between the importance of the parent in the life of the storyteller and the number of such figures interpreted as parents rather than other adults. This relationship, however, only exists when identification is with the child in the story. An adult may identify with the parents in his stories and in doing this is telling us that the role of parent has superseded his earlier role as a child.

E. Omission of Older Adults in the Picture

If older adults in the picture are omitted in the elaboration of a story it may signify either that parents and parental surrogates have ceased to be important or that the individual denies their existence because for some reason they are unwanted, dangerous, or otherwise unacceptable to him.

F. Number of Stories About the Family

A further index of the importance of the family is the proportion of stories concerned with the family rather than with love, work, or social relationships.

G. Length of Stories About the Family

The length of stories told about the family in comparison with the length of other stories also provides a useful criterion.

H. Intensity of Affect in Stories About the Family

An individual sometimes tells only one story concerning the family, but the affect of the storyteller and the affect attributed to the hero in the story are in striking contrast to every other story told by him. In such cases the individual may be attempting to deny or forget his own family and this is a single instance of the break-through of the feeling he is trying to control. However, if every story, whatever the theme, is characterized by intense affect this is a less diagnostic criterion of the relative significance of the family.

I. Conflict with Other Regions

The importance of the family may be such that it eliminates all possibility of conflict with other regions, or the family may have become so unimportant that no conflict exists. But if the individual is neither completely immersed in nor uninterested in the family, the intensity of conflict which he mentions between the family and other regions and the resolution of this conflict provides an index of the relative importance of the family and other regions. We are not referring primarily to stories of direct parental intervention in other regions, a topic which will be considered later, but to stories involving the hero's own conflict about the relative valences of the family and other regions. Such conflict, or the lack of it, is commonly expressed in response to picture 2, showing an older man and woman and a young girl.

In the following stories we shall illustrate the presence or absence of conflict, the oscillations that may occur, and the degrees of residual tension if the conflict is resolved either in favor of the family or another region.

As we have said, the hero may have a minimum interest in or conflict with anything outside the family.

> This picture gives a sense of the closeness of a family to the soil. They are all tied together in a common undertaking. The soil is fertile and these people have almost a religious feeling about their home. The mother's face denotes calmness and serenity indicative of her contentment. Her husband is bending his strength toward plowing, and although his .face is not visible, the degree of physical perfection which is his is shown by the musculature of his back and shoulders outlined by his toil. The daughter is obviously a student. She has a dreamy look in her eyes, dreaming of the summertime when school is out and she can spend all her time with her mother and father on the farm.

Or the heroine may, as in the following two stories, be interested in other values and leave the family, only to discover that the parental values are really her values; whereupon she returns to the family, experiencing no residual tension after her return.

This girl was brought up on a farm. The man and the woman are her mother and father, and she has just returned from the school, and she is looking over the land and wondering if it is worth all the energy and time to cultivate the land as they do. Later on she'll ask her mother and father for permission to go to the city to live with her aunt. When she gets to the city she enrolls in a very swanky girls' school. There she meets girls from different social classes than hers. To those girls the only important things are clothes and money, and she didn't like this new life. After a month of this kind of life she decides to go home. She now realizes that her mother and father's work—that her mother and father's work—is necessary, and she will devote her life to helping them.

A good old farm scene. The son has worked hard all his life on the farm and the father has worked beside him. The mother has slaved day in and day out with all the work of the house and feeding all the farm hands. They have gotten along all right in life without any real education. But what's this—the daughter of the family is carrying her beloved books around with her. She doesn't want to stay on the farm all the rest of her life. She reads every chance she gets. Why should she be stuck away out here—she wanted to go to the city and get somewhere. But her parents just laughed at her. What was good enough for them, was all right for her. And so she lived day and night snatching a couple of minutes when she wasn't doing some chore to read a little bit. She read at night when all around her was silent. Their farm was prosperous, but she never got away until one day she finally made up her mind to get out. She didn't tell her folks, but left one night when they were all sleeping. After being in the city for a long time she found out how stupid she had been to leave her family, home, and friends. So she came back meekly and she only then appreciated how marvelous her farm life was.

Or the heroine may intensely dislike home but stay, suppressing the wish to leave home.

This woman is trying to talk some sense into this girl. She is reading a preceptual passage to her but the girl's mind is far away. She does not want to listen to this woman her mother because she associates most of her previous humiliating experiences with her. She wants to get away, to be free. She has mixed feelings of self-pity, aggression, and a desire to start out on her own. However she makes an effort and suppresses this mood and listens to what her mother is reading.

Or the individual, although she rejects the parents and is interested in other values, may have no way of escaping them and remains at home, suffering much residual tension.

On a farm on a lake in Michigan lived a family who had had to toil hard to wrest a living from the unwilling soil. But in spite of their hardships and sufferings caused by the soil and its obstinate ways, they had all gotten to love it and were content to spend their lives working their sometimes beloved, sometimes hated, but always their own soil. Mother had come there as a young bride and there had had and brought up all her children, and Joe, the eldest son who was taking father's place, had really made the farm advance and was quite content to work there. But it is not right to say that all loved it there—leading that monotonous life with no chance for a higher development, for Martha, the daughter, hated it. She was sick of depending solely on the soil for an existence and being among people content to live there and never get anywhere in life. She wanted to learn all she could—and get out in the world, away from the farm and make a place for herself in the world that was really so fascinating if you only looked beyond the full sameness of the farm. But was there any plausible hope for getting away? No— only that of staying on the farm and getting some knowledge out of what books she could obtain. And she was right—for Martha never managed to get away. Though she did read many books and became more worldly-wise than the others of her family, in time she too was sucked into the soil, the farm, and the life there, as if by quicksilver.

But if the family values are unsatisfying the outside world may present different problems; the individual, unable to leave or to stay, may not resolve the conflict but live the kind of "between two worlds" existence described in the next story.

Ah a young woman in the country, a young girl rather, who is somewhat above average intelligence and some sensibility, who doesn't like, who didn't care for her family and for the life in the country and whose ambition was to get to college, and there was a little mountain college in the state, in her end of the state, and after much thrashing about she finally managed to, ah, get to the college but found that it, it didn't suit her either, or rather that she didn't suit it. She couldn't quite do the work and that people, ah, didn't, didn't care for her and so forth. She would come home at times she would go to college and be homesick and then get on a bus or something and come home and so in the mountainous part of the state and come home. Presumably when she was at home she would be miserable because she had not cared for her home in the first place. Ah, in the picture here she is [laughs] well, just as well, let's say just leaving, just going back on the way to college again, leaving her mother and perhaps mother and older sister at the farm. It's a kind of between-two-worlds thing where neither world is at all excellent, has no virtue in itself, but where one is not enough and the other is too much for this—ah, simple person.

Or the individual seeking other values may leave home but suffer a great deal of residual tension.

This girl lives all by herself. She comes home from work and retires to her lonely room. She sits in a chair and starts to ponder over what her life has been. She thinks of her childhood at home with her parents and of the many opportunities that were open to her. She thinks of her own stubbornness and selfishness. She wonders why she didn't take advantage of the opportunities. As a child she was given many things that other children did not have. When she grew older, a—she decided that she wanted to leave home and be by herself. She left home and went to a big city. There she got a job, thinking she'd be able to meet the kind of people she always wanted to know. But she finds herself one of many thousands of lonely girls with no close friends and no family to turn to.

Or throwing off parental standards, the individual may leave home and experience a minimum of residual tension. Rarely do we find an individual who has absolutely no attachment to or interest in the family, but that this interest may be slight and other values more important is seen in this story.

> This reminds me of a book. I can't remember the name of the book, but it was about a swamp and a girl. I think that the girl is seeing beyond the farm. That she is in deep thought. She was born with industrious, hard working parents. As she grew up, she saw all the toil of the farm. She has a desire to step out from the bounds of the farm. The book she is carrying bring this out, and the fact that her back is facing the farm. She doesn't hate it, but she wants to do greater things. Her parents are bound up with work, and her parents don't resent her going off. She is going to high school and is going through much trouble because of her queer appearance, but she has the strength of character that will make her successful. She will be successful. She has a hard time making friends. She will marry an eminent person—the professor type, and she will be very happy. She's not content to watch the world go by. She will be eminent in some field—either she's interested in painting or something along those lines—be famous. She'll be happier than if she were on the farm. She has character and foresight that her parents lack. No person to lead a humdrum life. She's not afraid of making rash statements, but will do what she thinks is right.

J. Range of Parental Impact Within the Family Setting

Another criterion of the relative importance of the family is the degree of parental impact within the family setting. By degree of parental impact we mean the extent to which the child's personality is actually shaped by the parent. Not infrequently the influence of the parent may be so pervasive that the child literally has no area of free movement. Whether the child identifies completely with the parent, is submissive to parental dominance, or rebels against the parent, his personality is the resultant of massive parental impact. At the opposite end of the continuum are parents who, either through indifference or complete submission to the child's demands, exert relatively little influence on the formation of his personality.

Parental impact is a complex resultant of parent-child interaction. There may, for example, be little influence on the child because the parent is either indifferent or submissive to the child, or if he attempts to govern or influence the child his influence may still be slight because of the child's indifference; or in the face of the child's resistance to any attempts to govern or influence him, the parent may retreat, abandoning any idea of trying to influence him or in some cases even becoming submissive to the child.

On the other hand, the parent may have great influence whether the child is submissive or rebellious to attempts to govern or influence him. In the case of the child who rebels the influence may still be great because his personality becomes the exact opposite of the parental ideal. The influence may also be great if the child identifies with the parent, whether or not the parent is instrumental in fostering this identification.

Between these extremes of maximal and minimal parental impact are many varying degrees of influence. The parent may exert some influence on the child indirectly by exposing him to other influences; parental ego idealism may extract half-hearted compliance from the child, or the parents may influence the child only on special occasions under special circumstances or for a certain length of time.

In the following stories we present a sample, ranging from a minimum to a maximum of parental impact. In the first story parental impact is slight; the child wishes the parents to do more for him than they're capable of doing and their lack is the stimulus specific to his development of independence and initiative:

> Well, it looks as though the violin is broken and he feels sad about it because he likes to play. Uh . . . he's about eight years old and he wants to be a violinist. His family can't afford to get him another one. He's probably thinking about how he can earn some money to get it repaired. He gets a job delivering newspapers and gets the violin repaired and takes up his studies again. Because of his interest he becomes a success.

In the next story parental impact is still very limited. The parents are capable of doing what the child wishes but the child is the instigator of their activity and they merely minister to his needs.

> Sitting there is a boy about 10 years old gazing at a violin. Ah—he's quite an intelligent fellow and ah—I think perhaps he wanted to study the violin. So his mother and father bought him the violin, and he started to take lessons. As the lessons progressed, he found there was more work involved than he had thought. He realizes that success wouldn't come as easily as he thought, and he will have to study and study before he becomes a great violinist. By the expression in his eyes, it looks as if he's wondering whether it's worth all the effort. As he grows older he stops taking violin lessons and listens to concerts. He will realize he was wrong to stop taking violin lessons.

The role of the parents in the following story is also limited; they minister to the child's needs as in the preceding story but they play a part in shaping the child's interest, even though indirectly, by exposing him to other influences.

Once when Frederick was a very, very, very, little boy his father took him along to hear a famous violinist play at the Opera House. During the performance and on the way home, Frederick had said nothing—nor did he for days afterwards. Instead he had a dreamy look of yearning in his eyes and he went around humming the pieces played by the violinist. Finally one afternoon his father, in his study, looked up to find the huge door being slowly pushed open by little Frederick. The boy came over to him and, with the same look of yearning in his eyes, asked if he could please, *please* have a violin of his own; that to play a violin was all he wanted ever in the wide world. His father didn't say much, but soon a big box came for Frederick. Hardly daring to hope, he opened it slowly, and lo—there it was—his *own* violin. He took it out gingerly and lovingly and set it on the table before him and just looked at it with that same loving, longing look. And do you know who that little Frederick is now? After studying and studying and studying, he became one of our famous violinists.

The parent in the next story attempts to play an active role in influencing the child, but the child's resistance induces the parent to conform to his wishes and the impact is limited.

I'll try to make them different. This one is hard to vary. He's obviously contemplating his violin with disgust. He's either disgusted or sleepy. Both indicate boredom at best. The violin was given him by his idealistic mother who thought it would be fine if Junior could become a virtuoso with the violin. She thought that her child ought to become artistically accomplished in one way or the other. Since her father used to play the fiddle in some church gatherings in the old days she thought it would be nice if Junior could maintain or at least establish a family tradition. The rub is that Junior doesn't go for the idea at all! This represents his attitude at the end of one week of playing and he is pretty fed up. His mother, who is also a sensible person besides being an idealist, decides that there's no point in her forcing him to do something that he is not willing to do, so she gives the violin to the U.S.O., and he is afterward unencumbered by the necessity of doing a slavish routine.

In the following story, the parents, having attempted to play an active role, retire in the face of the child's resistance as in the preceding story but continue to exert influence indirectly, inspiring the child by exposing him to other influences.

Well, some time ago this little fellow, his friend wanted, who is studying the piano and he thought he had heard of a violin so he thought he wanted to study the violin. He didn't realize the amount of time it would demand of him, but then anyway after he had studied several months he decided an hour a day was taking too much of his time and he decided after that, from then on he decided that he would rebel, revolt against the idea of practicing every day. This is, oh, a picture represents one afternoon about two and a half months after he had started his violin practice. He is very disgusted; this afternoon he doesn't want to practice his violin. His mother has been coaxing him but without much success and he is just as stubborn and persistent as his mother. He is sitting there and in a kind of a fit after the afternoon since he won't practice his mother has decided that, well, she is going to have to approach him in a little different way so she bargains with him that he can go out this afternoon on condition that he will practice his hour tomorrow without any trouble. That seems to be O.K. with him. It's a struggle when he comes down to practicing tomorrow but he carries off his part of the bargain. Ah, since he is a little fellow he is a, his mother has decided that her whole approach to music should be different. He shouldn't be forced to practice. He should be made to want to practice and so starting from this moment on she takes him to concerts and she gets, oh, small muscial biographies with which she tries to inspire him. Strangely enough, this is very effective and from that moment on he aspires, he starts to enjoy his practice. He aspires to greater things, undoubtedly the concert stage. Later on in his teens he is sent to a conservatory to study. He has become a, oh, a bit of an unusual player or he would never have been sent to the conservatory, but he decides to make music and the violin particularly his profession. Along in the past it became his, his life ambition to play on the concert stage. And of course, from his two-hour, two- and three-hour practice a day at home it is quite a jump in the conservatory where he has to devote seven to ten hours a day to his music, studying harmony, particularly the violin along with piano. Of course, after many struggles comes the big night when as, ah, the prize student of the conservatory he is asked to play with the shall we say the Boston Symphony Orchestra?—some famous concerto, Tschaikowsky's B Flat Concerto, and of course as an ordinary young genius he meets with success but it's just a sign of the success he will meet later as a great, as a great violinist.

In the preceding two stories it was the parent who realized the inadvisability of forcing her ideals on the child, but in the next story the child having conformed for three years suddenly rejects the parental dictate without waiting for parental sanction.

Little Jimmy is a normal little boy about eight years old. He is a member of the neighborhood gang and loves nothing better than to go out and hunt snakes, tadpoles and all sorts of insects. Besides that he is second base on the gang baseball team and now that it is four-thirty his mother calls him in to practice his violin. He has had to play the violin for three years and all the fellows razz him because he has to go in daily at four-thirty to practice and in his mind Jimmy can't understand why his parents make him play the violin when he is planning on some day being a fireman, and he doesn't plan on sitting around playing the fiddle like some emperor did. As he sits brooding over the violin Jimmy decides right then and there that he will not practice any longer and that this is all useless.

Dominance stemming from the parent's ideal for the child governs the behavior of the child through adolescence in the following story, but in early adulthood the child rejects the ideal and though the parent is dissatisfied he yields.

This little boy whose father was a musician forced his younger child into playing the violin. Somehow he had no desire to play, in spite of his father, and being forced into playing was torture for him. Day after day he would sit in front of his violin which lay on the table and with much discouragement, and hate would pick it up at intervals and try again but without success. This same performance went on for several years. At the age of eighteen he still had made no progress as his father had wished he would, and so he left his violin and took up the law which was what he wanted to do ever since he was a youngster. He was successful at law, and his father was pleased, but he was much dissatisfied that his son never became a musician like himself.

Although the child in the next story wishes to do something else and parental idealism extracts only half-hearted compliance and passive resistance, he does not completely reject the parental dictate as in the preceding two stories. Thus the parent exerts somewhat more influence.

After two years of daily practice, Billy still did not like to play the strings of his violin. But his father being a celebrated violinist in a symphony orchestra had one desire that this son should one day become a famous musician like himself. He instructed Billy twice a week, mostly in vain, because many a day Billy would just sit for hours looking at the wooden structure with strings on it. Strings, he thought, that probably came from a horse's tail. A horse that had probably broken his leg and had to be put away. Now that's what Billy wanted to do. He wanted to be a veterinarian and care for all animals.

The ideal of the parents in the following story is also foreign to the child's wishes but he conforms because he does not want to disappoint them. Parental impact is great and when he reaches maturity conformance with parental wishes has been sufficiently rewarding to bring about complete identification with parental values.

Many years ago a boy got a present for his birthday. The reason that they gave him a violin was because they wanted him to become as interested in music as they were. As the little boy sat looking at the beautiful instrument, disappointment showed in his face. He thought how much nicer it would have been if his parents had given him some toys. He realized how much the present meant to them so he tried to look as happy as possible. He was curious about the violin because he had never seen one before; he had only heard his father and mother talk about them, so he decided to see what it would do. He picked up the bow and drew it across the strings. He liked the sound and tried it again. Wouldn't it be fun to put all the sounds together, he thought. Now standing off stage at Carnegie Hall, waiting for the applause to die down, this great artist thanks his parents from the bottom of his heart.

But if, as in the following story, the child loves the parent deeply, parental ego idealism may hold him to a course in spite of occasional moments of resentment. In such a case the impact on the development of the child and on the resultant adult personality is massive.

Why must I practice so hard? and so long? and every day? And yet I love mother so. I must make a success of this violin playing. Oh I must! Mother is counting on it. It's everything to her; if 'I fail and can't become very famous as . . . well the Great Jonny Jerome or Mrs. Albert Jerome's Jonny Jerome . . . that would be better still, I certainly will deserve the booby prize. Then mother can dress up and feel very proud and forget her failure. Mother, gosh she must have been very pretty. Somehow they didn't see how talented she was . . . or maybe her voice was too small . . . it sounds so pretty here in the apartment but maybe it didn't sound like that in the big opera houses; maybe that's why she wasn't a success. I've got to work hard, real hard, terribly hard so she will be pleased. Tommy and Bud just don't understand why I'm so gone on this fiddle and catgut. It's mother—when some extra special sound comes out she is so happy. Gee, I want an awful lot of extra special sounds to come 'cause she seems to even have Dad with her in this room here on earth, not really but just pretend. . . . Now, Jonny Jerome, are you going to sleep when you have another hour to practice? Here goes . . . tum . . . tee tum. *The following is an excerpt from a local newspaper printed some 10 years later.* "A young, blond and handsome chap, known to this town's other young and handsome chaps as 'jonny' and to the 'olsters' as Mrs. Albert Jerome's son who plays the violin so well has been claimed by both 'chaps' and 'olsters' as the GREAT JEROME. Last evening he strummed and plucked those strings as no other seventeen year old since Paganini has ever dared. If we are not mistaken we see a brilliant future for this violinist. Mrs. Albert Jerome may well be proud of such a son."

I. SCOPE OF PARENTAL INTERVENTION IN OTHER REGIONS

The degree of parental influence is to some extent a function of the *scope* of such parental impact in regions outside the family. The parent may influence everything the child does inside or outside of the family, as in the following story.

The girl has been so watched by her parents that she feels herself going crazy. She has to tell them to the minute where she goes and what she does. Then her mind collapses and she spends years in an institution before she becomes normal again.

Every crucial region may be influenced by the parents but with less rigid control than in the preceding story. In the stories which follow, told by an eighteen year old girl, we see that work, love, and social relationships are all, to a great extent, under the influence of the parents.

What was a mother for but to comfort her child when in distress? If only she could think of something to say or do that would help her daughter. Mary had come to her in tears and sobs that shook her whole body. And no wonder—Bob had been such a rat about the whole thing. Ah, poor dear

Mary. Come, lean on me and sob it out. Yes, I know, it was ten times more awful to learn it from another person, and especially that silly mean Gertie. It would have been better if Bob himself had told you—but here's one consolation —now you know what kind of a person he is, so you can free yourself of him in time. And, Mary dear, you're young still, really very young, with the largest part of your life still before you. You can be happy you know— it is possible in spite of this part of your life. We can go away 'for a while and forget Bob and Gertie and let them do what they please. There are other men in the world. When we come back they will probably have left, and you can do some work and it will all turn out all right in time—really it will. Jane and her mother often sat together, Jane playing with her doll and her mother reading to her. But today was a little different. Jane couldn't sit back and comfortably become enthralled with the doll or the story, for she was waiting to go to a party. They lived out in the country and it was a rainy, bad day with the roads consequently turned into mires, so she knew it was likely her hostess' chauffeur would be later in coming for her. However, she also knew in her heart, but didn't like to admit it to herself, that it was very doubtful whether he could get through at all. Her mother was being very sweet and reading a lovely story to take her mind off that possibility, but still, she didn't want a story now, she wanted to go to a party. When Jane had just about given up all hope of going, she heard the sound of a car coming slowly and painfully down the drive. So she could go to the party after all! Her mother heard it too and put down the book and with a smile got Jane's hat and coat. They were ready and waiting when the car got to the door and Jane drove off at last to the party waving back to her mother with the happiest face.

What else could he have done—gone away and just never admitted it to her, in the hope she would just forget he ever existed? His own mother. Never! Being his own mother it probably would have hurt him more to desert her than to do as he had done and come back to tell her everything and let her know that she had brought her son up to be a total failure. But the look on her face when he had appeared. He'll never forget that! Of course she had known the minute he came in—for why would he have returned if he hadn't failed? She hadn't said anything, just turned away with a sad look that said "So, he's failed, which means I've failed, and now what is there left now?" Practically nothing. He could hardly bring himself to think of it. He had lost all his father's money—the money that his father and mother, and then just his mother, had scraped together and saved penny by penny, the money to start him out in this business. And now all their hopes and dreams as well as work, bound up in that money which would send their son on his way to success, were all gone for nothing. But he could still fight, couldn't he? He'd go out again and start without money—start on a less pretentious business and make a go of it. He could not bear to let his mother continue having that look on her face, or let it come back again.

But parents may be somewhat less ubiquitous. Very commonly the parent may allow the child considerable freedom in social relationships but take a strong stand about his choice of career or wife. In the following story, which is typical of this protocol, these two influences appear in the same story.

The young man, Peter, had become a great doctor in his home town, and his parents had made great sacrifices to give him the best education possible. Peter had decided to take a vacation and go to the city to brush up on city medical ideas and news. While there he met a girl and got engaged. She was the selfish debutante type and insisted that Peter give up his small town practice and move to the city where her father could set him up very well in his brokerage firm. Peter said he would go home, attend to some business and then come back to the city and be married. When he comes to tell his mother of his plans, she is very upset and will not take part in any of his wedding arrangements. She finally gives in and goes to the city for the wedding, but comes home afterward, broken-hearted because she believes Peter has given up his whole life. She refused to have anything to do with him, until two years later when there is a divorce and Peter comes home to resume his practice, a wiser man.

Less commonly the parents, frustrated in their own aspirations, center their influence on one particular region in an effort to achieve through the child what they themselves have failed to achieve. They may want the child to marry a wealthy person, achieve fame, know the "right people," or, as in the story below, be accepted in a good college in the East.

There was a certain young man who lived in a large family. His father was very overpowering and demanded that he do things just when his father wanted him to. Not much free choice. His father wanted more than ever for him to be accepted in a good college in the East. His mother wanted him to be accepted too. This is the one thing they were together on. Subjected all other petty grievances to gain that goal, and when this picture takes place, the boy just received an acceptance to M.I.T., and is dreaming of all the tremendous future and the chance that he has been given and is positive that he will be successful. Everything turns out very beautifully, very successful.

2. DURATION OF PARENTAL IMPACT

Parental impact may be further considered in its temporal dimension. The parents may, for example, control the child's life completely in childhood and relinquish or lose this control in late adolescence or after the child has left home. But the child may never leave home and the control continues, or in the extreme instance the child may leave home and continue to suffer the intervention of the parents in his own home or turn again to the parent for guidance and support. The stories that follow illustrate variations in the duration of parental impact.

The parent may be unwilling to relinquish control but the child on reaching adulthood may declare his independence.

This girl is tired of having her family tell her what to do, just because she's living at home and they support her. She wants to be her own boss so she goes out and gets a job and comes home and tells them and moves her things out. Now she is making her own money and can be her own boss with no one to tell her what to do.

On the other hand, the parent, although not completely willing, may relinquish control when the child reaches maturity.

The young man's mother had planned on her son becoming a great physician as his father had been. After going through pre-medical school he realizes that he will never make a good surgeon for he cannot bear to see others in pain. He knows that he will be a great baseball player if he wants to devote his energy to it. He tells his mother of his great chance to become a member of a professional team. When he breaks the news to her, her dreams are shattered. But realizing that her son is at an age where he must make his own decisions, she consents. It of course hurts the son to grieve his mother but he must go ahead with the work he loves to become a great hero on the baseball diamond. Later the mother is to find joy in seeing her son being cheered by millions.

But independence may be short lived, due not to parental intervention but to the individual's need for continued parental advice.

As always, age and experience tried to guide youth in its lack of experience, and youth, not using the advice, found out the same truth the hard way. In this case the father had had the business and then retired, handing it over to his son. Instead of taking his father's tried and true advice, the son had plunged ahead with his new ideas without thinking first, and so gotten the business in a terrible mess. He was just now realizing his mistake, ashamed and furious at himself and the whole business and coming to his father for advice on how to straighten the business out.

Or the relationship with the parent may be resumed at a later period, particularly when there are problems in the love region. The following is a story told by a man of 50.

A worried man with a problem, trouble with his wife, is asking advice from his mother who is also perplexed and worried. He has come to her with his problem and she evidently does not know how to answer him. He is nervous and troubled. She cannot solve his problem.

Finally, parental impact may continue throughout the life of the individual as in the following story.

This man and his wife are having mother-in-law trouble. The man has always been under his mother's thumb, and now that he got married it isn't any different. The wife can't stand the mother butting in all the time, but there isn't much she can do about it. When they have their first child the grandmother is there johnny on the spot to tell them how to raise the child.

And then the thing that the wife was afraid of most happened. Her husband's father died, and the mother came to live with them. The husband wasn't too crazy for this, but what could he do—it was his own mother, and she had no place else to go. They lived together for the rest of their lives, the husband henpecked by the mother and the wife, and they fighting each other. Amen.

K. Generalization of the Parent-Child Relationship

Perhaps one of the most important criteria in the determination of the importance of the family region is the degree of generalization of the parent-child relationship; the extent to which adults are cast in the role of parents; and the extent to which the individual's reactions to these surrogates are similar to his former reactions to his own parents.

If the psychoanalytic assumption of the importance of the family in shaping adult attitudes is true, we should expect to find the individual's childhood reactions continuing unmodified toward parental surrogates and sibling surrogates in the social, work, and love relationships of later life. To the extent that important differences occur we cannot invoke the doctrine of simple repetition. It is our experience that such generalization of parental impact is indeed found, but that the universality of this process needs considerable qualification.

Commonly, the narrator does not directly tell us the extent to which adults are cast in the role of parents or the extent to which his reactions to these parental surrogates are similar to his former reactions to his own parents. To determine this it is necessary to compare the stories in which the hero is a child with those in which he is an adult.*

Differentiation in Portrayal of Older People

We must consider first the differentiation between the portrayal of parents and other adults in the entire protocol. Do older people have the same characteristics as the parents portrayed in the stories? We find examples ranging from complete similarity to complete dissimilarity. There are protocols in which *some* older adults are similar to parent figures described in the same protocol, but *other* adults bear no resemblance whatever to the parents. We have found cases where a parental surrogate has actually had an important influence on the young adult's life and in these cases nonparental figures in the TAT sometimes resemble *the parent* and sometimes resemble *the parental surrogate* who was actually important in their early adulthood.

---

* The term "parent" will be used in this discussion to denote parents in stories in which the hero is a child. The terms "surrogate," "older adult," and "other adult" will be used interchangeably to denote adults in stories in which the hero is an adult. The use of the term surrogate in this way somewhat prejudges the issue, since individuals may react to older figures without regarding them as parent surrogates, but we are interested here in those figures who *may* in some cases be regarded as parent surrogates.

The Hero's Reaction

The continuities and discontinuities of the hero's reaction to parents and parent surrogates must also be examined. This is an independent variable, inasmuch as we find examples in which the parents and other adults *may be portrayed as similar,* but the hero reacts in one way to the parent and in another way to other adults. There are also cases where differences in the hero's reaction can occur only in response to those adults who treat him differently than he was treated by his parents.

Permeation of Other Regions

Finally, we must examine the extent to which this generalization of parental impact has permeated other regions. In the extreme instance we find that parental impact has permeated *all* regions. The work region is a replica of the family region, the boss playing the role of the father or mother and the co-workers cast in the role of sibs. In the love region the family romance is again recapitulated; the characteristics of the wife are those of the mother and the response of the husband is that of the son. In the social region older figures and younger people are also portrayed as if the human family were a replica of the individual's own family. This degree of generalization, however, is very rarely found in TAT stories. More commonly we find that most regions are relatively free of such generalization, but in *one particular region—* work, love or social relationships—the family constellation is recapitulated. Or frequently this type of generalization may occur *only under special conditions;* the usual adult reaction in the love relationship may differ from the child's reaction, but wherever a rival is introduced, the hero may regress to the reaction described in the stories of his childhood. Another example is seen in a protocol in which two different stories described the hero at work. In one the employer bore no resemblance to the father described in other stories and the individual worked well; but in the other the employer was described in much the same terms as the father and the hero lost his job for inefficiency. Here we are told in effect that when the environment resembles that of the individual's unpleasant childhood, he responds in the old ways, but if the environment is different, he responds differently. Thus we find individuals capable, in varying degrees, of distinguishing the realities of the present environment from the characteristics of their childhood environment. While achievement of this differentiation is the explicit goal of psychoanalytic therapy it is not an achievement peculiar to therapeutic intervention; differentiation of this type is one of the salient characteristics of the learning process in normal development.

The following examples illustrate varying degrees of generalization of the parent-child relationship. In the first story, told by an adolescent girl, we see within a single story the generalization of the family romance to her own later love life.

This young girl is a wayward youngster about 20, parents divorced, and she has always been left on her own. She was brought up in the poor section and had to shift for herself when she was too young. Extremely devoted to her father, intensified her hatred of her mother. At the present time she had lost her father and has now—is in grief and tears. She meets this young man and falls for him. She's a very jealous person and her love is so great she can't bear to see him go around with anyone else. The usual love triangle. He finally tells her off and seeing that she has a weak character, she commits suicide.

In the following story told by another individual we see again, within a single story, the generalization from a broken home to general social relationships. Generalization in this story, however, is not to adulthood but to another region in childhood.

The boy was sent to preparatory school not with the intentions of furthering his education but mainly because his parents thought it would be better for him. His family life had been a sad one. His mother died when he was seven years of age. . . . Later his father married again. After three years elapsed they became separated and finally divorced. While at school the boy imagined all sorts of things; that no one liked him or cared what he did. So he ran away. When the thick of night started to fall, he sought shelter in an old deserted barn. Here he spent the night. When signs of morning came, he set out for some unknown destination.

Generalization of the parent-child relationship may be tempered by later development and maturation, as in the following two stories, which illustrate the modification of the original mother-son relationship in adult marriage.

This boy had been playing out on the street with the other boys. His mother had called him a number of times but he hadn't heeded her. Finally she went after him and brought him home. She administered a sound spanking because he hadn't obeyed her. Here he is probably crying with tears of remorse. Tears of remorse maybe for a little while, then thinking how unfair for a boy not to be able to play all he wanted without having mothers spank such a big boy as he. In a little while his mother will probably call him to dinner, or perhaps lunch. Now he'll probably be a little more obedient, perhaps wipe his tears with his sleeve. His mother will tell him to go to the bathroom and wash up. He'll go without hesitation and come back to the dinner table a little bit refreshed, because of the cold water he probably washed his face with. He would probably eat slowly at first, gather up a little speed as the experience begins to wear off. His mother will probably admonish him not to do such things again, and he'll probably finish off a tall glass of milk with alacrity. By then his resentment will have gone.

This could mean so many things I don't know where to start. There's been a flood or it could be a fire. A fire would probably be more logical. Probably across the street from where these people are living. It's burning pretty badly by now. There may be somebody up in the building. The husband is very anxious to go up and help. His wife naturally wants to hold him back because there is a great element of danger involved. From the look of determination in his eyes and mouth, he'll probably put her gently aside in a little while and rush over and see what he can do. The fireman will stop him anyway, although he'll try desperately to cross the line. In a little while the fireman will have the fire under control and he'll walk back to his wife. No he won't walk back to his wife because she'll have been right there, have run over after him. The thing will turn out to be not as bad as they had feared. There'll be no loss of life, but the entire property will be ruined. He will offer his help to rebuild the home of the family.

Important continuities underlie the son's relation to his mother and his present relations with his wife. Both wife and mother are ubiquitous and wish to control the hero's behavior but there are important differences. The mother's dominance is at once more active, "Finally she went after him and brought him home," and more coercive, "She administered a sound spanking because he hadn't obeyed her." The wife however, *"wants* to hold him back" not because she insists on obedience to her dictates but, "because there is a great element of danger involved." She is less insistent and more considerate of the hero's welfare. She too will "run after him" but she will not drag him back and spank him for disobedience. The son ignores his mother when she calls him but after a spanking, "he'll probably be a little more obedient." He is overtly obedient to his mother's command that he wash before dinner, "He'll go without hesitation." The seeds of rebellion appear on the covert level in childhood, "tears of remorse maybe for a little while, then thinking how unfair for a boy not to be able to play all he wanted without having mothers spank such a big boy as he." By the time he finishes dinner his resentment will have gone. Since his resentment of this maternal dominance is freely admitted into consciousness, we might well have expected to find the same hero as a husband limiting the exercise of dominance by his wife and this is the case, "he'll probably put her gently aside in a little while and rush over and see what he can do." The continuity of behavior attributed to mother and wife appears in his afterthought: "and he'll walk back to his wife. No he won't walk back to his wife because she'll have been right there, have run over after him."

These stories are representations of actual differences between his original relationship with his mother and his contemporary marital relationship. The influence of the original relationship looms large but the seeds of its change were apparent in those feelings which the hero could not express towards his mother but was ultimately capable of expressing towards his wife.

The continuity between attitude toward the parent and later parental surrogate in the example above was marked. Less continuity exists in the following case. There is some generalization of a negativistic attitude toward work imposed by the parents, but this reaction is considerably modified in adulthood. Let us examine this relationship as it appears in the following stories.

> Little Jack was given his violin and told to practice for two hours, his usual practice time. Jack was wedded to his violin and would have rather played it than anything else, but, sometimes—well he wishes that he didn't have to give up the whole afternoon to practicing, practicing, practicing. Nevertheless, he began his scales and diligently tried to make himself a great violinist. For some reason, everything seemed to go wrong today, he couldn't play anything right. The voices of children playing on the grass suddenly captivated him. First he watched them, then he would look at his violin, wishing that he might play perfectly. Jack was finally tempted to join the other children for a short while. They played hard together for the rest of the afternoon, but suddenly he returned to his violin and found that for some reason, he could almost play perfectly. He had eaten his cake and had it too.

> Ellen was on her way home from school where she had been diligently teaching all day. How good it seemed to get out in the open and walk home after her long day. "Why do I keep this up?" she thought. "Why don't I work on a farm as my friends and the rest of my family do? They don't have to correct papers at night! They don't have lessons to give to twenty-five rude, indifferent brats. Wouldn't it be fun to plough and be with the animals all day?" "No" she finally thought after some meditation, "I'm just not the type to be a farmerette the children here need to be educated, and if I can do it, and do a little good for someone else, I think I had better stick to it."

In childhood the hero is "wedded to his violin." Despite this he wishes he "didn't have to give up the whole afternoon to practicing, practicing, practicing." He conforms to a certain point but finally is tempted to join the other children for a short while. On his return he "found for some reason he could play almost perfectly. He had eaten his cake and had it too." As a young adult that part of a task which is routine and mechanical is still rejected, "They don't have to correct papers at night!" But there is an important change in the consequences of this dissatisfaction. In the first story the child yields to temptation and on his return achieves his ends magically. In the second story the wish to do something else is never translated into action primarily because the heroine realizes the need of the children "to be educated and if I can do it, and do a little good for someone else, I think I had better stick to it." Not only is the wish not translated into action but the reason for this has changed. The older heroine is possessed of an ideal of service to others which was altogether lacking in childhood when work was done either because the parents insisted or because the child "would rather have played it [violin] than anything else." Further there is much greater realism in the second story. The heroine realizes that no longer can one have "eaten his cake and had it too." The attitudes of childhood have generalized into adult life only to the extent that there is dissatisfaction with boring means-end activity. No longer, however, is she a child resisting parental dominance but an adult governed by adult ideals.

In the preceding examples we have seen various degrees of generalization of the parent-child relationship both to another region in childhood and to adult attitudes. The examples which follow illustrate variations in the type of generalization.

Childhood may be important to the individual apart from the parent-child relationship and childhood attitudes not involving the child's relation to the parents may be generalized to adult life. Children of high intelligence, for example, may be sufficiently rewarded by the free play of their own curiosity to turn them in the direction of anyone who is intellectually stimulating in childhood and later life alike.

The following are stories told by a young woman whose major energies since childhood have been directed towards an eager exploration of the physical world and science in general. The parents could do no more than expose her to books and people who could answer her questions. As a child these were the people who mattered, and as a young adult this is still the case:

> Once when Frederick was a very, very, very little boy his father took him along to hear a famous violinist play at the Opera House. During the performance and on the way home, Frederick had said nothing—nor did he for days afterwards. Finally one afternoon his father, in his study, looked up to find the huge door being slowly pushed open by little Frederick. The boy came over to him and, with the same look of yearning in his eyes, asked if he could please, *please* have a violin of his own; that to play a violin was all he wanted ever in the wide world. His father didn't say much, but soon a big box came for Frederick. Hardly daring to hope, he opened it slowly, and lo—there it was his own violin. He took it out gingerly and lovingly and set it on the table before him and just looked at it with that same loving, longing look. And do you know what little Frederick is now? After studying and studying and studying, he became one of our most famous violinists.

> He was a funny little old professor, as absent-minded as they come and his course as stiff as the very devil to pass, but he was the favorite of the whole college. You could count on him for a warm and cheery greeting as

he passed, even if he didn't know you. In fact they all thought he forgot who he did know. He had been at the college for years and years—sort ot grown up with it. As long as anyone had known him there his hair had been tousled as if he had just gotten up and forgotten to brush it. It was a funny thing, you pay him a visit for the purpose of hearing him ramble on and on about any subject under the sun, in the hope of absorbing some ot his knowledge, but in the end, you always found yourself telling him of yourself, your home, your girl, your ideals and ambitions, while he listened attentively. Yes, he was beloved by the whole college, and when he died it was as if a great part—one of the most important parts of the college, had just ceased to be. It left an irreparable gap in the lives of the students as well as the professors.

Joe had always liked to read story books. He could as a rule be found curled up in the large old leather chair in the library completely enraptured by some story. Whether it was a good thing or not was a question because the stories affected him deeply. For days after reading a good book, he would be in a dreary state, imagining he was a pirate of yore, or an enchanting prince, etc. But Joe was a sensitive boy, affected by a great many things. If an odd stranger came to the house, or if Joe went to the museum, or just took a walk in the park among the birds and flowers, he could be seen looking up with wide dark eyes in wonderment. Many people didn't understand him at all. At the present time, Joe was thinking of the picture of that barbarian operation that was painted in his mind by the pirate story. How could they have really done such an awful thing as cut a man's stomach without giving him any anesthetic. But they did it in a kind way, he knew that, they just didn't know anything else to do. But now that people did know how to help humanity and save lives without pain, he wanted to do it! That was his ambition—the thing he must do. Think how those poor devils had suffered then, and to even think how they would suffer about the same way today—if enough people didn't become doctors and make sure that humanity was all saved from unnecessary pain and loss of life. As soon as he gets older, he would go to medical school.

The individual in his generalization of the parent-child relationship may reverse the roles. He does not act toward parental surrogates as he acted toward his parents, but he becomes the same type of parent and treats his children as his parents treated him.

Uh. . . . This girl lives in the midwest and uh, her folks own a farm. They belong to the middle class and they have a hard time keeping it up. Both her mother and father have to work hard, but they do their best to give her an education. She appreciates this and works hard studying and working around home so she won't be too much of a liability. She isn't dressed as fashionably and her hair isn't arranged in a modern style, but she wants to work hard in spite of the small inconveniences so that she'll be able to repay them for all they've done for her. Uh. . . . She has a strong attachment for her family and after she finishes her education and works for a while, she marries a farmer and raises a family and gives them the benefits her family has given her.

Occasionally we see a case in which two parent-child relationships have been generalized because either a foster parent or a parental surrogate has intervened in the life of the child. The impress of both the original parent and the foster parent may be traced in the TAT stories of such an individual; the later influence is superimposed on the earlier, with a blending of generalization. The following stories are those of a young woman whose mother divorced and remarried. In the first story we are told of her reactions to her new father.

> Poor little John—he had been playing so hard all day and now he was tired. His life was full of fun all day long, but something was lacking. He didn't know what it was. It wasn't a lack of love from his mother, but she couldn't be with him much. Now that his Dad was dead, she had to work. Yes that was it—he missed his father. He missed their hunting trips, the games they used to play, everything that his father had meant to him. He wanted his dad. Then who was this man that had been coming to see his mother. He resented his coming and showing so much attention to his mother. And she didn't pay so much attention to John when he came over. The great blow came when John's mother told him that she was going to marry that man. Now, he thought, I will be all alone. But things weren't like that. His new dad was a swell guy. They took camping trips and even his mom went along. Yes, he would be all right. Maybe he's not such a bad guy after all. And things did turn out very well and he even got more attention from this new comer than he did from his father. He found out in later years that his own father hadn't died after all but had been sent to prison and so things did turn out for the best.

This is a literal representation of her attitude toward her original father, the reception of her foster father and the restructuration of her attitude toward both fathers after she had achieved a secure relationship with the foster parent. A less direct expression of this change is reflected in the story to card 1.

> Poor Tommy! He had been taking violin lessons for four years now and although he was quite the child prodigy, he just learned that he couldn't go on with his lessons. Tommy, as young as he was, understood this and so in front of people he gave the appearance that he was tired of playing his violin, but when he was alone he would lay the violin on the table and look at it with longing eyes. When everyone was away from the house, he would go into his room and pick it up and play until he heard someone come back—but they were the same old pieces over and over again. However, one day he was playing his violin and a great musician heard him and was simply shocked by the beauty of what he heard. Everything turned out all right then because the musician made Tommy his protégé and Tommy got his fill of the thing he loved to do.

The effect of this change in her life and its generalization to later attitudes is striking. In almost every story told by this young woman the hero is faced with apparently insuperable difficulties which disappear as if by magic. The scar of her early childhood, indicated by the heroine of the next story who had been a cripple since she was born, has not been forgotten. She does indeed generalize on the basis of her early experience to the extent that she expects to meet many situations as unpleasant as her early home environment. But the experience of magical rescue has also been generalized. The resultant is a confluence of both forces in her contemporary expectations. These joint expectations are reflected in the following stories.

Marie has been a cripple since she was born and although she didn't show it outwardly, inside she cringed when she saw other children, running and playing. But then a miracle happened—something was done that most doctors said couldn't be done. She was cured. Naturally she was overjoyed but her joy came to light when her father came to the hospital and found that she was going to be well again. They sat enfolded in each other's arms, sobbing with joy and both talking at once. And then there was silence. Upon being asked what was wrong, she said that she didn't know how to play because she had always been alone. The other children had always made fun of her. But this was remedied by their moving to another city and here Marie became one of the leaders—and she didn't stop here. She went on and on and when she grew up she was one of the most successful people of her day.

Chris and Cherry had only been married a year. Yes, they were poor and things weren't turning out the way they expected. No, two couldn't live as cheaply as one. But Chris was proud and wouldn't let his wife work. She was silent about the affair knowing his feelings on the subject, but she just couldn't stand this poverty any longer. She went to him and told him that she wanted a divorce—she could get along by herself. Both their hearts were breaking because they loved each other very much, but pride came into the scene too. So Cherry left Chris. She didn't get the divorce, but she lived in another town and got a job and lived a little better. She had been living alone now for about six months, damning the day she left Chris and wanting him so badly. But the very next day, Chris came to her apartment and after the polite conversation was finished he blurted out that he had a very good position now and he wanted her to come back to him. All ended very happily and they went back together. He was successful in his business and she had her own little home and all that she never thought were possible.

Mrs. Kelly answered the door and there she found a young man who looked rather ill at ease. After inquiring if she was Mrs. Kelly, mother of Jane, he told her he had some rather unfortunate news. They had been in an accident and Jane had been hurt. "Oh, my baby" was all that Mrs. Kelly could say. She couldn't leave the house because her husband was upstairs in bed and he needed her near him every minute. What could she do? She knew that Jane needed her too. The young man told her that everything had been taken care of and Jane was resting quietly in the hospital. Everything did turn out all right and soon Jane was back home again feeling just as spry as she was before.

L. Changes in the Parent-Child Relationship

The parent-child relationship is not static; it undergoes change as both the parent and the child grow older. This change may or may not involve a change in the relative importance of the family for the individual. We may, for example, find in one protocol stories in which parental dominance is increasingly rejected as the child grows older and the parents completely lose their influence over him, while in another protocol the parents may be dominant but as the child grows older temper their dominance, offering advice only when the child seeks it and in this way continue to exert influence on him.

Any changes in the influence of the family during the life of the individual may be directly mentioned within a single story. This is common in the stories of those whose relationship with the family has been marked by dramatic changes which have not escaped the attention of the individual. He is aware of the changes and this awareness is reflected in his stories.

Frequently, however, these changes are so gradual and each one so slight that the total change is unnoticed. Wherever these changes have been of such a nature as to escape the awareness of the person they are rarely reflected in any single story. We can discover whether or not such changes are present in the stories only by a comparison of all the stories told in which a parent and child are the principal characters. In this comparison two important questions should be kept in mind. The first is the obvious question, *Is there a difference in the parent-child relationship when the hero is of different ages?* The second is of equal importance, *Can we be certain that the difference we find is a function of the age of the hero in the stories?*

In other words, is the difference in the age of the hero the only factor to which the change in the parent-child relationship may be traced or is there some other factor, perhaps unrecognized, to which this change may be attributed? If, for example, we were to find in a protocol one story in which a young child is submissive to parental dominance and another story in which a young adult rebels against parental dominance, we might assume that as the child grew older he became more rebellious. If, however, we were to find a third story in which a *young child* is rebellious to parental dominance we would question whether our assumption that this rebellion was a function of the age of the hero was true. We would then have to re-examine the stories for some factor other than the age of the hero to account for this difference in the hero's reaction.

This type of analysis was employed by the writer only after several years of what he must now regard as serious misinterpretation of TAT material. When confronted, in the past, with a protocol in which the hero expressed intense love for his mother in one story and equally intense hatred for her in another or rebelled against parental dominance in one story and was submissive in another, the writer assumed this to be evidence of an ambivalent attitude toward the parent or toward parental dominance. Or, to take another example, if the boy in picture 1 regarded the violin as the instrument through which he would achieve fame and worked hard toward this end, whereas the hero of another story was lazy, preferring the life of a hobo, to any kind of work, this was regarded as evidence of ambivalence toward "work" in general. This may be the case but such fine gradations of delineation of the parent-child relationship were found in so many protocols that the writer grew suspicious and reanalyzed a long series of protocols previously interpreted in this way. It then appeared that the majority of differences in the parent-child relationship found within each protocol could be better explained as an outgrowth of the individual's development. That, if the age of the hero in each story was considered, there was to be found in the microcosm of phantasy the impress of the individual's actual developmental sequence. If this proves to be the case the TAT offers us, in a two hour period, the possibility of tracing patterns of growth which would otherwise require years of laborious observation and study. This type of exploration might be more easily accomplished if a special series of pictures were employed depicting the parent and child together in a temporal series graded from infancy to maturity.

If one assumes that the TAT stories reflect the individual's personality, it is a small step to explain the further reflection of the developmental sequence. When presented with a picture of a boy facing a violin, the story is made congruous with a small boy's life and therefore with the individual's life as a child, and the same is true with older characters in succeeding pictures. If the individual tells us anything about himself, there is no reason to doubt that he can project himself into the past as easily as he can divulge his present preoccupations.

Determination of the generality of this type of projection presents an empirical problem of no small dimension, but we believe that further inquiry along these lines will be rewarding.

MODIFICATIONS

In the experience of the writer it is certain that such projection into the past is not in every case a "true" reflection of the sequence of development. There are at least two modifications of this mechanism limiting the inferences which may be made from this type of analysis.

First, there are instances in which important factors shaping the development of the adolescent may be projected back into childhood as though these same factors had been in operation earlier than their actual appearance in the individual's development. This type of modification will be discussed in detail in the case of Helmler.

Second, the individual's projection into the past may be a function of his present condition. This is a special case of a general phenomenon; it is well known that the picture of both the past and the future is to some extent a function of the individual's present condition. Thus frequently when a person is depressed he finds it impossible to believe that he ever was happy or that he ever will be happy again. We shall see in the case of Eggman how the present may color the past in the TAT, and when an individual's immediate problems seem insoluble or threaten to overwhelm him he may see all characters, whatever their age, struggling with the same problems.

This second type of modification places even more serious limitation on the inferences which may be made about the developmental sequence, but this is somewhat counterbalanced by the fact that it is easier to detect if we are familiar with the individual's present state, whereas only through a knowledge of the past history of the individual can we be certain whether or not the TAT faithfully mirrors the sequence of development or whether the image is blurred by the modification first mentioned.

THE CASE OF HELMLER

Past History

In a study by White, Tomkins, and Alper (106) of the personality of an individual whom we called Helmler, there is an example of telescoping in TAT stories. Helmler was frankly unimpressed with his father but very devoted to his mother until the age of 6. By the age of 6 this cathexis had been tempered by the presence of his brother five and one half years older who was "a long way off—a man" and who commanded the respect of both parents. Helmler was "irritated" because his older brother's "judgement was listened to, and mine was not." He was always "the baby" and dominated and teased by his older brother. Helmler chose him as his earliest masculine model: "When I was quite young I followed closely in my brother's footsteps." In adolescence, however, he was somewhat disillusioned—his brother turned out to be a "grind." His relationship with his mother was further complicated by the problem of the control of bodily impulses. A slip at the age of 3 or 4 in an automobile was the occasion of humiliation sufficient to create a dread of automobiles, overcome only at the age of eighteen when he first learned to drive. It also created a strong sympathy for "dogs not yet housebroken." Continence, he reports, was a matter of pride, but there were several slips (enuretic) at 8 years, which occasioned ridicule from his brother. He also reports being "fortunately scared out of" thumb-sucking at 4 or 5. Fingernail biting continued until he was 11; his mother would slap his hands for this.

Control of bodily impulses was not easy and its significance was somewhat emphasized by the presence of the older brother who was so superior to the "baby" in this as well as other accomplishments. At this time, too, a rich phantasy life appears, charged with anxiety. He had phantasies of being observed by God and great fear of punishment when he did anything wrong. His mother moreover was beginning to substitute dominance and more difficult expectations in the place of unquestioned admiration. The baby role, while denuded of its rewards, was nonetheless ascribed to him by mother, father, and brother. Helmler was more than willing to drop the role, but his mother was not so willing to relax her nurturant maternal dominance, and so Helmler seems to have experienced, at the age of 6, a striving for independence more typically adolescent. He sought the solution to this problem in the cultivation of his age equals and began to stay away from home. "I played mostly with people at school, not around home. That's my mother's chief complaint, that I was never at home. If we weren't playing we were involved in something down at school. I never hang around home. I never could understand being homesick. I was always glad to get out in the country in summer."

Although he acknowledges his mother's influence, "copied her likes and dislikes—tastes, almost unconsciously—clothes, as petty as that—music, movies, small things like that I've noticed . . . never stopped to figure out larger things, probably more influence than I know," his struggle for individuality issues in the following statement in his autobiography: "But by and large, I just grew without anything that seemed to me to be the conscious influences on the part of my parents."

Separation from the family was for some time a successful resolution of his problem. He was an active member of the neighborhood gang and at school "managed to keep honor grades throughout and stood close to the top. They elected me class president a few times and I liked to act in the little skits and plays which we presented." But though he sought out his age equals, this relationship could easily be spoiled if it derived in any way from his parents. "The only thing I can remember is resenting friends when my parents tried to make them for me: here's a nice little boy—why don't you play with him?—I didn't like that."

On entering high school, "I began to take an interest in school affairs. In school politics I attained some success, became president of the assembly, of the honor society, of various social science clubs, editor of the year book, and generally active in student affairs." The high point of this period of his life came with a scholarship to a summer camp dedicated to the development of democratic leadership. "The boys ran the camp as far as they could, with expert advice from a fine staff. There was equipment for the development of all sorts of talent, and encouragement to all. Three summers at this camp had a tremendous effect on my personality. I made about fifteen close friends whom I still call close friends. *And in an environment that lacked the watchfulness of home I began to know what it felt like to shift for oneself.* We were all given responsibility and in my last years I was given a good deal of authority as one of the camp leaders." Helmler's vision of the future, as described in his autobiography, further underlines the importance of this experience in shaping his life. "I visualize a world of a few large complementary powers who will be responsible to some competent world organization. I want the United States to play the chief role in this world, and therefore I want the United States to be ruled by competent men. I hope for a world governed by the modern version of the philosopher-king—the well educated statesman-politician who is ultimately responsible to the people. I look for a socialistic state where wealth is equalized, opportunities spread, and yet where man is not reduced to the average. The 'wise and the just' must be given enough power to rule effectively but not despotically. I like to picture myself in some position of importance in government, such as justice in a high court. I would like to have some power in enforcing and interpreting this complicated social system which would be necessary."

Helmler's adjustment during these years sprang from native intellectual and social ability, but his striving was greatly reinforced by both familial and endopsychic rejection of the "baby role," made especially intolerable by sibling rivalry. Equally important, however, were the substantial rewards for his independent strivings outside the family.

TAT Stories and Interpretation

In the light of this past history, let us examine a few of his TAT stories:

This picture would mean, ah, brings up the idea of some sort of a story for children perhaps on the tale of a little boy who had some sort of musical talent which he, he showed at an awfully early age, child prodigy perhaps in, in the violin, and ah a through some chance I will have to work that out—some awfully, ah fortunate happening, for instance accidentally, accidental fiddling with a great violin ah, brought him to the attention of some first-rate musician, took an interest in him and, ah here we have him gazing at this violin, dreaming of how happy he would be if he could have the advantages of good training and possess this violin, and this violin becomes the, the, oh, supreme good thing that ever happened to him and, ah we might have the rest of the story built around a struggle for some sort of recognition against, with a conflict of a family perhaps and, ah lack of money and, ah, the fact that he is such an awfully young fellow and nobody will pay any attention to him and that, at the end perhaps we could have him being awarded as the result of some recital a first-rate violin and ah, perhaps opening up a path toward development of his talent but not, nothing very complete or conclusive in the line of success. I don't mean that the end should have him a great violinist acclaimed by thousands or anything like that.

I walked into this apparent hole in the ground and looking with a good deal of wonder when a man walked up to me and said, "Take this and any time you need any help why merely ask it and take your tool and use it whenever danger approaches." I just walked along this . . . . Well, it was some sort of a shiny metal instrument and moon-shaped with various embossings on it almost like a shield a small one. And I walked along through, through what seemed to be the path of life passing these various dangers and for each one assuming different exteriors according to my need and protection, sometimes shell of an armadillo, at other times the spines of a porcupine and the scales of a fish and all sorts of horrible obstacles, sometimes webbed feet sometimes to cross water, other times feet equipped for climbing over huge stones. Finally the path went around, turned around and led to a, came to a fork in the road one side seemed to point outward toward earth and continuation of life and the other one toward more wanderings and more knowledge, more experience in the mysteries that I had been through. I don't know which one I took, though. Do I have to decide that? [Laughs] . . . Well, I took the one out to the earth and thought perhaps I could make use of some of the allegory and knowledge that I had picked up in my trip.

Oh Mr. Browdin was a share-cropper down in Alabama and he found that his situation was growing rapidly worse and worse and worse as years went on and he, and he found, somehow he never seemed to be able to make any sort of a profit, any sort of a subsistence level existence out of his land. His land was always bad and somehow or other there was always something coming up, drought or, or sickness or some special need each year or some new tax always took away any extra money that he might have. Finally there is a, finally there is quite a bit of excitement around their village when a radical labor agitator comes in and tries to organize the tenant farmers into some sort of union. There is a lawsuit and the planter tries to compel this, this union to go under and the union behind this ah, find Mr. Browdin is one of the best speaking witnesses of their group so they borrow a, borrow a clean collar and clean shirt and clean suit for him and bring him into court and we find him getting instructions from the union lawyer as to how he should act on the witness stand. He gets on the stand and pleads eloquently, ah, for some sort of rehabilitation for his group. As the result of a successful trial, ah the, ah, tenant farmers do form a, a substantial organization which gets them some improvements and a few guarantees for the next year, and in the last scene we have Mr. Browdin and his wife in the men's store buying their own suit and shirt.

Common to each of these stories is Helmler's concern with the achievement of success. In the first story it is "a struggle for some sort of recognition against, with a conflict of a—family perhaps." In the second story, "thought perhaps I could make use of some of the allegory and knowledge that I had picked up in my trip," and in the final story it is through the hero's efforts that there is a "successful trial" and the "tenant farmers do form a substantial organization which gets them some improvements and a few guarantees for the next year." Common also to these stories are the conditions favorable to this achievement. In the first story it is through the fortunate intervention of a benevolent and gifted outsider ("brought him to the attention of some first-rate musician, took an interest in him") and he is later "awarded as the result of some recital a first-rate violin, and ah, perhaps opening up a path toward development of his talent." In the second story an unknown man "walked up to me and said 'take this and any time you need any help why merely ask it and take your tool and use it whenever danger approaches.' " And in the third story, "a radical labor agitator comes in and tries to organize the tenant farms into some sort of union . . . and we find him getting instructions from the union lawyer as to how he should act on the witness stand."

Success is achieved through competence but competence requires the instruction and help of one who is already competent. Further, the instructor is an outsider, certainly someone outside the family. We can understand this in light of Helmler's past history. Most of his successes have been achieved outside the family and with the help of others. His success among his age equals, his experience in the summer camp, and his scholarship to Harvard were achieved "in a struggle for some sort of recognition against, with a conflict of a family, perhaps." But the crucial discrepancy in this projection backward into the story of the boy and the violin is that he *did not* receive this external help in his struggle against the family at the time when he was first breaking away from the family, at the age of 6. As we have seen, it was only when he reached summer camp as an adolescent that "in an environment that lacked the watchfulness of home I began to know what it felt like to shift for oneself." But this gratuitous assistance from the wealthy benefactor who supported the camp is projected into his earlier struggles for recognition against his family.

In Helmler's imagination this difference is of small import. He is telling us in effect, in all of these stories, that through the help of the competent outsider he has been enabled to maintain his individuality against the family. It is, however, important for the theory of interpretation to differentiate between phantasy and the actual course of events if we are to use the TAT as an instrument for diagnosis of the developmental sequence.

In addition to the telescoping of adolescent experience seen in the case of Helmler, this particular theme may represent a wish-fulfillment phantasy. The theme of the fairy godmother, universal in folklore, appears to represent the fulfillment of a need common to all children. Markmann (55) in her study of the relationship between TAT stories and the past history of the storyteller found that stories told to picture 1 most frequently reflected the individual's actual past history. However, the benefactor theme—in which the child, through the help of a benefactor, was enabled to succeed—showed the lowest correlation with the actual past history. This was found in one out of every three stories to have no basis in the past history of the individual who told such a story. Whereas other themes told to the same picture faithfully represented the childhood of the storyteller. Further research into the types of themes most commonly representative of the individual's actual childhood is required if we are to employ the TAT in the study of developmental sequences.

THE CASE OF EGGMAN

In the following case of a man of 50 whose problems were very acute and seemingly insoluble, we find attribution of his symptoms to the boy in picture 3.

> A tired child is sleeping on the floor in a sitting position with one hand and his head resting on a bench. The child has evidently fallen asleep while playing on the floor. The child will awaken sooner or later and resume his playing.

Inability to keep awake was not typical of this individual as a child, but is his *present* symptom.

Analysis of the temporal dimension must then proceed with caution, since there may be a telescoping of the temporal series in backward projections, juxtaposing elements from later life with those of early childhood, or there may be a complete restructuration of the past in terms of an immediate situation whose pressure is so massive that even the distant past is reinterpreted in terms of it. But despite these limitations we have found much .evidence to support the hypothesis that stories told to different pictures frequently do, in fact, represent a reliable picture of the individual's developmental sequence. Further exploration of these differences in the projective mechanism would in our opinion cast much light on general personality dynamics.

THE CASE OF MARNA

Let us turn to a few of these cases where external evidence supports evidence based on the TAT stories. Consider the following sequence:

> The small boy hates to play his violin and his mother has made him practice because she hopes that someday he'll be a great musician. He gets so angry that he breaks the violin and then is sorry because he knows he'll get whipped—and sure enough he does 'cause it was a genuine Stradivarius.

> The boy has come home to tell his mother about his marriage—he was out on a drunken spree and married the town's bad girl. She is heartbroken and refuses to allow him to bring home the girl. He has always been dominated

by his mother and is very unhappy at her anger and commits suicide. The mother realizing her failing brings home the wife and makes a lady out of her.

The girl has been so watched by her parents that she feels herself going crazy. She has to tell them to the minute where she goes and what she does. Then her mind collapses and she spends years in an institution before she becomes normal again.

A man is a great artist and is suddenly hit by a mad hysteria to kill—he shows this in his picture that he paints showing one old man lunging at another—then his desire leaves him and he knows that anything bad he feels can just be brought out in his paintings and he'll never do real wrong.

In the first of these stories the hero is a "small boy," in the second a "boy," in the third a "girl," and in the final story, a "man." The differences corresponding to these differences in the age of the hero are representative of similar changes in the personality of the young woman who told these stories.

They represent, roughly, childhood and early and late adolescence. The fourth story has been included, although there is no reference to the child-parent relationship, for the light it throws on the later sequelae of this relationship.

1. *Changes in Parental Dominance*

The first three stories show a parent-child relationship based on dominance. But there are changes in time. In the first story the child suffers a dominance somewhat limited in scope and intensity. The mother "has made him practice" and later whips him. In the second story "he has always been dominated by his mother" and the mother "refuses to allow him to bring home the girl," but in the third story dominance has increased even more, in both scope and intensity, "The girl has been so watched by her parents that she feels herself going crazy—she has to tell them to the minute where she goes and what she does." Not only does the dominance increase in scope and intensity in time, but there are changes in the reason for dominance. In the first story the mother is dominant because of the hope she cherished for her son. She makes him practice "because she hopes that someday he'll be a great musician," although she whips him because the violin was a "genuine Stradivarius." There is no dominance for the sake of dominance here. The motivation behind the dominance in the second story is similar. "She is heartbroken and refuses to allow him to bring home the girl" again because she was "the town's bad girl," presumably frustrating her aspirations for her son. Although in part responsible for her son's suicide she is able to realize her failing and "brings home the wife and makes a lady out of her." In this story the mother, again, is not pictured as someone who is domineering for the sake of domineering. In the third story, however, the parents, and this time it is not the mother but both parents, are presented as unreasonably domineering and with no other motive evident.

2. Changes in the Child's Reaction to Dominance

The *child's reaction* to this dominance exhibits more striking changes in time. The most striking change appears between childhood and adolescence. In the first story the child is openly aggressive and "breaks the violin." He also does something of which the mother disapproves in the second story; he marries the town's bad girl. But in the third story there is no evidence of rebellion. Moreover, his defiance of the mother's wishes in the second story lacks the spontaneity of expression seen in the first. There is no mention of anger in the second story or even of hating the mother's dominance and, secondly, the hero is portrayed on a drunken spree which seems to be a condition of his defiance. It is explicitly contrasted with his normal state in which "he has always been dominated by his mother." We see here the beginning of inhibition of self assertion and aggression which is completed in the third story.

3. Changes in the Hero's Reaction to His Own Defiance

The *hero's reaction to his own defiance* has also changed. In the first story the hero is not at all worried about the mother's feelings; his only concern is the whipping he may get—"then he is sorry because he knows he'll get whipped." In the second story, however, concomitant with the reduction in spontaneity and freedom of expression of his defiance, his whole concern is with his mother's reaction—"He has always been dominated by his mother and is very unhappy at her anger." It is a concern with the mother's state, rather than the consequences of the state as it was in the first story. Had the logic of the first story remained unchanged, the *consequences* of her anger, forbidding him to bring the girl home, rather than his unhappiness at her anger as such, would have caused him to commit suicide. Further reactions in this chain show similar changes. In the first story he is punished and that is all. In the second story he invokes the mother's anger, which is a variety of punishment that makes him unhappy, but the reaction to this is self destruction. In the third story, extreme parental dominance brings about mental collapse, which is not a striving but the end result of complete submission to extreme dominance.

These changes, then, are from overt aggression against limited dominance, and punishment which is tolerated, to inhibited aggression against greater dominance and maternal anger that cannot be tolerated leading to self destruction, and finally the most extreme dominance and complete inhibition of aggression, complete submission and mental collapse.

4. *The Fourth Story*

The end of the third story leads naturally to the fourth. In a mental institution away from the parents, the girl becomes normal again. In the fourth story, with no parent figures present, and the hero now a "man" he learns that "anything bad he feels can just be brought out in his paintings and he'll never do real wrong." We are told then that in later life aggression which could not be expressed towards the parents without fear of ultimate self destruction or insanity may be sublimated in painting. The changes delineated in these stories are a faithful picture of this young woman's actual development.

THE CASE OF KAROL

Let us consider the next three stories told by another young woman, Karol, in which the hero is a child and then a young adult.

For a long time the little boy has been wishing he could have a violin. His parents have at last bought him one and he takes great pleasure in just sitting and admiring it. He dreams of the day when he will be older and capable of making beautiful music with it after he has practiced for a long while. The violin will give him pleasure and relaxation when he is older and has mastered it.

Sally has always been a dreamer. When she was small it didn't matter so much, but now that she is 12 her mother is getting worried about her dreams of greatness and of doing wonderful things. Sally talks about extraordinary things she plans to do someday, and won't keep her mind on the things at hand, such as school. Her mother tries to divert her attention by reading to her and buying her dolls to play with, but though she is polite enough to listen and cooperate with her mother, she finds no joy in ordinary childish pleasures. Sally's father realizes that her dreams may be turned into something practical, so he encourages her to become a nurse, which Sally realizes is a truly great profession. She is willing to study when she grows older with such an aim in view.

Since Peg was a little girl she had been babied by her mother so that when she grew up to be 21 she was dependent on her mother for advice on everything. Peg's father had little to say in the matter, for like most fathers, he was "too busy." After finishing her education, Peg decided she would just stay home and look after her mother. Here is where the father came in. One evening the family was seated in the living room, and the subject of Peg's future came up. The mother said she wanted her daughter to stay home and be domestic. The father walked over to the couch where mother and daughter were sitting, and said to Peg, "What you need is a good spanking to make you wake up to all the opportunities open to girls these days." This speech shocked her mother, but it set Peg to thinking. The more she thought about it, the more she wanted to get out and see what she could do. In spite of her mother she did manage to get out of her over-solicitous control and she got a job in which she did very well.

1. Changes in the Characterization of the Parents

a) *First story.* Let us first consider the changes in the characterization of the parents as the individual grows from childhood to maturity. When the hero is a little boy, in the first story, the parents are not differentiated into mother and father. They are "his parents." Their impact on the child's life is a limited one. They neither instigate his wishes nor attempt to control them in any way. Ministering to the wishes of the child is their sole function. This however is not done immediately. The child has wished for the violin a long time and it is not until this wish has endured a "long time" that the parents "at last" bought him one. But having given the child what he wanted they play no further role in his life.

b) *Second story.* In adolescence, as portrayed in the second story, the role of the parents has changed considerably. Not only have they been differentiated into mother and father, but each parent exerts a very different influence on the adolescent's life. Parental impact on the adolescent is much greater than it was in childhood. The continuation into adolescence of childish characteristics is the explanation for this—characteristics which "didn't matter so much" when she was small and which as we have also seen in the first story were unnoticed by the parents at that time. But these now mobilize anxiety on the part of the mother and force her to play a more active role toward her daughter. The mother tries to divert her attention but is unsuccessful because she doesn't really understand her daughter. This lack of understanding was not explicit in childhood but might have been inferred from the role attributed to the parents in the first story. But the father has come, in adolescence, to play a new role. This may be explained in part by the influence of puberty, since at that time this young woman saw her father, for the first time, to be a "man," as she expressed it in her autobiography. The father is seen as less anxious and more intelligent in his insight; he encourages her to turn her energies into those channels which will provide the conditions necessary for her further development.

c) *Third story.* In the third story, the contemporary picture of the role of the mother and father is presented. This portrayal presents a difficult problem in interpretation. The mother is said to have "babied" her daughter since she was a little girl. Actually this is not the case. The historical sequence presented by the first two stories represents the actual course of events. Why then, in this story dealing with the contemporary situation, has this sequence, mirrored faithfully to this point, suffered such restructuration? Our hypothesis is that this represents a restructuration which is the consequence of her present wish for independence, in the manner in which someone who has just fought with a friend may convince himself that the person now detested was never a true friend, that he never really liked him. We have seen before that this process of restructuration of the past in terms of the present situation may reach back and distort characteristics of the past as they appear in TAT stories. The process in this case has not spread to those stories in which the picture presents a child, but it has influenced those stories in which the figures in the picture represent a contemporary situation. This, in short, is her present view of her past history. Craving independence she feels her relationship with her mother is too dependent, that her mother stifles her and, further, that this has always been so. The role of the father has also changed somewhat. He is still the more intelligent of the parents, but now the opposition between the parents has become clearer and more profound. The father not only understands his daughter better and is more effective in coping with this daughter's problems but he appears to have a less selfish attitude toward her future. The mother "wanted her daughter to stay home and be domestic," and to continue her complete dependence. But in adolescence the mother was "worried" about the child and, though not understanding, tried to remedy the arrested development of her childish adolescent daughter. Today, however, the mother is seen to be not only responsible for this arrested development but insistent that her daughter continue in this state of dependence. The father's intervention in adolescence was more successful than the mother's attempts but not in contradiction with the mother's ultimate purpose. Both parents were equally worried about her childlike characteristics. But in the contemporary situation the father's intervention "shocked her mother." These differences in part reflect actual growing opposition between the parents but they are also derived in part from the fact that she now faces the prospect of cutting the umbilical cord and leaving home and feels her father to be more interested than her mother in her ultimate well-being.

2. Changes in the Personality of the Hero

a) *First story.* Let us consider the changes in the personality of these heroes. The child is full of longing directed not toward the parents but toward the violin. He is dependent on the parents only in so far as they are instrumental in securing for him what he lacks. But in this respect he is the passive personality who waits for the action of others to satisfy his needs. When granted the object of his wishes, his reaction is on the perceptual level—"sitting and admiring it"—an aesthetic appreciation rather than an active manipulation. His activity is limited in effectiveness by his years. Turning to the level of irreality and daydream he projects into the future because of his lack of competence as a child. Achievement is thought to be the exclusive possession of the adult or at least the older person. But as a child he possessed the realistic awareness that means-end activity was a necessary prelude to competence and enjoyment of his potentialities "after he has practiced for a long while." Thus "he dreams of the day when he will be both older and capable of making beautiful music with it." But he recognizes that age and capability are not sufficient conditions of mastery, for these are qualified by "after he has practiced for a long while." Thus, although the hero as a child is passive, requiring the activity of the parent on his behalf, and although there is an aesthetic response rather than active manipulation and a turning to the level of daydreaming rather than behavior, he yet envisions a change in his future potentialities and competence. He will work hard when he gets older, and by virtue of both his age and his industry he will be "capable of making beautiful music." But the evaluation of this future achievement contains no social referent; neither the parent nor humanity in general inspire this future effort nor do they profit from it. It remains a solipsistic venture yielding the future adult "pleasure and relaxation." The achievement of "making beautiful music" is valued for no more than might be achieved through masturbation. It is in fact not uncommon for the playing of the violin to symbolize sexual experience. We lack sufficient evidence to know whether it is true in this case.

b) *Second story.* In adolescence the hero is still a dreamer and "has always been a dreamer," but it is now symptomatic of arrested development. Puberty did, in fact, intensify her cathexis for the level of irreality. This is, of course, not uncommon in adolescence, but since this adolescent characteristic was superimposed on a long established habit of daydreaming, the resultant was a withdrawal more marked than is customary at this time. The content of the daydream has become more, extravagant and less realistic. It is now "extraordinary things" which she "plans to do someday." Missing is the expectation of hard work and the knowledge of the means-end relationship. Achievement is still put off into the future but there is a change in her communicativeness; she now "talks" about it to others. But the most important change is in the fact that the daydreaming now has socially conspicuous consequences—"she won't keep her mind on the things at hand, such as school." There is more overt interaction with her mother— "she is polite enough to listen and cooperate with her mother"—but this is a very superficial interaction for "she finds no joy in ordinary childish pleasures." The wish to enjoy adult pleasures which we saw in her childhood has continued into adolescence but the path towards the fulfill-ment of this wish is less certain and less realistic. It is only through her father's intervention that she is restored to the former confidence in her own future and to her previous understanding that means-end activity is neces-sary for achievement. Finally, she regains her willingness to work "when she grows older." We see that even as an adolescent she considers herself incapable of beginning the work which she feels is necessary to achieve her goal. Since the goal is an adult one and not a "childish pleasure" she cannot begin to strive till she is an adult. The intervention of the father has however effected an important difference in this goal. As a child, goal achievement was measured in terms of personal "pleasure and relaxation." This aspiration has been socialized by the father and she now realizes that nursing "is a truly great profession." If a sexual symbolism is involved one might suppose that the solitary pleasure of masturbation has been transformed into a sexual aim with a human object, through the agency of puberty and new interest between father and daughter. But whether or not this is the case, the father has been instrumental in turning the adolescent dream towards social reality.

c.) *Third story.* The daughter as a young adult of 21 is a somewhat different person. We have previously discussed the reasons for this. In part it is the consequence of the hypertrophied level of irreality and daydream. The daydream which inspired her childhood was somewhat responsible for the arrest of development at adolescence but continuing into adulthood it has produced a 21 year old "baby," "dependent on her mother for advice on everything." The heroine attributes this to the fact that "since Peg was a little girl she had been babied by her mother." It is not attributed, as it should be, and as it was before to her own daydreaming, but to her mother—the same mother who became worried about her daughter for the first time in adolescence and who though incompetent meant to help her daughter escape from infantilism. Although this is her present picture of how her mother has always behaved, we have seen that this restructuration is something which the individual does not altogether believe is true—otherwise the actual historical sequence could not have been projected so faithfully in her first two stories. In those cases in which the past is completely restructured there is no evidence in the backward projections of the actual historical develop-ment of the child-parent relaionship. Evidence from other sources indicates that in all probability she pictures her mother as responsible for her infantilism because it is now completely unacceptable to her, having reached the age of adulthood, when according to her childhood dream she should have been "making beautiful music" and when according to her adolescent dream she should have been "willing to study" with "an aim in view." The mother has in effect become a scapegoat, to relieve the daughter of the unacceptable consequences resulting from an excessive immersion in phantasy. But in addition to this, she has been drawing closer and closer to her father and in her mind this involves rejection of the mother on the part of both father and daughter. The father's suggestions "shocked the mother," but in adolescence the same suggestion had no such effect, since the mother shared the father's interest in helping the daughter establish realistic social contact with her environment. There has been throughout the three stories an identification with the father, which is implicit in the first story, openly avowed in adolescence, and culminates in opposition between father, daughter, and mother in adulthood. Evidence suggestive of the family romance was also found in the other stories and autobiography. The third story tells us in effect that only as a young adult did she face this conflict openly. As a child there was the dream of playing an adult role. As an adolescent the father sustained the dream, and today her father will help her achieve the dream against the opposition of her mother. Though it shocks the mother and "in spite of her mother," she did manage to get out of her oversolicitous control. With her father's help, openly breaking with her mother, the adult heroine, just come of age, "got a job in which she did very well." This is the first reference to actual achievement. It is no longer placed in the future. This story represents a very recent change in her orientation. She does in fact plan in the very near future to follow the example of her heroine. It is noteworthy that the heroine is 21 years old, whereas Karol is not quite 21.

THE CASE OF LANS

The following three stories show the developmental sequence of an individual's increasing hostility towards his parents.

Little Johnny looked forward to a pleasant day outside playing baseball with his pals. Before he got half way to the front door, mother grabbed him, and led him by the arm into the music room, and sat him down in front of a violin. "Practice your lesson for an hour or you can't go out to play today." Johnny sat and looked tearfully at the violin. What will the outcome be? Very simple—he will practice for an hour on the violin.

They were seated around the dinner table. Father and son were violently arguing. Father was very angry. Junior's grades were not what they should be. Father sent Junior from the table when Junior remarked on father's grades during the days of his youth. Junior retired to his room angrily, and finally was practically dissolved into tears when he thought of the injustice of it all. He was hungry too. After a while, father knocked on the door and came in. He put his arm around the boy, and Junior leaned on his shoulder feeling exceedingly sorry for himself. Father did not scold. He talked in a quiet voice and told the boy to please try to work harder in school. Junior relented and promised. He actually believed that he would. And at first he did, but gradually lapsed back into laziness again.

Joel came in the door. He was mad. His father could see that very plainly. The usual chip was on his should. He must have a talk with Joel. He must learn to be more even tempered, and not fly off at any small thing. The father said "Joel come here son, I want to talk to you." Joel said, "I know what you're going to say father, but I can't do anything. Please father, it's no use. Some other time" and left the room.

Changes in the Expression of Aggression

We have seen before that aggression, freely expressed in childhood, may later suffer severe inhibition. In these stories the opposite developmental sequence is illustrated. In the first story the hero's reaction to parental dominance is one of tearful compliance. In the second story paternal dominance evokes anger but the hero retires to his room at his father's insistence. There is again a regression to the original response. He "finally practically dissolved into tears when he thought of the injustice of it all." The father then comes in and puts his arm around the boy, and as a result the boy determines to work harder in school although he "gradually lapsed back into laziness again." That this individual should be divided within himself between anger and tears is probably a result of his father's oscillation between stern dominance and sympathetic nurturance. In the third story, however, the hero has come to terms with his conflict. He is now capable of expressing more unambivalent aggression: "He was mad. His father could see that very plainly. The usual chip was on his shoulder. He must have a talk with Joel. He must learn to be more even tempered, and not fly off at any small thing." In response to his father's dominance he "left the room" but not to dissolve in tears. The hero has accepted his own personality with all its limitations and will not allow himself to be swayed by his father. "I know what you're going to say father, but I can't do anything. Please father, it's no use. Some other time and he left the room."

THE CASE OF BRINT

In the following two stories there is a delineation of the development of an ego ideal.

Joe has been given one of his greatest wishes. A violin. He had, during his short life, dreamt of becoming a great violinist. Strange, he never knew why, but he did. But now that he had received this precious gift he realized his future task would not be as easy as his dream. It meant work, hard work, long hours of toil and probably agony for everyone else, but he was still very young, and his mind was set and his heart and mind were as determined as his face. And he'll reach his goal; I feel sure of that!

It's only natural for a son to want to follow in his father's footsteps—or is it? Well, in the case of young Dick it was so. His father was a surgeon and Dick had watched many operations. His mother didn't approve of that but she did wish her son to follow his father. Dick didn't care about being famous, he just wanted to help people and the sooner he could get to it the better. He was still very young, but he could do it, he would do it—and he did!

The hero in both stories is driven by an ideal which determines his life. It is of little moment that one of these wishes is to be a violinist and one to be a surgeon. These differences may be attributed to the fact that the first story was told to the picture of the boy and the violin, and the second to the operation scene. But what is of import is the difference in aim and in awareness of the origin of the ego ideal. In the first story the child does not know: "Strange, he never knew why but he did." But in the second story he is clearly aware of it's origin, "It's only natural for a son to want to follow in his father's footsteps or is it? Well, in the case of young Dick it was so." Although aware of this origin, the remarks of the subject—"or is it?"— suggest some question of the naturalness of this aspiration. A young woman told these stories and the fact that "his mother didn't approve of that" may indicate anxiety about identification with the father against the mother's wishes and may further explain why the younger boy did not understand the origin of his dream of becoming a great violinist. Whatever the meaning, it is clear that there has been an important change in both awareness of the origin of his dream and in its direction, "he just wanted to help people and the sooner he could get to it the better." He is no longer interested as he was in his career as a violinist in "being famous." The ideal of becoming a great violinist had a less social meaning; there was no mention either of an audience or of giving pleasure through his playing or pleasing his parents.

There is also an increased confidence that the goal may be attained. In the first story success is placed in the future and the storyteller is "sure" he'll reach his goal: "He'll reach his goal, I feel sure of that!" But in the second story success is actually achieved in the future: "He was still very young, but he could do it, ne would do it, and he did!" These differences again reflect the importance of the avowed identification with the father as the hero matures.

THE CASE OF FRANK

The following two stories are representative of a not uncommon sequence concerning the emancipation of the child from parental ego idealism.

The little boy has just been told that he must practice on his violin and is looking at it with hatred for he knows there is a baseball game going on outside. After a while he will pick up the violin and practice without any thought of what he is doing but just go through the motions of it without any thought.

The young man's mother had planned on her son becoming a great physician as his father had been. After going through pre-medical school he realizes that he will never make a good surgeon for he cannot bear to see others in pain. He knows that he will be a great baseball player if he wants to devote his energy to it. He tells his mother of his great chance to become a member of a professional team. When he breaks the news to her, her dreams are shattered. But realizing that her son is at an age where he must make his own decisions, she consents. It of course hurts the ,son to grieve his mother but he must go ahead with the work he loves to become a great hero on the baseball diamond. Later the mother is to find joy in seeing her son being cheered by millions.

The mother is a dominant figure in both stories. In the first story, "The little boy has just been told that he must practice on his violin," and in the second story, "The young man's mother had planned on her son becoming a great physician as his father had been." As a little boy he pays lip service to the maternal dictate—"go through the motions of it without any thought." He "is looking at it with hatred" however because there is a baseball game going on outside. In the second story he realizes that the career planned for him by his mother is not for him. There is neither "hatred" nor mechanical compliance. Although it shatters the mother's dreams, he tells her of his plans to become a professional baseball player, which is what his mother would not allow him to do when he was younger. He eventually not only achieves his goal but proves that he was right and his mother wrong in her plans. "Later the mother is to find joy in seeing her son being cheered by millions." His mechanical compliance with maternal dominance in early childhood has been transformed into an assertion of his own individuality and a realization of the potentialities previously so misunderstood by his mother.

In these few samples of temporal sequences we have seen that quite apart from later changes in personality which are a resultant of the diminution of interaction with parents there may be marked changes in attitudes of both child and parent within the family setting as they adjust to each other's increasing age. Stable inflexible parent-child relationships there are, but development is the typical characteristic of the maturing child and may temper the rigidity of the parents' later years.

SUMMARY

We have attempted to provide criteria useful in the assessment of the relative importance of the family region for the individual. Our purpose was twofold: first, to provide techniques for determining the relative importance of any region, whether it be the region of work, family, love, or social relationships, and second, to examine the relationship between childhood and the adult personality. We found that the importance of the family might be indicated by direct references in the stories, but that because this was uncommon more indirect techniques had to be employed. Such techniques included consideration of the introduction of parental figures, the interpretation of ambiguous figures as parental figures, the interpretation of older figures as parental figures, the omission of older adults in the picture, the number of stories about the family, the length of such stories, and the intensity of their affect. More important was the criterion of the degree of conflict with other regions. The importance of the family may be such that no conflict between the family and other regions is possible; the individual is completely absorbed by the family or the family may mean so little that no conflict is involved. The individual may leave home with no conflict and find his chief values elsewhere but where there is a conflict the outcome may provide a measure of the relative importance of those regions which have created divided loyalties. We examined the extent to which the parents influenced the child within the family setting. There were found to be parents who through either indifference, incompetence, or complete submission to the child's demands exerted relatively little influence on the formation of his personality. There were also parents whose influence was so pervasive that the child's personality bore the heavy impress of the parental mold. We also examined the subtle interplay and mutual adaptation which may occur between parent and child, each influencing to some extent the personality of the other. We found it illuminating to examine the scope of parental intervention in other regions; the parent may intervene in everything which concerns the child within and outside the family or limit such intervention to one particular region, such as the choice of a career or wife. We next considered the duration of parental impact, and found that a child may reject parental influence very early or continue to depend on parental help throughout his life. These differences could be attributed either to the child or the parent. The parent might continue intervention despite rejection by the child or in response to appeals for parental help. We also examined the generalization of the parent-child relationship, the extent to which the individual casts others into a parental role and reacts to them as if they were his parents. We found evidence of varying degrees of differentiation between the child's reaction to his parents and his later marital, work, and social relationships. Finally, we examined the changes in the nature of the parent-child relationship as the child developed into maturity. We found the TAT to reflect faithfully actual developmental sequences. We found, however, two types of distortion of this projection into the past, which necessitated caution in the use of the TAT for diagnosis of the individual's development. First we showed that events occurring in adolescence might be telescoped and attributed to the hero's childhood. Secondly we found that contemporary problems may be projected back into the past, so that all the heroes struggle with the same problem that concerns the adult who is telling these stories. In those protocols which are not modified by these two types of distortion, we found marked changes in attitudes of both child and parent within the family setting as they adjusted to each other's increasing age. We saw that development is the typical characteristic of the maturing child and that it not infrequently tempered the rigidity of the parents' later years.

CHAPTER VII

DIAGNOSIS OF PERSONALITY: THE REGION OF LOVE, SEX, AND MARITAL RELATIONSHIPS

A knowledge of the individual's adjustment in the love, marital, and sex region is necessary to an understanding of his personality. Aspects of personality not revealed in more general social relationships may be revealed in love relationships. Moreover, discrepancies between this and other regions often shed considerable light on personality structure. Adjustment in this area may be crucial to the individual's total adjustment.

In part, the individual's expectations, wishes, and fears in a love relationship bear the imprint of the family, as we have seen, but the two regions are sufficiently different to justify further analysis. Let us consider those dimensions of the love relationship crucial to the diagnosis of an individual's adjustment in this area.

I. DIMENSIONS OF THE LOVE AND MARITAL REGION

A. THE NATURE OF THE RELATIONSHIP

I. THE DEFINITION OF THE SITUATION

Of primary importance is the individual's definition of the nature of the love relationship. What role does the individual wish or expect to play; what does he expect from his love object? Is there a discrepancy between the role he plays and his ideal role? The stories which follow are a sample of the more commonly expressed phantasies. Perhaps one of the most common definitions of the love relationship is seen in the first story, in which love is defined in terms of gratification of dependency wishes (vector "on").

> This is a young girl who has been waiting for the right man to come along. She has never liked boys her own age because they don't understand her. She wants someone older that she can talk to, someone she can rely on to stand by her and take care of her, someone that she can depend on. Then she went to work for Mr. Rogers and in the course of working together they discovered that they had a lot in common. They spent long hours talking together and finally woke up to the fact that they had fallen in love. She is ecstatically happy because at last she has found the man she had dreamed about.

We see at the beginning of the story a discrepancy between her actual role and her ideal role which is remedied when she meets "the man she had dreamed about."

These wishes not infrequently are overlaid with a fear of loss of respect.

This woman is blissfully happy because she had found someone who returns her affection with equal intensity. The man here is a little amused at her childish clinging because he had thought her so mature and self-contained. She on her part is happy because she can cling to him as much as she likes without fear of his ceasing to respect her on that score; she wants to feel thus protected and cherished always so that she might in turn be a source of strength and faith.

Through the gratification of dependency without fear of loss of respect, the heroine of this story is enabled in turn to "be a source of strength and faith" (vector "for"), whereas the gratification of dependency in the previous story was an end in itself.

This wish to help the love object (vector "for") appears in purer form in the following story.

All she asks of life is a chance to make a home for him and to take care of him. She pictures herself waking him in the morning, fixing his breakfast and seeing him off to work and then spending the day doing things in preparation for his return. That is the way marriage should be, she thought.

Here the wish to be of help to the love object is as unfettered as was the wish to be helped in the first story.

A second definition of the love relationship is in terms either of governing or being governed (vectors "over" and "by"). In the following story the heroine governs her love object.

She is the kind of woman who has a strong influence over her husband. She believes that she knows best about everything and she has convinced him of this. She loves him but she just can't let him make a decision by himself. This has been going on for so many years that he has given up any idea of trying to change it.

The heroine of the next story is submissive, governed completely by the wishes of her love object.

Well, anyhow here is a very timid woman. She has the kind of husband who's very overpowering, a very strong character. She spends her whole life trying to please him. She likes to have things the way he wants them and whenever he tells her to do anything she hurries to do it. She wants very much to please him and he's her whole life.

These needs are complementary as were the needs to depend on or take care of the love object. Conflict, frustration, and an unstable relationship may result if an individual having one of these needs enters into a relationship with someone whose needs are not complementary. We see this in the following story in which the man's wish to care for the woman is frustrated by her self sufficiency.

She had everything she wants, and doesn't take him seriously, and he wishes there were something he could do for her that would make her conscious of him. He wants to take care of her, but she's so self sufficient that he doesn't ever have a chance. One afternoon when she's been out riding he has his chance. She's become very tired from riding and he takes her to his little house that's out in the field. He tells her to go to sleep and she lies down and he comes over and tells her a story, and she reacts very well. In fact she goes to sleep while he's talking. While she's asleep he's making elaborate plans to get her something to eat. He gets exotic foods around the house, cheeses and wines, etc., and he plans a very happy evening together, but suddenly she wakes up and realizes that it's late, and so she rides off and says good-bye. So he very sadly put away all the preparations and yet he thinks it's nice that she had been sleeping there while he fixed dinner, and that for a little while he had been able to feel that she was his and depended on him.

A third type of love relationship involves neither nurturance, dependence, dominance, nor submission, but a sharing of experience (vector "with") as its essential characteristic.

Margaret and John have been married for three years and are a wonderful couple. They enjoy going places together, sitting home reading, listening to records on the Capehart, talking things over together and lead a very happy life.

A fourth definition of the love relationship is in terms of acquiring and possessing a love object (vector "from").

He married her because she was the most beautiful thing he had ever seen and he desired to possess her as he might possess any other beautiful thing. He never let her out of his sight. He had to know that she was always there and that she was his.

A fifth variety is based on the aesthetic enjoyment of the love object (vector "toward").

As he looked at her he marveled at how lightly the years had touched her. They had been married for fifteen years and every time he looked at her the miracle of her beauty was a new discovery. Her deep brown eyes had softened a little and her hair had been touched with gray, but she still had the same proud grace that had made him fall in love with her.

Although such direct references to the nature of the definition of the love relationship are not infrequent, there are protocols which require more indirect techniques to elicit this material. There may be stories in which only the threat to a love relationship is elaborated, but implicit in the threat is the meaning of the love relationship.

Thus, in the following story, the threat of disruption of the love relationship is essentially a threat to the hero's need to govern the behavior of his love object.

> She has just told him that she's going to leave him. She said it calmly and quietly as though it were an everyday happening. He can't believe his ears. She's always been a model wife, so different than other guy's wives. At first he thinks she's kidding but then he realizes she isn't. Then he thinks there's another man, but she says she just wants to live by herself and run her own life. He can't understand it, but he's sure she'll come back.

2. THE RECIPROCITY OF LOVE

Another important dimension is the degree of reciprocity in the love relationship. Does the individual see his love returned in equal measure? The following three stories represent the middle and end points of a continuum ranging from complete mutuality to complete lack of reciprocity. Love in the first story is completely mutual.

> These are two people probably married for some short period of time who, at the point of this picture, had made one small step further in reaching a fundamental understanding of each other. They are now both content with full realization of their deep love for each other. They are both fairly intelligent people and their deep desires to establish complete mental harmony are the controlling factors in their entire life. Their marriage is a happy one and the ability to overlook each other's defects and to appreciate each other's qualities enable them to lead a very full life.

In the next story, however, mutuality is achieved; at the beginning of the story the heroine "isn't too interested in him yet." But her attitude changes and "they will make a very interesting and happily married couple."

> She isn't too interested in him yet but he has decided that she is the girl that that he will make a play for—not just a play for he really has his eye on her . . . . She is still sore as far as the subject of men is concerned and has a rather self-sufficient hands-off-me attitude but she just can't put this man in his place, he is too smart and she realizes, not without some hostility and ambivalence that he is a man she will have to reckon with. After he slapped her down at the right times and showed tenderness at the appropriate times they will make a very interesting and happily married couple.

In the third story, the end point of the continuum, we see a complete lack of reciprocity.

> Well, I think he's going to war. She says she wants him to go. "You are an American she says and I want you to fight for your county and die for it," she says. She's bidding him farewell. "I must tell her before I go," he says, "but I don't know how." There's someone else in my life. "She's in love with me but I'm not in love with her." You see she's in love with him

but he's not in love with her. "I don't believe in marriage without love," he says. "She's in love with me but I'm not in love with her and I must tell her there's someone else." And she's saying, "I want you to die a noble and honorable death in the service of your country because I know you don't love me." She wants nobody else to have him if she can't.

3. THE INTENSITY OF LOVE

The intensity of the feeling of love is independent of the nature of the love relationship and the extent to which love is reciprocated. These three stories represent the middle and end points of the scale.

This man has lost his wife to his best friend. He is so terribly in love with his wife that he looks only for her happiness and gives her to his best friend.

This woman has led an ordinary life. She has a happy family, probably two or three children. And she has a business-like husband whom she respects deeply but never passionately loved. At the point of this picture—this is late at night—her family's in bed—she has just finished reading. She's going around turning out lights and shutting windows in preparation for bed herself. Her life will continue as it has been before.

Camilla was married to John. It was a forced marriage sort of a family wish, and even though they didn't love each other there was no way of getting out of it.

4. TEMPORAL CHARACTERISTICS

a) *Maturation*

Another independent dimension of the love relationship is its temporal characteristic. The maturation of the relationship should be examined. Does the hero speak of falling in love at first sight, as in the following story, or does he describe a long acquaintance which gradually ripens into love?

It was at a hotel in New York at which this handsome young man planned to stay. There was also a beautiful woman, who stayed also. Both came down to breakfast at the same time. Suddenly, they apparently were in love at first sight. They couldn't believe it, but it was so, so true that they began to plan their marriage. This doesn't seem practical, but yet it was probable. They fixed their wedding day—October 25, 1829—and planned to be married by that day. They couldn't believe that those two were to be together. The night before the wedding they were all excited, too excited to think of anything else. As the time passed they sat silently waiting for the hour, the minute, the second for them to be united as one.

That love may not be so spontaneous a phenomenon is laboriously elaborated in the following story told by a cautious young woman.

Jill had lived a most unexciting life; she had gone to school and then started working at the 5 and dime store which was more monotonous than it was exciting. One day a strange man came in the store and bought a bag of candy which was where Jill worked. Two days later he came back and bought another bag of candy but this time he stood and stared at her for quite some time. On the third day, he came back again and bought another bag of the same cheap stuff and then he began to make conversation with Jill by asking her her name. He finally got around to asking Jill if she would pose for a picture he was going to paint. He knew that this was a most unusual way of getting a model but after seeing her the first day he was in he knew that she had the type of face that he wanted to use in his new work. He assured her that everything would be on the up and up and that she could come nights and sit as he too had a job in the day time. At first she was a little afraid but then after the first night she knew that he was really on the level and in spite of everything he said he was really a good painter, but then she was no judge of these things. There was one thing that Jill didn't count on and that was her falling in love with Chris which she did in a very short time but it was only natural for they were together every night for such a long time and he was the first man who had ever paid any attention to her in her life with the exception of a boy with red hair back in the tenth grade who used to take her out and buy her ice cream sodas. Jill was excited by this new thing that had happened to her and for her life had taken a new turn. When the picture was finished she suddenly realized that everything was over and that again she must go back to the same type of life she had been living, store, home to dinner, and be back to the store again. Jill was determined that this was not going to happen to her for after all she had spent so much time trying to make something of herself, but little did she know that Chris had fallen in love with her also and that soon again he was going to ask her to pose for another picture so that he could be near her. Both of them were too proud to come out and tell the other that he was in love with the other so time passed, two years to be exact, and the war had been declared and Chris was leaving for the camouflage department before he told Jill of his love for her and asked her to wait for him.

Not infrequently, the rate of maturation of the love relationship may differ between the lovers.

The man has just asked the girl to marry him. Uh, she is very much in love with him and although he doesn't know it, the minute she saw him she decided that he was hers. She started an intricate campaign and ran away from him, uh so much that he became interested.

b) *Duration*

Duration is another temporal characteristic of the love relationship which must be considered. How long does the relationship endure? In the story which follows, the relationship endures for only a short time; one of the lovers dies "in her teens."

When a young boy, Roger Rollins brought his girl, Mary Caudry, to this tree and carved their initials on it. Later in her "teens," Mary died; and Roger every year makes a pilgrimage to this tree.

That the relationship may be long-enduring is seen in the next story in which a couple are celebrating their fiftieth wedding anniversary.

Pictured here are a man and wife on their fiftieth wedding anniversary. Their children and grandchildren have made them a surprise wedding anniversary party. When the evening draws to a close, they retire to their room and start to reminisce. They remember all the years they have spent together. They think of the troubles they have gone through, the sacrifices they have made for one another and their children and also the many happy moments they have shared together. They admit to one another there have been times when they wondered if perhaps they would have been happier if they hadn't married. But when they think of all the wonderful years they have spent together, they realize that theirs has been the perfect marriage.

Fine gradations in the portrayal of the duration of the love relationship are found between these end points. In the following story for example, we see a love relationship which is neither short-lived nor long-enduring.

Man is deeply in love with a woman. He has come to tell her that their love cannot endure due to extenuating circumstances. She is sobbing and he is deeply moved. They both appear strong. She releases him in spite of her great love for him. He tries but never is able to get over the great love of his life.

These stories reflect differences in the duration of the love relationship; we must, however, also inquire into the duration of the *feelings of love*. The relationship may outlast the feelings of love; the feelings may continue after the relationship is broken; the feelings may continue only as long as the relationship is maintained; or the relationship may be maintained only as long as the feelings continue.

Following is a story in which the individual breaks off the relationship at the moment his feelings change.

He wasn't very capable of loving anyone for very long. He fell in and out of love as easily as a fish swimming in and out of the waves, and Anne was no exception. He loved her passionately, but not for long, and she couldn't hold him.

Or the duration of the feelings may be a function of the maintenance of the love relationship; when this is broken the feelings change.

This woman has a weakness for men. She's rather oversexed but she is a woman with lots of style, rather sensuous and quite wealthy. One day out in the country she was riding, and she came to an open field where she saw a man working. So she went to talk to the man just because she thought it would be fun and that he would naturally be thrilled to talk to her. Before very long, a couple of weeks, they were in love. He doesn't love her quite the way she loves him. She wants to marry him. He likes to have fun with women. At this point, he has just told her that he can't tie himself down. This hurts, but she decides that she won't cry over any man, and she goes back to her old way of life and falls out of love quite easily.

Feelings may continue for varying periods of time after the relationship has been broken. The heroine of the following story adjusts in a relatively short time to the broken relationship and "begins a new life for herself."

I'd say that this girl had just received a telegram from the government telling her that her husband had been killed in action. She doesn't know how she'll be able to live without him because she has centered her whole life about him; but, because she is still young, she later becomes adjusted to the fact that he won't come back and, uh, begins a new life for herself. Later on, she remarries and, uh, had a very happy life with her husband and family, and her life becomes broader since she has known grief.

Whereas it takes the heroine of the next story "a long, long time to get over it."

This girl is crying desperately—the man she loves has just been there and told her that the whole thing has been a mistake—that he thought he loved her but the war has changed everything and he doesn't feel that he can marry her—she faces a dark and desolate future—all her dreams are shattered and at this moment she doesn't know what she'll do. She feels helpless because she still really doesn't know what's wrong—why he changed his mind. She feels very alone and it'll take her a long, long time to get over it but eventually she'll meet someone she can trust who will always love her and never leave her and she'll be happy with him.

And the heroine of the following story never recovers from the broken relationship; her feelings continue until she dies.

This picture, to me, depicts an old woman, about seventy years old, peering with longing in her eyes. She is alone in this house in which she lives, and has been alone there for the past ten years since her husband left—died, I mean. They were a devoted couple and loved each other dearly. His death shocked her and since they were childless, she was left positively alone. The past ten years haven't at all worn off his absence. At times the sense of loneliness so greatly overcomes her that she begins searching the house for him believing he is still there, sitting and reading. This idea which she holds, that he is still alive and present in the house, so overwhelms her as years go on, that eventually, one night, she imagines seeing him in a chair and goes over and speaks to him. The next morning some neighbors, missing her, search the house and find her seated in a chair very comfortably opposite an empty chair. She had died of a heart attack during the night.

Less frequently do we find references to the maintenance of a love relationship after the feelings have changed. The following story was told by a disenchanted woman of 40.

These people are middle aged. They've been married for years. They were once in love a long time ago. But they've gone their separate ways. Nothing but the habit of living together through the years keeps them together. They're just used to each other, and will probably live together for the rest of their lives, going on in the same way. They're just in a rut.

A preoccupation with duration and constancy may signify more than the temporal characteristic of the love relationship. In such cases, the type of love relationship is no longer a primary consideration. The concern with constancy and duration supersedes the individual's more specific love needs. In the following example, the individual who is suffering a basic lack of self confidence cannot enjoy the love relationship, afraid that it will not last.

Ever since the night he had proposed she had been afraid she couldn't hold him. She had lived in fear of this day. She had been the plain girl of their crowd and she knew people had whispered when they became engaged, "I wonder what he sees in her." Now she knew it was over—all her worst fears were realized. She wouldn't put up a fight—what could she do against a beautiful, clever girl like Jane? She was just the plain girl of the crowd who had married a wonderful man and had been foolish enough to hope against hope she could hold him. Tears streamed down her face.

B. The Vicissitudes of the Love Relationship

1. THE SOURCE OF DISRUPTION

The love relationship, vulnerable to diverse threats, may be threatened or disrupted by purely exogenous forces.

For seven long months, Dick had been waiting for this day. At 8 p.m. the train was to arrive that would bring his fiancée, Jean, to Boston to be married that next week. Dick waited until 9 and was not too upset for trains are usually late these days anyway. He passed another hour or so, and then the news arrived that the train had been wrecked going over a washed-out bridge, and that a list of casualties would follow. Dick waited anxiously until 1 a.m. and word came through that Jean had been killed. Dick was beside himself, and being almost alone in the station he found it easy to overpower a shore policeman and take his gun. Dick made his way to a secluded section of the station waiting room, put a bullet in his head, and slumped onto the bench. He had no relatives and no one to care for him except Jean. So maybe it was the best thing to happen to a young person of such weak character.

Or disruption may stem from sources partly exogenous and partly endogenous. Thus, in the following story, both dissatisfaction with the love object and a more desirable love object who is available contribute to the disruption of the original relationship.

A woman is married to a man who has a great deal of money but whose other qualifications for a successful husband are nil. He is several years older than she, and she is still young and beautiful. It is not surprising, therefore, that after three years of married life she should have a lover. He comes one afternoon when her husband is working and has tea in one corner of the sumptuous living room. She is bidding him good-bye at the door when her husband comes home. The three of them quarrel and the lover decides to leave town for good. The table and teacups remain behind as mute evidence of a flame that died.

The threat may, however, be primarily endogenous, stemming from dissatisfactions arising completely within the relationship.

Lydia is a perfect lady and great fun but during two years of married life she has not been a companion to Edward. He's a very sincere person who works hard, wants and expects much love from his wife and had thought of marriage as a happy, companionable life for two people in love—who wanted more than anything else to share the same interests, a home, etc. He finally comes to the point where he tells Lydia that he isn't happy and he thinks it best that they "call the whole thing off" and each go his own way. Lydia's the type that doesn't need too much love and home life and is content to live as they have but she begs him to stay, promising him that she'll always be kind to him and bear his children, if he wants them, and be a good mother to them. He decides that she may grow to love him and that she is a good wife and that, after all, maybe one can't expect too much.

2. THE MAINTENANCE OR DISRUPTION OF THE RELATIONSHIP

Let us consider now the extent to which these threats disrupt the relationship.

The threat may be overcome and the relationship maintained intact.

Mary and Jim had been engaged for three months and had their first fight. It wasn't a very big argument but it worried each of them. Finally, because he was sure that it was his fault, Jim decided to go and ask Mary to forgive him. When the maid at Mary's house answered the door, she was sure that Jim had come to break his engagement to Mary—at least, she gathered that from what Mary told her about their serious quarrel and how it was all her fault. When the maid saw them come in the living room a half hour later beaming at each other, she decided never to try to understand human beings, especially those in love.

Or, the threat may not disrupt the relationship yet produce important changes.

I think I have been reading too many *Ladies' Home Journals*. I think some one has told him gossip about the girl. She is at present pleading with him not to believe what he has heard. She is a very attractive young woman. So it wouldn't be difficult for people to misunderstand her actions. I believe he wants to believe that she is right in her denial of the gossip and yet he is man enough to be hurt by what he has heard. I think he will accept her side of the story but with—with slight reservation. Ah—a slight reservation will—ah—cast a shadow on their future relationship because he will never be able to fully believe in her.

Or the threat may completely shatter the relationship.

> Jane stood behind the tree and watched the girl in the blue evening gown run down the beach. Jane knew what was going to happen. She hadn't meant to spy. The girl ran on. A man rose up from the rocks at the other end of the beach. They clasped each other in their arms. Jane gasped, turned, and scrambled back up the rocks to the house. She didn't want to look. She didn't want her husband to see her. She told him their marriage was over when he returned.

a) *Maintenance of the Love Relationship*

If threats to the love relationship are successfully met, how is this achieved?

In the following story, the relationship is maintained by the husband's tolerance and the heroine's new appreciation of his qualities.

> The wife came back after leaving home for a little affair. She appreciated her husband after she left him. He loves her and is patient and willing to wait. He is older and knew she was subject to these little flights. He expected it because she is very beautiful. He knew she really loved him. They live happily ever after because now she appreciates him.

The couple may be reconciled through a common sorrow.

> The wife is resentful, of course, of the other girl and is justified. The husband in the meantime is drawing away from the other woman and closer to his wife. Her pleading and begging have made an impression in his mind and he realizes that his wife means more to him than anyone else. Through an unfortunate accident, she dies while in childbirth—no, make it the baby who dies being born. But the two have been reunited in their grief.

Or through reformation on the part of the hero.

> Here the impression is received that the young lady has discovered her lover or husband being unfaithful and is pleading with him to leave the girl with whom he has been conducting his infidelity. Possibly the reason for the lover or husband, which ever the case may be, being there is that he met the young lady of his unfaithfulness at a bar while under the influence of alcohol. Having been caught in the act and through his true love's pleading, he mends his ways.

Or the hero may be reconciled to a lower income of love.

> He finally comes to the point where he tells Lydia that he isn't happy and he thinks it best that they "call the whole thing off" and each go his own way. Lydia's the type that doesn't need too much love and home life and is

content to live as they have but she begs him to stay, promising him that she'll always be kind to him and bear his children, if he wants them, and be a good mother to them. He decides that she may grow to love him and that she is a good wife and that, after all, maybe one can't expect too much.

b) *The Sequelae of the Disrupted Relationship*

If the love relationship suffers disruption, what are the sequelae?

The individual may never relinquish the possibility of future reconciliation.

Roger was an artist of little note and lived with his wife in a small village. He decided that he must go to the Nudist Colony to paint as most of his works were like those of many of other artists, and that he would become famous through this work as no one else had portrayed such a life. He left his wife in the small village to give birth to his son and started painting at the Nudist Colony. The son, Reuben, is born and, after three months, the wife takes him to the Colony in order that her husband might see their offspring; but instead of being happy to see them, he tells her that he has fallen in love with a girl at the Colony and points to his painting to show that this new love gives him inspiration that he needs for his work. The wife is deeply hurt but takes the child back home, hoping that he'll return someday.

Or he may achieve symbolic reconciliation in death.

Eugene was deeply in love with Ruth and they were to be married in June. All plans were made but on May 20, Eugene received a call to come immediately to Ruth's home. She's had a heart attack; but, before Eugene could get there, Ruth had died. He worshipped the girl and almost went insane. Each night he would dream of walking through the cemetery and lingering for hours over her grave. He finally took poison so that he might die and be nearer Ruth.

The disruption of the love relationship may result in further disruption of the individual's life. In the extreme case it may even result in insanity or death.

After Louise's death, he was a different man. He lost all his glamour, ambition, and his ability to converse with immediate friends. At night, instead of going out to make a friendly call on some of his friends, he would stay in complete darkness and stare out of the window, his body only illuminated by the moon. In the distance he saw nothing, but kept gazing at the sky for hours in hopes of seeing Louise. After several weeks of the same performance, he went literally insane, and was put away.

The old man is looking at his wife's grave. He is very dejected. He doesn't know what to do with himself. He's thinking over all the things they did together before she died. He goes to visit her grave pretty often. He's sort of hoping he'll die himself before long—he has nothing to do on earth. He does a lot of praying. He dies himself before pretty long.

The individual in such cases is telling us of the importance of his love need and how unyielding his fixation to a love object might be. This type of story has been told by individuals who have never permitted themselves to enter into a love relationship because of their expectation that it would be disrupted and their lives shattered by the experience.

Another reaction to disruption of a love relationship is the quest of a new love object. This is achieved with varying degrees of effectiveness and residual conflict. In the two stories which follow the development of another relationship in one case and the hope of one in the other enable the individual to cope with the disruption of the original relationship.

When she went out to garden this morning she had been perfectly happy. She had had everything—a home, family, fiancé, pleasant work to do and wonderful things to look forward to. But she hadn't been out there more than an hour or so when she had seen her lover walking along the wood path with another girl. From that moment on, it seemed as though the bottom had dropped out of her life, present and future, the most important thing and her fiancé being gone as far as she was concerned. And walking with his childhood sweetheart! She had known he still held a small place for her in his heart, but had hidden from herself the possibility of its outgrowing her own place there. All this she thought as she was sitting down to rest before lunch. What could she do now? Well, she finally realized that the only thing to do was to say nothing and let him tell her when he wanted to. Which is just what he did, and soon after married the girl who "had always had a small place in his heart." But time went on and she grew older and wiser and realized she had missed nothing by losing him. As if in reward for these thoughts, she by and by met a man who really appreciated her and understood her. And this man gave his whole heart to her.

A few years ago, in a rural town, there lived a handsome young man, a young girl, and an older woman who was determined to have the young man for her husband. The two younger people were really in love, but by means of deceit and treachery, the older woman was able to make the man forget about the other girl and marry her. Now they live on a prosperous farm where he plows and keeps his family protected. The young girl has to pass the farm on the way to school, and the wife pretends not to notice her, for she knows how much she would like to be mistress of that farm herself. The farming family will continue to live together, but without any love or companionship. The young girl will get her fill of "book learning" and be a career girl while waiting for another "true love" to come along.

In other cases, the individual, incapable of seeking a new love object or unwilling to do so, turns to some other region to cope with the trauma suffered in the disruption of the love relationship. In the following story, the heroine turns to work to forget.

This woman is pleading with this man to leave his work for a while and relax. She offers herself to him. The man here seems to be hesitating between his duty and his love, but actually he knows which really matters to him. Besides, he will soon grow tired of the woman and the temporary pleasure is nothing compared with the rewards of his work. So he fools around with her for a while and then throws her off without a remorse because after all she got what she wanted and he gave as much as was his to give. The woman takes it badly at first but she recovers and throws herself into her own work with greater determination. She is thrilled to find how well she makes out on her job.

But the activity may be something other than an attempt to forget. The individual may wish to preserve the memory of the love object and prevent similar tragedies in the lives of others.

John Smith was an average American man. He worked in a defense plant and earned a pretty good living and felt on top of the world. He felt that everything was going OK for him. He was married to this woman. She complained of severe pains in the chest. She went to a doctor and was told that she was developing tuberculosis. She told John nothing of this for she did not want to worry him. He was doing very well in his job and had been promoted to floor manager. She continued suffering in silence. Her illness required nothing but a few months' rest at a sanatorium with the proper climate, food, and attention. One night, John came home from work and found his wife lying in bed gasping for breath. He immediately called the doctor, who pronounced her case as advanced tuberculosis. She was sent away to the sanatorium. But she did not recover and, instead, died. After the first shock of her death, he continued working and became head of the defense plant, which was now converted back to civilian manufacturing. John Smith became a wealthy man and gave huge sums of money to the tuberculosis fund so that other women, children, men, and boys, would not have to suffer from this dread disease.

Activity which has its origin in the attempted suppression of painful memories may be the basis for a regeneration of interest, which had been blunted by grief.

The girl on the bridge lives down on the waterfront. She often goes down in the morning to watch the longshoremen loading and unloading the boats, ships I should say. Usually her surroundings gave her a feeling of contentment. They are all that she had ever known and they are all she wants to know. This particular morning however, her surroundings bring back only painful memories. Painful in the sense that she will never experience them again. Her fiancée had worked as a longshoreman on these very docks. And they'd been very happy planning their future together. When the war came, he joined the Navy and yesterday they had received notice of his death. As she looked about her, and down into the murky waters of the river below, she wondered whether it was worth while to go on living without him. Lacking the nerve to heave herself off the bridge into the river, and as she was a practical person, realizing that the men were near enough to fish her out if she did, she decided the best way to sever connections with these painful surroundings was to leave the city and try to make a life for herself elsewhere. That afternoon she packed her bags and got on the train, her destination being another city quite some distance from her home. She found a place to live and got a job in a war factory. Soon she made friends among the girls working in her department. Soon she began to enjoy the interests and plans of her friends. She, uh, went to a dance at the U.S.O. and made friends there. With all these new contacts, she soon forgot about the grief she thought was going to color the rest of her life.

Although this may happen, for many individuals substitute satisfactions never altogether replace the lost love relationship.

This ex-service man comes back to meet the woman with whom he thought he was in full accord before he left to find that she's not the same girl he dreamt about in the horrible days of war. At the point of this picture, some fundamental misunderstanding has come up. The man is determined that he cannot overlook this and the woman is pleading with him to do so. He leaves her because he's a man of determination and strong will, but finds out later that in his strength—in his trying to be strong—he had lost the woman he'd loved. But he resigns himself to this fact, and leads a life of superficial happiness.

The disruption of the love relation may produce misery and resignation, the quest of a new love object or substitute satisfaction. But, frequently, the most conspicuous sequelae involve aggression directed either at the love object, or the self, or both.

The story which follows is representative of the purely extrapunitive reaction.

A husband—no, change it to a lover, I'll make it real good while I'm at it—in his jealous rage has killed his beloved. Through his grief one thought still shines—escape. Tripping down the stairs, bumping into the little old lady on the first floor, he runs blindly to the street. Escape running through his mind, the shock of her death has turned him into an unbalanced person. Running down the street at a terrific pace, not knowing where to go, he is led on by his conscience pounding "escape" in his brain. Stumbling along, he goes to a movie so he will not be caught. Planning every motion carefully in his twisted mind, he sets out after dinner to the hall where she would have given her concert tonight. As far as he could see he had not made a slip. On entering the hall he heard thunderous applause. Wondering who it could be for, he went into the auditorium where he saw her, bandage on her head but otherwise all right. Muttering to himself, "I killed her, I killed her," he leaped forward, took her white neck in his hands and slowly drained the life from her. Like a madman he leaped up realizing what he had done, but it was too late. The wheels of justice had already begun to turn and, as they took him away, he was still muttering, "I killed her, I killed her."

Aggression incited by disruption of the relationship is not always so directly expressed. Thus the hero may be the instrument of the death of his love object, even though no overt aggressive act is committed.

> This is the ghost of a lover come to keep his tryst by the street lamp. Both he and his girl have long been dead but still he comes. She used to be a passionate girl and, for a long time, he resisted her. However, when he finally veered around, her feelings for him had cooled somewhat. In fact, she had found a new interest. He did not realize this. One day, he asked her to meet him at a certain place. She never turned up. He waited and waited, refusing to believe that she would not come. It was a· bitterly cold night and, as the hours wore on, a numbness overcame him. The next morning, they found him lying in a heap by the lampost more dead than alive. He died of pneumonia in the hospital. When the girl heard of this she was, of course, sorry in a way, but she said what was she to do? It was silly of him to wait so long. Besides when she had wanted him to love her, he wouldn't. If he had returned her love then, things might have been very different.

Or the hero may be the instrument of the accidental death of the love object.

> Late one night, this man came home and found that the door to his house was locked. He had no key. So he thought that the best plan would be to get the stepladder out of the garage. He put the ladder up to a bedroom window where the light was on because he thought it would be easier to get inside if he could see what he was doing, and it was his and his wife's room. He realized that, because the light was still on, his wife must still be up. When he climbed to the top of the ladder, he saw his wife standing in the middle of the floor facing him. She couldn't see him because the room was so light and it was so dark out in the night. She must have mistaken her husband for a burglar, because in her hand she held a gun. Before the man could think she pulled the trigger. When she discovered her mistake she was glad—glad that she had killed him. He had been out with that other woman for the last time.

Or death of the love object may be wished, although the hero will not commit the aggressive act.

> Well, I think he's going to war. She says she wants him to go. "You are an American," she says, "and I want you to fight for your country and die for it," she says. She's bidding him farewell. "I must tell her before I go," he says, "but I don't know how." There's someone else in my life. "She's in love with me but I'm not in love with her." You see, she's in love with him but he's not in love with her. "I don't believe in marriage without love," he says. "She's in love with me but I'm not in love with her and I must tell her there's someone else." And she's saying, "I want you to die a noble and honorable death in the service of your country because I know you don't love me." She wants nobody else to have him.

It is of interest that individuals who are capable in phantasy of killing their love objects often feel no guilt for their aggression.

Consider now the hero who turns his aggression against himself.

This girl is the girl about whom the "Bridge of Sighs" was written. Now before she jumps, she is thinking how bitter has been her life, how pointless, how futile. She curses the man she had trusted and jumps.

In this story, there is hostility towards the once trusted love object, but we are uncertain of the extent to which her suicide stems from her bitterness, or, the futility of her life. The behavioral vector in all suicide stories would be scored vector "against" with the self as subject and object, but the Freudian concept of free-floating aggression which may be turned outward or inward is debatable. Rarely do we find in the "intrapunitive" response to frustrated love any evidence for an aggressive wish toward the love object simply redirected against the self. Aggression against the self, as we shall see in some of the stories that follow, may be an act in the service of a variety of motives.

Thus, in the next story, suicide is the means of escaping depression and remorse and a social situation which has become unbearable.

This is the most peculiar cemetery that I have ever seen (long pause—laughs— long pause). This story took place many years ago. This man had married a nice girl. Throughout his life, he was a respected person in the community, but, unknown to most people, he was extremely unkind to his wife, finding many subtle ways of making her unhappy. He frequently limited her social activities and refused to give her the things she most enjoyed. She died in middle life and, as the years went by, her husband gradually became remorseful. He became depressed and seclusive. People came to look upon him as a town character. Finally, he could stand it no longer. So on a very dark night he went to her grave and committed suicide.

Suicide, in the following story, is the result of a realization that "he had lost the only person who really liked him or could stand him," and he had become a social outcast.

Paul Avon and his wife had been very much in love and were very devoted. But he was always rather conceited and hot-headed and wanted everything the way he liked it. She was very devoted to him but was very popular and social. She would have given up anything for him, but his constant nagging, jealousy and sureness of himself killed in her all she loved in him, and, in mental anguish, finally left him and remarried later. Soon after her marriage, he realized he had lost the only person who really liked him or could stand him. And in the world he became an outcast because of his eccentricities, and rather than bother her any more, he killed himself in a gas-filled room under an assumed name.

Another example of suicide as a means of relieving a situation which has become intolerable is the following story.

This man has lost his wife to his best friend. He is so terribly in love with his wife that he looks only for her happiness and gives her to his best friend.

After their marriage takes place, they are killed by an automobile, which mangles them to death. The man becomes so despondent that he is sent away to a hospital for the insane. The environment plus his sorrows leads him to committing suicide, which he has just done. He slumps down on the floor, happy that he is out of his misery.

We have evidence for truly aggressive wishes directed against the self, but these rarely involve wishes for physical self destruction. The individual may criticize himself for his inadequacy in the love relationship, or feel remorse for hurting the love object, but, if he takes his life, he does this to escape his inner misery, which may be caused by loneliness, his sense of inadequacy, social ostracism, or his feelings of guilt, which are unbearable. There is rarely, however, a hero who "wishes" suicide for its own sake. For this reason, the extreme intrapunitive response must be regarded as typically a means to some other end rather than an end in itself. He may "hate" himself as he once hated his love object, but killing the love object is an expression of the hatred, whereas self-destruction is very rarely a direct expression of self hatred.

II. DIMENSIONS OF THE SEX REGION

Although love and marital adjustment are closely related to sexual adjustment, there is, in our society, sufficient discrepancy in the expression of these related needs to justify a separate scrutiny of the dimensions of these two regions. Precisely the same dimensions used in the analysis of love can be employed in the analysis of the sex need.

A. The Nature of the Sex Need

I. THE TYPE OF SEX NEED

a) *Varieties of Heterosexual Relationships*

Inspection of TAT stories reveals that every type of love relationship has its sexual counterpart, but that for any individual the love relationship may be defined quite differently from the sexual relationship.

In the following story, the sexual experience is exciting because of its fusion with the wish to be cared for (vector "on").

Janie has just come in from a thrilling date with Bob. She started to get ready for bed. She is so excited she's walking on air. She sits dreaming about it, treasuring over every moment. He's so wonderful, the most exciting man she's ever known. When he kisses her, tiny shivers run up and down her spine and she just melts. He's so tall and handsome and makes her feel so warm and protected. A girl likes to have a man she can lean on.

The complementary wish, to help the love object (vector "for") is fused with the sex need in this story.

When she met him she liked him immediately. He reminded her of a lost pup. She immediately took him in hand in her friendly way and they started having dinner together after work. Then one evening he suggested that she come to his apartment so they could talk. She went and he began to tell her how much knowing her had meant to him. She was very touched and then the last thing she expected happened. He came over and kissed her passionately and told her that he wanted her. She tries to look shocked but he's so impulsive and childlike that she finds herself kissing him back. She's more excited than she ever thought she could be. Suddenly, she wants to give herself to him—his need of her is so great

The wish to govern the love object (vector "over") may be fused with the sex need.

This guy brought this girl home after doing the night spots. He asked her if he could come in for a while. She isn't in favor of it, but he finally convinces her. She mixes him a nightcap and he starts pawing her. She objects, but this only adds fuel to the fire and the idea of making her give in makes him more ardent. He's doing fine until her roommate comes in.

Or the complementary need to be governed (vector "by") may be satisfied in the sexual experience.

This scene shows a seduction which has just taken place. She was a virgin and didn't quite want to do it. But he was so masterful and she got so excited she couldn't help giving in.

Sex may also be the vehicle of shared intimacy (vector "with").

A woman who has slept with her lover for the first time, sitting and dreaming about it. It was a wonderful experience. She never felt so close to anyone in her life. She knows now what they mean when they say united as one.

Or it may be based on esthetic enjoyment of the love object (vector "toward").

All during the war, in the foxholes and on the battlefield, he could still see her as she had been that night, lying in bed, half naked, her beautifully curved body relaxed, her lips slightly parted. He grew hot and cold by turns as he thought of the way she had looked.

A variation of the same wish is expressed in voyeurism.

This is a picture of a Peeping Tom who's been causing a great commotion in the neighborhood by looking in windows and watching the women get undressed. The men of the neighborhood have organized a group to look for him. He hears them coming and slides down the rope to try to get away. He gets away this time, but they finally catch him.

Still another variant is the exhibitionistic wish to evoke interest in the self as a sex object, (wish-other object-vector "toward" object-self).

> The better he got to know them, the more he desired them but he desired both of them equally and he had an idea that some day he'd go over and pull his penis out in front of them and see how they both reacted. So he did. But they weren't even shocked and still he couldn't choose between them.

The sexual experience may have as its primary meaning the acquisition and possession of the love object (vector "from").

> This man is standing at the open window thinking about the evening he just spent. He's gone with this girl for a long time but he's never really possessed her, sexually, that is. He's tried but she always seems so unapproachable. He wants this very much and he's dreaming of the day when she will be his completely.

There is also a type of sexual satisfaction fused with the wish to hurt (vector "against").

> This guy's a "queer", some sort of a sex pervert. He gets a big kick out of beating women and hearing them scream, and then, when they're just about passing out, he lays them.

Related is sexual enjoyment in being hurt. This may be expressed as wish-other object-vector "against" object-self.

> They've been fighting, having an awful row about something. All of a sudden he loses his temper completely and slaps her. Instead of making her mad, it excites her, she doesn't understand it. It has a strange effect on her. In the future she finds herself deliberately provoking him and aggravating him to the point where he'll slap her again.

b) *Varieties of Homosexual Relationships*

We must also examine the stories for evidence of homosexual wishes. Stories are sometimes told by men in which the storyteller identifies with a woman in a sexual or love relationship. We see this in the following story.

> She's in love with him but she suspects that he's been seeing other women. She finally finds proof of this—something in his bureau drawer—and she's completely broken up. She was all right until she knew it for sure, but now she has to face the fact and she can't. She alternates between crying and cursing him. She commits suicide rather than have to live with this knowledge.

Identification with women, based on identification with the mother, is not infrequent in American society and is reflected in the TAT's of many heterosexual males. Whether or not this results in an "effeminate" male is to some extent determined by the personality of the mother with whom the son identifies. In many cases, the mother's personality coincides with the cultural definition of the masculine character. Conversely, there are sons who, in identifying with an "effeminate" father, are less masculine than those identifying with masculine mothers. For this reason we cannot assume that female identification in the stories is related in any simple manner to homosexuality.

We must further distinguish an unconscious identification with the opposite sex from a *wish* to be of the other sex. The male may know himself to be a man and wish to be a woman, or think himself effeminate and wish he could be a "real man." In the following story, told by a girl who had been a tomboy in her youth and relinquished the masculine role with regret, we see another aspect of this problem—the person who wishes to be of another sex and *also* loves objects of that sex.

> She's sitting in a room looking out of a window and she's watching her brothers and their friends outside playing baseball. It's spring. She's very proud of her brothers but she's also wishing she were a boy and could play with them too. She's about fifteen years old. What happens to her is she reverts from her tomboy wishes and aspirations and becomes extremely feminine in a couple of years. She sort of realizes she can't be a boy, unconsciously, and she decides that, if she can't, at least she wants them to notice her some way or another, and she does it by becoming very popular so that all her brothers' friends take her out.

In this case, the heroine did not *identify* with boys, since she knew she was not and could not be one, but she did wish to be a boy. But not so that she might indulge in lesbian activities, since her preferred love objects were also male. There are also males who wish to be females and who have females as love objects.

The following story illustrates the case in which the individual feels *identified* with the opposite sex, but wishes he were a better representative of his own sex.

> This boy was raised by two maiden aunts who insisted that he wear Little Lord Fauntleroy suits and learn to play the violin. He doesn't mind this when he's small, but when he grows up and goes to college, especially when he starts going out with girls, he feels that there is a difference between him and the other fellows and the girls seem to feel it, too. He wishes there were something he could do about it but he doesn't quite know what.

As we have seen, the choice of homosexual or heterosexual object is independent of the sex with which the individual feels identified or the sex he wishes he were. Either heterosexual or homosexual objects may be sought by men who are either identified with men or women or who may wish to be either masculine or feminine.

In the following story, we see the homosexual object choice on the part of the effeminate man.

A weak, effeminate, most repulsive-looking character. A boy who grew up in a world of his own. No one ever understood him. He may have been a musician, dramatist—might have been an actor—became weak and fleshy. He's enjoying being in the clutches of this man. He gives himself up freely (I wanted to find someone who would rule my life). He has a strong sensuous feeling about it. He is on his way out now. He will end up by suicide. Or, having lost his self respect completely, he will sink down into the depths of degredation.

We next see the same type of object-choice on the part of a man who wishes to be a woman only because he wishes to enjoy homosexual objects, but his wish is not to be a woman per se.

This guy is a prize fighter—a real rugged guy. He's never gone out with women very much. He always liked men better. He's a little peculiar and sometimes he dreams of being a woman so he could have a man.

The homosexual object-choice may also stem from a man's wish to be a woman, per se.

Is that a man or a woman? I think he's a man—but a queer. He wants to be a woman and he dresses up in a woman's clothes and imagines himself feeling like a woman and flirting with men.

Another variety of homosexual object-choice is based on masculine identification and masculine object-choice. The man has no interest whatsoever in women and enjoys homosexual experience for its own sake. This type of story is extremely rare in the protocols of heterosexual males but not infrequent in the stories of overt homosexuals.

A picture of a sailor climbing a rope. He's been going to sea ever since he was a kid. He's a homosexual and part of the attraction of the life at sea is that all the other men are too. He was introduced to this by the first mate and continued it ever since then.

Or the individual may have purely homosexual wishes which he cannot accept and which he feels are degrading.

Hm, interesting picture, a young boy who (I'm getting a sexual reaction from this picture) he was put to sleep by the man. The boy has tendencies toward weakness. He either lived with the man or was drawn to the man. He couldn't help himself. The old man has hypnotic power over him and is putting him in a deep trance. The man is very bitter with life and he found a young man clean of mind and body. The boy comes back to the man. The old man has degrading thoughts. The old man will drag him down. . . .

In some cases, previous homosexual experience may interfere with the development of heterosexual interests.

Young man in youth had had homosexual relations, and these always made him fear to have sex relations with women, which he really wanted. On one occasion, such a relationship did develop and he became tormented because the idea of homosexual relations were always on his mind; he couldn't enjoy her— it made him very unhappy. After this relationship, he went out and committed suicide.

That the interrelationship between homosexual and heterosexual wishes may be complex is illustrated in a story told by an individual whose primary conflict centered on his feelings of inadequacy as a male.

Hard to determine sex and what's on the floor. I can think of a story but it's so disgusting I'm afraid. This person is a boy, but he's always wanted to be a girl. One day, he's so sick of fighting it off, or trying to make believe he's like other boys, that he dresses up as a girl. He stuffs artificial breasts into his dress, etc. He decides he's going to fuck himself. So he looks around for something that'll look like a penis. He hasn't decided where he's going to put it. So he finds this old splinter of wood that's on the floor and he wraps a cloth around it so it won't hurt. He sticks the thing in between the cushion and the frame and it's sticking out like an erect penis. And then he gets all ready and he himself is sexually excited and he becomes frustrated because he realizes that there's no place in his anatomy to fit this thing   So he masturbates, and while he's masturbating, he takes the role of the male and has a heterosexual revery while he's masturbating. Then, when he's all done, he feels disgusted just because he's masturbated and because he's dressed up like a girl and he feels he shouldn't be. So he sits down and he cries. And while he cries, he feels how hopeless it is; he feels he needs a male in his arms and although it is not sexual, he feels he needs a male to protect him. And he doesn't know what to do.

Of interest in this story is the reference to masturbation. Although the practice of masturbation is admittedly common, this is one of the few protocols, in our experience, in which there is direct reference to the practice. This is puzzling inasmuch as other equally tabooed wishes· and practices are mentioned far more frequently by normal subjects. We have not, however, been able to find an explanation for this.

2. RECIPROCITY IN THE SEXUAL RELATIONSHIP

Let us consider the degree of reciprocity in the sexual relationship. Is the ardor of the hero returned by his sexual partner or is the hero more or less responsive than she? Sex in the following story is completely unreciprocal; the hero rapes the girl, who "is unaware of the action that has taken place."

This is an obvious case of rape from the picture. The girl is motionless, indicating that she is unaware of the action that has taken place. The man, from the pained expression on his face and the fact that he has his arm in front of his eyes, is terribly ashamed and full of remorse. He sits beside her until she comes to in an attempt to square himself with her. He appears to have some strength of character in his face despite his cowardly act.

In marked contrast, sex is completely reciprocated in the next story.

Ahhh . . . He's just sort of weary . . . Well, let's see now. Can't figure why he's got his clothes on. Well, he got a date with this gal and they've been necking; they're always necking. But tonight, it's petting pretty heavy . . . pretty heavy petting. Oh yah, and they're going further and further and then suddenly someone's turned the light and he jumps up fast. And he's got his hand over his face. He's feeling faint. You know how you feel faint when you get up fast. And the light's in his eyes. It's a very traumatic moment. She looks the other way and she'll pull the covers over her head. Her roommate in the apartment house. This is her room but she lives with a girl friend who's as shocked as they are. But she didn't know the girl would be in this position she is. And so she goes out quietly and leaves the light on. They're very disturbed. But they leave the light on and talk awhile about public relations and sex and finally they convince themselves that the public be damned. He undresses and snaps the light off and they have a fine time. They're even happier now, because now they've talked about it. They hadn't verbalized it before. And talking all these things over made it all right.

Between these two points we find the same range of variability that we saw in the reciprocity of the love relationship. In the following story, for example, there is neither complete reciprocity nor a complete lack of reciprocity in the sexual relationship.

This poor guy wants to go to bed with this girl, but he's so afraid of being impotent that half the time he ends up that way just because he's afraid. She's luring him on and gets into bed with her breast exposed. He's excited but he's so afraid of making a fool of himself that he walks out and leaves her wondering what happened.

3. INTENSITY OF THE SEX NEED

Direct references to the intensity of the sex need are relatively infrequent; more common are references to the degree of enjoyment or excitement in sexual experience. Although this may be a resultant of the basic sex need, modified by inhibiting forces, it yet provides an index of the intensity of the need as it operates within the total personality. The three stories which follow are a sample of the range of variability of enjoyment and excitement.

This guy has had his first experience with sex, and, if he were to be perfectly frank about it, he would admit that it was a little disappointing. He enjoyed it, but he wonders what the hell everyone has been raving about for years.

These two people met at a dance hall and end up in bed together. Afterwards, he leaves. He enjoyed himself a lot because he hadn't been with a woman for a long time. He goes home feeling very good.

It's hard to think of these people as real. They look so unreal and so fictitious. She's a famous singer in a night club in New York. He has met her; he's a janitor; he comes to clean up. He's very dumb—handsome but dumb type. He's met her after hours while he's cleaning up around the place. He feels that she'd be a good lay and vica versa to put it bluntly. The trouble is, he feels he's so inferior to her because he realizes he has no talent and is kind of dumb. But she's asked him up to her apartment. (This is habitual and, every time he's gone up, he's laid her.) Well, she's very kind and she understands how he feels and she's always trying to give him confidence in himself; but the more gentle she is with him, the more he resents it and feels she's patronizing him. One afternoon he goes up to the apartment (she asked him up) and she tells him she wants him to learn to play the drums so he can play in the orchestra in the night club where she sings. He resents this because he feels that she just wants to keep him around because she likes his body and there's nothing else about him which she values. And so instead of just laying her today, he suddenly becomes very vicious—very aggressive, I should say the word is—and he gets her on the bed and rips off her clothes and starts to bite her breasts. She is—it hurts her—and she's sort of struggling, but she's tremendously excited sexually—so he starts to slap her hard and she starts to cry—and he feels at this point that he's triumphed and then after this triumph he becomes very gentle, very tender with her and gives her the best screwing she's ever had. (I like this story—makes me feel kinda good.) He agrees that he'll learn how to play the drums and he works terrifically hard at it and he makes a success and they get married and live happily ever after.

4. TEMPORAL CHARACTERISTICS OF THE SEX NEED

The temporal characteristics of the sexual relationship may be analyzed in the same way as those of the love relationship.

a) *Maturation*

Does the hero typically engage in sexual activity or have sexual wishes on first meeting or only after a longer acquaintance? In the three stories which follow we see a sample of variability in maturation.

These two people met at a dance hall and end up in bed together. Afterwards, he leaves. He enjoyed himself a lot because he hadn't been with a woman for a long time. He goes home feeling very good.

When she met him she liked him immediately. He reminded her of a lost pup. She immediately took him in hand in her friendly way and they started having dinner together after work. Then one evening he suggested that she come to his apartment so they could talk. She went and he began to tell her how much knowing her had meant to him. She was very touched and then the last thing she expected happened. He came over and kissed her passionately and told her that he wanted her. She tries to look shocked but he's so impulsive and childlike that she finds herself kissing him back. She's more excited than she ever thought she could be. Suddenly she wants to give herself to him—his need of her is so great.

These people have known each other for years. They both work in the same place and were always interested in each other. One night they're leaving the office, both having been working late at night. He waits for her to turn out the lights and as she comes through the hall they're very close together and there's a sort of animal magnetism in the air. The next thing they know, they're in each other's arms.

b) *Duration*

Duration of the sexual relationship is a dimension which may vary independently of its maturation.

This is a girl this fellow has picked up. Here we see him full of remorse. He vows he will never see her again.

Shown here are a man and his mistress. They have come to a parting of the ways. They have had a lot of fun together but lately they are getting on each other's nerves, and this is it.

He's married but he's been having an affair with this woman. They can't get married because of his wife and children. So I guess they'll just go on like this.

B. The Vicissitudes of the Sexual Relationship

It is a commentary on the relative importance of the love and sex need in American culture that although the heroes of TAT stories are concerned with the duration of the love relationship, it is a very exceptional hero who is anxious about the duration of a strictly sexual relationship. Though the hero's life may be shattered by the disruption of a love relationship, there are no such sequelae to the disruption of a sex relationship nor are the poignant attempts to reconstitute a disrupted love relationship ever paralleled in the quest of a lost sex object. But if the sex need is taken less seriously in this respect, it is nonetheless beset with anxieties peculiar to the particular pressures of American culture.

I. DEGREE OF INHIBITION OF SEXUAL BEHAVIOR

The most extreme degree of inhibition of the sex need is exemplified by those individuals who are incapable of experiencing sexual feeling of any kind or of entertaining any sexual phantasies. We sometimes find this extreme inhibition attributed to the hero of a story.

This woman never married. She's an old maid. She's not like most old maids. She was never interested in the things that interested other women, and she never wanted to get married. She spent her life doing good works among the poor and she's perfectly content.

A less severe degree of inhibition allows the individual awareness of his wishes but at the cost of severe endopsychic conflict.

This man is being torn asunder by the struggle between his natural desires and the voice of his conscience. He finally masters his feelings and his conscience gives him peace.

Somewhat less inhibited is the individual who can accept his own sexuality but who fears the rejection of his wishes by other individuals.

He's thinking of the girl he met tonight. He's thinking of how he would like to take her in his arms, but he's afraid that she would be shocked by the depth of his feelings. Finally, he goes to sleep.

Fear of the consequences, or anticipatory guilt, may completely inhibit the expression of the sex need, as in the following stories.

He's wondering if he should sleep with her. Maybe he is wondering if he will get V.D. if this is someone he has picked up, or maybe he is wondering if he will be impotent. He decides it isn't worth taking the chance.

The girl is tight and the man has taken her home. He knows that he could seduce her tonight, but he knows he'll feel ashamed if he does. So he leaves.

Or sexual behavior may be permitted some expression but never consummated because of guilt, fear of the consequences, or feelings of inadequacy.

This young impulsive young man has been violently in love with this woman. He has known her but little and has at no time been with her in any intimate situations. Through a coincidence, he and the girl manage to end up in his small apartment. He makes an attempt to become familiar with her in a physical sense and she refutes him. He offers her a soft drink which he dopes, then undresses her, puts her in his cot, and covers her over. At this point of this picture, he has just picked up the cover to see her bare breasts and is instantly struck with the deep sense of having done wrong. He dresses her, revives her, tells her that she has fainted, and they part friends, the woman never knowing what has happened and he all the more capable of controlling his emotions for the present.

The couple in the picture have sneaked up to her room in the boarding house to have some fun. They're both a little tight and quite excited. But, as he starts to undress her, they both start to think of what might happen—supposing she gets pregnant, supposing someone finds out about it. This has a sobering effect on both of them and it doesn't seem like as much fun as it did—they feel sort of let down. So he kisses her goodnight and leaves.

This poor guy wants to go to bed with this girl, but he's so afraid of being impotent that half the time he ends up that way just because he's afraid. She's luring him on and gets into bed with her breast exposed. He's excited but he's so afraid of making a fool of himself that he walks out and leaves her wondering what happened.

Or the sexual act may be consummated, with remorse or fear of consequences following the act.

The girl has just previously had (illicit) sexual intercourse for the first time in her life. Now she is very unhappily thinking about the consequences. The chances of having a baby, of getting a bad reputation, etc., all run through her mind. This experience will greatly affect this girl, who, because of the surroundings, seems to be poor. She will in the future try to do nothing amiss and aim her relationship with males towards marriage.

This fellow has just had intercourse with this woman. It is the first time for both of them. She's asleep and he's disgusted with himself because he realizes that he doesn't love her and that she will be hurt. He leaves her a note saying that it will be better if he never sees her again, that he leave before he does any more harm.

This is an obvious case of rape from the picture. The girl is motionless, indicating that she is unaware of the action that has taken place. The man from the pained expression on his face, and the fact that he has his arm in front of his eyes is terribly ashamed and full of remorse. He sits beside her until she comes to in an attempt to square himself with her. He appears to have some strength of character in his face despite his cowardly act.

Strong inhibition of the sexual need may appear in the stories in a more oblique way. Thus in stories told by individuals who suffer severe anxiety or guilt concerning their sexual wishes, the hero may be allowed to consummate the sexual act, but the consequences are extreme. The individual either takes his life, is imprisoned, or killed.

They had been posing for a portrait. That was all right, in and of itself. But, they were also very madly and emotionally in love. The artist had gone out of the room for a few moments, and in that time the two models had been behaving outrageously. They were making love in a barbaric way. Just then the artist's wife appeared in the room carrying her baby. She was furious and disgusted. The female model was shy and afraid, but the other model wasn't the least bit worried. The wife asked them to dress immediately and leave. Her husband was far ahead enough in his work so that he didn't need them any longer. But the wife didn't leave it at that. She spread the story about and made it appear as filthy and disgusting as possible. There was really no need for that. The young couple were not accepted anywhere, either as friends or as models. Finally, they gave up in despair and committed suicide together.

This is a picture of a Peeping Tom who's been causing a great commotion in the neighborhood by looking in windows and watching the women get undressed. The men of the neighborhood have organized a group to look for him. He hears them coming and slides down the rope to try to get away. He gets away this time, but they finally catch him.

Stories of sexual wishes or behavior which end in guilt on the one hand or punishment by some external force on the other, are generally representative of the degree of introjection of conscience with respect to sexuality. The individual who feels remorse for his sexuality has introjected the parental or societal dictate to a greater extent than the individual who sees himself being imprisoned for sexuality. This is illustrated in one case * analyzed by the writer in which either guilt or punishment by the law followed the consummation of the sex act. These sequelae occurred, however, in alternation so that when the hero of the story felt guilt there was no external punishment and when there was external punishment, no guilt feelings were expressed. In the following two stories from this protocol we see the alternation of these sequelae.

The man has succeeded in getting the woman drunk and then having intercourse with her. Now, he is getting ready to leave but he cannot quite coordinate between drunkenness and sleepiness. He knows he must leave but he doesn't know why. He forgets his suit coat, and out on the street he is arrested.

The man is very drunk. In this condition he has gone to see the woman shown here. She has gotten undressed and into bed and is now pretending to pay no attention to him and to be disinterested. He is getting undressed in order to get into bed with her. In the moment shown, he has gained some of his faculties and is at this moment thinking how wrong it is to do this thing he has contemplated. Immediately, however, liquor will cloud his mind and his body will take control. Afterwards, he will probably be very upset about it.

In another story from the same protocol the hero himself tells us of the existence of this alternation.

The boy is a collector of old wood and is very much attracted to the block holding the library bell up. When the guard is not looking, he whittles off a piece and rushes out. Later, he comes back and starts to glue it on but is caught and put into jail for 99½ years. He escaped from jail but then he failed to get guilt feelings. So, he got so worried he turned himself in.

Finally, there are stories in which the consummation of the sex act proceeds without incident. This does not necessarily signify that the individual telling the story enjoys the same degree of freedom in sexual behavior. In the case just cited, for example, where references both to remorse and to incarceration and death for the expression of sexual wishes are frequent, we also find the following story in which the hero is unhampered by inhibition.

* This is the subject who was given daily TAT's.

The woman has been lying in the dark, naked. A man she knows is staying in the same house. She has had the servant tell him his room was the one she is now in. The man has opened the door and the light shines on her body. Realizing the charms of her body, she merely turns her head aside as if to betoken modesty. He stammers an apology and starts to leave but seeing that she doesn't seem to mind his presence he stays to "chat." They spend the night together.

The key to an understanding of this paradox lies in the phrase "she doesn't seem to mind" as well as in the woman's general initiative in the sexual relationship. Whenever the hero initiates the sexual relationship, either the woman minds very much, breaking off the relationship completely, or he is overcome with remorse or imprisoned. The story tells us the unique condition under which he might be able to express his sexual wishes. Contrast the above story with the following, also told by this subject.

This couple are dancing together. They have been old friends for a long time. Now the man tells the woman that he loves her. He kisses her lightly on the forehead. In a moment, he'll kiss her passionately on the lips. Then she'll tell him that she doesn't love him and not to put her in a position where she'll have to forfeit his friendship by not allowing him to see her.

The man while suddenly kissing the girl on the cheek bit her cheek. He apologized profusely—he could [slip of the pen] tell why he had done it. No avail—their acquaintance was broken off.

Stories of uninhibited consummation of sexuality may be told by extremely inhibited individuals, as above, but they may also mean what they seem to say: that sex is not beset with crippling anxieties. As in any interpretation of a single story, this can only be determined by an analysis of the entire protocol.

2. NATURE OF INHIBITION OF SEXUAL BEHAVIOR

Having considered the range of inhibition of the sexual need, let us turn to a closer examination of the nature of these inhibitions.

a) *Exogenous sources*

As we have noted in previous examples, sexual behavior may be inhibited by a variety of fears stemming primarily from exogenous sources.

Common to both men and women is a fear of pregnancy, particularly in premarital relations.

Joe was always a conscientious guy and he worried a lot about the family's financial situation, and Paul was, on the contrary, very heedless. He didn't have any sense of responsibility. As they grew older, started getting aware of life, they sort of broke away from the gang. They started going around about 14 or 15—very young—with girls who were going around with each other and they also started quite early having sexual intercourse with them. Joe was always afraid of it and was afraid if she were to have a baby—and Paul didn't worry much because he wasn't responsible. Joe, when he was about 17, he became, against his wishes, a father. So he married the girl. He was poor and she was poor and he didn't have money to support the girl and he had to help his mother, too.

Another source of anxiety is the possibility of disease.

He's wondering if he should sleep with her. Maybe he is wondering if he will get V.D. if this is someone he has picked up; or maybe he is wondering if he will be impotent. He decides it isn't worth taking the chance.

Or the individual may fear general social disapprobation if his sexual behavior should be discovered.

This couple have just had intercourse and he's worried about how he's going to get out of the building without being seen. He tiptoes all the way out and jumps at his own shadow. When he finally gets out, he breathes a sigh of relief, but he thinks they shouldn't go on like this—supposing he had been caught.

Or more specifically, he may fear arrest or imprisonment for his sexual behavior.

This guy has just committed rape. He raped this girl. She's passed out and he knows he's got to get out of there. He's afraid he'll be caught. He passes a cop on the street and he has a terrific impulse to run. He's afraid the girl will report it; so he takes the next train out of town.

Rejection, however, may be feared only from the sexual object.

The guy's worrying. He's been out for the evening and come in and he can't sleep. So he's standing in front of the open window, worrying. He's worried. He was out with a girl he likes a lot. He kissed her goodnight and almost was more passionate than he meant to be. He's worried about whether she noticed it and whether she thought he was too forward.

b) *Endogenous Sources*

The individual's anxiety may, on the other hand, have its primary source within the individual. Thus, he may feel generally inadequate and sexually impotent.

This poor guy wants to go to bed with this girl, but he's so afraid of being impotent that half the time he ends up that way just because he's afraid. She's luring him on and gets into bed with her breast exposed. He's excited, but he's so afraid of making a fool of himself that he walks out and leaves her wondering what happened.

Or his ideals may conflict with the free expression of his sexual wishes.

> This man is being torn asunder by the struggle between his natural desires and the voice of his conscience. He finally masters his feelings and his conscience gives him peace.

Or the inhibition may stem from the social definition of acceptable sexual expression which the hero has introjected.

> This girl and boy are both virgins. They're going to be married and they decide there's no sense in waiting—a few days doesn't make any difference. They're in her room in the hotel and she's half undressed and they're both pretty much carried away by emotion—but all of a sudden he gets up and says "No, it shouldn't be this way, everything should be perfect, we'll be married in a few days and then you'll be my wife. We can wait until then."

III. INTERPRETATION OF THE DIMENSIONS OF THE LOVE, MARITAL AND SEX REGIONS

Having sampled some of the dimensions important in the analysis of the love, marital, and sex region, we shall now consider the interpretation of these dimensions for the light this may throw on the adjustment of the individual in the love and sex region and to illustrate techniques of interpretation which may also be used in the analysis of parent-child and social relationships.*

Case of Nancy

It should again be stressed that there is no simple relationship between phantasy productions and the personality of the individual. We cannot on inspection of a story, for example, which ends in suicide after an unhappy love affair, assume either that the individual has had an unhappy love affair or expects to, or that he is going to commit suicide or expects he would if he were rejected. As we have seen in the previous discussion of multifactor analysis, it may have one of many meanings. Its exact meaning can be ascertained only by a comparison of this story with other stories told by the same individual and, sometimes, only by further information from other

---

* We have omitted this type of analysis in the family and social regions so that we might consider in greater detail other types of regional analysis, which are also applicable to this region. Thus we might have inquired in the case of love and sex, as we did in connection with the family, into the general importance of the region in the economy of the individual. The same criteria, e.g., introduction of love objects, number of love stories, range of impact of the love region on other regions, and conflict with other regions, may be used in the assessment of the importance of love and sex for the individual. We may also analyze changes in the love relationship as a function of the age of the hero. The impact of other regions on love may also be analyzed. We will assume that the application of the general methods employed in other regions does not require detailed illustration here.

sources. In general, we must employ those techniques of analysis outlined in Chapter IV, if we are to avoid the pitfalls of our own projective mechanism in interpretation.

Consider the following story told by a young woman, whom we have called Nancy.

> It's very late at night and this girl has come down to the beach by herself. This other girl in the picture isn't there at all, this is just an image of the other girl as she sees herself. She's very depressed and alone and has come to the beach because she wants to dream. She's thinking of a time in the past when she was down here with a man. They were at a dance and came here and had a quarrel and she ran away and he didn't follow her and he just left and she never saw him again. It was a couple of years ago. What she does is come down to remember him and see herself as she was. I don't know what happens to her. She never sees him again but jumps into the water and drowns herself.

How shall we interpret this story? Is this individual on the point of suicide? Has she been rejected? Is this a picture of what she would do if she were rejected? On the basis of this story any of these interpretations are plausible. But let us turn to another story.

> She isn't half as miserable as she looks. She's had a fight with someone in the other room behind her, probably a man. She wants him to think that she's quite miserable. She's young and she's seen too many movies and she's waiting for him to call her back. She really isn't crying underneath that hair. He's too smart and he doesn't call her, and she has nothing to do but close the door. After that she really is unhappy and so she learns her lesson and grows up.

Here we see the story of another quarrel and another rejection, but there is no suicide even though she "really is unhappy." Why then does she commit suicide in one case and not in the other? We can clearly discard one hypothesis—that rejection is the cause of suicide—since she is rejected in both stories. Nor can we now accept the hypothesis that she is on the point of suicide since this is not an invariant outcome. We must then examine these two stories for those differences which might provide an explanation. In the second story, she solves her problem by this formula: "She learns her lesson and grows up." Is there anything in the first story which would make it impossible for the heroine to "grow up?" We are told that she has "come to the beach because she wants to dream." This suggests an antithesis between introversion, the cathexis of the inner world, and a more realistic "growing up." With this as a hypothesis, let us see if there is any corroborating evidence that introversion is dangerous and that it leads to suicide. We find this evidence in another story.

This is a girl who has—she's like Miniver Cheevy, sort of, she's looking at the various paintings, and she wishes she could be living in some other time and she's just a schoolgirl and an introvert and she thinks also that the girl in the picture she's looking at is someone like her, a dreamer, and also wishing she were somewhere else besides the farm. This girl wants to get away from school and all the things that everybody else is doing. She wants to be free of all conventions. She "looks and looks and goes on reading" instead of "drinking." I don't know what will happen to her, I think that she'll probably commit suicide like Virginia Woolf. She won't ever be happy.

This is further evidence for discarding the hypothesis that it is rejection which produces suicide since suicide is here otherwise produced, and as we saw before, rejection may or may not result in suicide. We now can better understand why "dreaming" and "introversion" lead to suicide, since this inner life is centered on a wish to throw off convention. On the basis of this evidence, a further hypothesis is suggested: that the contrast between introversion, dreaming, and growing up is also a contrast between an unconventional and a conventional life, and that the unconventional life ends in suicide. If this were the case, we should expect to find other stories in which people who live unconventional lives also commit suicide. We find, on inspection of other stories, evidence that women who do unconventional things die, although they do not commit suicide.

This is a very nice fine girl. And she is a secretary to this man. She came from Peoria to New York City, very nice and innocent. He asks her to go out with him and he takes her up to his apartment. Right here he's asking her if she'll have a drink and she's very shocked and then he convinces her it's all right to drink, it's the thing to do. She takes a drink and gets drunk and he seduces her. Then she tries, the next day thinks whether she should go back to Peoria or stay in New York, now that she's a little confused about everything. All sorts of awful things are going to happen to her; she's such a dope! She has an abortion and she dies and that's the end of her.

We have evidence, then, that an unconventional life may lead either to suicide or death. Suicide is preceded by the wish to lead such a life; death by the innocent and transitory unconventional act. We also find a story in which a woman is reviewing her life and remembering a feeling of excitement and then goes back to Italy to die.

This is an old woman talking of the time when she was young. She's—the time she's thinking of is when she first came to America. She came from Italy and she's remembering herself and how glad she was to get here, the whole feeling of excitement and life, and she's thinking of the life she's had. At this point now, she's on a ship going back to Italy. She's going back to die.

Thus we see that, in addition to an unconventional life, the memory of a feeling of excitement is followed by death. Our hypothesis would then have to be that leading an unconventional life or dreaming about it or remembering a feeling of excitement may be dangerous. We must look, then for negative evidence. Do people who act unconventionally or who are dissatisfied with the prosaic, everyday quality of their lives, ever escape death?

We find such negative evidence in the following story.

> This man's tired of his life, tired of the common prosaic things; and he's looking up into the sky thinking that there is something real because he's found nothing real in his life. After a while he closes the window, puts on the light in his room, and comes back to things he had to do. Possibly studying, possibly he's a student. He forgets pretty easily that he was so discontented for a minute.

How can we explain the fact that this story presents an individual tired of the common prosaic things, but for whom there is neither suicide nor death? We might first suppose that it is because he "forgets pretty easily that he was so discontented for a minute." We have seen before that the girl who "learns her lesson and grows up" escapes suicide. It may be the characteristic of the mature individual in general. But it may stem from the fact that the hero is a man. If this were the case, we should expect to find that, when men do what is unconventional, there are no serious consequences; but that when women do the same thing, they die. This proved to be the case, as we see in the following two stories.

> This girl killed her sister. Her sister is, er, younger than (she). She's always been the more attractive and intelligent and the girl who's killing her has been jealous. And the climax came when the younger sister stole the other girl's boy friend away from her. They had a terrible fight and the younger sister is still talking now and saying, "You won't kill me"; and finally, the older sister stops; she doesn't kill her; and eventually she kills herself.

> This is Jack the Ripper. It's in London and he has with him the heads of the bodies inside the bag he's carrying. He's had a very interesting evening! Killed a few people here and there, lots of fun. He's going back to his room and nail the bodies up on the wall or something. I'm not quite sure what he does with them.

In the first story, the heroine kills her sister, but later decides she cannot go through with it, and kills herself. In the second story, however, a man, Jack the Ripper, commits murder which results in nothing more than "a very interesting evening." Men, then, can either accept the prosaic more easily or behave unconventionally with relative impunity. If this difference in the sex of the characters is the crucial one, we might expect that this young woman would rather be a man; and such is, indeed, the case, as we see in the following story.

> She's sitting in a room looking out of a window and she's watching her brothers and their friends outside playing baseball. It's spring. She's very proud

of her brothers but she's also wishing she were a boy and could play with them, too. She's about fifteen years old. What happens to her is, she reverts from her tomboy wishes and aspirations and becomes extremely feminine in a couple of years. She sort of realizes she can't be a boy, subconsciously, and she decides that, if she can't, at least she wants them to notice her some way or other, and she does it by becoming very popular so that all her brothers' friends take her out.

The conflict between her wish to be a boy and the knowledge that she can never be one is here resolved by her "adoption" of a feminine role. The outcome here, as in the story in which she "grows up" is not an altogether unhappy one. There is no suggestion of death or suicide. But her preference for the male role is indicated by her portrayal of men as either more capable of easily throwing off discontent with a prosaic life or more able to commit antisocial action without punishment or death.

Summary of the Case of Nancy

From an initial story of a suicide which appeared to be the result of rejection in love, we saw that rejection need not lead to suicide if the heroine "learns her lesson" and "grows up," and that the heroine who did commit suicide comes to the beach "because she wants to dream." From this, we hypothesized an antithesis between introversion, with too much emphasis placed on dreaming, and extroversion, which is realistic and free of the dangers of introversion. We found further evidence that day-dreaming and intro-version led to suicide, and that this introversion concerned itself with the unconventional life, away from the everyday prosaic life of the heroine. This suggested the hypothesis that the antithesis between dreaming and "growing up" reflected a conflict between two ways of life—the conventional and the unconventional—that dreaming of the unconventional life, as well as living it, was dangerous, and that growing up and leading a more conventional life was safe. We found evidence for this hypothesis in the fact that illicit sexual relations ended in death for one heroine and that the memory of a feeling of excitement in the case of another heroine was followed by death. Negative evidence appeared in the story of a man who, discontented with his prosaic life, was able easily to forget his discontent. The question arose whether he was able to do this because he was a man or because of his maturity. We tested these alternatives by looking for differential outcomes for males and females committing the same type of antisocial behavior and found that the difference in sex was the crucial factor. A man who killed enjoyed himself; a woman who killed, or wished to kill, killed herself. We had, therefore, to qualify our hypothesis and say that unconventional living or excitement is followed by death or suicide only in the case of women, and for this reason supposed that this woman would rather be a man. This proved to be the case. Consequently, the dichotomy between the danger which issued from excitement and unconventional living, or daydreaming about such a life, and the safety engendered by a mature, extraverted acceptance of the prosaic life, had to be broadened to include a conflict between a masculine, active, and unconventional way of life and a feminine, passive, prosaic life.

We have thus been told why there is a dichotomy between an active, exciting, unconventional life and a passive, prosaic way of life. The difference is that between the life of a boy and the life of a girl who wanted to remain a tomboy. Even in later life, the male is portrayed as the unfettered executive of his most antisocial wishes. We have yet to explain why a man may lead an exciting life without danger, but a woman dies or commits suicide as a consequence of unconventional living or as the consequence of even the wish to lead such a life or the feeling of excitement in remembering such a life.

The answer to this question is not to be found in the TAT. This protocol was originally analyzed "blind," without any knowledge of the case, and this was as far as the analysis could be carried on the basis of the protocol itself. The most crucial factor in this case found no direct reflection in the TAT. Nancy had in her childhood been a tomboy, but at the age of 5 contracted rheumatic fever and was taken to Florida each winter until she was 12. She reported that she was not much handicapped by her condition since "almost all the kids down there were sick," but that when she came back to New York each spring she did notice her restrictions. Her mother never told her how serious her condition was, although Nancy understood this from the fact that her mother always talked to the doctor alone and tried to keep her from overhearing. She has been told to smoke no more than three cigarettes a day but ignores this completely. There are limitations on her physical activity, however, which she does observe. Thus, she would like to take up modern dancing but "won't be allowed to."

We see, then, that Nancy's fear of the unconventional, active, exciting life has a very realistic basis in the possibility of heart failure and that it was complicated by her wish to be a tomboy, which was renounced with regret. It is of considerable significance that this was never mentioned in the TAT, although the derivatives of this fear do appear. We have no explanation for this, and it is the more puzzling in view of her short stories concerning which she tells us, "My short stories used to be very psychological. People would be very frightened of something. And they'd end up dying of heart failure, or something of that sort."

We have followed the leads presented by one story through these complex interrelationships to illustrate the meaning which may underlie a simple love story, and to show that although the protocol may be self illuminating, its complete interpretation may call for knowledge which must be sought from sources other than the TAT.

The story of an unhappy love affair revealed in the final analysis that a certain way of life may lead to death. This was discovered by an examination of the conditions under which love affairs ended in suicide and the conditions under which they ended less unhappily.

Thus suicide in a single story may mean that the conditions in this story are dangerous for the individual. In order to prove this it must be demonstrated that when the conditions which led to danger in the initial story are different in other stories there is safety for the heroes of these other stories. In the discussion of multifactor analysis in Chapter IV, we saw that any story might be an expression of the individual's central value, threats which beset him, invariances characteristic of the individual, or an expression of the conditions necessary for any element within the story.

In further illustration of this method of analysis, let us reconsider the first suicide story in the case just discussed, and see what meanings it might have had if the other stories in the protocol had been different.

I. CENTRAL VALUES

Let us suppose that the story had been an expression of the fact that satisfaction of her heterosexual love wish was her central value. If this had been the case we would have found other stories in which any threat to her love life would have seriously disturbed the heroine. We would have found, moreover, that in stories in which there were threats to her career, her family, or general social relationships, the heroine was not so disturbed.

2. THREAT

If however, the story had been an expression of her vulnerability to any threat of loss we would have found other stories in which the heroine suffered the loss of friends, parents, or job and reacted in the same suicidal fashion.

If, on the other hand, the story had been an expression of a general fear of any kind of frustration rather than fear of the specific threat of loss we would have found other stories which expressed a variety of frustrations all resulting in the death of the heroine.

Or the story might have expressed the individual's differential reaction to one type of threat—the threat of loss—and in that case other types of threat would have been more easily tolerated. We would have found other stories involving loss which resulted in death for the heroine, and still others involving another type of threat—lack of love objects, friends, or parents, for example—in which the heroine overcame these deficits.

Or the story might have expressed the individual's differential reaction to losses of varying magnitude. If this had been the case there would have been other stories involving losses of less serious magnitude which resulted in less serious disturbance. It would not be love as such which was crucial in this case, but the importance of the particular love object, or the permanency of the loss. For example, a lover's quarrel which was later resolved might cause distress but not suicide, since the loss of the love object was temporary; loss of one love object might be disturbing, whereas the loss of another more important love object might cause the heroine to commit suicide.

3. INVARIANT CHARACTERISTICS

Let us suppose that the story represented an invariant characteristic of the individual. If the story had expressed her invariant expectation that she would be disappointed in love, every other love story would have portrayed a rejected or frustrated heroine.

Or it might have expressed the more general expectation that she would inevitably be frustrated in all her wishes. If this had been so there would have been other stories in which her wishes, no matter what their nature, were frustrated.

It might, however, have been an expression of the fact that she invariably withdraws to the level of phantasy when she is frustrated. If this had been so there would have been other stories in which the heroine turned unhappily to introversion following frustration but was happily extraverted in stories in which she could satisfy her wishes.

The story might have been an expression of a basic self-destructive wish. Had this been the case all other stories, whatever else happened, would have ended in suicide.

Had this story represented the invariant reaction of a suicidal wish following rejection in love, we should have found other love stories in which there was no rejection and no suicide, and stories in which she was rejected by friends or parents and did not commit suicide.

4. NECESSARY CONDITIONS

On the other hand, the story might have been an expression of the necessary conditions for any element in the story. It might have defined the specific conditions which create suicidal wishes in the individual. If this had been the case there would have been other stories in which the heroine was not rejected and did not commit suicide or in which she was reconciled with her love object and did not commit suicide.

Thus we see that we may determine which of the conditions preceding the suicide in our single story, is actually responsible for it, by examining the conditions in other stories which do not lead to suicide.

RANGE OF VARIABILITY

This is the logic of multifactor analysis. Before it may be applied, however, the dimensions of the stories must be identified, and we must then determine the extent to which these dimensions vary. There are protocols in which the range of variability of any particular dimension is zero and others in which the range of variability is very great. The duration of a love relationship may be invariant in one protocol—all love relationships are eternal or transitory; but in other protocols some love affairs are transitory, others are of moderate duration, and some are eternal. These differences in the range of variability are found in every dimension we have considered. Where the range of variability of a dimension is zero, we may consider this presumptive evidence that the specific value of this dimension (that all love affairs are transitory, for example) represents some invariant characteristic of the individual telling the stories. It may represent his wish, his expectation or his behavior. This must be determined in other ways, but whatever the level, the invariance of the specific value of the dimension found in the stories generally represents something equally stable in the personality of the individual. In some protocols we may have no indication of the specific value of a particular dimension. For example, there may be no references whatever to the length of time required for the maturation of the relationship. In such cases, we would also consider the range of variability to be zero. The actual value of this dimension remains indeterminate; but, whatever its value, since we find no mention of it we assume that it is a constant in the mind of the storyteller. Suppose no outcomes are ever given. We do not know whether the individual cannot see an outcome to a love relationship or whether there is a typical outcome which is never mentioned; but, in the light of our evidence, we would assume zero variability for outcomes.

INTERPRETATION OF VARIABILITY

Although uniformity in any dimension is diagnostic of stable elements in the personality of the storyteller, variability in any dimension does not necessarily imply an *equivalent variability* in the personality. That is, if all stories end unhappily, we may assume that there is a particularly rigid expectation of unhappy outcomes to any love relationship into which the individual may enter. But, if some stories end happily and others end unhappily (with fine gradations of happiness and unhappiness in outcomes), we cannot assume simply that the individual expects sometimes to be happy and sometimes to be sad in the ratio of happy to unhappy endings. Again, if all stories tell of a long maturation and the slow ripening of acquaintance into love, we may assume that this is the individual's characteristic way of entering into a love relationship, or the conditions under which he might enter into a love relationship. But, if some of the stories depict hasty marriages and other stories tell of childhood sweethearts marrying after years of acquaintance, we clearly cannot assume that he will sometimes enter into hasty marriages and sometimes into more carefully considered relationships in the ratio in which these appear in the stories.

In general, variability which appears in any dimension must be explained in one of two ways. It must be shown either that this variability is the effect of differences in preceding conditions if in two or more stories or that these differences produce different effects in the stories into which they are introduced, or both.

For example, consider the following two stories.

These pepole work together in the same place. At first, he didn't pay much attention to her. But she was very kind and considerate and one day she offered to stay after work and help him finish his work. This makes a big impression on him. He accepts and afterwards he notices more and more how she always goes out of her way to do nice things for him and he comes to love her deeply.

This man and woman have known each other for a long time. They like to do things together, like going to plays and concerts together. They have a lot in common, and he likes her a lot. They will always be very good friends.

In these stories, the variability in intensity between "he comes to love her deeply" and "he likes her a lot," are effects of two different conditions. We may infer from these two stories that women who nurture the hero elicit intense feelings of love, and that women who are companionable elicit less intense feelings. We cannot be certain either that he actually has two such relationships or would wish to. We know only that different kinds of behavior on the part of women elicit variations in the intensity of his feelings.

In the stories which follow, variations of intensity of the hero's feelings produce variations in the outcome of the relationship.

This man loves her desperately. He has never before been so completely swept off his feet. He has just finished telling her of his feelings. She tells him that she likes him, but she can't marry him. He feels that she is laughing at him.

This is a picture of a proposal. He has just told her that she means a great deal to him and asked her to marry him. She says she will and they're sealing their engagement with a kiss.

In these two stories, we are told that, if the hero's feelings of love are too intense, they will not be returned in kind and that he will interpret this as rejection; but, when his feelings are less intense, they may be reciprocated.

Utilizing this type of analysis, complete interpretation of each region requires an explanation of the variability of those dimensions which exhibit any degree of variability as well as an examination of dimensions which are invariant. And, finally, these two sets of dimensions must be examined for their interrelationships.

Each of the dimensions illustrated in the love, marital, and sex region is capable of variation which is either the effect of variation in another dimension or the cause of such variation. Actually, such variability is not infrequently the resultant of the concomitant variation of a number of other dimensions. But were we to restrict our analysis to those cases in which the variability was a function of only one other dimension, we would find that the inter-relationships between the definition of the situation, reciprocity, intensity, temporal characteristics, source of disruption, maintenance or disruption without further specification would number thirty. In any one protocol, however, the important functional relationships are usually simple and limited. But if one considers the population of all TAT protocols, the actual variety of such functional relationships, while finite, is extremely great, since specific aspects of each dimension may vary independently and a dimension may vary as a function of the variability of sets of dimensions.

Documentation of these varieties of functional relationships would require encyclopedic treatment beyond the scope of this book, but we shall present some of the more common and more simple of these functional relationships which have been found in the analysis of a variety of TAT protocols. These examples are, however, but a sample of even the most common of these relationships.

A. DEFINITION OF THE SITUATION

1. *As a Cause*

As a dimension responsible for variation in any other dimension, some common resultants are the following: a) *Reciprocity*. The hero reciprocates nurturant love and rejects dependent love. The hero reciprocates the love of companionable love objects and rejects domineering love objects. The love object rejects the love of a dependent hero and reciprocates the love of a nurturant hero.

b) *Intensity*. The hero feels strongly toward nurturant love objects and less so toward companionable love objects. He has little intensity of feeling toward love objects he possesses and feels more strongly toward love objects who are aloof. The hero's feelings toward a beautiful love object are intense, and less intense toward a love object of less beauty, or he has intense feelings toward a beautiful love object and less intense feelings toward a nurturant love object. The love object responds to the hero's dominance with intense love and to his nurturance with less intense love.

c) *Temporal characteristics.* Marriages based on nurturance and dependence endure while those based on companionship are short-lived. Relationships based on dominance and submission endure while those based on the esthetic quality of the love object do not endure.

d) *Sources of disruption.* Relationships based on the esthetic quality of the love object are subject to disruption from exogenous sources, while relationships based on companionship are not subject to disruption from exogenous sources. Relationships based on submission to dominance result in disruption from endogenous sources while those based on dependence do not.

e) *Maintenance or disruption.* If disruption is suffered, the type of relationship determines whether reconciliation is possible. Thus, a relationship based on companionship is reconciled while a relationship based on possession of the loved object can not be reconciled. When the love object is submissive to the hero the relationship is reconciled but when the love object dominates the hero the relationship cannot be reconciled.

Where the relationship is based on possession of the love object, finding another love object may be impossible, but where it is based on esthetic enjoyment of the love object, the hero finds someone else he can love. Where the relationship is based on companionship, the hero is able to find satisfaction in another region; but where the hero dominates the love object this is not possible.

2. Definition of the Situation as Effect

a) *Reciprocity.* If his love is reciprocated, the hero wishes to take care of his love object; but if his love is not reciprocated, he wishes to dominate the love object. If the hero is uncertain of the reciprocity of love he wishes to be dependent; when love is reciprocated then the wish is to take care of the love object.

b) *Intensity.* If the hero's wishes are not very intense he desires no more than companionship; when his wishes are more intense he desires another type of relationship, e.g., to be possessive.

c) *Temporal characteristics.* If a relationship has existed for a long period of time, then sexual relations suddenly become possible; whereas if the relationship has existed for only a short period of time, the hero does not have sexual relations.

d) *Sources of disruption.* An exogenous disrupter changes a relationship from one of dependence to one of possession; but if there is no exogenous disrupter it remains a dependent relationship.

e) *Maintenance or disruption.* Reconciliation of one type changes a relationship from a possessive one to one based on companionship, whereas reconciliation of another type leaves the possessive relationship unchanged. If there is no disruption there is no change in the relationship; if there is disruption, however, there is a change in the kind of relationship desired by the hero.

B. RECIPROCITY

1. *As a Cause*

a) *Intensity.* The reciprocity of love increases the intensity of the hero's feelings of love; lack of reciprocity decreases their intensity.

b) *Temporal characteristics.* Reciprocated love produces an enduring relationship. If love is not reciprocated the hero's feelings do not endure.

c) *Sources of disruption.* Unreciprocated love leaves the individual open to exogenous sources of disruption. Reciprocated love, on the other hand, leaves the individual open to endogenous sources of disruption.

d) *Maintenance or disruption.* Unreciprocated love allows no reconciliation in the event of disruption of the relationship. Reciprocated love allows reconciliation after disruption.

2. *As an Effect*

a) *Intensity.* The more intense the feelings of the hero, the more they are reciprocated. If the hero's feelings are less intense they are not reciprocated.

b) *Temporal characteristics.* In enduring relationships the hero's feelings are not altogether reciprocated. In relationships which are transitory the hero does not altogether reciprocate the feelings of the love object. Slow maturation results in reciprocity on the part of the love object; fast maturation results in a lack of reciprocity.

c) *Sources of disruption.* Exogenous disruption leads to reciprocity of love afterwards, Endogenous disruption leads to the hero's unreciprocated wish for the love object.

d) *Maintenance or disruption.* Reconciliation leads to a new reciprocity of love; no reconciliation leads to the hero's unreciprocated wish for the love object.

C. INTENSITY

1. *As a Cause*

a) *Temporal characteristics.* Intense love relationships do not last; less intense relationships are more enduring.

b) *Sources of disruption.* Intensity of feeling on the part of the hero leads to endogenous disruption. Less intense feelings on the part of the hero lead to exogenous disruption.

c) *Maintenance or disruption.* Intense feelings lead to reconciliation in the event of disruption; less intense feelings lead to no attempt at reconciliation.

2. *As an Effect*

a) *Temporal characteristics.* If a relationship has endured, it results in increased intensity of feeling; if the relationship has existed for only a short while, feeling is less intense.

b) *Sources of disruption.* If the disruption arises from exogenous sources, the hero's feelings decrease in intensity; if the disruption arises from endogenous sources, the hero's feelings increase in intensity.

c) *Maintenance or disruption.* If there is reconciliation after disruption, feelings decrease in intensity; if there is no reconciliation, feelings increase in intensity.

D. TEMPORAL CHARACTERISTICS

1. *As a Cause*

a) *Sources of disruption.* If the relationship has matured slowly, it is open to disruption from exogenous sources; if the relationship has matured rapidly it is open to disruption from endogenous sources.

b) *Maintenance or disruption.* If the relationship has been long-enduring, reconciliation is possible; if it has existed for only a short time and there is disruption, reconciliation is impossible.

2. *As an Effect*

a) *Sources of disruption.* If the relationship has been disrupted from exogenous sources (the death of the love object), the relationship is preserved in the memory of the hero. If the relationship has been disrupted by endogenous forces, the relationship does not endure, and neither the hero nor his love object wish that it had endured.

b) *Maintenance or disruption.* If the relationship is reconciled it endures, but, if it is disrupted and there is no attempt at reconciliation, it does not endure.

E. SOURCES OF DISRUPTION

1. *As a Cause*

a) *Maintenance or disruption.* If disruption arises from exogenous sources, the lovers are reconciled; if it arises from endogenous sources, no reconciliation is possible.

2. As an Effect

a) *Maintenance or disruption.* If a relationship has suffered disruption and has then been reconciled, it is open to further disruption from endogenous sources.

We have, in these samples of functional interrelationships, considered primarily the variations in specific values of the dimensions of the love region. The same type of analysis may be applied to the sex region. Further, the same type of analysis may be applied comparing the variability of dimensions in both love and sex. For example, it may be asked whether the definitions of the love and sexual situations are the same, or different; and if they differ, in what direction and for what reason. It may further be asked whether there are differences in the duration, the relative intensity, liability to disruption, and potentiality of regeneration.

In these illustrations of the functional relationships between dimensions of the love region, we have excluded from consideration all the interrelationships which may and do exist between this region and other regions and between this region and the personality structure of the individual whose activity in this limited region has been isolated from the larger matrix.

SUMMARY

In Part I we considered those dimensions of the love and marital region important to the individual's adjustment in this area. We first examined the nature of the relationship, inquiring into the individual's definition of the love relationship. It was shown that different individuals are in quest of diverse gratifications in their love life. Some of the more common of these are wishes to be dependent, to care for the love object, to govern or be governed, to possess the love object, to share intimacies, or derive esthetic enjoyment from the love object.

We next considered the degree of reciprocity in the love relationship, illustrating relationships which represented the middle and end points of a continuum ranging from complete mutuality to complete lack of reciprocity.

The intensity of the feeling of love was seen to be independent of the nature of the love relationship and the extent to which it might be reciprocated.

We next examined the temporal dimension, illustrating differences in the rate of maturation of the love relationship and the length of time the relationships endure. We said that the relationship might outlast the feelings of love, or the feelings continue after the relationship is broken; that the feelings might continue only as long as the relationship was maintained or the relationship might be maintained only as long as the feelings of love continued.

We then inquired into the vicissitudes of the love relationship, examining first the sources of disruption. There were seen to be threats either exogenous or endogenous in origin. We then considered the extent to which these threats might disrupt the relationship. We saw that if these threats were successfully met this might be achieved through a common sorrow, or reformation, or the hero's new appreciation of the qualities of the love object, or through the acceptance of a lower love income. When the relationship is completely disrupted the individual may never relinquish the possibility of future reconciliation or may seek symbolic reunion in death. The disruption of the love relationship may result in further disruption of the individual's life, or he may seek another love object, or satisfaction in some other region. These attempts may or may not be successful. Another sequel of a disrupted love relationship is aggression directed either against the love object or the self. Suicide was seen to be an instrumental act providing an escape from inner misery rather than an expression of a wish to destroy the self.

In Part II we examined the dimensions of the sex region, since there is, in our society, sufficient discrepancy in the expression of love and sex to justify a separate scrutiny of the dimensions of these two regions. In general the same dimensions were found useful in both regions. But although every type of love relationship has its sexual counterpart, the individual may define the love relationship quite differently from the sexual relationship. Thus an individual may seek gratification of his dependency wish in love or marriage, but wish to dominate his sexual partner. We then examined stories for evidence of homosexual wishes. We distinguished identification with the opposite sex, wish to be of opposite sex, and love objects of the opposite sex. We saw that these were independent variables, that whether one loves members of the same or the opposite sex is not determined either by identification with same or the opposite sex or by the wish to be of the opposite sex or one's own sex.

We then examined the degree of reciprocity in the sexual relationship and the intensity and the temporal characteristics of the sex need.

Next we discussed the vicissitudes of the sexual relationship. We noted that although the heroes of TAT stories are concerned with the duration of the love relationship, it was a very exceptional hero who was anxious about the duration of a strictly sexual relationship, and that although the hero's life might be shattered by the disruption of a love relationship, there are no such sequelae to the disruption of a sexual relationship, nor are the poignant attempts to reconstitute a disrupted love relationship ever paralleled in the quest of a lost sex object. But if the sex need is taken less seriously in this respect, it is nonetheless beset with anxieties peculiar to the particular pressures of American society. We examined first the varieties of degree of inhibition of sexual behavior, ranging from the individual who is incapable of experiencing sexual feeling to those who may consummate the sexual act but with acute remofse or anxiety thereafter. Less frequently in TAT stories does the hero consummate the sexual act with enjoyment and no remorse or fear. We saw that the sources of this inhibition might be exogenous or endogenous.

In Part III we undertook the interpretation of these dimensions of the love, marital, and sex regions. We examined one protocol in some detail to illustrate the dependence of interpretation on the pattern of the whole protocol, and in this case on information which was not revealed in the TAT. We examined again the multiplicity of meanings which any single story may express, using the techniques of multifactor analysis outlined in Chapter IV. We saw that the meaning of a single love story of a girl who takes her life, depended entirely on the concomitant variation between elements of this story, and other stories. We said further that the dimensions of any region must first be described in terms of their range of variability. Those dimensions which were invariant were assumed to represent stable elements in the personality of the individual telling the story. Those dimensions which varied throughout the protocols had to be explained either as the cause of other effects in the stories in which they were introduced, or as the effects of other causes. Finally, in interpreting the protocol, the invariant and variable dimensions had to be related to each other.

We examined systematically some of the more common functional relationships between dimensions of the love region. We excluded from consideration all the interrelationships which may and do exist between this region and other regions, and this region and the personality structure of the individual whose activity in this limited region has been isolated from the larger matrix.

CHAPTER VIII

DIAGNOSIS OF PERSONALITY: THE REGION OF SOCIAL RELATIONSHIPS

Every region thus far considered involves social relationships to some extent: interaction between parent and child, between employer and worker, and between lovers all constitute social relationships. But since these have been considered elsewhere, only the residuum will be the topic of this chapter. We have further limited the scope of our inquiry, even within this narrowly conceived sphere, to antisocial behavior. We have focused on this sector of social relationships in view of the importance of the control of antisocial wishes in the socialization of the individual and the difficulties inherent in investigating wishes which the normally socialized individual usually guards from public scrutiny. As we have seen before, the TAT is peculiarly sensitive in exposing antisocial wishes which are deeply imbedded in the recesses of the personality.

Part I will be devoted to the illustration of dimensions of antisocial behavior, and Part II will be devoted to the interpretation of these dimensions

I. THE DIMENSIONS OF ANTISOCIAL BEHAVIOR

A. The Form of Antisocial Behavior

We must first ask what form the antisocial behavior takes. The behavior may take the form of aggression (vector "against"), as in the following story, in which the hero kills his best friend.

> The man has been jealous of his best friend and kills him. He goes to his grave begging forgiveness and drops dead over the tombstone.

Or it may take the form of acquisitiveness (vector "from"), as in this next story in which the hero, who is a spendthrift, steals to supplement his salary.

> We'll call this one "Justice." Reynolds had lived a careless life. He had never felt the importance of duty and responsibility he owed to himself and others. He had been primarily concerned with his own pleasure. As a young man, he became a spendthrift and very soon the small salary he earned as a clerk in a brokerage firm did not suffice to supply him with his wants. The firm had hired Reynolds as a gesture of appreciation to his father who had worked for it previously. Before many months passed, questionable items began to appear on his accounts. Becoming suspicious, the owners of the firm warned Reynolds, then proceeded to watch him. Unfortunately for him, having spent all his week's wages in a nearby tavern, on gambling and drink, Reynolds

decided to return to his office to replenish his cash out of the firm's safe whose combination he knew. Upon opening the safe, at this late hour, without authority, he was apprehended by several detectives who laid hands upon him and took him into custody. He was found guilty of attempted embezzlement and would have been jailed for a long time had not his employers pleaded leniency for him in the hope that in some other position and with this experience as a bitter lesson, he would make good. There is certain justice following the deeds of men.

Or it may take form of desertion (vector "away from").

Might be a soldier who deserted. He never believed in war anyhow and he thought his own skin was more important than a lot of flag waving by a bunch of war profiteers. So he just upped and walked out, got himself some civilian clothes and went about his business. Some MPs have caught up with him and are taking him to the guard house. He'll probably be court marshalled.

Or the antisocial behavior may take the form of dominance (vector "over"), as in the story which follows: a hypnotist who uses his power to make his subject do things against his basic nature.

A hypnotist is trying his practice out on a subject. He has in mind to perfect his technique beyond that of normal hypnotists—that is to a degree where he can command the subject to do things that are against the subject's basic nature. When he thinks that he has his technique worked out he will try it on someone who will come out of the spell and in a spell of anger hurt the hypnotist or threaten him with the law (poetic justice).

B. Motivation of Antisocial Behavior

What are the conditions that motivate such behavior? In the story which we again reproduce, jealousy (vector "from") incites aggression.

The man has been jealous of his best friend and kills him. He goes to his grave begging forgiveness and drops dead over the tombstone.

Antisocial behavior may also be motivated by the wish to help someone (vector "for") arising from a previous poverty (condition lack), as in the following rescue phantasy.

The boy has just told his mother about committing a robbery. Before they were very poor and he decided to give his mother luxuries in her last years. He robbed a bank and told his mother about it. She is unhappy but tells her son to give himself up. The son does this and spends the next ten years in jail.

Antisocial behavior may also be motivated by the desire to be like others (level-wish-object, condition abundance) arising from poverty (condition lack).

Joe didn't have much education. He lived on the other side of the tracks, and his friends were limited. He used to love to play Cops and Robbers. His parents didn't care much about him, and they were very poor. Joe was very self conscious about his feeble clothes, he wanted to be like other boys, and it was in this way he got tangled up in a murder situation, and was forced into committing a crime. We find him in this picture just after the crime has been committed. He knows he's done wrong, and is upset.

Or there may be a wish to get what other people have (vector "from") arising from poverty (condition lack) and the hostility it arouses (vector "against").

Dave had been brought up in the slums of one of our big cities and received his education from his own imagination. He thought he was wronged in being born in poverty and always bore this grudge against the world. Instead of making an honest success of himself, he strove to get what he wanted and what other people had through crime. He became brutal and hard. 'Til one day, upon escaping in a stolen car, he chose to run down an elderly woman rather than risk smashing up. She was an old scrubwoman, mother of seven children, whom she slaved to bring up right and turned out to be an old neighbor of his. When later caught and faced in the morgue by the mangled body, he could not bear it and screeched for mercy before collapsing. He later died, coward as he was, in the electric chair, still with a distorted mind. But we were supposed to regard our lives as luxuries rather than sacrifice.

Or the inciter may be a wish which the hero must obey (vector "under," object self).

This old servant has been caught stealing food out of the pantry. He is a well-fed servant but he feels he must steal and not desiring to steal something valuable he steals food. This inner urge has gotten him into trouble before in the same manner, and this time he is fired. He has no place to go and he is turned out until weak with hunger he goes to the poorhouse.

An antisocial act may be caused by the hero's behavior itself, which passes beyond the control of the hero (vector "under," object behavior-object self).

The woman facing us has been showing the other woman some neck holds. Suddenly she lost control, as is shown, and began really to choke her. The woman lost consciousness and at that point the woman facing us gets a grip on herself, and stopped choking. Immediately afterward she has hysterics. The other woman tries to show her that everything is all right, but she is really afraid, and their friendship will be broken by fear on the one hand and self-mistrust on the other.

Or antisocial behavior may be the consequence of drinking (Special State).

The man shown is drunk. He's a perfectly respectable citizen when he is sober, but he's a terror when he's drunk. He gets mean and wants to fight everybody, and doesn't quite know what he is doing. He was in a bar and had had a few too many and he started a fight with the guy standing next to him and there was a free-for-all, and in this free-for-all he hit the guy over the head with a bottle and killed him. He's being led away by the police here and he's still too drunk to know what happened. When he wakes up in the morning and finds himself facing a murder rap he's going to be stunned.

Or it may be incited by feelings of inferiority (feeling-object condition lack).

She's a hunchback and her deformity has affected her life. It made her a very bitter, malevolent person because she feels inferior to other people, and feels that they are always looking at her and pitying her. She comes to hate people, particularly young girls her own age, who are going out and enjoying themselves in a way that's impossible for her. A friend of hers came to see her, not to gloat or to pity her as she thought but because she really wanted to see her. They were sitting talking when she was suddenly seized with a burning hatred, all the years of feeling inferior and hating burst forth, she scarcely knew what she was doing and she picked up the nearest thing she could lay her hands on and came toward this girl with her arm upraised ready to crush her skull. The girl saw her coming and ran screaming from the room. The hunchback collapsed on the floor realizing what she had almost done, she was afraid. She started to cry, it really didn't matter what happened to her she knew that she could never be happy.

Or it may have its inception in a growing hatred (vector "against") arising from submission (vector "under") to extortion (vector "from").

The wicked looking old woman in the background is a blackmailer. Years ago she found out something about the younger woman and since then she has demanded money or she says she will tell the woman's husband. The young woman despises her but she has had to pay the money, there's not much else she could do. She has stood it for years and is fast reaching the point where she can't stand it. She gets so she hates the old woman more and more and the next time she comes for her money the young woman pulls out a gun and shoots her. She feels no regret, the old woman was a parasite on society and shouldn't be allowed to live. The old woman has no friends and if she disposes of the body no one will ever wonder what happened to her. She disposes of the body and lives in peace after that.

Or the antisocial behavior may be a consequence of rejection by others (vector "against") which incited counteraggression (vector "against").

The story of a young man who has first been apprehended for having committed robbery and later many murders. Being presented with the picture taken of him just after one crime—he was forced by police to face the camera— begins suddenly to realize that there was more behind this picture than might appear to anyone else. It might help in the solitude of his own imaginings, and explain them as such to a visiting prison psychologist, that his hands reminded him of constant clutching that was going on in his life pulling him back into crime whenever he tried to break away from it. He told him how in early life he had been thwarted and many mixed-up circumstances . . . to his complete self-satisfaction. That constant rebuffs which he received in early life so sensitized him against society that he could never really appreciate it. These rebuffs he experienced in early childhood . . . his entrance into his own male world of friends, since they considered him a spoiled child and taunted him with their dislike, and instead of trying to overcome it, he let it affect him and thus this fear of rebuff had a grip on him, prohibiting him from a normal young life. When he came into age of entrance in mixed society, there was shown the same regard towards women, no, by women, because by that time he had developed such a cynical personality, something which was innate although not totally deserved by him. This situation affected him, so he had eventually turned from society and turned to crime and a revengeful attitude. Whenever he did stop to realize what he was doing, and would try to make an attempt to turn away from these fears, inhibitions, and repressions, his sensitive feelings seemed to grip him, and pull him back and say, "Stay away— don't want them," till, finally, one crime led to another. The result was ultimate apprehension, and while waiting to die in the electric chair, he donated his time fully to psychical research, and social writings for the benefit of any other starting out with the same predicament, and after death donated his body to a nearby medical school, showing his innate liking for society although overshadowed by a superficial distaste for it.

C. Direction of Antisocial Behavior

Against whom is the antisocial behavior directed? It may be directed against an individual.

The young man had gone through a trying mental period such as Dostoievski might describe. He finally decided to murder an acquaintance. The thought tormented him, seared his brain, yet was not entirely unpleasant to him. He laid out the details of the murder carefully, but when it came time for the actual deed, he stood before the sleeping victim who was lying on the couch and couldn't shoot. The victim awoke—went screaming out of the room, the man realized he had failed due to weakness he hadn't counted on, and realizing that there is no use fleeing, he shot himself as shown in the picture. No future.

Or it may be directed against some particular class or group.

This guy is a Marxist. He's in some South American country trying to start a revolution. Things are pretty well organized. They're out to get the capitalists and to persuade the proletariat to join them. Everything goes pretty well, the revolutionists run through the street firing capitalistic establishments and yelling "Down with the capitalists, the revolution has come." But the capitalists get the soldiers after them and this guy, the leader, just manages to escape by climbing this rope over the side of the ship. They're disheartened that they've failed but are determined to try again.

Or it may be directed against the social order.

The man is an instigator of a revolt. Having laid his plans he now has gone home and standing at the window with the room darkened he watches the explosion in a gov't building which is a signal for the revolt to begin. Mingled emotions are experienced by him at this instant, fear for an instant, then excitement and joy—trust of his companions.

D. The Role of the Hero in Antisocial Behavior

1. the instigator

Who instigates the behavior? It may be instigated by the hero.

Jimmy was a notorious little prankster around the neighborhood. He was regarded by all the storekeepers and pushcart peddlers and other commercial institutions around the slum district in which he lived as a general nuisance. He stole whenever possible and upset ashcans and was generally being chased by the police for some prank or misdeed of some kind or another. Jimmy had a gang. The gang's reputation, if anything was worse than, than Jimmy's and together they pulled off some of the best bits of small sized larceny, small scale, larceny that any group of school boys could ever be, could ever hope to do, ah, however, on this particular occasion they were engaged in breaking into a candy store one evening about ten o'clock and they were apprehended and rushed off to the nearest police station. Jimmy's father a hard-working truck driver, was quite upset when he heard about this and rushed down to the jail heard Jimmy's story, Jimmy was full of tears and protests and sobbed that he would reform absolutely if dad would only see to it that they didn't take him away and put him in the reformatory and I guess we'd best round it off by having him put away, or rather not put away but let loose and returning to his old existence of small scale robbery and such like troubles.

Or the hero may instigate the behavior and persuade others to join him.

This guy got a bad start in life. He was kinda smart alecky when he was in school and he wasn't in school as he should have been. I mean he didn't go much. He thought he was smart. He formed a gang, told the other kids that they weren't smart, that they should get smart and not waste their time in school either. They formed a gang and he was the leader. At first they didn't do much but run around and get in trouble, they were hoodlums and got in trouble for not being in school and for breaking windows. But this guy who was the leader got big ideas and thought maybe they'd swipe some stuff. The other kids weren't for it, but he was the leader and he talked to them and told them to be smart. They started swiping things and the things got more and more, the things they swiped. When they got older they were regular crooks and the police were on the watch for them. One night they planned to rob a bank but what they didn't know was that somebody had tipped the police off that they were going to do it and they were waiting for them. There was a lot of shooting and the leader and some other guys were shot up and the police wagon came down the street and took them off to jail.

Or someone else may persuade the hero to undertake antisocial behavior.

This is the story of a weak minded man who had no will power, he let a friend of his talk him into taking money from his firm to bet on the horses.

The friend kept on saying they would win and he could pay it back. He was weak minded, had no self control so he let himself be talked into it knowing all the time that maybe he couldn't pay it back. They won some money, not very much but some and he wanted to pay the money back but the friend said they needed the money to make more money and after that they started to lose and didn't have enough to pay it back and they went on betting until they lost it all. The friend left the man to hold the bag and went off to find another sucker. The man realizes that he's never going to be able to get that money and he doesn't know what to do. He goes home and puts a bullet through his head.

Or someone may coerce the hero leading him into a life of crime.

Some bandits had been kidnapping boys for their own use. One boy, David Johnson, was brought to the chief who taught him many tricks and changed him from a weakling to a strong boy. He gave him a gun so he could practice shooting, robbing, and killing. In his younger days, he didn't like to fool with guns, but his master had told him to, so he had to. At first, the jobs were simple—hold-ups. Then robbing banks. Then kidnapping and sabotaging. But this was not to be slightly disregarded by the police; they had found that the ringleader had kidnapped the boys who robbed and killed, not because they wanted to but because they were made to. One time, the boy David began a hold-up of a bank with fifty thousand grand. At first, he killed the cashier, took the money and went by the couch, but was intercepted by the police. His gun fired but his shot went high. Sharpshooters of the police found their mark. He slowly and defiantly slumped to the floor. This is one of the awful ways in which to die.

2. THE SOCIAL CONTEXT

Is the antisocial act done by the hero in the company of others, or does he act alone? The hero may have an ally.

Steve and Jim has been pals together back in Brooklyn when they were kids. They hated school and hardly ever went, they took to hanging around pool rooms instead and living how you pleased. They hear the men in the pool rooms talking about easy ways to make money and decide to try their hand at it. They start stealing cars. Steve drives them while Jim˙ watches for the cops. It was fun and exciting even though a little risky at times. They sell the cars and for the present they haven't a care in the world and they aren't worrying about the future. One night Jim sees a cop coming and warns Steve to get away in a hurry but it's too late. Steve gets shot trying to get away and Jim ends up where most lawbreakers do.

Or he may be a member of a gang.

Hm, we got a, here we have a guy who's a member of a gang of crooks, a dope ring. They have men who smuggle the stuff in for them and they sell it in this country, peddle it. This woman who's his girl has heard that the FBI is on their trail and she's trying to get him to get out of it before they get caught. She's trying to make him promise but he's trying to get away from her to warn the others. She won't let him go until he promises so he does.

Does the hero regard himself as a member of an in-group or out-group in his antisocial behavior? In the story that follows the criminal has an out-group feeling. In his activities, he is opposed to the rest of society, which constitutes an in-group.

> The story of a young man who has first been apprehended for having committed robbery and later many murders. Being presented with the picture taken of him just after one crime—he was forced by police to face the camera—begins suddenly to realize that there was more behind this picture than might appear to anyone else. It might help in the solitude of his own imaginings, and explain them as such to a visiting prison psychologist, that his hands reminded him of constant clutching that was going on in his own life pulling him back into crime whenever he tried to break away from it. He told him how in early life he had been thwarted and many mixed-up circumstances . . . to his complete self-satisfaction. That constant rebuffs which he received early in life so sensitized him against society that he could never really appreciate it. These rebuffs he experienced in early childhood . . . his entrance into his own male world of friends, since they considered him a spoiled child and taunted him with their dislike, and instead of trying to overcome it, he let it affect him and thus this fear of rebuff had a grip on him, prohibiting him from a normal young life. When he came into age of entrance in mixed society, there was shown the same regard towards women, no, by women, because by that time he had developed such a cynical personality, something which was innate although not totally deserved by him. This situation affected him, so he had eventually turned from society and turned to crime and a revengeful attitude. Whenever he did stop to realize what he was doing, and would try to make an attempt to turn away from these fears, inhibitions, and repression, his sensitive feelings seemed to grip him, and pull him back and say, "Stay away—don't want them," till, finally, one crime led to another. The result was ultimate apprehension, and while waiting to die in the electric chair, he donated his time to psychical research, and social writings for the benefit of any other starting out with the same predicament, and after death donated his body to a nearby medical school, showing his innate liking for society although overshadowed by superficial distaste for it.

This story illustrates both an out-group feeling on the part of the criminal and a later wish to be a part of the in-group. It was the frustration of this wish which caused him to become a criminal.

In the following there is an in-group feeling amongst criminals who are a closely knit group, loyal only to each other and opposed to the rest of society as an out-group. There is only for an "instant" a feeling that society is the larger in-group.

> The man in this story is a member of a gang of criminals. They are carefully organized and they pride themselves that there are brains behind their activities.

Every operation is carefully conceived and cleverly carried out. No member has ever been caught. The only loyalty they know is to each other and it is a practical kind, a bond of self preservation. They are linked together by the knowledge that a chain is only as strong as its weakest link. This night one of the men has been placed as sentry to wait by a lighted lamp post for the policeman who walks the beat. He is there to be seen by the policeman and then with the greatest speed he is to be whisked to another part of town far away to commit a crime. The object of tonight's operation is a great loot of money. It will be necessary to kill a man but murder has never deterred this crowd. These men know no fear, but just for an instant, as the man stands by the post, carrying out the first step of the plan, he almost feels that through the fog, eyes are peering at him and civilized mankind is learning the guilty secret. Soon the foot steps of the policeman are heard and he sighs with relief. He never liked waiting. Killing, stealing, tricking, these things never bothered him, but waiting if he ever made a misstep, he knew it would be when he was just waiting. The policeman left, the plan rolled on like clock work. It was his gun that shot the man, but he felt no remorse, no regrets.

3. THE ACCEPTANCE OF RESPONSIBILITY

Does the hero assume responsibility for the act? He may feel that he is really innocent.

Hunger made this man steal some food. He felt that he hadn't done wrong, that the world owed a man enough to eat. But the manager of the store and the police don't agree with him and he goes to jail for thirty days.

Or that he is not responsible for his behavior.

He's a madman. Strange spells come over him when he doesn't know what he's doing. Some nights he comes out of these spells to find himself wandering through dark and desolate sections of the city, places he's never seen before. In his sane moments he's haunted by the fear of what he might do when in one of these spells. He tries to lock himself in, but he always manages to get out. He reads in the newspaper about a series of murders in the section of town near the wharfs where he had found himself on several occasions. Knowing that he isn't responsible for what he does when he's in a spell he's frightened and thinks that he might be the murderer. No matter whether it's true or not he has to know. He rushes over to look at the clothes he wore the night before and is horrified to see deep blood stains on them. He drops to his knees trying to think. He wonders if he should give himself up, if he told anyone about these spells they either wouldn't believe him or they would say he was insane and put him in an institution. The thought terrifies him and he commits suicide.

Or that he was intoxicated and didn't know what he was doing.

The man shown is drunk. He's a perfect respectable citizen when sober, but he's a terror when he's drunk. He gets mean and wants to fight everybody and doesn't quite know what's happening. He was in a bar and had had a few too many. He started a fight with the guy standing next to him and there was a free-for-all, and in this free-for-all he hit the guy over the head with a bottle and killed him. He's being led away by the police here and he's still too drunk to know what happened. When he wakes up in the morning and finds himself facing a murder rap he's going to be stunned.

Or he may assume complete responsibility for his behavior.

As far as the present is concerned this woman has had quite a career. She was exposed to lots of money and she stole some—I can't think of the term they use for stealing by forging numbers in accounts, but anyway she did it. She needed money for something very important. But after she had taken it she realized what a wrong thing she had done, and somehow the thing she had taken the money for didn't seem so important—she went and confessed. She couldn't give the money back because she'd spent it, so she went to jail. But she never did anything wrong again.

E. The Duration of Antisocial Behavior

Antisocial behavior may represent an isolated incident or the way of life of a hero. Further one may ask how enduring are the consequences of the behavior, whether isolated or repeated? In the following story the act represents no more than an isolated incident, although its consequences are never forgotten.

This picture reminds me of the hero in *Jane Eyre*. He's a man who at some time in his life has done what he considers a great wrong but which the world for the most part would excuse him for. His deep faith has given him a burning desire to reconcile himself in the eyes of his God. He considers himself shackled to this need for reconciliation and is at the point of this picture wondering what great thing he can offer God. He toys with the idea of giving his life, but considers this sacrilegious in the sense that he's taking the easy way out. He will go on leading an unhappy life and die at some great catastrophe.

Or antisocial behavior may represent the hero's way of life, with enduring consequences.

Mr. X was a criminal who had committed many crimes, including murder for which he was sentenced to pay for with his life. His attorney an old gray haired man did not believe that he was alone in this, for it was his firm belief that there had been a gang of criminals involved in these crimes. Mr. X did not admit that he was alone but he would not tell the names of the other people involved no matter how much his attorney pleaded with him. Mr. X was a man with a moral code, even if it was the code of criminals which was the only code he had ever known and rather than give up his code he went to the chair without revealing the names of the other men.

F. Sequelae of Antisocial Behavior

What happens to the hero as the result of his antisocial behavior?

1. PUNISHMENT

The hero may suffer punishment for his antisocial behavior.

a) *Punishment from Exogenous Sources*

Punishment may come from exogenous sources. The hero may be punished by the representative of legally constituted authority, as in the following story.

> Here a man is being apprehended by a policeman. This man has probably been wanted for murder for some time and had been in a state of worry or fear in his attempts to lose them. Now that he has been caught it is with an expression of relief and his reluctance to struggle, for he is a large man and possibly could put up a great struggle, make it appear that he is glad the chase is over.

Or he may be punished by his victim.

> This is a fellow—a young guy, 27, 28, got started in life in wrong way, dishonest in business, selfish jaw shows this. Someone he hit badly came in and murdered him. This is the scene of the murder. This is the arm of the other person involved in it. The fellow might have been strangled.

Or by another criminal.

> Ah, this, ah, fellow and his friend, they grew up on the other side of the tracks and ah they became—back to crime again—they started of course during their, oh, petty thievery and ah—before they got very old they were committing more major crimes. It happened on a robbery in which they had taken about, this fellow, the other fellow had done the hard work in it. He had taken the money while this fellow stood guard. The other fellow didn't want to split fifty-fifty on it for some reason. This fellow went into a rage and pulled out a gun and shot his friend. This is the moment just after he shot him. He realized that he was wrong. He has fallen on the floor. He is weeping. He actually loved his friend and, and he has, the fellow has, he has just dragged him out the door and now he is just sitting and he doesn't know what to do. This is a case, it's after this while he is crying the police come in. Somebody has reported the shot, and they do come in and the fellow gives himself up. He admits everything and the murder and the crimes that have been committed. He is given a twenty-five year sentence in the penitentiary. Its point is that crime doesn't pay.

Or by some natural force as in the following story where the hero escapes only to be drowned.

> The impression is that this man is up to no good. He looks like a criminal type—narrow eyes. I've got it now. He stole a lot of money, make it

$100,000 and was skipping to another country where he would live in luxury and no one would know his background. The ship was sailing along and he was very satisfied with himself and relaxing now that he has escaped. But a storm blew up which wrecked the ship. All hands were lost so he didn't escape his fate after all.

Or the punishment may come from a supernatural force.

This shriveled old man was once a pastor in a small town in New England, a God-fearing righteous man. But something turned him from the path of God. People in the village say he sold his soul to the devil. Whatever it was he turned away from God and people and was seen abroad in the company of the ne'er-do-wells of the village and often walked by himself in the cemetery in the dead of night, and you have to be on friendly terms with the evil spirits to do that. Then the scandal broke that rocked the village. The pastor turned out to be no more than a common, ordinary thief. He had been stealing from neighboring villages for years and burying the money in the cemetery. The indignant villagers gathered together and marched to find him. He heard that they were coming and hurried to the cemetery hoping to dig up the money and escape. As they marched, the people heard ominous sounds in the sky, great black clouds gathered and when they reached the gates of the cemetery, they saw a sight that none of them will ever forget. The pastor stood in the midst of the tombstones, busily digging, when there was a terrible thundering, the heavens split and a great tongue of lightning reached down and struck him where he stood. Many said that God has wanted to punish him and had chosen this way. There may have been a few who doubted but no 'one raised his voice.

1. *Nature and duration of exogenous punishment.* What is the nature and duration of the punishment which follows antisocial behavior? The punishment may be death, as in the following story where the hero is electrocuted for his crime.

Dave had been brought up in the slums of one of our big cities and received his education from his own imagination. He thought he was wronged in being born in poverty and always bore this grudge against the world. Instead of making an honest success of himself, he strove to get what he wanted and what other people had through crime. He became brutal and hard. 'Til one day, upon escaping in a stolen car, he chose to run down an elderly woman rather than risk smashing it up. She was an old scrubwoman, mother of seven children, whom she slaved to bring up right and turned out to be an old neighbor of his. When later caught and faced in the morgue by the mangled body, he could not bear it and screeched for mercy before collapsing. He later died, coward as he was, in the electric chair, still with distorted mind. But we were supposed to regard our lives as luxuries rather than sacrifice.

Or, it may be life imprisonment.

These two girls were put into a reform school for committing a crime at a very young age. They never had much to do except sit around in a cell, and look at the scenery outside. They were never allowed to go out, but remained in their cell until death.

Or, imprisonment for a specific number of years.

The boy has just told his mother about his committing a robbery. Before they were very poor and he decided to steal to give his mother. luxuries in her last years. He robbed a bank and told his mother about it. She is unhappy but tells her son to give himself up—the son does this and spends the next ten years in jail.

Or the hero may be imprisoned but released for good conduct before his term has been served.

This man has just committed a terrible crime and his conscience is bothering him so that he thinks that people are looking at him and that he is being seized by policemen who know of his wrong doings. In desperation (for he feels as if people are running after him all the time) he goes to the police and confesses his crime, and is put in jail and sentenced to life imprisonment. Later, however, he is let out for his conduct is like that of any upright citizen. He has learned his lesson from his conscience.

2. *Attitude of the hero toward exogenous punishment.* What is the hero's attitude toward such punishment?

a) *Resistance.* The hero may resist apprehension by the law.

This one has to be dramatic. That's a weird looking house or whatever it is. It's in the dead of winter and this house is completely covered with snow. Some crooks are hiding out in it. For months the police have been trying to catch up with them, but they're hidden in the country and you can hardly tell the house from the snow except for the chimney which sticks up like a periscope which in fact is what it is, so that the crooks can see anyone who comes up the road. One of the crooks named Tony is posted at the periscope and he sees cars moving along the road, he yells to the other men, he's the head of them and tells them to stick their guns out through the windows in case there is any trouble. The police surround the house thinking that they can't be seen, not knowing that the crooks have guns trained on them and are watching their every move. The police yell to them to surrender but they just answer by firing the guns. Meanwhile they are arranging to escape by means of an underground passage. While the police are too busy firing at the house to notice, they sneak out one by one and are far away by the time the police notice that they are the only ones firing. They keep doing this kind of thing and are never caught.

Or give himself up.

This man has just committed a terrible crime and his conscience is bothering him so that he thinks that people are looking at him and that he is being seized by policemen who know of his wrongdoing. In desperation (for he feels as if people are running after him all the time) he goes to the police and confesses his crime and is put in jail and sentenced to life imprisonment. Later, however, he is let out for his conduct is like that of any upright citizen. He has learned his lesson from his conscience.

But though his wish may be to avoid punishment he may yet give himself up.

This man has just murdered a woman. He was overcome with remorse and stunned. In a little while his mind snaps into action—he must cover this up some way, no, he must not cover up. He better confess the whole business. No, a terrible thing. His mind becomes more and more alert. He began to think of a means of getting away without arousing suspicion. He turned her over, covered her up and softly left the room. As he went down the stair stealthily, he thought he heard a door open on the second floor. He pressed against the wall but the noise stopped. He got down the stairs. He walked out on the street, looked back once or twice and walked quickly away. He had better get out of town. He walked for a number of blocks. His mind became hazy; he didn't know what to do. Gleaming lights of a Police Station were blinking a few blocks away. They seemed to be beckoning to him. Yes— no—they were calling to him he walked deliberately up to them—walked up to the desk and gave himself up. He was sentenced to 25 years for manslaughter.

b) *Attitude toward apprehension.* How does the hero regard the fact of his capture? He may have lived in a state of anxiety and fear but be glad when he is caught that the chase is over.

Here a man is being apprehended by a policeman. This man has probably been wanted for murder for some time and had been in a state of worry or fear in his attempts to lose them. Now that he has been caught it is with an expression of relief and his reluctance to struggle, for he is a large man and possibly could put up a great struggle, make it appear that he is glad the chase is over.

Often the hero's attitude toward apprehension is implicit. But in some instances the hero may describe his feelings of hostility.

This man held someone up with a gun on a dark street. The man put up a struggle and they were fighting when a cop heard them and came up and asked what was the matter. The man who was doing the robbing got in a fight with the cop who tried to arrest him and it wasn't 'til some other cops came because they heard the noise that they were able to drag this man off to jail. He cursed and tried to get away the whole time until they got him to the jail and when they put him in a cell he was still yelling he wanted to get out.

c) *Conflict.* Is the hero in conflict about whether or not to give himself up? The heroine of the following story has no such conflict.

As far as the present is concerned this woman has had quite a career. She was exposed to lots of money and she stole some—I can't think of the term they use for stealing by forging numbers in accounts, but anyway she did it. She needed money for something very important. But after she had taken it she realized what a wrong thing she had done and somehow the thing she had taken the money for didn't seem so important—she went and confessed. She couldn't give the money back because she'd spent it, so she went to jail. But she never did anything wrong again.

But the hero may be undecided.

Here we find a young man who has committed a crime, and has been living under cover ever since it occurred. The police are after him, and he ponders over the fact, whether he should give himself up or not. He goes to a very close friend, who always helped him out of his troubles. In this picture we find him sitting quietly, but worried listening to the elderly gentlemen, as he gives him advice, and is trying to persuade him to give himself up.

If the hero is undecided he may resolve his conflict by giving himself up.

All those hands, like the hands of a Hindu statue are symbolic. They are dragging the man this way and that. He can't decide what to do. Over and over in his mind he tries to decide. He has committed some atrocity and he can't sleep and he can't eat. He wonders if he should confess his crime and take his punishment, he tries to forget but he can't. He loses weight, he can't eat. At last he is so weak he thinks he's going to die and he drags himself to the police and confesses. He goes to prison but he sleeps peacefully for the first time since he did it.

If the hero is guilty of antisocial behavior and has been caught, is there a conflict about whether he should take his punishment or try to prove his innocence. The hero of the story that follows has no conflict. He does everything he can to prove his innocence and escape punishment.

A guy who's trying to beat a murder rap. Probably has done it before and uses all the angles, hires a smart lawyer, fixes an alibi, has dozens of witnesses who swear they saw him someplace else at the time of the murder. Probably even has his mother come and cry at the trial. Of course there's some smart detective who sees through it and breaks his alibi. I've probably been listening to the radio too much.

In the following story the hero has an option between accepting his attorney's offer to try to free him on a plea of insanity, or proving his sanity and taking his punishment. He decides on the latter and is sentenced to hang.

A week before this—this is a court scene—the defendant here has been able to get this majestic or this handsome, white-haired man to defend him. The gray-haired gentlemen is a very prominent lawyer. He offered, he offered to take the case of this, this fellow. He is a criminal. He has I guess committed some sort of fantastic murder and the gentleman decided that he would try to free the fellow, and ah, the fee in the case would be very good and it's the money that this fellow is interested in. . . . Oh, it's one of those. I was thinking. I thought of a, oh, of a trunk murder. I don't know why that came in my mind, but ah, we'll just leave it a trunk murder and ah, ah, the lawyer is just telling him now that he thinks the case is absolutely hopeless and he is going to try, there is one way that he can free him and that is to try and prove that he is insane. The fellow is sitting there and he is listening. He doesn't know quite what to do. His reaction is kind of nil. He is ah. . . . He realizes he has been in the wrong. He has committed this horrible crime and he decides while the lawyer goes on to prove him insane; he talks himself out of it and he proves his sanity and he is convicted of this murder and sentenced to hang.

The heroine of the following story also has a similar conflict which she resolves in the opposite way.

This lovely young woman has come from a murder trial in which she was the defendant. The man with her is her lawyer, who's a little in love with her and who defended her and got her off. Of course she is very young and lovely which helped. He is telling her that he never doubted that she was innocent for a minute. At which a strange look comes over her face. She says, "You're wrong I really did commit that murder. I tried to bring myself to confess it but I'm too young to die, I couldn't stand the thought and I knew you could get me off if you believed I was innocent." He looks at her shocked and disillusioned. He's furious to think that she made him a party to her deceit and treachery and turns away from her in rage. He says that he'll reopen the case. She looks at him sadly but says, "You can't do that, no one can be tried twice for the same crime."

3) *Success or failure of resistance to exogenous punishment.* Is the hero able to resist apprehension successfully? The hero may never be caught as in the following story:

The hands belong to a sort of Robin Hood character. He steals from the rich to give to the poor. He and one of his gang are sticking up this wealthy guy. They do a lot of good and are never caught.

Or he may wish to avoid apprehension but be unsuccessful in his attempt.

A second story man. He broke into a house and was using this rope to get away when someone spotted him and called the police. He's hanging on the rope in midair, and goes up the rope and tries to make his getaway over the roofs of the houses. The police chased him and also surrounded the buildings so if he tries to get down he'll walk right into their cordon. The chase goes on for a couple of hours but they finally get him.

If the hero has been imprisoned and attempts to escape, is this attempt successful? The hero may be captured in his attempt to escape:

This a jail break, he's using this rope to lower himself over the prison wall. The sirens are screeching and the cops are shooting at him. He's just about to drop to the ground when a bullet gets him in the shoulder and he falls. The cops rush down and capture him. His leg is broken and he's shot up but they take him to the prison hospital and he gets well.

Or there may be some uncertainty about the success of his attempt:

A prisoner is shown escaping by means of a rope from a prison. He is a husky fellow and might succeed. If he does he will be very careful for a while but soon will get more and more careless. Probably he will be retaken. According to him it is worth the risk for a little freedom at the least. Right now though, he is thinking of nothing but his escape and is on sharp lookout for a place to run when he gets down.

Or the hero may escape from prison, never be retaken and live to enjoy his ill-gotten gains.

I see a pirate ship in the Caribbean, flying a Jolly Roger, a very colorful ship manned by swarthy sailors wearing gold earrings with daggers through their belts. The captain of the sturdy ship is Spanish John a very bloody pirate whose reputation has followed him around the world. He takes particular delight in plundering the ships of the British who are his old enemies and have been trying to capture him for ten years. It's been a merry chase, but they caught up with him in a little harbor and blocked the mouth of the harbor, he was completely outnumbered and had to surrender. The British were jubilant and put him in irons, but not for long. He made a daring escape and sailed away to the island where he has headquarters and lives the rest of his days in luxury, leaving only to plunder an occasional ship.

But this type of story is rare and it is noteworthy that it is placed in a remote and romantic setting.

4) *Relatedness of crime and punishment.* The hero may or may not be explicitly aware of the connection between crime and punishment. There are stories in which this connection is not made. The hero may, for example, commit an antisocial act for which he is not punished but then suffer an accident which is not connected either by the hero or the storyteller to the crime for which it might have been a punishment. This may be taken to mean that the individual is not altogether aware of the connection between his own antisocial impulses and the punishment which he expects. Ordinarily this connection is explicitly made in crime and punishment stories, indicating that for most individuals the sequence of crime and punishment is something so dramatic and painful that awareness of this connection is inevitable. That it is possible for an individual to be relatively unaware of this connection is illustrated in the following story in which death due to an accident follows antisocial behavior with no statement of any explicit connection between the two.

This is a man who had a great difficulty in establishing himself as a youth in his own mind. So he turned to crime as a means to power and glory. One foggy night he was finishing up a robbery and the man woke up, he had to kill him. He walked out of the building and out into the street not looking where he was going and a car ran him down and killed him.

b) *Punishment from Endogenous Sources*

Punishment may issue from within the hero rather than from exogenous sources. He may suffer guilt which prevents him from leading a normal life. In the following story the servant, although not directly responsible for his master's death, suffers guilt which makes him withdraw from the society of others.

A servant has wronged his master. As an indirect cause of this wrong the master has died. The master was quite poor and the servant liked his master— he wasn't mercenary. Now the servant has gone to the grave of his master seeking in some way to get relief from his feeling of guilt. He is truly penitential. This feeling of guilt will continue to bother him and he will tend to be around people less than before.

Or he may be tormented by thoughts of his deed and commit suicide.

This man has committed a murder. Some force greater than that of other men is preventing him from leading a normal life. He is tormented by the thoughts of his deed and is, at the point of this picture, attempting to walk off his state of mind. He feels very tired, has a tremendous pressing in his head. He doesn't know which way to turn or where to go. He carries on like this quite a long while and then takes his own life by drowning himself.

c) *Punishment from Both Endogenous and Exogenous Sources*

Punishment may stem from sources not entirely exogenous nor purely endogenous. In the following story the hero is tormented by his conscience and gives himself up to exogenous punishment.

This man had just committed a terrible crime and his conscience is bothering him so that he thinks that people are looking at him and that he is being seized by policemen who know of his wrongdoing. In desperation (for he feels as if people are running after him all the time) he goes to the police and confesses his crime and is put in jail and sentenced to life imprisonment. Later, however, he is let out for his conduct is like that of any upright citizen. He has learned his lesson from his conscience.

Or he may place himself in a position where he knows he will be punished by natural forces. The hero of the following story goes to a cave of vampire bats knowing that they will destroy him.

Having just committed some crime, this South American has gone to a cave of vampire bats, intent on leaving the world in their beaks. He knows that they are instruments of the lower regions, that he won't have to sit very long for judgment in their hands before descending to Hell, whence they will quickly guide him.

Or exogenous punishment may lead the individual to inflict further punishment on himself.

> Because of having done something fiendish this man is in prison. He spends all his time staring out the window at the people doing everyday things. His sentence is life and he knows that he'll never leave these walls again, and tears roll down his checks. The next time a friend comes to see him he asks him to slip him a knife which he does and he kills himself, death is better to him than a life in prison.

2. REFORMATION

The sequel of antisocial behavior may involve reformation by the hero, rather than punishment.

a) *Sources*

How is reformation incited? In the following story the reformation of the hero is effected primarily through external agencies. Religion, love, or friendship leads to a realization of the error of his ways and to his reformation.

> This might have been the case of a man who lived a life of crime and evilness, and obscenity, and did not realize his evil ways, till one day through religious experience or the finding of a pure love or perhaps the making of a real and true friend he sees the real light. Crossing the threshold and leaving behind forever this life of unhappiness—not unhappiness but evilness. He is constantly working away from it in a reactionary way, and thus one day becomes the epitome of success and decency in his own community.

In the next story, punishment is the exogenous agency inciting reformation.

> This man might be a criminal and he's finally cornered and thrown in jail with all these bats and owls. Seems to be resigned to his fate, and spends his time in jail writing. There's writing paper and some kind of pen down there. When he started on his life of crime he never expected to land in jail and it has a big effect on him, the horrible monotony and lack of company almost drives him out of his mind. He finally gets out and is so glad, he resolves never to risk having to go through that again and he gives up crime forever.

Reform may stem from the confluence of an external agency, and a spirit which had never been wholly dedicated to evil. In the following story the mother is the immediate inciter to reform. She persuades him to return the money, but the hero had always been a "good hearted fellow."

> This story starts, this fellow is his mother's pride and joy from child, from child, from the time he is born. He is an only child and of course has become very spoiled through these years. He grows into a reckless young man, too reckless. He becomes a sort of, oh, he gets involved in, in small crimes and ah, yes, oh, particularly robberies and so forth. He is a good hearted fellow but

he just gets involved and his mother is aware of this and it, it hurts her very much but ah, she is one of those mothers that, she can't reproach him for anything and of course he is always very honest with her and he comes to tell her all of his problems when he does get into these scrapes. Up to this time, however, he has gotten involved in a major robbery and in making their escape they have gone around a corner and some old gentleman has been hit by the car that he is driving and he wasn't driving fast but he was trying to get away in a hurry and he hit this old man and because he had taken, he had stolen enough money from this concern so that it was actually a major robbery but that isn't the thing that bothers him. He is afraid that the old man was hit hard enough so that he was killed. He didn't stop so that he naturally is a hit-and-run driver too to add to all this trouble. He goes home and tells his mother of all this mess. He of course is being hunted by the police now. Ah, the mother of course is very worried. She doesn't know what to say. She has turned away. She is angry. She realizes that she has made mistakes in raising of her son. She gets the boy, she has talked him into returning the money that he has stolen and they, she is, she is a religious woman and, and she starts praying for this old gentleman. Well, the fellow returns the money and gives himself up to the police. He is a kind of a, it's a kind of a change of heart; like I said he was a good fellow at heart and so the mother in her prayers decides that she will go and see the old gentleman that the fellow had hit on the street and very fortunately the gentleman, the gentleman is recovering and when the mother and this old fellow get to talking they realize that, that they are childhood playmates. They haven't seen each other for several years now but ah, when they, she tells the old gentleman his story he is about to, well he withdraws his charges against the young man and the fellow for having returned the money and these charges against him were withdrawn by his, this old gentleman and he is released and from then on the outcome is that he lives a very straightforward and happy life.

Or the inciter of reformation may be completely endogenous.

It seems to be a symbolic thing, this man has difficult mental and psychological problems. He might have gotten in with a bunch of gamblers and been unable to pay his gambling debts and thus drifted into a life of crime doing what the gamblers wanted him to. In time he got the money to pay the debts but by then he was in so deep he just drifted along. But now it has suddenly hit him in the face what's happened to him, how low he has sunk, robbing and even killing one man. He's afraid to get out of it, but he is so filled with loathing at himself that he can't live with himself if he can't live a decent life. No matter what happens he has to be able to live with himself or die. He goes away to another part of the country with the hope of starting a new life.

b) *Duration of Reformation*

How enduring is the reformation? The hero's character may never again suffer moral relapse.

Awful lot of hands, poor man. He wouldn't be seized by so many hands unless it's in his imagination. He's probably murdered a lot of people and sees these hands coming to take him to prison. The fright is so terrible that he mends his ways and leads a life of perfect virtue from that time on. The hands never come back.

Or the reformation may be relatively short lived.

Joe had always been the tough guy of the neighborhood, but when he grew older, he used to get into serious difficulties with the law. His father had warned him that it was easier to go straight than take the risks he did with his mob of petty gangsters, but Joe liked the profit his illegal doings brought him. One day he and his pals were caught robbing a warehouse, and they each got five years in jail. Joe came out resolved to go straight, but he needed a start, so he went to his father who could set him up in his business. Joe's father refused to have anything to do with him and turned him out of his house. Joe makes several other attempts to find honest work, but no one wants to hire a man with a jail sentence. He finally goes in with another gang, and is shot during a bank hold-up.

3. ATONEMENT

If the crime represents an incident rather than a way of life, the hero may atone for his act rather than reform.

From this picture I gather the impression the young man is in a mental state of anxiety and befuddlement because he has shot his best friend while in an argument. The life of his friend whom he shot is in doubt and only this possible operation can save him. The young man is indeed sorry for his action and is waiting and praying in his befuddled state that the operation may prove a success so he may atone for his act. The operation does prove a success and the boy does atone for his act and a lasting friendship develops.

4. AMORAL SEQUELAE

Although the individual may suffer or escape some form of punishment or reform or atone for his antisocial behavior, the hero may commit antisocial behavior in a completely amoral fashion with no thought of punishment or guilt. Such a hero is presented in the following story.

This is Jack the Ripper. It's in London and he has with him the heads of the bodies inside the bag he's carrying. He's had a very interesting evening! Killed a few people here and there, lots of fun. He's going back to his room and nail the bodies up on the wall or something. I'm not quite sure what he does with them.

II. INTERPRETATION OF ANTISOCIAL BEHAVIOR

Interpretation of the variables illustrated in Part I follows the general method we have employed in the region of love, sex, and marital relation-ships. Wherever a single dimension is constant throughout all the stories there is presumptive evidence that this invariance is a reflection of a stable element within the personality of the storyteller. We must first determine the extent to which antisocial behavior is attributed to heroes. Not infrequently, the entire sphere of antisocial behavior is conspicuous by its absence from a protocol. The heroes' values and problems may be of an entirely different kind. Dedication to the service of humanity, an all consuming interest in achievement or the counteraction of some inferiority, a desperate sense of loneliness and an attempt to achieve communion with a love object—these and other values may polarize the main energies of the individual. In the pursuit of these ends, antisocial wishes *may* be of slight import. Conscience is the representative of but one member of the family of man's values—the moral value. Various other values of equal import may be represented in the democratic organization of the individual's motivational systems. There are, of course, those for whom the moral value is central in a hierarchical organization which subordinates all other values to the moral imperative. No less frequently however, the hierarchical organization may subordinate the moral value and it's representative—the super-ego—to some other central value, such as achievement or the counteraction of inferiority. The following two stories told by different individuals illuminate the basic differences between an individual who is concerned with antisocial wishes and the moral problem of their control, portrayed in the classic image of the taming of wild horses and the individual whose allegory concerns the dangers inherent in the path of life and the knowledge requisite for competence in coping with such dangers. For both individuals control is basic, but one needs to control his own antisocial impulses and the other external forces which are dangerous and which he must learn to control and use to his own advantage.

> Hm, we got a, here we have a bunch of cowboys out on the ranch. They, they are also horse thieves and at the present time they have just had a heavy day drawing up, they have left the farm and they have come out to the, to a, oh, a little ah, just kind of hole in the ground where they draw up their plans for a big raid on a ranch tonight where they expect to get a lot of horses, men with which to start a ranch of their own. I think there are, oh, there must be six or seven of them lying around. We only have four in this picture, and, ah, anyway ah, they have just made up the plans and now they just kind of, they think life is so easy and they have lain down to rest up for the night and, ah, there happens to be one double-crosser here. It's the guy that's looking directly at us in the picture, and he is making plans, they have drawn up all the plans and he figures well that if, the plans they have doesn't take seven men to do it so ah, ah, he decides that he will do it all by himself. He doesn't know what he's going to do about these guys but he figures that if he works pretty well and can slip away he will be able to finish things off and finish them too. He's kind of a heartless guy and a few minutes after this picture is taken he, he tries to slip away and another guy wakes up and decides to follow him and when they have got over to this ranch and are ready to open the gates and

start the horses stampeding out, running away. It, it can be done on account of this corral is, is several miles from the house of the ranch owner and this fellow, the one fellow has disposed of the two guards that have been watching the corral tonight and so all he has to do now is, is stam, get the horses out and start them away, running away on a stampede. Well, just as he is opening the corral this, the fellow that's behind him in this picture comes up to him and wonders what he has been doing, double-crossing and all that and the fellow who has started double-crossing the first time decides well, maybe the two of them might just as well do this little job together and share the profits that they can get and start their own ranch and so being both ruthless fellows they make this agreement and they don't give a hang about the other guys. Well, they open the corral and chase out the hundred and fifty head of there, the, these horses out of the ah, ah, corral and ah, it's kind of funny. They find out that the, the horses that have been in this corral are wilder than they thought. They are just, they don't know why, they are wild horses but they are wild horses, but anyway, they actually start on a stampede. They are unable to control them and so they start running down the valley and they are headed for the spot where these fellows have been asleep. There are still five fellows lying on the ground, and, ah, and, ah, and, ah, they are not aware that these, this stampede of horses are headed in their direction. I don't know why these, these two fellows should get all excited and kind-hearted all at once but they decide they had better warn the guys that the horses are coming; so they try and dash around and, ah, and, ah, head the fellows off but they are not making much better time than the stampeding horses but as they get down there they yell at the guys and they jump off their horses, shake 'em, and get them all up and just at that moment when they are climbing on their horses the stampede comes dashing into them and the guys are knocked on the ground and the whole, this whole, all seven of the guys are just trampled to death and of course whatever happens to the horses, they are set out on this wild plain again and will have to be, ah, ah, caught if they are ever going to be tame.

I walked into this apparent hole in the ground and looking with a good deal of wonder when a man walked up to me and said, "Take this and any time you need any help why merely ask it and take your tool and use it whenever danger approaches." I just walked along this. . . . Well, it was some sort of a shiny metal instrument and moon-shaped with various embossings on it almost like a shield a small one. And I walked along through, through what seemed to be the path of life passing these various dangers and for each one assuming different exteriors according to my need and protection, sometimes shell of an armadillo, at other times the spines of a porcupine and the scales of a fish and all sorts of horrible obstacles, sometimes webbed feet sometimes to cross water, other times feet equipped for climbing over huge stones. Finally the path went around, turned around and led to a, came to a fork in the road one side seemed to point outward toward earth and continuation of life and the other one toward more wanderings and more knowledge, more experience in the mysteries that I had been through. I don't know which one I took, though. Do I have to decide that? [Laughs]. . . . Well, I took the one out to the earth and thought perhaps I could make use of some of the allegory and knowledge that I had picked up in my trip.

If the protocol does reveal antisocial behavior, the variability of the dimensions illustrated in Part I must be examined and explained. If in one story the hero tries to escape but is ultimately punished for his crimes by imprisonment we could not interpret this story until we had compared this with other stories concerned with immoral behavior. If all other stories revealed a hero who expressed antisocial behavior only to suffer imprisonment after an unsuccessful attempt to escape this punishment, we would assume that the individual feared external punishment for any expression of his antisocial wishes but had not introjected moral norms sufficiently to experience remorse or guilt. But if we found other stories in which the hero suffered acute remorse rather than punishment for his misbehavior we would have to explain this difference. We have found that the same individual may experience guilt for one kind of sin and fear punishment for some other sin—he will, for example, feel guilt for sexual misbehavior but fear punishment for antisocial aggression. Or the hero may, in two stories, experience guilt or fear external punishment for the same kind of sin but the difference may depend on the violence of the crime. Thus a hero who injures a person may fear the law, whereas a hero who kills someone experiences intense guilt. Or it may depend on the hero's role in the crime. There will commonly be found heroes who fear punishment for crimes committed with the cooperation of allies, but who feel guilt for crimes committed without the cooperation of allies. Again, guilt may be the sequel to crimes instigated by the hero, fear of punishment the result of crimes another person has persuaded the hero to commit.

Stories vary not only in the internality or externality of punishment but in the heroes' attitude toward the punishment and in the severity and duration of punishment. There are important variations in the type of antisocial behavior expressed, the targets of such behavior and the part played by the hero in crime. All these variations between stories in a single protocol can usually be explained either as the effect of some important cause which varies in these stories, or as a cause of different effects which result from variations in any of these dimensions.

Any story of antisocial behavior must also be analyzed with due regard to the possibility of the expression of repressed wishes. Thus the objects toward which antisocial behavior is directed may express varying degrees of remoteness. The role of the hero in antisocial behavior may indicate those conditions which are sufficiently remote and safe to permit the expression of repressed wishes; for example, when someone else persuades the hero to commit a crime the individual may express a wish which he could not express if he felt that he was directly responsible. The social context may provide similar remoteness and safety. As we saw in the case of Z, the assistance of allies permitted Z's heroes to aggress upon father surrogates. The story of the slaves who murdered their master is an example of this.

One must also consider the temporal characteristics of antisocial behavior. Whether antisocial wishes have their origin in childhood, or in later life is a matter of import. In order to determine this we must compare stories concerned with antisocial behavior in which the hero is a child, an adolescent, and an adult. We must then examine the extent to which the hero's wishes have changed from childhood to adulthood. Thus, there are protocols that delineate a childhood turbulent with moral conflict which continues unresolved into adulthood. In other protocols adulthood is portrayed as relatively free of the moral conflicts of childhood. Analysis of the age of the heroes who are concerned with these problems may indicate that these conflicts were resolved in late childhood, adolescence, or in early adulthood. There are also protocols in which childhood is marked by freedom from moral conflict but adolescence is particularly stormy, with serious sequelae in adulthood. Finally there are protocols which indicate that the individual suffered acute moral problems in early childhood, solved these problems in late childhood but suffered reactivation of the same conflicts in adolescence or adulthood. In the analysis of such sequences one may use the technique employed in the investigation of changes in parent-child relationships. Stories of antisocial behavior should be placed in chronological order, according to the age of the hero in each story. Changes which may be attributed to differences in the age of the hero should then be analyzed to illuminate exacerbations and resolutions of moral conflicts as these fluctuate in time.

We may also examine the impact of antisocial behavior on other regions. It is possible through such an examination to illuminate the importance of other regions for the individual whose heroes express antisocial behavior. If the hero who commits a crime is concerned with the effect this will have on his family, this indicates the importance of the latter to the hero and to the storyteller. When an individual tells a story of crime he has the option of describing the consequences of his behavior either in terms of his own fear or remorse or in terms of the effect which this will have on his family or love object or on his work or career. In the following story, for example, the consequences of antisocial behavior for the hero's marital relationship are such that the hero ultimately reforms.

> There was once a young scientist in the late nineteenth century who became a genius in the use of explosive chemicals. He loved a young girl very dearly and married her. They were married a great many years, during which time he received great amounts of money from various countries. But the various explosives he invented were for uses of destruction. He gradually acquired a great desire, or lust, for money and power and he continued to invent these deadly explosives, each one more powerful and deadly than the other. But

beneath this lust was imbedded his love for this girl for whom he thought he was doing best by showering on her these fabulous riches. Day after day, she pleaded with him to give up this business and devote his time to medical science instead. But his lust grew until, one day, after having made a terrifically explosive powder, he left it in his laboratory while he went off to negotiate for its sale. While he was gone, for some unknown reason which we can attribute to nature, this powder exploded, blowing up the house and killing his wife. Though still a young man, the loss of his wife suddenly made him realize the power of nature and his wrongdoing. The loss of his wife affected him so that within the next few years he aged almost twenty years. He gave up his malicious lust and turned his ability to medical science. Day after day he visited the grave of his wife, until finally he died an old man with great accomplishments in the medical field behind him and a full realization of what his lust had cost him.

The parent-child relationship is disturbed by the antisocial behavior of the hero in the following story. The mother persuades the son to return the money. He has a change of heart and reforms.

This story starts, this fellow is his mother's pride and joy from child, from child, from the time he is born. He is an only child and of course he has become very spoiled through these years. He grows into a reckless young man, too reckless. He becomes a sort of, oh, he gets involved in, in small crimes and ah yes, oh, particularly robberies and so forth. He is a good hearted fellow but he just gets involved and his mother is aware of this and it, it hurts her very much, but ah, she is one of those mothers that, she can't reproach him for anything and of course is always very honest with her and he comes to tell her all of his problems when he does get into these scrapes. Up to this time, however, he has gotten involved in a major robbery and in making their escape they have gone around a corner and some old gentleman has been hit by the car that he is driving and he wasn't driving fast but he was trying to get away in a hurry and he hit this old man and because he had taken, he had stolen enough money from this concern so that it was actually a major robbery but that isn't the thing that bothers him. He is afraid that the old man was hit hard enough so that he was killed. He didn't stop so that he naturally is a hit-and-run driver too to add to all this trouble. He goes home and tells his mother of all this mess. He of course is being hunted by the police now. Ah, the mother of course is very worried. She doesn't know what to say. She has turned away. She is angry. She realizes that she has made mistakes in the raising of her son. She gets the boy, she has talked him into returning the money that he has stolen and they, she is, she is a religious woman and she starts praying for this old gentleman. Well, the fellow returns the money and gives himself up to the police. He is a kind of a, it's kind of a change of heart, like I said he was a good fellow at heart and so the mother in her prayers decides that she will go and see the old gentleman, the gentleman is recovering and when the mother and this old fellow get to talking they realize that they are childhood playmates. They haven't seen each other for several years now but ah, when they, when she tells the old gentleman his story he is about to, well he withdraws his charges against the young man and the fellow for having returned the money and these charges against him were withdrawn by his, this old gentleman and he is released and from then on the outcome is that he lives a very straightforward and happy life.

Or the hero may, as in the following story, think of his lost career as he is going off to jail.

> The hands belong to the law and they are taking this man off to jail. There is a long train ride before they reach the penitentiary and this man has plenty of time to think over what he's done. Particularly he thinks about his job and how he hoped someday to be a great lawyer, but the mess he was in now had queered that. Even if it weren't for the jail sentence which would make passing the bar impossible he'd be too old when he got out, he'd be lucky if he could get any kind of a job.

Because antisocial behavior in the TAT usually represents suppressed or repressed material, it will be found most frequently in the protocols of normal, neurotic and psychotic individuals. It will in general be found less prominent in the protocols of those whose behavior is actually antisocial. Kutash's study of psychopathic defective criminals (49) revealed these individuals to be much more concerned with separation anxiety, ambition, and guilt than with the wish to commit antisocial behavior. Whether these same individuals might have described more antisocial behavior in their stories had they been tested before they were imprisoned we do not know. But we do know that the actual antisocial behavior of the individual telling TAT stories may have no representation whatever in his stories. It has been the writer's experience in "blind" analysis of the TAT's of children and adolescents who presented serious behavior problems that he has, in almost every instance, misdiagnosed the specific behavior problem which was the concern of the parent and therapist. Paradoxically, this was not infrequently the virtue of the diagnosis based on the TAT protocol. Thus the stories of a 7 year old boy revealed a terrified young hero who faced a physically threatening world alone, his parents conspicuous by their absence or death. His heroes were obsessed with the problem of time, centering on the time of the parents' return. In response to the violin picture, the hero misses the presence of his mother: "And maybe his mother's away and he wants to show it to her." In the third story, rather than complaining of coercive parental dominance the hero laments the absence of his parents: "Well this guy might be crying because probably his mother or father died and he's all alone." When he is with his father the hero is aware of physical danger but he believes his father can cope with this.

> And they're going to go out in the boat pretty soon. And the boat won't sink and it doesn't have any leaks in it. And the father will row. Well, it'll end up that it doesn't sink. Nobody gets hurt and they'll get back safely.

However, the child feels capable of coping with this dangerous world if his parents have taught him how to take care of himself.

> I think the guy is in a log cabin. He's wondering and he's seeing something. And he wonders inside if he should get his gun. And he doesn't have any mother or father. His mother and father are dead, or they're away. He's about ten and before his father and mother left they taught him how to work and he shoots his own supper and breakfast and gets fish out of a brook.

Incidental remarks made during the inquiry were the only clue to his overt behavior. He talked about how strong he was, how he had cut down an oak tree and could pull nails with his hands. He boasted that other boys were afraid of him. The discrepancy between the tone of these remarks and the characteristics of his heroes made it clear that this was the façade of an anxious child. I was not prepared, however, to learn that he was responsible for setting fires. The TAT had been administered in an effort to discover the motivation of this behavior. Analysis of the TAT, however, revealed neither a preoccupation with fire setting nor evidence of *any* type of antisocial behavior. The physical dangers of a threatening world in the absence of his parents, his relative security in the presence of a beloved and powerful father— these were his preoccupations. Setting of fires was instigated by a more dominant and more active playmate who persuaded this child to join him. A short time after this, his playmate moved away. This frightened and lonely child never set another fire, partly because the other child's influence was removed and partly because his parents were persuaded to give him more attention and guidance. The precise meaning of his overt antisocial behavior was never determined, nor did the TAT illuminate its meaning, although it provided reassurance that the wish to destroy per se did not underlie the subject's antisocial behavior.

Let us consider another "blind" analysis, that of a protocol of a 14 year old girl. In this case the only information available to the writer was the fact that both mother and father were living, and that she had one younger and two older brothers. Analysis of this record revealed a deeply repressed hostility towards the brothers and an intense longing for the exclusive affection of the mother. In the following story there is a wish fulfillment phantasy indicating what this girl hoped she might mean to her mother.

> This one's not too hard. This woman had a great happiness come into her life and she's bursting into the room trying to find her daughter to tell her about it. Oh dear, I can't think. Her daughter is nowhere to be found. She looks every place for her. After giving up hope, she finally hears that her daughter was killed. Murdered. After this the woman has great sorrow and never lives a happy life again since she lost her daughter.

Contrast the effect of the daughter's death on the mother with the effect of the son's death.

This woman has just been to a party and something terrible has happened to her. A child has been drowned out in the ocean. She hears him calling and goes running out. When she goes out to meet him she finds he's dead. This woman up above standing behind the tree is the child's nurse and she's trying to find what's the matter with the child's mother. The mother after this is very unhappy about life and she didn't think there was anything to live for after her child was gone. She's living in the country, not the city, at the time and she moved out in to the country and with her husband and the nurse lived very happily and she never had any more children.

There is also a wish expressed here. She would like the younger child to drown so that she might live happily ever after with the mother and father. The condition of such happiness would be that the mother have no more children. Clearly this girl is tired of playing the role of nurse to the younger child. In the story "she's trying to find what's the matter with the child's mother." There is no thought that the nurse might be interested in the child whose care is her responsibility. This story avoids direct expression of her hostility. It is a nurse rather than a daughter. The son drowns through no fault of the nurse and the nurse continues to live with the mother and father. This accidental death of the boy is not the nurse's expressed wish. In the story that follows there is again an indirect expression of the girl's hostility towards her brothers.

This boy is kissing his mother and he's just come home from the service and he's so excited that neither of them are laughing or crying, just very sad. The boy's twin brother was with him but he was killed in the war. This boy was the only one who came home out of three. He starts to tell his mother about all the horrible adventures he's had. She's so grief stricken by it that she faints. After a few months the mother dies and the boy is left all by himself. He gets married. After a few months he gets divorced and is left all by himself to be a bachelor. That's a very unsuccessful ending.

Again, no overt aggression is expressed toward the brother but the mother is taken away by death and the brother is eventually "left all by himself to be a bachelor." Nor is he permitted the satisfaction of a substitute mother. Thus far there has been no indication of any hostility toward the brother. Our evidence, such as it is, is the result of inference. We have found only that she separates mother and son and contrives to unite "nurse" and mother and permits the mother to have no more children. Though she had been able to forget the death of her son, the mother is grief-stricken and inconsolable at the separation from her daughter. In none of this is there any evidence of aggression, except by inference. No one has committed a single aggressive act, nor has there been mention of any feeling of hostility. Inasmuch as we suspect some repressed aggression motivating these stories, where shall we look for evidence of it? According to our theory of repression we would expect some aggression to be expressed under more "remote" circumstances. We have noted before that card 11 depicting a dragon in a prehistoric setting is peculiarly capable of eliciting aggressive phantasies because the animal and the setting are sufficiently remote to allow aggression to be displaced. If the aggression were directed toward the parent we should expect that one of the human figures might be pitted against the dragon in a life and death struggle. If an Oedipus complex existed we might expect the struggle to terminate in the rescue of the parent figure from the clutches of the dragon. But these common displacements do not appear in this case.

> Are these animals? This is an animal that's about to attack the buffalo. And this animal is getting ready to jump out of a cavern and he's about ready to attack. And the buffalo sets a trap for him. Just about as the animal is about to attack the buffalo, his foot slips and over the cliff the buffalo goes. The ledge below saves him and the animal that was about to attack the other animal hits his head looking down at the buffalo. The animal loses his balance and falls over onto the next ledge where the buffalo is. The buffalo won his battle. I guess that's all.

Although the picture provided the possibility of conflict between human beings and the dragon, she has elected to disregard this possibility. The struggle is made more "remote" than is customary for this card; since it is a struggle between two animals rather than a person and an animal. We would suppose that this happened because of the very strong inhibition of her aggression, and the possibility that two animals better symbolize her self and her sibling. Further indication of the strength of the repression of her aggression is seen in the fact that although the "battle" is won by the buffalo, the animals never come to grips with each other. "Accidents" happen even in this "battle."

Let us turn then to the card in the female series designed to elicit aggression, card 18 GF (a woman has her hands squeezed around the throat of another woman whom she appears to be pushing backwards across the banister of a stairway). We would predict that the somewhat ambiguous figure of the woman who is being strangled would be changed to a young boy, but not portrayed as her brother and that the older woman would be changed to a girl. We would further predict on the basis of the inhibition of aggression thus far evidenced, that the story would either be completely unaggressive or that if aggression were expressed, it would appear to the heroine as a completely "foreign" impulse which might be disclaimed as an abnormality or if not disclaimed would produce overwhelming guilt.

> This boy and girl were playing together when the girl became very angry with the boy. She's about to strangle him. She's putting her fingers in his

ear and pushing his eardrums in. The boy screams for help but that does no good because the woman has got her fingers in his throat. The woman—the girl has the boy almost dead when she suddenly realizes what she is doing. She stops then and there and leaves the boy and runs out of the house. She's so terrified that she goes and commits suicide. The boy lives to be happy ever after.

The aggressive woman is portrayed as a girl, although there is an oscillation between these alternatives. The other woman has been turned into a "boy." No reason is given for the suddenness of her anger, and there is no elaboration of the transition between this feeling and the resultant behavior. After she "became very angry" the next moment "she's about to strangle him." This she does quickly. She is so intent on this that "the girl has the boy almost dead when she suddenly realizes what she is doing." We had predicted that the aggression would be something "foreign" and disclaimed by the heroine. This was not an altogether mistaken expectation, but the story suggests certain qualifications. The fact that the girl could become "very angry" while playing with the boy suggests that her aggression is both intense and volatile under certain conditions. But the immediate translation of this feeling into behavior was permitted only because it was not so intense that she wished to kill the boy. It is only *in the act* of aggression that the girl's hostility grows more intense, until finally "the girl has the boy almost dead when she suddenly realizes what she is doing." Presumably she would not have expressed this aggression had she realized *before* the full extent of her wish, since "she stops then and there and leaves the boy and runs out of the house. She's so terrified that she goes and commits suicide." In atonement for this act she permits this young boy "to be happy ever after." All other brothers have been killed, separated from the mother, or left to lead lonely lives. We are told then, that if she ever expressed her hostility, its intensity would know no limit. But if she *were* to realize the extent of her wish she could not completely express it. The heroine commits suicide because of her *realization* of what she has almost done, and not because she has murdered the boy. He is permitted to live happily ever after. But her terror at the realization of what she has *almost* done is sufficient to cause her to take her life. Her aggression can never be completely expressed and even its partial expression would overwhelm her with terror, *if* she were to realize the extent of her aggression. It was for these reasons that the writer doubted that the problem presented by this child was one of aggressive behavior. But the form it might take could be no more than guessed. The problem which concerned the parent and therapist was compulsive stealing. It is unclear whether this derives from her wish for her mother's attention or her hostility towards her brothers, or both. It would seem more likely that it is an expression of her longing for her mother rather than an expression of hostility, since the former is to some extent a conscious wish, and to some extent repressed in so far as it is connected with killing the siblings. She is capable of a wishful phantasy in which she as nurse lives happily with the mother but she is incapable of expressing her aggression towards her brothers in her stories. We would suppose that the compulsive stealing stems from her wish for love, on the basis of our assumption that the more deeply repressed the wish the less counterpressure is capable of producing either symptom formation, anxiety, or a breaking through of the repressed impulse.

The wishes of these two individuals, as they are expressed in the TAT, and their overt antisocial behavior bear no obvious resemblance to each other. But if we were not able to explain the meaning of the antisocial behavior, we have at least been given insight into the psychic soil in which this behavior took root—insight which enabled therapy to attack the causal conditions of the symptom despite relative ignorance of their meaning.

SUMMARY

In Part I we illustrated dimensions useful in the analysis of antisocial behavior. We first examined the form of antisocial behavior and then the motivation of such behavior. We saw that these were independent dimensions—any motive might lead to any type of antisocial behavior. Aggression, for example, might be the consequence of jealousy, the wish to be like others, or the wish to help someone. A feeling of inferiority might lead to aggression, stealing, or antisocial dominance. We then examined the direction of antisocial behavior and saw that it might be directed against an individual, some particular class or group, or against the social order. The next dimension of analysis was the role of the hero in anti-social behavior—whether the hero or others instigated antisocial behavior. Then we examined the social context—whether the hero committed his crime alone or with the cooperation of allies, and whether the hero regarded himself as a member of an in-group or an out-group in his antisocial behavior. We next examined the acceptance of responsibility—whether the hero assumed responsibility for his behavior or felt that he was really innocent or not responsible for his behavior. Examining the duration of antisocial behavior, we saw that this might represent an isolated incident or the hero's way of life. We then examined the sequelae of antisocial behavior—whether the hero suffered punishment and whether punishment came from exogenous or endogenous sources. We examined the nature and duration of exogenous punishment and the attitude of the hero toward such punishment—whether he resists punishment or gives himself up and whether there is any conflict about the latter. We examined his attitude toward apprehension—whether the hero was relieved that the chase was over or hostile toward his captors. We then examined the success or failure of resistance to punishment. We saw that successful resistance to punishment is uncommon and usually placed in a remote setting indicative of a repressed wish. We also examined the extent to which crime and punishment are connected. Usually the punishment is the consequence of a crime, but occasionally one finds stories in which this connection is not explicit. This usually signifies that the story-teller is not altogether aware of the relation between his antisocial wishes and their punishment. Another sequel of antisocial behavior was reformation on the part of the hero, either incited through external agencies or the result of inner promptings. Such reformation we saw might be permanent or short-lived. A third sequel of antisocial behavior was atonement, when the crime represented an incident rather than a way of life. Finally we examined amoral sequelae in which the hero commits crimes in a completely amoral fashion with no thought either of punishment or guilt. These are uncommon stories, and the remoteness of either object, time, or setting which is character-istic of these stories signifies deeply repressed material.

In Part II we considered the interpretation of these variables. We said first that the general techniques employed in analyzing the dimensions of love, sex, and marital relationships could be employed in the region of antisocial behavior. We must first examine the extent to which antisocial behavior is mentioned in the protocol, since other values may be much more important to the individual than moral values. If the latter finds representation we must determine whether any dimensions are invariant in the protocol, since these represent stable elements in the personality of the storyteller. When the dimen-sions vary from story to story it is the task of interpretation to explain such variation as the cause or effect of concomitant variation of other elements within the stories. We said also that attention must be paid to the possibility that repressed wishes may be expressed in any story concerning antisocial behavior. We next examined the temporal characteristics of antisocial behavior and sug-gested that the techniques employed in analyzing changes in the parent-child relationship could be applied to changes in antisocial behavior. We also examined the impact of antisocial behavior on other regions for the light it shed on the importance of these regions for the individual. We then examined in some detail the protocols of a child and an adolescent, both of whom presented behavior problems. We saw that the TAT shed little light on the meaning of the antisocial behavior, which was indeed conspicuous by its absence from the protocol; what it did reveal however, enabled the therapist to attack the root of the problem despite a relative ignorance of the meaning of the symptoms.

Chapter IX

DIAGNOSIS OF PERSONALITY: WORK AND VOCATIONAL SETTING

Contemporary vocational guidance, not unmindful of the relevance of personality diagnosis to an assessment of the individual's abilities and capacities, employs the interview and questionnaire methods for this purpose. These, however, may be more profitably employed if supplemented by projective techniques.

Assessment of an individual's needs in the work region differs in no essential manner from any other variety of personality diagnosis. It is as simple or as complex as a determination of the conditions of a neurosis and of no less urgent import to the individual. We do not believe that every individual who seeks vocational guidance is, or should be, in quest of psychotherapy. In the writer's experience only a small percentage of those seeking vocational guidance require psychotherapy. In the majority of cases seen by the writer the individual in quest of vocational guidance has accurately diagnosed the region of his life most crucial to his future well-being. He may, however, on first appearance in the office of the vocational counselor, be anxious and confused and appear to be more in need of therapy than guidance. Nonetheless, accurate diagnosis of the individual's work needs, his acceptance of the diagnosis, and its translation into specific vocational behavior may ultimately result in the integration of the individual.

An accurate assessment of the precise meaning of work to the individual is of considerable import in such diagnosis. The irreducible minimum of conditions necessary if he is to work at all, the conditions which are "ideal" and mobilize the individual's best energies, and the conditions which inhibit or seriously interfere with his functioning in the work region must all be determined.

We shall turn our attention first to the characteristics of the individual's work and the variety of meanings implicit in work.

I. THE CHARACTERISTICS OF WORK

A. The Meaning of Work for the Individual

The goals for which individuals in American society strive and the satisfactions they enjoy or hope to enjoy reflect the varieties of motives generated by a complex social order. Although all work is to some extent motivated by dissatisfaction, it is profitable to distinguish between work oriented primarily away from unpleasant or frustrating circumstances and work oriented primarily toward some positive goal which excites and mobilizes the individual's energies. The former type of work is undertaken by those who are driven by a sense of inferiority, by poverty, by unhappiness in love, by the wish to be free of dependence on others, or by any anxiety, whatever its source. Such an individual's work is rewarding insofar as it removes him from these frustrations. But an individual may also work for more positive goals. The vision of future fame or competence or the wish to create something of value or to dedicate himself to the welfare of others may excite and inspire the individual and sustain his work. For many individuals both types of motivation are found together, with varying proportions of the negative and positive components.

Let us consider first a sample of stories illustrating work which is motivated by forces essentially negative in quality.

I. WORK NEGATIVELY MOTIVATED

In the following story, work is motivated primarily by the hero's feeling of inferiority, which he strives to overcome through hard work.

> Here is a picture of a young man participating in a gym class. This young man was probably underdeveloped as a young child and consequently was subject for the taunts of his fellow youths for his inability to play or participate in the more strenuous games. With a feeling of inferiority he made up his mind that he would take every means at his disposal to develop himself. Entering into gym classes he worked hard and in time did develop the bulging muscles and the stamina that seemed so necessary to win the respect of his fellow youths. Here in this picture he is winning the rope climbing event and, from the expression on his face, a great deal of satisfaction.

He may work to overcome poverty and financial insecurity.

> They're very poor and down and out, and this poor guy works like a dog to keep his head above water. He's hoping, if he works hard enough, the boss will notice him and maybe give him a raise. He's got to get some money to pay bills, his wife's been sick and he has to pay the doctor. But it doesn't seem to do any good. No matter how hard he works his pay check is the same at the end of every week, and it isn't enough.

Or to overcome rejection by a love object. In the following story a woman, rejected in love, finds satisfaction in work.

> This woman is pleading with this man to leave his work for a while and relax. She offers herself to him. The man here seems to be hesitating between his duty and his love, but actually he knows which really matters to him. Besides, he will soon grow tired of the woman and the temporary pleasure is nothing compared with the rewards of his work. So he fools around with her for a while and then throws her off without remorse because after all she got what she wanted and he gave as much as was his to give. The woman takes it

badly at first but she recovers and throws herself into her own work with greater determination. She is thrilled to find how well she makes out on her job.

Or to overcome the psychological effects of a physical handicap.

The woman has just had a fit of crying for she is horribly deformed and rushes into her father's arms for comfort. Everyone excludes her from their social circles because she is so ugly. Her father tells her that the thing that counts most is the real person, not one's physical appearance. She determines that she is not going to let this ruin her life. She takes up the study of psychology and turns out to be a great authority on the subject. And people are so interested in what she has to say that they forget what she looks like.

Or to be free of dependence on others.

He's a veteran home from the wars, and at first he's happy to be home and to see his family again. They're very happy to see him and everyone is very nice to him. But after a while he feels that he wants to get out on his own, he wants to get a job. He can't go on being dependent on his family forever. He talks to them about it but they can't seem to realize that he's grown up in the years he's been away. They tell him to wait awhile and then to go to college, and then to think about getting a job. He tries to explain that he couldn't take it being dependent on them for four more years, that he's grown up in the years he's been in the army, he's not a baby any more. He wants to get out and make his own money. They don't understand and he feels it's hopeless to try to explain any more. So he packs his things and leaves. He's saying goodbye to his mother here.

Or to overcome his aggression.

A very impetuous man. He's just had a fight with his boss. They're talking here and in a minute they'll have a fight, and both will say a lot of things they don't mean. The man will come out of the boss's office still mad and will sit down to work. Furiously working, calms him, and gradually he will begin to feel sorry and will go and apologize to his boss.

Or to overcome anxiety.

She looks worried. She's worried and she doesn't quite know what she's worried about. She's just worried about everything. She tries to get her mind off her worries and throws herself into a book. She's studying. The time it's time for her to go to bed, she's feeling much better, not worried any more.

2. WORK POSITIVELY MOTIVATED

But work may have more positive meaning for the hero. He may work to become famous.

The girl is daydreaming. She wants to become a great artist, the kind that people admire. She is a very smart girl and she wants to make a name or reputation, for herself. So she studies diligently and develops into a renowned person.

Or to become great.

This looks like a little boy who wants to become a great violin player. He, I mean now he is just dreaming about what a great man he will be. He eventually becomes a great violin player and is acclaimed by the world.

Or to create something of beauty.

This man is very young. Ever since he was a small child he has been interested in music. He has never been able to express his feelings about it but he has always wanted to take lessons. His favorite instrument is the violin. He has begun to take lessons and he likes it very much. As he first begins to undertake his instrument, after he has studied a while he realizes the difficulty of what he has undertaken and compares his playing with that of the old masters. He realizes how different it is. What he is learning and doing for the first time is getting insight into the meaning of genius. As he looks at the violin he is trying to understand how some great composer could compose music, a beautiful melody, out of wood and strings and bows. How could he put together such music? Did he do it in his mind, or did he run his fingers over the strings, or with the bow? He feels that he, too, would like to compose such beautiful melodies for the instrument. But he feels that he has a long way to go before he can reach such heights. This is his state of mind, which is encouraging for the future. One day he will learn that he can. As he draws his bow over the strings an entirely new melody comes, simple and beautiful, and he realizes that this is something at least akin to what the great artists have done. This is only the beginning, and seems to have come spontaneously, through no effort of his own. He can't explain how. And several things might happen. Possibly he could become a composer, or perhaps only come to realize that everyone can create beautiful music, and that this creation is only the energy one has in them. Music might come from everyone. It might not be beautiful music but it might be an expression of what was in people. So the man dreams about music and his experience, out of love of music, will give him more understanding into life and into his fellow men.

Or work to excite applause.

She had always wanted to act, but she had been a poor girl and didn't think that she would ever get the opportunity to study drama. As a young girl she worked hard to help the family along financially. But every chance she got she would study drama. She would stay awake reading all the books she could get her hands on, long after all of the rest of the family were asleep. And she finally did get a chance to go and try out for a play. It was her big chance and she knew it. It wasn't a big part, but if she could do it perfectly she would be given another chance, no doubt. So she sat in her room practicing and re-acting her lines until she had them down pat. The day came and the performance was given—The stage was set and there she was, seated in a chair, in a pensive mood. The play went along smoothly and although she was nervous in the beginning she was confident of her part. And she did magnificently. As the curtain went down, she heard a roar of applause. She was complimented after the play on her brilliant performance.

Or to excel a rival.

These men went to school together when they were young. They're rivals, always have been. They were always the first two in their classes and each worked hard to be first. This continued all their lives. Whatever one had, the other worked to get something better. Whatever one did, the other had to do better. They're meeting now and talk about calling a truce. They will both agree that this is childish. But it won't work. The minute they separate, they will be up to their old tricks, each working to outdo the other.

Or to be as good as another person.

This little boy admires his father and wants to be as great a violinist as his father is. He can play a little bit and he realizes how much effort it will take to be as good as his father. But he will work hard and practice. And someday he will be as good as his father.

Or he may wish to work with others.

This boy is blind, and has been blind since birth. His parents are quite musical. In fact, they are so wrapped up in their music and in each other that they have had little time to spend on the boy during his formative years. They cared about him enough to see that a competent person was always around to see that he did not get into trouble. But they themselves gave him little attention. He has now gotten old enough to be curious about his parents and they, not understanding him, have hit upon the idea of teaching him how to play the violin. They have given him the instrument, had him feel the parts of the violin with their guidance, and now have left him alone with it. The boy was quite happy when they were with him, but now he feels that once again he has been thrown on his own. He feels that he can play the instrument but he would get much more enjoyment out of playing it with them. So now he is deciding what to do. He will decide upon the simplest procedure. He will pick up the instrument and make a few sounds on it. But he knows that they will lose interest in him and his progress and that, once again, he will have to fall back on the companionship of the person who looks after him.

Or he may wish to work to help others by means of his skill.

We'll make a doctor out of him. Albert had dedicated all his life toward becoming a physician. From very early days he felt a sympathy for things, for beings in distress, in pain. There was the time when he healed the sick squirrel back to health. And the time that he reset the front paw of Fido, the fox terrier pup of one of his neighbors' children. Always in his heart was the desire to make people and animals happy and well. Pain and deformities seemed to him out of place. During his high school years he seriously decided to study medicine. Then came the hard years through college and medical school, and finally he hung out his shingle. Late the first night he started practice, a neighbor called him to visit his sick wife who appeared to be dying in an asthmatic attack. Albert raced over, and after a long time it seemed that he was about to lose his first case. Nothing he did seemed to do any good. He almost despaired and was about to give up, when realizing that a human life was at stake and that he had to save it. He went back to work again with renewed faith in himself and his efforts. Shortly afterwards, the woman began to regain her breath her natural color, after her hard struggle and almost suffocation. With a sigh of contentment, Albert mopped his brow and thanked God for not allowing him to fail in the first great test of service.

Or he may wish to repay others.

The young girl is looking at her family plowing in the fields. She knows that they have worked hard all their lives and have spent all their money to send her to school so that she will not have to go through all this, too. She is determined that she will educate herself so that some day she will become a great woman and repay them for all they have done for her, so that they will never have to toil in the hot fields again. She of course will achieve her goal and make for her family a house of luxury where they can sit and waste their time away as other women of riches have done.

Or to help others to a fuller life.

The impression received is that of a young girl returning from school and stopping to refresh her memory with the fact that these people are hard-working people, people who have to live close to nature and have material and practical things, not enjoying many, if any, of the pleasures of life. It is her ingrained hope that through close attention and diligence to her studies she will be able someday to help these people, particularly her own, to a life filled with a few more pleasures.

Or work may be a means to spiritual fulfillment.

This is an ambitious girl, a dreamer. But not merely a dreamer. She accomplishes much because of her determination. She was born in poor circumstances but she had made headway. She is planning to go to another city. She wants to see the world. She has great dreams to fashion. But her heart is tied to the soil. In fact, the best work she will ever accomplish will be in connection with the people of the villages, the farmers, the tillers, the downtrodden. Here she is thinking of a beautiful poem she could write about these rude folk. She is inspired by the sight of the soil and the man at work. However, the sight of the fine strong-muscled man also stirs in her a different emotion and she feels the inadequacy of her personal life. The woman at the back symbolizes this sex-urge, which has the power to defeat this girl's other life. The expression on the symbol, the woman's face, suggests how confident she is of triumphing over the girl. The girl thinks what terrific happiness it would mean to gratify this desire and be a mother of children and serve the needs of this strong man. But she also realizes that such happiness would be transient and that soon she would yearn for spiritual fulfillment. She thinks of Madame Curie and others who have accomplished much through denying themselves, and she thus manages to control herself. She eventually becomes a great poet.

Or happiness may be found only in work.

He's restless. It's night and he's through working for the day but he can hardly wait for tomorrow to come. He's fascinated by what he's doing and he's only completely happy when he's working. His work for him is his whole life.

Or work may be the means to future security.

These are two patient old people. They've worked hard all their lives. They are not exactly misers but they've worked hard and saved so that they would have security in their old age. Now the time has come for them to stop working. They will spend the twilight years of their lives together in peace.

Or the hero may work to achieve power and money.

There was once a young scientist in the late nineteenth century who became a genius in the use of explosive chemicals. He loved a young girl very dearly and married her. They were married a great many years, during which time he received great amounts of money from various countries. But the various explosives he invented were for uses of destruction. He gradually acquired a great desire, or lust, for money and power and he continued to invent these deadly explosives, each one more powerful and deadly than the other. But beneath this lust was imbedded his love for this girl for whom he thought he was doing best by showering on her these fabulous riches. Day after day, she pleaded with him to give up this business and devote his time to medical science instead. But his lust grew until, one day, after having made a terrifically explosive powder, he left it in his laboratory while he went off to negotiate for its sale. While he was gone, for some unknown reason which we can attribute to nature, this powder exploded, blowing up the house and killing his wife. Though still a young man, the loss of his wife suddenly made him realize the power of nature and his wrongdoing. The loss of his wife affected him so that within the next few years he aged almost twenty years. He gave up his malicious lust and turned his ability to medical science. Day after day, he visited the grave of his wife, until finally he died an old man with great accomplishments in the medical field behind him and a full realization of what his lust had cost him.

Or to raise his socio-economic status.

Mike was a poor boy who early in life decided that he was going to climb the ladder from the lowest to the highest rung, a typical Horatio Alger. He started with the usual job—a paper route. Whatever there was to do he was a jump ahead of anyone else. He didn't waste time looking at rich kids and wishing he could be like them, he worked to be sure he would be. People liked him for his frankness and rung by rung he climbed the ladder until he finally stood at the top. He married the boss's daughter and settled down to raise a bunch of kids like the ones he never had time to envy.

Or he may work to earn his living.

> A haggard young transient had been searching for the past few years for a steady job. He was not looking for a handout but a good hard job where he could earn his own living. But his weak, haggard appearance prevented any employer from hiring him for the least position. But one day, while walking near a river, he saw the entire outfit of some well-dressed man who had discarded them. He put them on, and with a clean-shaved appearance he returned to town to look for a job, and there rose rapidly because of his dignified appearance and ability to work hard. He saw that it was clothes that made the man.

Or because of a cathexis for money per se.

> This is the story of a miser. All he wants in life is money. That's all he cares about. He slaves for years and carefully carries the money home and adds it to his growing hoard. He loves to handle it and count it. This goes on for years and every week he cashes his pay check and adds it to his hoard. Then he dies. The moral of this story is, "You can't take it with you."

Or to earn money for marriage.

> He's an artist and although he does his best he can't seem to earn any money. He's got to earn money or this girl's family won't let her marry him. He works day and night hoping to paint something that he can sell. Without his knowing about it she takes one of his pictures and enters it in a contest like the Pepsi-Cola contest or whatever it is. She doesn't tell him anything about it and he wins a prize of $5,000 which is enough for them to get married on.

This is a sample of the more common meanings of work as reflected in TAT stories.

B. Level Analysis

Our concern here is with the sequence of levels characteristic of the work of the individual. One of the more important relationships to be examined is that between the level of daydream and the level of behavior.

There are those for whom the daydream is a tonic spurring the individual on and sustaining his work. This is seen in the following story.

> The girl is daydreaming. She wants to become a great artist, the kind that people admire. She is a very smart girl and she wants to make a name for herself. So she studies diligently and develops into a renowned person.

For others the daydream is either a retreat from work or so exciting that the intention to work is short-circuited in the daydream.

> This young kid is daydreaming about being a doctor, I mean a surgeon, and presumably looking forward to being one of the better known and able ones. Judging from the mustaches on the doctors, he may be thinking of some

earlier pioneer in medicine operating with relatively simple tools, and rustic surroundings.

Daydreaming in the next story is a retreat from work which the hero is unable to continue.

It's a lazy spring night and this boy is standing at the window thinking about the studying he should be doing. But it's such a beautiful night he just stands looking out until finally he realizes that it's getting late and rouses himself and gets to work. He works for about an hour but then he can't seem to concentrate. He starts dreaming about the good time he's going to have this summer. He's sleepy, so he closes the books and goes to bed.

The daydream following the esthetic experience (levels of perception and feeling) in some cases not only enables the individual to work more effectively but may constitute an important part of creative work. This may be true of any type of work in which the behavioral component is a relatively minor element, as in the following story.

An artistic soul who likes to watch the sky [long pause]. This young man is very fond of music. He's worked very hard for several years as a music student and is especially interested in composition. During the past few weeks his experiences have given rise to a wide range of emotions. A brother was killed in action in Europe; a sister was happily married; friends have come to visit him. He felt unsettled and had difficulty working. He opened the window and watched the stars. As he pondered about the universe, his family, and his friends, new and beautiful melodies surged into his mind. He began to write furiously. All night long he worked and produced his symphony of night, which marked the beginning of his real career.

The esthetic experience may renew and enrich the individual's work.

This boy was spending the evening at home, working. As the evening wore on the whole atmosphere became oppressive. He went to the window to breathe in fresh air and as he looked out the beauty of the twilit sky overwhelmed him. He felt small, insignificant, and yet part of a mighty universe. The experience both saddened and uplifted him; he felt purified and returned to his work with a feeling of having found his perspective. His work acquired a heightened quality thereby.

The level of daydream, as such, may have differential effects, depending on the specific content of the phantasy. In the following two stories, told by the same individual, the daydream concerned with work is a tonic to further work, but the daydream of love disrupts work.

This is a Harvard graduate student, and, uh, he's been burning the midnight oil. He's studying some science like anthropology and he starts dreaming about the different peoples all over the earth. And he gets an exciting picture of all these peoples blended into a harmonious whole, working together for a better life for everyone. He's very excited and he goes back to work and works hard, with the idea that the work he's doing will enable him to do his part in bringing his dream to reality.

The girl in the foreground is a student on her way home from school and she passes this farm everyday on her way home. Today she notices that they have a new hired man working in the field. She stops to talk to the woman, curious, and hoping that she'll meet him. But he goes on working and she goes home. That night after supper as she's doing her homework she finds herself dreaming of his strong muscular back and his nicely shaped head. Something stirs within her. She tells herself that this is nonsense and tries to get back to work. But she can't seem to. She begins to plan ways she can get to meet him.

The content of the phantasy, however, may not affect the outcome. Any type of phantasy may disrupt work, or work may continue no matter what the content of the phantasy. In the following stories told by an individual compulsive in his work, we see an example of the latter.

A very ambitious man, a junior executive in some big firm. He's having lunch with the vice-president who's telling him how pleased he is with his work, and to keep it up and someday soon he'll get a promotion. By the time he gets back to the office he's walking on air and sits at his desk dreaming of the day when he, too, will be a vice-president. But he snaps himself out of it with the thought that there's a lot of work to be done before then and starts to write a report on a big account he's just gotten.

A young man who's very hard-working. He's brought some work home from the office to do. He's interested in getting ahead. He works for awhile and then goes to the window to get some air. He looks out at the city below. He's thinking of his girl and how much he'd like to be out with her tonight. Then he shuts the window. There'll be other nights and he has work to do.

This is, in fact, a person compulsive in his work behavior. It makes no difference whether he dreams of promotion or of an evening of pleasure with his girl. The daydream yields to work in both cases.

The following story, however, shows the opposite trend: phantasy, no matter what its content, is disruptive to the activity of the individual.

"We are all of us dreamers of dreams." That's what Anne thought, as she passed her sister leaning against a tree. She was probably dreaming about the new baby that was coming, what it would look like and what it would say. Other people dreamed and Anne couldn't understand why she was always being told to keep her mind on what she was doing, and not to dream so much. But she couldn't help it. The pictures in her history book brought dreams of the days of old and the Kings and Queens who had ruled then. She forgot to do her lessons. When she was supposed to feed the chickens she would find herself trying to hear what they said to each other. And it was time to go to school before she remembered to feed them. When she was sent to get water from the well she would imagine that it was a wishing well and all she had to do was to make a wish and it would come true. One morning she was in Bagdad before she heard her sister calling from the house. It was worse in school. The clouds made such beautiful pictures that she couldn't turn her eyes from the window. And one day the teacher spoke to her three times before she turned from the window. And she had to stay after school. It would be so nice if people would try to understand and not keep after her. But she guessed that when people got as old as her sister and teacher they were just like that.

Another level of psychological function important for the work process is the level of thought. Individuals differ significantly in the extent to which their work is governed by conceptual activity. For some individuals such activity typically precedes work. Others prefer initial trial and error activity and only later turn to the conceptual level for further clarification. Such reflection may or may not lead to further work.

In the following story the hero, initially uncertain of his competence goes to work and discovers that he is in fact incompetent. He then turns to the level of thought. His "pondering" does not, however, lead to further work.

This boy is looking at the violin. He is thinking—wondering whether he will ever be able to play it. He started playing the violin and found that the sound produced was not as perfect as the sound he had heard from other violins. The outcome is that he has set the violin down on the table with the bow and is now pondering what he can do to make the sound coming from the violin more perfect.

Yet, as we see in the next story, such withdrawal to the level of thought may bear fruit in further work and ultimate success.

It's a boy contemplating a violin. More than likely he has been practicing. Having found difficulty with the sheet in front of him, he has placed his violin down and wonders why he can't produce the music that he knows should be gotten out of it. I say he has been playing because of the position of the violin. On the whole, his attitude is one of study and wonderment. More than likely he will resume his playing of the instrument. Having spent time studying it once, he will go back with renewed determination to finish the score before him. As a result of this interest and contemplative study of his, he is probably headed to be a good musician. It is quite possible that he may become one of the world's greatest violinists or composers because he has shown the qualities of consideration of his instrument, contemplation and an attempt to understand his instrument which brings about a love of the instrument and greater productivity, all of which point to a productive later life. Other facts, he's well groomed, his hair is neat, and the care with which he has put his bow on the table, indicate later success.

The level of thought may, however, lead neither to a dead end nor to further work and success but rather to confidence in future work and success.

A young boy looks out of his open window into the moonlit sky. He is a college student and this night he went to bed. But his mind was not tired. He was working vigorously. First he turned over in his mind the lecture he had heard during the day. Little bits of each one came to him, exciting intellectual thoughts, but his mind leaped from one to the other. Regarding each he thought, "This I must know more about." Then he began to think of when he would learn all these things, when he would find the answers, how he would find the answers to the thrilling and exciting problems that arose every day. At this point he got up, went over to 'the window. He looked off into space as though somehow the breadth of the vista before him might find him some perspective. He thought of what he might do, what career he might choose. He did not think of people. He thought only of ideas. At this moment he felt himself a kind of intellectual giant in whose hand lay the whole world. He would learn about it, he would know all about it, he would have power over it.

C. Differentiation of Means and Ends

Does the individual differentiate between means and end? The nature of the work may be such that it cannot be broken down into means and end. This is especially true of work which offers no particular problems; either it is simple and never required much training, or it is complex but has become habitual and presents no further problems. For the creation of such a distinction there usually has to be some discrepancy between the wish and the achievement. No distinction is made between means and ends in the following story because of the routine nature of the work.

Her first year as secretary to Mr. Jones was drawing to a close. Somehow she wished she had never wanted to take a white collar job. How could she have ever wanted to work, work, work. Up at 6:30. How? The alarm of course. Turn on the electric lights, make toast on the toaster, go to work on an electric trolley, go to the 16th floor by elevator and work all day on the typewriter, adding machines, machines, electricity, everything mechanical. Everything is scheduled, nothing free, natural, unhurried from 6:30 to 5:30 every day, day in, day out. Why, you'd think she was a mechanical man, or robot, or something. Oh, to get away from it all. Never to have to even set the alarm clock, much less turn it off. To be free to do as you please! Never to have to catch the 8:30 bus. Thank heavens her vacation was so near. Perhaps she might quit this job. Joyce had spoken of another job that had sounded like less monotony. Yes, that was what she wanted to do. Mr. Jones was disappointed to hear her proposal. She was an attractive receptionist, efficient, and had become completely familiar with the routine of his office. To train a new girl, and most likely one not as good, would take several months. So it was with this in mind that he gave her the chance to come back after her vacation if she should happen to reconsider. The vacation was ideal. She and Joyce went together and just basked in the sunshine, not caring what hour of the day and without a care in the world It was a change all right and at first it was heaven. But somehow the contrast to a hard working day seemed too great and was not as appealing to her as she had thought it would be. By the end of her vacation Anne realized that she really wanted and craved some sort of routine and planned work. She had always loved a sense of accomplishment and actually craved a certain amount of it. So it was with eagerness that she went back to Mr. Jones and remained his secretary for many years.

In the next story, however, means and ends are differentiated. We see that the conditions necessary for this distinction exist; there is a difference between the hero's desire to be a doctor and his achievement of this end.

We'll make a· doctor out of him. Albert had dedicated all his life toward becoming a physician. From very early days, he felt a sympathy for things, for beings in distress, in pain. There was the time when he healed the sick squirrel back to health and the time that he reset the front paw of Fido, the fox terrier pup of one of his neighbors' children. Always in his heart was the desire to make people and animals happy and well. Pain and deformities seemed to him out of place. During his high school years he seriously decided to study medicine. Then came the hard years through college and medical school and finally he hung out his shingle. Late the first night he started practice, a neighbor called him to visit his sick wife who appeared to be dying in an asthmatic attack. Albert raced over, and after a long time, it seemed that he was about to lose his first case. Nothing he did seemed to do any good. He almost despaired, and was about to give up, when realizing that a human life was at stake and that he had to save it. He went back to work with renewed faith in himself and his efforts. Shortly afterward, the woman began to regain her breath, her natural color, after her hard struggle and almost suffocation. With a sigh of contentment, Albert mopped his brow and thanked God for not allowing him to fail in this first great test of service.

If there is a differentiation between means and end, to what extent is this differentiation elaborated?

D. Means-End Cognizance

An examination of the protocol for means-end cognizance is useful in assessing the realism of the individual in the work situation. Does he wish or expect to achieve his ends through means-end activity or does he fail to consider the necessary means?

The hero may possess *no* means-end cognizance.

A little boy, about six who is dreaming of being a very great and wonderful violinist, one who leaves his audience spellbound with the power and beauty of his music. And then we see him years later receiving a tremendous ovation, his dream come true.

Or he may possess *some* means-end cognizance.

The boy is gazing at the violin with a dreamy, rapt expression on his face. He is a music lover and hopes someday to be a great musician. He knows that it means hard work but he will accomplish his aim and play in all the great cities all over the world.

Or he may possess a *high degree* of means-end cognizance.

It's a boy contemplating a violin. More than likely he has been practicing. Having found difficulty with the sheet in front of him, he has placed his violin down and wonders why he can't produce the music that he knows should be gotten out of it. I say he has been playing because of the position of the violin. On the whole his attitude is one of study and wonderment. More than likely he will resume his playing of the instrument. Having spent time studying it once, he will go back with renewed determination to finish the score before him. As a result of this interest and contemplative study of his, he is probably headed to be a good musician. It is quite possible that he may become one of the world's greatest violinists or composers because he has shown the qualities of consideration of his instrument, contemplation and an attempt to understand his instrument which brings about a love of the instrument and greater productivity, all of which point to a productive later life. Other facts, he's well groomed, his hair is neat, and the care with which he has put his bow on the table indicate later success.

The highest degree of means-end cognizance, however, is found where there is greatest elaboration of means. This is seen in the following story told by a business executive.

This looks like a scene from the Lost World. A number of explorers have been investigating this territory—perhaps in the vicinity of New Mexico. They come upon this path through a canyon. There doesn't seem to be any living thing whatever in the entire. vicinity. Everything is one monotonous color, a sort of dirty, brownish ivory. In a little while their eyes become accustomed to the light and coloration and notice various shapes—one in particular of a dinosaur, seems to be dormant, but its outspread webbed foot seems to indicate that it may be alive. As they approach a natural bridge, toward the dinosaur, they are confronted with a spider-like creature or a bug-like creature, except that it appears to be gigantic compared with an ordinary bug. This, too, this is moving. The creature however seems to pay no attention. They're fearful of going on and decide to return with weapons and some means of carrying out these creatures if they could be captured. Strangely enough when they return a day and a half later both creatures are in the same spot—as they had previously been. The bug still moved about and the men advanced slowly. The bug's horrible face and ugly legs put fear in the men's hearts. They decide not to capture him alive. A number of men let fly with high powered rifles. They aimed for his head and all shot accurately. The bug crumbled to dust. By some strange phenomenon the injury to his head disintegrated the entire body. The men were extremely disappointed and downcast. They decided not to try the same tactics with the dinosaur if he were alive. They approached warily, but the dinosaur made no move They got closer and closer to him until they were able to throw a lasso around his neck. They carefully tied it in a slip knot and all the men took hold of the rope and with one—at a signal, with one great tug, they pulled the monster from his place. He came very easily. There was no weight to him at all. As a matter of fact he was just a hollow shell. The back half of him crumbled as he hit the rocks. They rushed forward in an effort to save what was left. His body had been broken in too many pieces and they decided to cut up certain pieces which appeared that they would break in transportation. They transported the animal out in 45 wooden cases. It would probably take years to assemble him again. Took only one case to assemble the remains of the bug. They would get to that problem later. Perhaps they would let some of their assistants experiment with the dust. They had not originally expected a find as extraordinary as this, but now that they had found it and seemingly not captured these creatures correctly, they were a little bit disappointed. Their disappointment was forgotten in the years that they labored on reconstruction, and they looked with pride on their accomplishment when their creature was unveiled to the public at the museum of natural history.

Such a degree of means-end cognizance may, however, have pathological sequelae. This is seen in the following story where the hero's high degree of means-end cognizance paralyzes action.

In the foreground is a young boy and I guess what's above is his dream—a dream about being a doctor. This dream comes from a book he's read about doctors, Arrowsmith or something like that and he wants to be a doctor. He's thinking about the years of hard, grueling work entailed. He's have to study biology and chemistry and physics in college and then go to medical school for years, and learn anatomy, physiology, surgery and all the other sciences and then he'll have to be an interne and take care of people in hospitals and then be a resident in a hospital. It would be very hard work and take years and years. He never does become a doctor.

MEANS-END ELABORATION IN DAYDREAMING AND BEHAVIOR

We cannot assume, however, that because we find no means-end elaboration on the level of daydreaming that this is also true on the level of behavior. It may be that the absence of means-end cognizance on the level of phantasy merely represents a short-cut between wish and achievement not found on the level of behavior. To ascertain whether or not this is so, it is necessary to compare the individual's work stories on the level of daydreaming and the level of behavior. In the following two stories from the same protocol we find an example of this. The first story will be recognized as one in which the hero possesses no means-end cognizance on the level of daydreaming:

A little boy, about six, who is daydreaming of being a very great and wonderful violinist, one who leaves his audience spellbound with the power and beauty of his music. And then we see him years later receiving a tremendous ovation, his dream come true.

In the next story, however, the hero possesses a high degree of means-end cognizance on the level of behavior.

These men went to school together when they were young. They're rivals, always have been. They were always the first two in their classes and each worked hard to be first. This continued all their lives. Whatever one had, the other worked to get something better. Whatever one did, the other had to do better. They're meeting now and talk about calling it a truce. They will both agree that this is childish. But it won't work. The minute they separate, they will be up to their old tricks, each working to outdo the other.

It is important to note that at the beginning of these two stories the heroes are approximately the same age. The factor of age must be controlled in this type of comparison. It would otherwise be impossible to tell whether the difference in means-end cognizance is a function of the difference in the age of the hero or a function of the level of the story.

E. Cathexis of Means

Cathexis of means may be either positive or negative. The hero of the story which follows found the means so arduous that he abandoned his goal.

The little boy wants to learn to play the violin and he's looking at it and wondering if he ever will be able to. It looks so complicated and the music looks hard. He'll have to learn to read music and then to make the music come out on the strings with the bow and then he'll have to learn to play scales. Then he'll have to practice everyday for hours. He's very discouraged and decides maybe he doesn't want to learn.

Whereas the hero of the next story is positively cathected to the means.

This man is very young. Ever since he was a small child he has been interested in music. He has never been able to express his feelings about it but he has always wanted to take lessons. His favorite instrument is the violin. He has begun to take lessons and he likes it very much. As he first begins to undertake his instrument, after he has studied a small while, he realizes the difficulty of what he has undertaken and compares his playing with that of the old masters. He realizes how different it is. What he is learning and doing and for the first time he is getting insight into the meaning of genius. As he looks at the violin he is trying to understand how some great composer could compose music, a beautiful melody, out of wood and strings and bows. How could he put together such music? Did he do it in his mind or did he run his fingers over the strings or with the bow? He feels that he, too, would like to compose such beautiful melodies for the instrument. But he feels that he has a long way to go before he can reach such heights. This is his state of mind, which is encouraging for the future. One day he will learn that he can. As he draws his bow over the strings an entirely new melody comes, simple and beautiful, and he realizes that this is something at least akin to what the great artists have done. This is only the beginning and seems to have come spontaneously through no effort of his own. He can't explain how. And several things might happen. Possibly he could become a composer, or perhaps only come to realize that everyone can create beautiful music and that this creation is only the energy one has in them. Music might come from everyone. It might not be beautiful music but might be an expression of what was in people. So the man dreams about music, and his experience out of the love of music will give him more understanding into life and into his fellow men.

1. MEANS WHICH BECOME ENDS

A familiar phenomenon in work is the transformation of means into ends. Any activity which is pursued for a long period of time may eventually become an end in itself, although it was originally a means to some other end. Thus the hero of the following story worked originally in order to support his family, but a lifetime of such work renders him incapable of retiring from work when there is no longer the same reason for continuing it.

This fellow has worked hard all his life. He's raised a big family and it wasn't easy meeting all the bills but he kept at it day in and day out, never took a vacation—but somehow he never seemed to mind it—in fact he used to laugh to himself when his family pitied him for the hours he had to work—he really enjoyed it and when he got old enough to retire he wouldn't. He had plenty of money now, but he just couldn't see himself sitting around doing nothing.

2. ACTIVITY VALUED AS MEANS TO AN END

The individual may, however, cathect means only as they serve another end. The end may be something completely outside the realm of work, as in the following story where the hero reforms and starts working, "so that if he falls in love he won't have to wait for a good job."

This is a young man who lives an ordinary life without any particular ambition. All he cares about is getting enough money to live. One night just before he goes to bed, he turns off the lights and is looking out of his window. He realizes he has spent a good deal of his life with no purpose and it is time to settle down. It is not because his conscience troubles him but just because he feels he is missing something in his life. He needs someone to love him and to love. He wishes now that he had something to offer a girl if he fell in love with the right one. He decides that now he will reform and start really working so that if he falls in love he won't have to wait for a good job.

Or the means may be cathected as a means to an end within the realm of work.

The girl is daydreaming. She wants to become a great artist, the kind that people admire. She is a very smart girl and she wants to make a name or reputation for herself so she studies diligently and develops into a renowned person.

3. ENJOYMENT OF BARRIER SOLUTION

Certain aspects of the total work process may be cathected. One of these is the barrier which presents itself before the end may be attained.

Thus, although the hero of the following story is primarily interested in making money from his business, he derives pleasure in breaking down the sales resistance of a particularly difficult client.

The young serious man is trying to sell the other man insurance. This is a very big deal, it may mean a $100,000 policy if he can put it across. This guy is a tough customer but it doesn't faze him. In fact he enjoys it and prides himself on knowing just what to say to men like this, how to flatter them but not so that they get suspicious. First a little shop talk to show that he knows his business and then he tells them that every intelligent man should have insurance and quotes figures and mortality statistics. It works well with this one and by the time the afternoon is over the deal is closed.

F. Complexity of Organization

Does the individual attribute complexity of organization to the work of his heroes? Does the work involve the organization of a large number of parts into a whole? This is important in estimating the complexity of organization of work of which the individual is capable since he cannot attribute to his heroes a degree of complexity of organization of work which surpasses his own capacity. We see this in the following story, told by a gifted individual who attributed his own subtle intelligence to the hero.

Mr. Pritchard was not an ordinary mathematician. His chief delight lay in reducing to mathematical formulae the creations of artists both in the fields of music and drawing and of reproducing these conveniently according to the formulae which he had derived. His system was the old one of reducing lines to multiples of simple wave forms. He could reproduce a face with as few as fifty multiples of a sine wave and had even developed methods for doing landscapes. But, as he grew older, he became more and more enchanted with his own success, and seized on every opportunity to make pictures of figures. Finally he conceived the idea of finding the hidden meanings in the Old Testament by developing a formula including all the numbers quoted there and then transforming it to a picture. This he did. The result being a huge drawing containing sections which were more or less units in themselves. It was one of these that finally drove him mad. It was the picture of an old man riding on the shoulders of another, goading him ever onwards. He read into this the story of his own defeat.

G. Temporal Characteristics of Work

I. TIME PERSPECTIVE PLANNING

Time perspective in work must be differentiated from complexity of organization. An individual may possess a long time perspective and carefully plan his work over a long period of time but the work may be simple and lack complexity of organization. These two dimensions may, however, be combined, as in the following story where the work is complex, well organized, and planned over a long period of time.

This looks like a scene from the Lost World. A number of explorers have been investigating this territory—perhaps in the vicinity of New Mexico. They come upon this path through a canyon. There doesn't seem to be any living thing whatever in the entire vicinity. Everything is one monotonous color, a sort of dirty, brownish, ivory. In a little while their eyes become accustomed to the light and coloration and notice various shapes—one in particular of a dinosaur, seems to be dormant, but its outspread webbed foot seems to indicate that it may be alive. As they approach a natural bridge toward the dinosaur they are confronted with a spider-like creature or a bug-like creature, except that it appears to be gigantic compared with an ordinary bug. This too, this is moving. The creature, however, seems to pay no attention. They're fearful of going on and decide to return with weapons and some means of carrying out these creatures if they could be captured. Strangely enough when they return a day and a half later both creatures are in the same spot—spots, as they had previously been. The bug still moved about and the men advanced slowly. The bug's horrible face and ugly legs put fear in the men's hearts. They decided not to capture him alive. A number of men let fly with high powered rifles. They aimed for his head and all shot accurately. The bug crumbled to dust. By some strange phenomenon the injury to his head disintegrated the entire body. The men were extremely disappointed and downcast. They decided not to try the same tactics with the dinosaur if he were alive. They approached warily, but the dinosaur made no move. They got closer and closer to him until they were able to throw a lasso around his neck. They carefully tied it in a slip knot and all the men took hold of the rope and with one—at a signal, with one great tug. They pulled the monster from his place. He came very easily. There was no weight to him at all. As a matter of fact he was just a hollow shell. The back half of him crumbled as he hit the rocks. They rushed forward in an effort to save what was left. His body had been broken in too many pieces and they decided to cut up certain pieces which appeared that they would break in transportation. They transported the animal out in 45 wooden cases. It would probably take years to assemble him again. Took only one case to assemble the remains of the bug. They would get to that problem later. Perhaps they would let some of their assistants experiment with the dust. They had not originally expected a find as extraordinary as this but now that they had found it and seemingly not captured these creatures correctly they were a little bit disappointed. Their disappointment was forgotten in the years that they labored on reconstruction, and they looked with pride on their accomplishment when their creature was unveiled to the public at the museum of natural history.

2. ENDURANCE

How long does the work actually endure? Endurance is a dimension of the work region which varies independently of time perspective. The hero may have a long time perspective but his actual work may not endure for long. Or, as we saw in the story above, both the time perspective and the endurance may be long, or the hero, although he works for a long period of time, may have no time perspective. Endurance is implicit in any work story although it may not be mentioned directly. We see this in the following story. The heroine does not tell us how long the work endures, she tells us that "eventually her sacrifices bear fruit and she becomes a great poet." Implicit in this is the long duration of the work.

> This woman is crying because she is lonely. She is isolated emotionally because of her own peculiar personality. She is a very gifted woman and therefore eccentric enough to make her isolated. At the same time she would like to be liked, to have someone passionately fond of her, to be understood and appreciated. The people who do get attached to her are usually of a lower caliber while those for whom she could care always have some impediment. She has been looking at the twilight scene beyond and with the first coming of the stars she feels a tumult and breaks down in tears. Immediately, however, she masters herself and resolves to brave life. She fortifies herself with the thought that suffering is necessary in order to accomplish anything great. Eventually her sacrifices bear fruit and she becomes a great poet.

The individual, however, may describe directly the endurance of the work. The following stories illustrate varying periods of endurance. Work **may** endure the greater part of the hero's life.

> This elderly scientist who, having spent the greater part of his life in search of a means of prolonging youth is at the point of this picture about to culminate his work with this great experiment. . . . His whole theory is based on the fact that organic decay can be combated by a state of mind. He fails in his work and dies realizing that the only thing man is sure of—no, no, no—that man can pass on is the will to do good in the eyes of God and cannot in any way violate the laws of nature.

Or it may have a medium period of endurance.

> Well, this is a young man who has been working for a couple of years, and ah, he has been doing very much run-of-the-mill desk work. Life has been pretty dull. He has really gone to the office and sat there, been more or less of a stenographer. He has ideas of wanting to get ahead. His pictures are pretty good. After two years of that drudgery, he is given a promotion. Somebody thinks his ideas are pretty good and he is given the opportunity to work on the advertising copy, wording, drawing, advertising, what he thinks is pretty interesting. He is pretty happy about it. He has spent more time being happy about things than actually accomplishing much. He has gone home after a party. He's been to a party and he has gone home from a party he's been to and thought he had better accept this thing. He likes his work, and so he sits down at his desk and starts work . . . and somehow it is a much better time for work than the office where everyone is watching, and he expects to accomplish something. It is more like a vision. He draws out the picture, carefully figures out the coloring and where it will go and where the wording will go, works on that until it gets pretty well smudged, takes a new piece of paper,

tries to make it the final copy, figures out where the letters will go and the words and the heading. It's in sort of a diagonal heading. At the bottom he puts something fine, almost poetic, and gets it down. And he is very happy over it when he gets it done, happier than he was when he got the promotion and he thinks about it and what he will say about it the next day when he will try to sell it. He looks and sees that it is about five o'clock. It's getting light outside. He goes to the bathroom and washes a bit and comes back and sees it is light outside and goes to the window, happier than he's ever been, and he stands there looking out into the light and you see him here.

Or the hero may work only for a very short time.

It's a lazy spring night and this boy is standing at the window thinking about the studying he should be doing. But it's such a beautiful night he just stands looking out until finally he realizes that it's getting late and rouses himself and gets to work. He works for about an hour but then he can't seem to concentrate. He starts dreaming about the good time he's going to have this summer. He's sleepy so he closes the books and goes to bed.

3. CHANGES IN EGO IDEAL OR WORK HABITS AS A FUNCTION OF TIME

We have seen in the family region that the hero's relation to his parents or to parent surrogates may change as a function of time. The same type of change may occur in the work region. When analyzing the work stories of any individual, the age of the hero should be taken into consideration and stories compared to see if there is any change in ego ideal or work habits as a function of time. The hero of the following two stories has a different reason for work in childhood and adulthood:

This little boy admires his father and wants to be as great a violinist as his father is. He can play a little bit and he realizes how much effort it will take to be as good as his father. But he will work hard, and practice and someday he will be as good as his father.

He's restless, it's night and he's through working for the day but he can hardly wait for tomorrow to come. He's fascinated by what he's doing and he's only completely happy when he's working. His work for him is his whole life.

Thus we see that as a child and as an adult the hero is hard-working. However, the child regards the work as effort and works to "be as great a violinist as his father is." The man, on the other hand, works because his happiness lies in work and for this reason work requires little "effort."

II. RELATIVE IMPORTANCE OF THE WORK REGION

In this section we shall apply more briefly some of those criteria used in the determination of the relative importance of the family region.

A. Direct Reference

As illustrated in the family region, the protocols may directly refer to the importance of any region to the individual.

He's restless, it's night and he's through working for the day but he can't hardly wait for tomorrow to come. He's fascinated by what he's doing and he's only completely happy when he's working. His work for him is his whole life.

B. Number and Length of Stories

Other criteria which may be used in evaluating the importance of this region are the length of the stories told about work in comparison with those dealing with other regions and the number of stories in which the work region is treated. The most striking example we have seen of the number of stories concerning the work region was one protocol in which work was the principle theme in seventeen of the twenty stories.

C. Affect and Intensity

The affect and intensity in stories about this region also provide a means of estimating its importance. In the following story the affect towards knowledge and learning is marked.

A young boy looks out of his open window into the moonlit sky. He is a college student and this night he went to bed but his mind was not tired. He was working vigorously. First he turned over in his mind the lecture he had heard during the day. Little bits of each one came to him, exciting intellectual thoughts, but his mind leaped from one to the other. Regarding each he thought, "This I must know more about." Then he began to think of when he would learn all these things, when he would find the answers, how he would find the answers to the thrilling and exciting problems that arose every day. At this point he got up, went over to the window. He looked off into space as though somehow the breadth of the vista before him might find him some perspective. He thought of what he might do, what career he might choose. He did not think of people. He thought only of ideas. At this moment he felt himself a kind of intellectual giant in whose hand lay˙ the whole world. He would learn about it, he would know all about it, he would have power over it.

D. Introduction of Strivers

We may also obtain this information by examining the way in which the individual treats the figures in the pictures. Are strivers introduced? This question may be asked about those pictures which present passive figures. In the picture of the cowboys stretched out on the grass, a cowboy may not be

seen as the hero but someone who is characterized as a striver may be introduced, as in the story that follows.

> It's been a very tough climb for these men. They had been going up toward
> the summit of the peak since early this morning. And now at noon they were
> exhausted enough for a little sleep. One man who seems to have a little more
> energy than the rest has probably had enough of a stop and is anxious to get
> on, but seeing the others reposing so peacefully he does not awaken them.

E. Interpretation of Ambiguous Figures

Are ambiguous figures interpreted as strivers or failers rather than as
sinners or lovers? Ambiguous figures in this sense are those figures in the
picture who are not engaged in any particular activity. Such interpretation
would indicate that the individual's thinking about people tended to be in
terms of work rather than any other value. This is illustrated in the story
following.

> Looks like a girl who lives on a farm has just come home from school and is
> going to start work on the farm or is going to school and is watching her
> parents working Looks like she's thinking about the work she's gotta do now
> that she's home from school. What she'll probably do now is change her clothes,
> start milking the cow or something. That's about all on that. She'll continue
> living like she's been. Going to school in the day, coming home and going to
> work.

F. Restructuration of Passive Pictures

Passive pictures may be restructured as a preparation for activity.

> These are a bunch of cowboys who have been working hard all morning.
> They've just had lunch and are resting a bit because they will have to work
> hard to get all the cattle rounded up in the afternoon. They're just resting a
> minute and will go right back to work.

G. Omission of Passive Figures

The individual may omit passive figures in the picture from the stories
he tells. The following story was told to picture 12M (the picture of an older
man bending over a younger man reclining on a couch).

> This is a man who does this for a living. He's on stage and he's giving a
> demonstration of his powers as a hypnotist.

H. Identification with Active Figures

The individual may identify with active figures when both active and
passive figures are present in the picture. This may be ascertained by the
story told to picture 12M. The following is an example.

This is a kindly old doctor—a psychiatrist who wants to help this patient. He has been giving him some sort of therapy but it hasn't been too successful and he's decided to try hypnotizing him and telling him that he's going to be all right. He's just about to bring him out of it and he hopes it will be successful.

I. Rejection of Passivity

A further criterion is the individual's affective rejection of passivity or his affective acceptance of activity, or of figures he sees as either active or passive. The following stories from the same protocol illustrate such an attitude.

These men are a bunch of lazy bums. They're supposed to be working and they're getting paid for it, but what are they doing—loafing on the job. It's a disgrace to the country to pay men for loafing. Somebody ought to take a horsewhip to them and get them back to work.

Good people—these are good hard working people. The backbone of the nation tilling the soil, working from sunup to sundown. Probably came over from the old country to make a new life for themselves and have worked hard to make this beautiful farm and to send their daughter to school.

J. Conflict

The relative importance of the work region may also be revealed by examining the protocol for stories of conflict between work and any other region. The degree of conflict, the way in which it is resolved, and the degree of residual tension afford indices of the relative importance of work and other regions. In the following story we see a conflict between love and work which is resolved in favor of the latter.

This is an ambitious girl—a dreamer. But not merely a dreamer. She accomplishes much because of her determination. She was born in poor circumstances but she has made headway. She is planning to go to another city she wants to see the world. She had great dreams to fashion, but her heart is tied to the soil. In fact, the best work she will ever accomplish will be in connection with the people of the villages, the farmers, the tillers, the downtrodden. Here she is thinking of a beautiful poem she could write about these rude folk. She is inspired by the sight of the soil and the man at work. However, the sight of the fine, strong muscled man also stirs in her a different emotion and she feels the inadequacy of her personal life. The woman at the back symbolizes this sex-urge which has the power to defeat this girl's other life. The expression on the symbol, the woman's face, suggests how confident she is of triumphing over the girl. The girl thinks what terrific happiness it would mean to gratify this desire and be a mother of children and serve the needs of this strong man. But she also realizes that such happiness would be transient and that soon she would yearn for spiritual fulfillment. She thinks of Madame Curie and others who have accomplished much through denying themselves and she thus manages to control herself. She eventually becomes a great poet.

There is some residual tension but the importance of spiritual fulfillment in work provides integration for her personality, enabling her to control her wish for sex and love.

K. Impact of Work on Other Regions

Another story by the same individual illustrates a further important criterion—the impact of work on other regions. There may be an ego ideal centered on work which structures the personality and allows the individual to tolerate frustrations in other regions. In the following story the heroine is enabled through success in her career as poetess to tolerate frustration of her wish to be loved.

> This woman is crying because she is lonely. She is isolated emotionally because of her own peculiar personality. She is a very gifted woman and therefore eccentric enough to make her isolated. At the same time she would like to be liked, to have someone passionately fond of her, to be understood and appreciated. The people who do get attached to her are usually of a lower caliber while those for whom she could care always have some impediment. She has been looking at the twilight scene beyond, and with the first coming of the stars she feels a tumult and breaks down in tears. Immediately, however, she masters herself and resolves to brave life. She fortifies herself with the thought that suffering is necessary in order to accomplish anything great. Eventually her sacrifices bear fruit and she becomes a great poet.

III. THE CONDITIONS OF WORK

In the love and sex region we undertook a systematic inquiry into the functional interrelationships between the dimensions of that region in an attempt to demonstrate that the variability of any dimension between stories could be treated either as the effect of differences in preceding conditions in two or more stories or as the cause of different effects in the stories in which they appeared. The application of this type of analysis to the work region will be illustrated here.

The following two stories were told by the same individual to the same TAT card (14) within a two month period.

> Well, he's been working hard all day and on into the night. Some work that he isn't very much interested in. Finally he was stiff and tired and his mind was getting sleepy. He stretched and got up and threw open the window and just looked out at the world around him. He's thinking about how beautiful the wonderful world is. He'll go to bed, go to sleep very soon.

> Well, this is a young man who has been working for a couple of years, and ah, he has been doing very much run-of-the-mill desk work. Life has been pretty dull. He has really gone to the office and sat there, been more or less of a stenographer. He has ideas of wanting to get ahead. His pictures are pretty good. After two years of that drudgery, he is given a promotion. Somebody

thinks his ideas are pretty good, and he is given the opportunity to work on the advertising copy, wording, drawing, advertising, what he thinks is pretty interesting. He is pretty happy about it. He has spent more time being happy about things than actually accomplishing much. He has gone home after a party. He's been to a party and he has gone home from a party he's been to and thought he had better accept this thing. He likes his work, and so he sits down and starts work on an advertisement for perfume or something, and he has come in from a party or something, about one or two o'clock and he sits down at his desk and starts work . . . and somehow it is a much better time for work than the office where everyone is watching, and he expects to accomplish something. It is more like a vision. He draws out the picture, carefully figures out the coloring and where it will go and where the wording will go, works on that until it gets pretty well smudged, takes a new piece of paper, tries to make it the final copy, figures out where the letters will go and the words and the heading. It's in sort of a diagonal heading. At the bottom he puts something fine almost poetic, and gets it down. And he is very happy over it when he gets it done, happier than he was when he got the promotion and he thinks about it and what he will say about it the next day when he will try to sell it. He looks and sees that it is about five o'clock. It's getting light outside. He goes to the bathroom and washes a bit and comes back and sees it is light outside and goes to the window, happier than he's ever been, and he stands there looking out into the light and you see him here.

As we read these stories we see that the physical settings and the duration of the work are very much the same in both. There are however, two striking differences between them, a difference in length and a difference in affect about work in the two stories. The first story contains a brief reference to the fact that the work is uninteresting; no positive affect is expressed. In the second story, however, a minute description of the nature of the work and the work process is given accompanied by frequent affective comment.

The factor responsible for this difference in affect in these two stories is the nature of the work. In the first story the individual tells us that he is doing work "he isn't much interested in." In the second story, however, "he is given the opportunity to work on the advertising copy, wording, drawing advertising, what he thinks is pretty interesting" and "he likes his work."

We are told here that interesting work creates positive affect, and interesting work upon examination proves to be creative work.

These stories reveal both the conditions under which this individual will work and the conditions which seem to him ideal. He seems to prefer to work at home and at night, which "is a much better time for work than at the office where everyone is watching." He works hard in both stories, despite the fact that he is doing work in the first story which "he isn't very much interested in." But his ideal conditions for work are seen in the second story where he is doing work which he considers interesting creative work. It is of interest, in the light of these findings, that the individual who told these stories planned a career in creative writing.

In the protocol of another individual we find two stories which illustrate the conditions under which the individual will stop work, rather than the ideal conditions for work.

> Workers, yes, workers, fruit pickers. They work different seasons in different parts of the country, picking fruit, whatever crop needs picking, I guess. They like the work, like picking fruit, no one to boss them. They can go as fast or as slow as they like. Here they're taking a snooze before going back to picking. No one to tell them what they should do.

> Looks like a mother and a son. Neither looks happy, the son must have quit his job, guess that's it and he's telling his mother. Feels bad, he liked the work. Had a fight with the foreman, I guess, got mad, told him he'd be damned if he'd be told by him what he should do, and quit.

An examination of these stories reveals that in both stories the individual likes his work. Why then does he continue to work in one story and stop in the other?

We find that dominance is the factor responsible. In the first story he tells us that there is "no one to boss them"; in the second story, however, the foreman tries to tell him what to do, he gets angry and quits.

In the next two stories another individual tells us the conditions which sustain his work.

> This young fellow has just come home from looking for a job. He's pretty downcast at not finding one, particularly since he's a college graduate. He's been out of school for about six months. He still hasn't landed anything. Here his father who is evidently a man of experience is consoling his son: He has a great faith in the boy and is sure he will get a position of which he is worthy. He talks to the boy for a while comfortingly and pats him on the back. The boy will feel much better because his father has faith in him and the next day he will go out looking for a job with a new determination that he is going to justify his father's faith. And he will.

> This takes place after the school day is over. The woman with the books is a discouraged school teacher. She came to teach in a little country school in the midwest and she was full of enthusiasm. She was going to bring modern educational methods to these people. But instead of being eager for them, the people were outraged and ridiculed all her attempts at modernization. They thought the way they had been taught was good enough for their children. Finally she couldn't stand their scoffing and ridicule any longer and decided to leave.

The hero of the first story is downcast about his work at the beginning of the story but is filled with a new determination at the end. The heroine of the second story is enthusiastic about her work at the beginning and becomes

discouraged. The factor responsible for this difference is the attitude of others
—whether they reject the individual or have faith in him. In the first story,
the hero, consoled by his father, who has faith in him, eventually succeeds;
the heroine of the second story meets with ridicule, becomes discouraged and
decides to leave her job.

The following two stories from another protocol illustrate the effect of
recognition on the work of the individual.

> This is a man and his wife celebrating. He has just received a promotion
> and he's telling her what happened when he got the promotion. What the
> manager said and he tells her what a good guy the manager is and how he
> said they were pleased with his work and he was promoted. She tells him to
> work hard and he says he'll kill himself working. He suggests to her that they
> go out and celebrate and they go out and celebrate.

> This is a fellow who's drunk. When he was younger he was a very hard
> worker and never drank. He worked in one place years. He kept telling him-
> self the only way to get ahead was hard work. But after a while he began to
> think he was a fool. Nobody ever noticed how hard he worked, it was for
> nothing. The boss sat in his office and never noticed anything or anybody. He
> thought he was too good for the rest of them. There was no sense in anybody
> killing themselves for him. He took to having a little drink in the afternoon
> and now you see what's happened to him. He's drunk and some guys are
> helping him home.

In both of these stories the hero is a hard working man; in the first story
the couple are going out to celebrate the hero's success in work, and he
resolves to work even harder. In the second story however the hero has
failed in his work and is being helped home because he is drunk. There is
a difference in the hero's attitude toward authority. In the first story he tells
his wife "what a good guy the manager is" but in the second story the boss is
described as someone who "sat in his office and never noticed anything or
anybody. He thought he was too good for the rest of them." The factor in
these stories responsible for this difference is the recognition accorded the hero.
In the first story he gets a promotion, a symbol of recognition and the manager
tells him that "they were pleased with his work," whereas in the second story
"nobody ever noticed how hard he worked, it was for nothing." This is in
fact an individual who is a hard worker but one who continues to work hard
only if his effort is rewarded by recognition.

The next two stories reveal an individual's cathexis of stable, unchanging
work conditions.

> This man, the younger one, is a clerk in an office and doesn't make much
> money but his job suits him. This day the head of the office calls him in to talk
> to him and asks him if he would like to try his hand at selling. The younger
> man is rather startled by the idea, he likes what he's doing now and doesn't

want to change. But he doesn't know what to say. He finally mumbles something about wanting some time to think it over and leaves. He tries to think of some way to say no. He finally leaves and gets another job as a clerk—the lesser of two evils.

This woman is an old school teacher, she looks like one. She's been teaching the same class for years now and she loves it. She knows every brick in the school building. She's taught in the same old classroom. The only thing that ever changes is the pupils and even they don't change much, they look like their parents did before them. She loves teaching beloved subjects, which don't change through the years.

The hero in both of these stories likes his work. In the first story, however, he leaves his job and in the second he doesn't. He leaves in the first story because he is asked to change the work he is doing. But the heroine of the second story loves her work and continues doing it because it does not change "through the years." Change as such is negatively cathected. Any change in the stable conditions of the work environment may disrupt the adjustment of such an individual.

The individual may, however, have no wish whatever to "work." In the case of one person seeking vocational guidance, the TAT protocol indicated that his interest lay primarily in impressing others. He asked the vocational counselor what type of work he "should" seek, confessing that he had no preferences. The following stories are representative of his present confusion.

This fellow apparently feels held back by uncertainty. He doesn't look overly energetic but I suppose he's trying to shake the repressed or lethargic feeling off. He ought to make the effort and I suppose he will succeed when he makes up his mind in which direction to dodge.

I could imagine a man who once, when younger, sat on a curbstone watching the fire engines whistle by, thinking of all the choices for careers he had before him. Now the man feels he has already unconsciously and indirectly made some choice, although he never did make up his mind but rather drifted along, trying several kinds of work but never clearly preferring any one or doing any one well. He thinks maybe I should have made up my mind then on the curbstone and stuck with it. He could do a lot of things, but diffidence and idleness confuse him and have taken away his momentum. He lacks drive, gets to be too submissive. Maybe he can start over again now. Or on the other hand maybe he is already too old to do some of those "from the bottom up" stories himself. So he will continue to drift, stay near the edge of his polite society and continue his job, as, say, file clerk because he never felt the urge to accomplish better things.

Tough life for this fellow, no friends, nowhere to go. Or if he can go to some of his old haunts, his friends who have established themselves will turn up their noses to learn that he is still where they passed him five or ten years ago, not having accomplished as much. He is trying to make up a good story to tell them, to justify himself, before he starts off to anywhere where he might meet the old crowd of classmates. He is really in the fog. He will finally get up enough gumption to move and when he gets to the old haunts will probably find a lot of new faces anyway which partially solves the problem but he will still be concerned more with the "story" than with the performance.

He is clearly more concerned with the "story" he is going to tell his friends than with his actual performance, but he "never felt the urge to accomplish better things." Although he would like to impress others, there is no urge to do anything which might earn him such applause.

As we might have supposed, those heroes who experience any enjoyment in what they are doing are indulging in exhibitionism. Although all heroes would like to be impressive there are only two heroes for whom this satisfaction is possible. These two stories follow.

Maybe this is some kind of hypnosis demonstration. Easier to imagine myself doing the hypnotizing than being the patient. Can't figure out why this should be going on. (In the old days, so I'm told, hypnosis used to work as a cure for certain ailments.) Maybe this fellow is demonstrating before a radio audience. Will make the kid do a couple of tricks while "under the influence" to impress the audience.

This chap is having a grand time swinging on a rope in the gym. He likes to show off. Maybe he imagines he is a sailor. He is climbing to the top and asking if anyone else can match him. There are some other fellows who accept the challenge and try their mettle.

When told by the counselor that his basic interest was exhibitionistic he was somewhat disturbed but also relieved. "I have always known I was not really interested in any job for its own sake," he said. A week later, however, this individual was less certain that the counselor was right. As he expressed it, "there was something to what you've said" but he seemed to have reservations.

For reasons which need not concern us here, this person was incapable of completely accepting advice either from his father or father surrogates. He had previously consulted a psychiatrist and another psychologist whose advice he had accepted only with many reservations. Such an exhibitionistic wish might of course have been gratified had he chosen to be an entertainer. Since this was not possible he was advised to choose from among the jobs open to him the one which would offer him the greatest rewards for his exhibitionism and demand the least expenditure of energy. Psychotherapy previously undertaken had not altered his basic personality sufficiently to warrant any expectation that his exhibitionistic need could be modified. Consequently the counselor chose to regard this need as the "given" in the situation, directing the individual into those areas where the need might be less frustrated than it had been for most of his life.

SUMMARY

We have attempted a delineation of dimensions pertinent to an analysis of the individual's adjustment in the vocational setting. Work, we said, may have a positive or negative meaning for the individual. Examples of some of the negative motivating forces were work to overcome inferiority, poverty, and financial insecurity, or to overcome the psychological effects of a physical handicap. On the positive side we found work to create beauty, to excite applause, or to become famous or great.

The sequence of levels characteristic of the work of the individual was considered and the relationship between the levels of daydream and behavior was seen to vary between individuals. Daydreams, it was found, may have a tonic effect on some individuals, spurring them to work and sustaining them, whereas for others they provide a retreat from work or the individual finds them so exciting that his intention to work is short-circuited in the daydream. Phantasy may, however, constitute an important aspect of creative work.

Phantasy, regardless of its content, may inhibit or excite work for some individuals while for others the effect is differential: certain types of daydreams are disruptive to work while others are stimulating.

Conceptual activity, we saw, was the typical forerunner of work for some individuals, whereas others turned to this level only after initial trial and error activity. There was not always further clarification or work from such reflection.

Differentiation of work into means and ends was discovered to depend on the nature of the work. Work which offered no problems was not so differentiated. For the creation of such a distinction there had to be some discrepancy between the wish and the achievement.

An examination of the degree of means-end cognizance appeared useful in assessing the realism of the individual. Too high a degree of such cognizance, however, might paralyze action. We distinguished means-end elaboration in daydreaming from its counterpart on the level of behavior. These were sometimes found to be different in the stories of the same individual.

It was shown that means might be cathected only in so far as they contributed to some end or that such means might, through experience, come to be positively cathected for their own sake. Certain aspects of the total work process might be cathected, and one of these is the barrier which must be overcome before the end may be achieved. The conquest of barriers may in fact become an end in itself.

The complexity and organization of work attributed to heroes was shown to be an index of the individual's actual capacities.

We next examined the temporal characteristics of work. We differentiated time perspective from complexity and organization of work. We found that an individual might possess a long time perspective, carefully planning his work over a long period of time but that the work might be relatively simple, lacking complexity of organization. We also differentiated the dimension of endurance, since the hero might have a long time perspective and yet work for only a short time. Finally, we examined changes in the ego ideal or in work habits as a function of time. The hero as a child, and the hero as an adult were seen, not infrequently, to work in different ways to achieve ends which were conspicuously disparate in character.

We addressed ourselves next to the criteria used in the determination of the relative importance of the work region. Direct reference, number and length of stories concerning the work region and the affect and intensity of stories were shown to be useful in such assessment. Further criteria were the introduction of strivers, the interpretation of ambiguous figures as strivers, the restructuration of passive pictures as a preparation for activity, the omission of passive figures, identification with active figures, and rejection of passivity. The relative importance of the work region may also be revealed by an examination of the degree of conflict between this and other regions, and the resolution of such conflict. Related is the criterion of the impact of work on other regions. We found evidence that there may be an ego ideal centered on work which structures the personality and enables the individual to tolerate frustration in other regions.

Finally, we inquired into the conditions of work, illustrating that work for different individuals depended on such conditions as the stimulating character of the work, a minimum of coercive dominance from the employer, the faith of others in the worker, recognition from the employer, unchanging conditions of work and sufficient reward for exhibitionistic wishes. These represented only a sample of the conditions which commonly determine the individual's adjustment in the vocational setting.

Chapter X

DIAGNOSIS AND PSYCHOTHERAPY

A. Diagnosis *

The use of the TAT as a diagnostic instrument is limited by the uncertainty of inferences based on this procedure. No less serious is the admitted inadequacy of present-day classification of mental diseases. These do not, in our opinion, represent homogeneous entities even at the level of symptomatology. It is for these reasons that correlations between TAT results and these entities cannot be far reaching. Such effort would be better applied to the reclassification of mental disease on the basis of homogeneous test patterns.

It is accepted dogma that one cannot altogether trust what the patient says of his own condition. Yet much of present-day psychiatric practise proceeds on the basis of evidence derived from the interview situation. The interview material one must indeed have, but there may be crucial gaps in the material necessary for diagnosis and therapy if some "depth" technique is not employed in addition to the interview. The TAT affords a relatively economical method of exploration before therapy is undertaken.

Typically we find a contrast between what the patient is willing or able to tell and his covert or unconscious antisocial wishes. These are generally sexual or aggressive wishes which occasion the individual anxiety. But there are many instances in which the suppressed or repressed wishes are not antisocial and are more readily capable of being assimilated into the adult personality if they can be discovered and brought to the individual's consciousness.

In one such case, mentioned previously, the individual, while in the armed forces, had worked in a laboratory under the direction of a medical scientist. Under the paternalistic and benevolent guidance of this man he had worked effectively. Then one day he was bitten by a dog. The entire year following this he lived with the intense fear that he might have contracted rabies. He had experienced anxiety attacks before he had come to the laboratory but while there he had been free of such attacks. During the year following his injury, however, there was a reappearance and exacerbation of his anxiety. Then he was discharged from the armed forces. When first seen he had renounced his plans for marriage and his medical career. He complained of a complete lack of self confidence and an inability to concentrate on his work. He was afraid to resume his medical studies because he could not work,

---

* By diagnosis we mean the general assessment of any pathological condition rather than the determination of a specific nosological entity.

afraid to marry lest he be an inadequate husband and his wife turn away from him if she were to appreciate the extent of his inadequacy. There was an important sense in which these fears were realistic. His anxiety was so intense that at crucial moments, while taking an examination, for example, his real ability was so reduced that he was indeed incompetent. Although the original anxiety may have been based on unreal expectations, the sequence of anxiety, paralysis, and reduction in competence provided a realistic basis for further anxiety.

One would expect in such a case to find a TAT protocol weighted with anxiety and feelings of inadequacy. But this was not altogether the case. In striking contrast to his verbalized feelings an optimistic forward-looking picture emerges in much of his TAT record. In these stories there are defined the particular conditions under which this individual once did, and might again, function without fear. It is noteworthy that his "slips of the tongue" in interviews were in the same direction. He said on certain occasions "this set me up, I mean upset me very much." Let us examine the first story told by this individual.

> A picture of a young boy with a violin who seems to be sitting in complete awe upon reception of a new violin. He possibly was a child protégé with a deep and complete understanding of music and his receiving of the violin has presented his opportunity to go on and develop his talent and great love into becoming one of the world's great artists.

Looking into the past he pictures himself as a child protégé who has been presented with the opportunity for development and future achievement. Notice that this was mediated through an unmentioned benefactor. In the next story we are told something of his adolescence.

> Here is a picture of a young man participating in a gym class. This young man was probably underdeveloped as a young child and consequently was subject for the taunts of his fellow youths for his inability to play or participate in the more strenuous games. With a feeling of inferiority he made up his mind that he would take every means at his disposal to develop himself. Entering into gym classes he worked hard and in time did develop the bulging muscles and the stamina that seemed so necessary to win the respect of his fellow youths. Here in this picture he is winning the rope climbing event and from the expression on his face, a great deal of satisfaction.

This represents almost a literal page from his own youth. He did strive to overcome feelings of physical inferiority by taking boxing lessons and became a good amateur boxer. When he later joined the armed forces this was partly the basis on which he won the respect of his new friends. Notice that the conditions for success are here more specifically documented. This is accomplished through instruction and his own strenuous effort. In another story we see his work under the medical scientist.

Here the impression gained is of an old man—a man who appears to represent success, possibly a successful doctor who has trained the young man in the picture trying to pass on all the wisdom he has accumulated over long years. The time has come for the older man's retirement and he is having one of his last long talks with the young man he has selected and trained to be his successor who I would say does "carry on" as successfully. The picture could be entitled "The old master and his successor."

This is a picture of the self confidence which was actually his while he worked for the older man in the medical laboratory.

Tracing the changes from early childhood to this point, we see that his self confidence varied at different ages; as a child he was relatively self confident, as an adolescent, he had a feeling of inferiority which was overcome and as a young adult he had complete self confidence under special conditions.

The conditions for his achievement have also undergone changes in time. In childhood we were told only that someone presented him with the opportunity; in adolescence he received impersonal instruction in the "gym class." But in early adulthood the instruction is seen to be crucial, and this instruction has to be given paternalistically by a "successful" doctor whom he can respect. Inquiry revealed that he could work only for a distinguished scientist whom he respected and from whom he felt he could learn. For this man he would work late into the night in order to profit from his apprenticeship. He rejected other scientists in the laboratory who respected him for his knowledge of the more recent literature. In fact he turned down the offer of partnership in a medical practice with one of these men because "he wanted to learn from me and I couldn't learn anything from him." It is important to differentiate his need from that of passive dependency. His wish is that the older man teach him all he knows so that he will later be able to function adequately by himself. The interruption of this apprenticeship, his injury and his discharge from the armed forces exacerbated his anxiety.

We are next presented with a picture of his present state.

A young man, a soldier suffering from some neurotic disorder possibly a partial paralysis is receiving the benefits of physical neurotic medicine. Clinically it has been proven that the young man suffers from no organic disorder so he has been referred to the psychological clinic. Here the doctor through hypnotism is attempting to unlock from his mind the possible cause of the paralysis. The doctor is, of course, successful and the young man's condition is "cleared up" or the paralysis goes.

It is of interest that although he actually suffered a bite on the hand there is here mention of partial paralysis. Whether this symptom might have appeared had the anxiety level increased we cannot say. Notice that despite the neurotic disorder the soldier has faith in the older doctor who practices the techniques of modern science. The doctor is "of course" successful. It was just this confidence which the patient verbally disclaimed.

We see in another story that where the problem is less serious, he thinks his own resources are adequate.

> Here is a picture which could be entitled "Lonesomeness." This young man portrayed in the picture has severed the ties of home and gone off to a strange section of the country to work. Having not previously been away from home he of course suffers many periods of lonesomeness. At times the feelings are so acute he is about to give up and return to home and familiar surroundings. However, being a young man possessed of a lot of the good old-fashioned "stick-to-itiveness" he hangs on and with time meets people, develops comradeships with them while slowly but progressively losing his periods of lonesomeness.

This individual was living at home and one of the reasons he hesitated either to resume his medical education or to marry was his avowed "fixation" to his family, and yet we see that he does possess confidence in his ability to cope with new situations and with "lonesomeness"—another contrast to his verbalized feelings.

When confronted with his own stories he disclaimed their relevance. He insisted that they were simply "stories" and that he could have made them much more pessimistic had he tried. A few days later however he volunteered the information that he felt better in the presence of the therapist. It was at this time that I pointed out to him that when he had worked for the medical scientist whom he respected he had also been free of anxiety. This he admitted somewhat reluctantly. I then pointed out that this was reflected in his stories— his confidence was great when he was instructed or helped by someone who was expert—he expected that he would "of course" be cured. He again resisted the interpretation and it was not until some weeks later that he himself saw these relationships and decided to act upon them—to carry out his plans for marriage and to resume his medical studies, planning to work again under the personal guidance of a distinguished medical scientist.

This individual had been "reassured" by others to no avail. He had resisted all attempts to tell him that he was "all right." Transference for him was based not on love but on respect, and more particularly in later years, respect for the man of science, the adult prototype of the omniscient parent. In this particular case it was of no little importance that the diagnosis rested on a "scientific" test. His primary phantasy involved learning the wisdom of the parent and then taking his place. This he hoped to do with the loving cooperation of the parent. But the parental surrogate today must be someone who stands in the same relation to the adult as the father did to the child.

B. Therapy

I. ELICITING REPRESSED MEMORIES

It is problematical whether the recovery of repressed memories is an agent of cure or whether it is simply the resultant of an increased tolerance for these memories achieved in some other way. Whatever their ultimate worth, memories long unavailable to consciousness may be elicited through use of the TAT. In the intensive study of Z reported previously, interviews by myself and others failed to elicit memories of material particularly prominent in the TAT. These interviews extended over the entire testing period. In this ten month period pointed questions revealed very few early memories and none pertinent to the TAT stories. After he had completed all the TAT stories, Z was confronted with the following sample of the stories he had told during the school year.

At first, this picture reminded me of a fish but after looking at it a little while it appears to be a thumb with a drop of fluid on it. Perhaps this fluid is blood and this is a cue to the solution of a crime. All in all, the picture is striking and has an appearance of cold about it.

The picture is one of a big toe. An anatomy student has cut it off a body and put it into the tux pocket of another fellow. At a formal dance this student took out his handkerchief and this toe fell out on the refreshment table.

This thumb has been severely burned. It belonged to a criminal and skin grows back on with a different thumbprint. This causes havoc in the field of criminology and many theories are advanced as to the reason of this exception. The criminal later escapes and commits crimes that for a while baffle the police because of the prints. This, of course, is many years later. Before they catch him again he commits suicide.

This man is an Indian fakir and he is climbing up a coil of rope that he has stiffened. Halfway up he sees a purple bird which is a bad omen. The rope becomes limp, he falls to the ground, breaking a leg.

The upper woman had a pet dog she loved dearly. The other woman accidentally stepped on the dog's foot and caused it to whine. The mistress became infuriated and strangled the woman.

There has just been a murder committed. The man has killed his sister and dazed and stunned stumbles out and stubs his toe. Gangrene sets in and his toe is cut off. Then he is hung.

Another idea is that the baby lost its right hand and the possessor of the large hand is thinking how limited the growing boy will be. However, the baby will astound everyone with its one-handed achievements.

Bats and owls. Man has become thoroughly soused. The bats pick all his hair out. He is bald. He is very much ashamed of becoming drunk. He has a fixation for bats now because he is bald.

Confidentially if I were that guy I'd get a hair cut. Me I need a hair cut too. Oh you with the power of life and death. I refuse sir. I writhe in torment. . . . And the orange fell in little pieces and the little pieces turned into shears and cut off his hair and one of them slipped and cut off his ear, and that's how I lost my left ear.

The boy is an engineer and is wondering how the mechanics of a violin work. When he grows up he'll become a physicist and work on the problems of sound and acoustics. In the midst of the work an explosion deprives him of both hearing and sight. After a long recovery he starts to work again, never accomplishing much.

This man is blind and he is thinking back over the days when he couldn't see and wishing something or other. As he thinks, a river rushes by and the noise opens his eyes. He sees green cocktail shakers and then becomes blind again.

Milton went blind. I'd be crushed by blindness. I couldn't see a damn thing. Have to live within myself and I'm a horrible being.

This old lady has been having trouble with her eyes and so she has sent away to a mail order house to get a prescription. They seem to help her, but after a couple of weeks her eyes once again bother her and she goes to a doctor who examines her eyes and her glasses and tells her not to wear her glasses and to rest her eyes. Later she goes blind from a hereditary weakness.

Similar phantasies were also prominent in his dreams:

I was arguing with mother whether babies' umbilical cords should be stepped on or cut. I said that if they were cut the baby would get some terrible disease.

After reading these stories Z expressed surprise at the degree of mutilation anxiety they indicated and thought they referred to "something" but didn't know what. Then suddenly there was a burst of memories which shed much light on the origin of these fears of castration and body mutilation. The most significant of these was the memory of the time his mother caught his brother masturbating. He overheard the threat that she would "cut it off and put it in the soup" if he ever did it again. Another memory dates from the age of 8, when he caught the skin of his penis in a loose nut of a fire hydrant where he had been playing. "The experience was painful, especially because there was a short period in which I didn't think I could get it free. I didn't tell anyone about it and I guess I fairly well repressed the memory but not the fear that went with it." He also remembered his mother saying that she didn't like to leave children with a nurse because nurses taught children to play with themselves. He remembers masturbating with both his left hand and left foot. His father ran over his foot with a motor car. He was not sure whether this was a fact or phantasy. It probably is phantasy. He says "my father running over my foot probably happened between the ages of

4 and 7 and it didn't hurt." He was warned by his father not to masturbate "and it was with strong guilt feelings that I continued it. Although my religion was a weak one, I had fears that those among the dead who knew me were watching and condemning me. During this year I had my first shave. Curiously it was under threat from my father and brother who threatened me that they would shave me in bed. Most adolescents are only too proud to shave for the first time. I still dislike shaving. Freshman year at college I had a long siege of anxiety about losing my hair and becoming bald before I graduated. The external cause was dandruff, but the fear was great. I almost have a compulsion about entering haircuts in my diary. I tried to rationalize it, that it was to keep a record of how often I had a haircut. I came to college with 20-20 vision. That same fall I went home and because my eyes had been bothering me I saw a doctor who gave me glasses. According to test I was nearsighted. Two years later my eyes got worse. They are now 20-70 and 20-50. Sometimes I feel horribly tense and when I go to sleep I can hardly relax my eyes. Recently I've been trying to relax them." Whether this decrease in visual acuity was the resultant of increased anxiety and tension we do not know.

The recovery of these memories excited the subject, gave him insight into some of the sources of his anxiety and was a cathartic experience. So far as could be determined, however, the ultimate therapeutic gain was slight.

2. ASSESSMENT OF ATTITUDES TOWARD THERAPY

More important than the eliciting of repressed memories is the use of the TAT to determine the individual's attitude toward therapy and toward the therapist. While prognosis is not necessarily correlated with this attitude, a knowledge of it will be useful in deciding such questions as the degree of directiveness or nondirectiveness therapy should employ. It is of some importance to know in advance exactly what the individual wants and expects from therapy and whether he gives any indication of willingness to change.

Stories in which these attitudes are revealed may be told to any picture, but the picture of the younger man and the hypnotist (12) is of particular value in eliciting such material.

The following story gives at once the patient's attitude toward his own problem and his attitude toward the therapist.

Hypnotist hypnotizing some young man—trying to mesmerize him—no he's fast asleep—he'll awaken sooner or later—trying to solve his problem that way— Don't know the outcome—think he'll be helped to solve his problem.

He is uncertain about the therapeutic outcome and equally uncertain whether it is he or the therapist who will be able to help him. This person suffered from a pathological need to sleep; he was hardly able to keep awake during the day. This story tells us that sleeping is not only a defense but an attempt to solve his problem.

In the following case, we see a definite rejection of the therapist.

This boy has been studying very very hard—been reading a lot, taken many examinations and the mother was worried. She finally decided to send him to a psychiatrist. Here the psychiatrist is putting the boy at ease, perhaps even putting him under the influence of hypnosis. The boy is a brilliant one. He has not been overworking or overstudying—although he has been doing quite a bit of each or both. His mother feels that there may be something in his mind that he cannot bring forth hence the psychiatrist. The boy is put under an hypnotic spell and is made to talk by the psychiatrist, talks of very many things, but one significant thing to the psychiatrist is—seems to be—a key to the solution of this boy's trouble. He talks of his fear of the water—of how he had been pushed into the river by older boys in an effort to make him swim when he was just a youngster. He talks about this for quite a while and then stops entirely. The doctor lets him sleep for about one-quarter of an hour and then induces him to awaken. He talks with the boy about various things, his activities at school or play, recreation, feelings toward girls—takes notes as he goes along. The boy seems to be a willing patient. The questioning goes on for about ten minutes longer. He thanks the boy and tells him to go home. In a day or two he has a report for his mother. The woman comes to his office. He gives her what seems to her long and detailed explanations of her boy's condition. When she asks the doctor to boil it down to simple English —it comes down to the simple fact that the doctor sees nothing really wrong with the boy. He is a normal boy who has gone through a nervous stage and will snap out of it suddenly. The mother seems to be rather disappointed. It couldn't be as simple as that, she feels, and after having spent so much money in consultation with this man—she is a little bewildered. Thanks the doctor and walks out of his office thinking to herself that all these psychiatrists are fakers.

This was an individual who was, in fact, willing to travel a few hundred miles for vocational guidance and who said he was very much impressed with modern diagnostic methods. But this story would indicate that he covertly resented the money involved and felt that the scientific aspect of the whole procedure was both pretentious and trivial.

Z, who it will be remembered suffered excessive castration anxiety, told the following story to the hypnotist picture.

The man lying down is in a coma. He is suffering from a painful disease and is in the last stages. The other man is a doctor. He realizes there is no cure for the sick man who is a close friend of his and as he sits there he places a hand on his forehead and offers a prayer that his friend's pain may soon be over.

The therapist's intentions are good. He is a "close friend," but the malady from which the patient suffers is beyond help.

In the following case there was a more realistic expectation of the nature of the therapeutic relationship.

> Obviously a psychologist who is using the mode of hypnosis to relieve the tension of the subject's mind. Subject being a boy of 17, lying flat on a couch. The psychologist has just completed the seance and is about to bring the boy out of it. Boy has interesting story. He has come to the psychologist because he had conflict between his own desires and those of his family concerning his future. His family wished him to become a pillar of the church and perfectly acceptable normal man. When he had gone to college he had discovered much more enjoyment in life besides the grim austerity of a puritanical background. Being a loyal son, he finds it difficult to reconcile what he wants to do with what his family wants him to do. The psychologist has not been entirely successful because tension is still evident on boy's face. It will take more than one seance to bring the boy to a successful appraisal of his difficulty. He will realize that he has his own life to live, own responsibilities to himself, and family will become less and less important.

This individual expected help but realized this could not be effected in one "seance" and that he would have to assume some of the responsibility for his cure.

In another case this picture did not elicit such phantasies, since the subject identified with the hypnotist who loved to show off before an audience. But in a story told to picture 7 (a picture of an older man and a younger man) we find a portrayal of his attitude toward paternal authority, which reflected the attitude transferred to the therapeutic situation.

> This might be a father and son scene. (A) Maybe they are hatching plans for a vacation together or (B) maybe the father is giving advice to the son. Father has slightly more pleasant expression than the son. If (A), they will go off together and have a good time, though maybe they aren't too well acquainted, if (B) son will accept advice, but with private reservations that maybe father doesn't understand.

As vocational counselor I wondered whether he would show the same "private reservations" about my advice. This seemed likely, inasmuch as he felt the psychiatric treatment he had received previously was of doubtful value and he had been to a university vocational counseling service which he also felt had not helped him. When I revealed to him his need for recognition and his exhibitionism, he was somewhat upset but also relieved, admitting that he had always known that he was not really interested in any job for its own sake. When I saw him a week later, it was clear that his "private reservations" had nullified much of the insight he had achieved. In his words "there was something to what you've said" i.e., partial acceptance as it was delineated in the father-son story but with "private reservations."

We reproduce again, for the sake of contrast, the story of the individual whose anxiety state was precipitated by the bite of a dog.

A young man, a soldier suffering from some neurotic disorder possibly a partial paralysis is receiving the benefits of physical neurotic medicine. Clinically it has been proven that the young man suffers from no organic disorder so he has been referred to the psychological clinic. Here the doctor through hypnotism is attempting to unlock from his mind the possible cause of the paralysis. The doctor is, of course, successful and the young man's condition is "cleared up" or the paralysis goes.

TAT as Play Therapy

The TAT is also useful, in some cases, as a type of play therapy. It must be admitted that the conditions under which it may and may not be useful in this connection are still obscure. We shall present in some detail a case in which the TAT was used by the writer as a diagnostic instrument but in which it served a useful therapeutic purpose although this was not intended.

This child aged 6 suffered a variety of phobias and a generalized chronic anxiety. He was afraid of running water and would grow panicky if anyone ran water into a basin or tub which was plugged, begging to have the plug released. When he flushed the toilet he would run away. These fears appeared to have their origin in an experience where water overflowing the bathtub spread through the house. His parents were away at the time. He also feared noises in general and the noise of the oil burner in particular and refused to go near the cellar when it was on. He is afraid of strange places and strange people. When he visits the houses of strangers with his parents he sometimes prefers to remain alone in the car for several hours rather than go in with them. He will no longer play with his former friends because they now play around the corner from his house, on a strange street. He refuses to go to the neighborhood movies with his brother, who is three years older, or even with his mother. He cannot easily be left alone by his mother. On the one occasion when she was out of town for a day, she returned to find him in a severe anxiety state. After this he refused to go to school. There is general anxiety about going to school and he frequently vomits his breakfast on the school bus. When his brother joined the school orchestra club and couldn't accompany him home from school one afternoon a week, he refused to go to school. On these mornings he would wake at five o'clock and cry until it was time to go to school. He refuses to eat very much. It makes no difference whether his parents cajole, threaten, or ignore him. He is possessed of low frustration tolerance, frequently whining and crying and refusing to participate if he can't have his way. He also appears to have marked feelings of inferiority and when encouraged to show his skill complains that "he can't do it" and will generally make no attempt. If he does try, his interest is short-lived; he lacks perseverance and will often fly into a rage at his own lack of skill or give the task to someone else to complete.

When the child was three his father went off to the army and saw him only infrequently in a three year period. During this time he stayed with his mother and brother. His mother, having suffered an excessive amount of maternal dominance in her own childhood, leaned over backward in treating her own children dispassionately.

It was in this context and in light of the age and distractibility of the child that the writer undertook to administer the TAT as a game. Both he and the child were to tell stories. This appealed very much to the child and we went off to another part of the house. He regarded it as a secret shared only by the examiner and himself, refusing to allow his older brother to be present at the session or to play the game until he had completely finished. The testing was distributed over a week, and the child constantly asked the examiner if they could play the "game." The child was also encouraged to participate in the stories told by the examiner, who pretended not to know what to say and allowed the child to demonstrate his superiority. The examiner treated in his own stories those themes which he knew were sources of anxiety to the child. The stories which follow are those told by the child himself.

The first two stories of the protocol tell us little. They may show either inertia in beginning or resistance to revealing his phantasies.

> Boy writing—looks like and he's looking at something—I don't know what this thing is here—I don't know what this thing is—he's looking at the violin—there's some paper underneath the violin—the boy was probably playing the violin and then he put it down on a piece of paper and then (now I'm up to the other thing) then he didn't play any more and he put it down on the piece of paper—think that's all I think.

> There's a lady—she's holding her books in her hands—this looks hard. And there's a horse there and—I don't know what this is [E answers] that's a field and the horses are going on it and there's a lady over watching the horse looking at it. There's a house, a few barns, mountains and brushes and stuff and trees and everything—looks like that's all.

In the third story we see the beginning of the recital of his fears.

> Is that a man or a boy or a girl or what. She's laying on a sewer pipe and she's sitting on the dirty floor where the rats are and there's a mouse coming and she ran away and she runs upstairs cause she's afraid of the mice and the rats and everything—so the exterminators come and squirt (water)—bugs all over the cellar then—then the exterminators come again and squirt water all over the bugs and then they go home—then the girl came down again and she found water all over and the exterminators came again and then she saw the pipe broken and then they called the plumbers, and the plumbers couldn't do

it—and the pipes kept leaking and water got all over and then they didn't have any water left—so they had to move to another house and the new pipes were so high that it wouldn't fit into the house—they broke the other house and took some of the stuff they needed—like a door—and they used it—like to make a darkroom. So when the girl went down that cellar—there was a coal gas explosion—then she went upstairs and told her mother and then when she came down the next day—she saw an oil burner and she was so glad. And then the next day—the oil burner went on—she got so scared that she ran upstair crying—so after that she got so scared that she got happy again and she didn't know it was Christmas and she got so many toys—she asked her mother if it was Christmas and her mother said yes "it was"—so when she heard that it was Christmas—She got so glad that she got too many toys to play with (she didn't have time to use all those) she put some away in the cellar—so next Christmas she still had those and she didn't know it (she forgot) after she found them (next Christmas) she still had those toys from the last Christmas to the third Christmas (she didn't know) but after she found out that her mother buys toys before Christmas. She looked for them and she found them then after she found them she didn't let her mother see them—she saw that they were swept away from the diathermy with a broom so she looked in her son's room and she found those toys and she didn't give it to her son till the fourth Christmas and that's all.

In story 4 we see the introduction of the magician, who is to play a very important part in these stories. He is later seen as the agent of therapy.

Once upon a time there was a girl and a man and they were cousins so once there was a baby born and after they got that baby they got married and after the baby got big he came to be a magician and he was the best magician in the whole world—know who he was—he was Houdini and after Houdini was big enough he got so big that he died and after that the next day he was buried—and after he was buried he wasn't buried any more—he jumped out because he was a magician and he died—so he jumped out because he was a magician and after he died (funny stuff) he went up to Heaven and came down—went up again and came down and after he came down from heaven— he made everybody in the whole world disappear—even God (God would never disappear—would he? or Jesus?) and after that—I'm finished this story and I'll start some more. One day a little boy came to the magician's house and the magician gave him some stuff and one of them was a tin soldier and that was Blackstone the magician—and after that the mother and father dies and this boy was a man and he got married. (Who?) He married Mrs. Hamintush—and after Hamintush died he died and there was nobody to marry—and after that everybody else lived happily together. Only two what was living that was God and Jesus. After that twenty funny came in—he was a new baby—he got so big he got married and after he got married he died. And after he died there's mister Eighty skillion million billion—he got married to the other one—they both died together with their eyes open and looking at each other and got buried and jumped out of the hole—that was funny.

This story shows a preoccupation with thoughts of death and dying. There is little in the past history to give us a clue to the origin of these phantasies. When asked why people die he said, "it's because they eat the wrong food." When asked what the wrong foods are he gave them as germs, clorox, and ammonia. There is a strong possibility that this phantasy is closely linked with his refusal to eat, either because he believes that food is poisonous or because he believes that food might cause him to grow too big and he would then die. But there is no definite proof of either of these hypotheses and no explanation of the association between death and marriage which appears in these stories.

We do, however, see that the magician is a kind of superman who has the power to return from death and even from Heaven at will and that he possesses the power to make God disappear, although the child seems a little doubtful that either God or Jesus would disappear.

The first three stories were told in the first session, and the fourth in the second session. In the third session we begin to see evidence of some therapeutic gain.

> This woman was afraid of water and she couldn't drink water and when she got thirsty all of a sudden she got brave and she took a drink of water. It didn't hurt her. One day she got over being afraid. Maybe she was a baby and then she was a big girl.

This change, as revealed by the TAT was accompanied by behavioral evidence reported by his mother. He undertook to clean the sidewalk of snow and remained at the job despite the cold until he had finished, in marked contrast to his usual abortive effort. Moreover, he offered, despite some anxiety, to go to the movies with his brother.

In the final session, however, he is less concerned with overcoming his fears and gives his first happy ending, which endures ever after.

> After they got married they got some children and a magician came to their house, just when the children were 5 years old. The magician showed them some tricks. After the magician left they did some of the tricks. Then they had a broken pipe and a hole in the cellar floor—the exterminators and plumbers came—went away, and the children lived happily ever again.

The magician has taught the child magic which enables him to live "happily ever again," despite the broken pipe. This therapeutic gain resulted in considerable diminution of his general anxiety level. His report at school changed. He had previously been something of a problem to his teacher because of his lack of confidence. An improvement has been reported in his adjustment in school and he is described as much more confident. He no longer vomits his breakfast on the school bus and is willing to go to school.

His fear of running water has abated and he flushes the toilet without running away. When the examiner saw him a month after the testing the child manifested an intense interest in magic and tricks. He demonstrated an experiment he had done in school, calling it a trick, appeared boastful in exhibiting his skill and insisted that the examiner watch him.

There is still much to be desired in the reduction of this child's anxiety, but we are certain that the opportunity to express his fears through the medium of TAT stories in the permissive atmosphere this game provided was of therapeutic efficacy.

3. USE AS AN INSTRUMENT FOR CATHARSIS

The TAT may further be useful in inducing catharsis of feelings which were not adequately expressed in a traumatic situation and were isolated because they threatened to overwhelm the individual. The TAT may be particularly effective in therapy of the repressed grief reaction. The individual in this case is aware of the death or loss of the loved object, suffers apathy or depression but refuses to renounce the object, and is hence incapable of developing new love relationships.

The experience of telling TAT stories may be of therapeutic gain with children. But with adults it is generally more effective to give an interpretation and then read to the patient the stories on which the interpretation is based. This was the procedure employed in the following case.

This individual had suffered much insecurity throughout his life. He was first sent away by his mother following her divorce from his father. After sixteen years of marriage his wife deserted him. Two relationships followed which ended as unhappily. After the final rejection, there was a sharp but brief grief reaction which was consciously suppressed and never allowed full expression. Instead he preserved objects which he had shared with his beloved—souvenirs, dolls, curios, and phonograph records. A variety of experiences painful in memory—going to the ballet, drinking tea, etc.—were avoided. He experienced severe 'depression and apathy followed by loss of interest in love and sexual relationships. He transferred his remaining affect and energy to his work, overworking to keep from thinking of his grief. He was aware that he could not tolerate another rejection but was unaware of the depth of longing and grief still suppressed and isolated.

The TAT proved to be most valuable in unlocking this affect. After a preliminary interpretation telling the individual that he was still suffering from this experience, the examiner read to him a few of the stories which revealed his suppressed longings.

This boy or girl (boy probably) looks sad—perhaps past crying—at first you might think he fell, but the position does not bear that out, so he is crouching.

Even if the objects on the floor to the left be some broken toy or more valuable article that should be handled carefully, the grief could not be caused by so trivial a matter. This is despair. It looks as though he had been out playing and had suddenly heard some devastating news—the death of someone perhaps —and he came in from play and was going to go up to his room, when it hardly seemed worth the effort to go up the steps—after all, his room would be no different from here—from anywhere—especially if he has lost someone so dear—so the world blows up in his face, and he collapses at the foot of the steps. How long will he be there? Only ten or fifteen minutes. By then he will have gotten hold of himself and will go up to his room. Things will look different in the room. Nothing will have much meaning. What brought him joy—an aquarium, a toy boat he made—now looks so useless so meaningless. To him the room is empty—the world is empty. What to do? Yes— what to do? Why of course, one does what one is supposed to do. Whatever it is that one would have done before the bad news. Now what would that have been? Nothing has happened. And he won't want people to talk to him about what has happened to him. After all, who can understand—who can care really—so why listen to the drivel they spill on him with such righteous satisfaction that they are doing him a favor—so for a while he will go about his business as usual, and gradually he will come out of it—get over it— apparently, and perhaps even forget it, apparently. And he will be a little more patient and understanding with people who have suffered a similar loss—but he will not sympathize with them to weaken them, rather he will show them how to grin and bear it—the only way to overcome anything. And—all other things being equal—he can advance through life ready to absorb still more still greater disappointments—so that what he is suffering now will seem trivial—but this may be his first great hurt so it will stay with him forever.

This projection into the past envisioned a future of disappointment, which he would "grin and bear." In stories concerned with the contemporary situation, there is a different technique of dealing with the same problem.

What do I see in this blank card? Helpless men—if alone; happy, productive men if cooperative. So at first they wander about alone, each striving for his own existence, even fighting each other if threatened or even if the possibility of a threat appears. But as they kill each other off they stop to realize that there must be a way out of the fighting, if only all will look for it. And so science helps, whether to raise more food to feed more mouths, or to control births if there is not enough food, and then I see these men entering into peaceful pursuits with peaceful minds and hearts, not quite including the preachers though. But with these supplanted by sociologists, psychologists, experts in every area of peaceful purposeful productive living. So the scene has changed from fighting to helpfulness, from mere helpfulness to abundant productivity and consumption, with no solitude of mind, spirit, or body, but communion of all three with their kind without restraint. And the inevitable is accepted without question or quarrel—is prepared for, is anticipated, so that the pain that accompanies death and its minor forerunners will be minimized both in the sufferer and in his loved ones, not through will power or great fortitude, but through proper concepts, proper conditioning, proper perspective, and so full a life for all of us that none of us is too important to any of us—yet where bonds should be close they can be much closer than now—and yet the pain accompanying the dissolution of the bond should be less—there should linger only a pleasant glow because of the richness of the good experiences that accompanied the forming of that bond. And the picture changes to the ultimate catastrophe of the world—it is blotted out by a comet and all is for naught.

Here is the same preoccupation, but it is now through "proper concepts," rather than "will power," that it is "hoped" the problem may be solved. This is clearly a new wish and a hope, but there is no certain conviction that the problem is soluble.

In the next story the patient gives us a more accurate diagnosis.

If this is sorrow—phewy. The man should be sorry in his home—who wants to stand by a grave? Whomever he has lost was not appreciated as an experience which can not pass so long as memory persists. The carcass he stands over is nothing. So his sorrow is wasted. And his prayers too are wasted. And the whole concept of a life hereafter is not to be dwelt upon. We should not delude ourselves with any feeling of continuing consciousness, and if there is no consciousness on the part of the departed one, why worry about them— worry about the one left—so my hearty, go home about your business, and let the dead past bury its dead. If you were not smart enough to build into your life anything other than what is under your feet now, it is a little late, but you'd better do so at once. But he looks like such a dope that he may not take my advice and may mope and mope and mope. But if he has any of this world's goods (and is not mentally deranged—too much anyway) some woman will undertake to console him as a means to a more complete life (not to say a more leisurely life) of her own—always hoping of course that he too will get something out of the new arrangement—which he should be able to if he will indeed bury his dead. So he will ultimately marry for convenience in a nice way—not too cold-bloodedly. Now if this is his daughter—then he certainly is wasting his time.

Here we see a realization that something was lacking in the past relationship and that he cannot enter into a new relationship unless "he will indeed bury his dead." He is not certain that he can do this, and the outcome is therefore conditional.

In his last story (picture 20) we are told why he hesitates to attempt a new love relationship.

Looks like a giant caterpillar from upper left and about to devour the man. He seems indifferent to life—not just out for a stroll. Yet not despondent. He's hardly even wondering what to do next. He'll just wait until the spirit moves him, so to speak; then he'll decide what to do. Meanwhile he is just standing there leaning up against the lamppost. Perhaps he feels he should be doing something else, but what special difference does it make? So many things not done "on time" turn out not to be necessary after all. Important things usually have a way of making themselves known and are taken care of so he is just letting time pass. He probably has finished his day's work, had his dinner, and doesn't want to go to bed, yet has no place to go. No wonder he is dejected—at least slightly. It would have to be a very special sort of person—man or woman (but no children please) that might be welcomed by him for a brief chat. Who wants to hear most people's opinions on the elections or styles or strikes or atom bombs or the next war? So he is a bit lonely—especially since, should that special person come along, he or she would soon have to keep' on going about his or her business—as he would have to too. So it is almost preferred not to meet that interesting person if the contact is to be so short. Yet, no matter how wise one's own thoughts, they are not enough, so he may settle for the stupidities heard around a bar— or a dancehall—or anywhere but alone in the park. Yet I wonder if he will get up enough desire to seek out suitable companions, he seems too listless. So I'll have him go to a bar, have a few drinks, be bored, and go home disgusted—next night he will try another outlet—always the same—so he settles for work—and even if that gets boring eventually, at least is an intellectual boring, not a stupid boring, and he feels the difference, much as he might profit by a good belly laugh—and much as he may wish for such an environment, his duty, his work, or his morbid memories or something just seem to keep him from being able to get himself into that desirable environment. Yet I think he'll persist and eventually have the good luck to find a partner who seeking the same thing can find it in him as he just found what he sought in the other.

We are told that "it is almost to be preferred not to meet that interesting person if the contact is to be so short." So he buries himself in work, his "morbid memories" blocking any solution to the problem. And yet he thinks that eventually he may meet the right love object.

Reading these stories to the patient was sufficient to release the affect which had been isolated from his memories of the mourned love object. The patient was shaken with grief. The catharsis afforded by this experience shattered the apathy which he had suffered since the disruption of his love relationship. This brief abreaction was followed by a further massive grief reaction, in which the original affect attending his loss was allowed full expression. Following this there was a slow regeneration of his interest in another love object.

4. DIRECTIVE THERAPY

In the case of individuals who are either too old or too inflexible or wherever intensive psychotherapy is impossible or inadvisable the TAT may be useful as a guide to directive therapy.

As an example let us consider the case of a man in his middle fifties whose symptom was a curious inability to make correct change. When given a five dollar bill on his route, he would return change as though it had been a ten dollar bill, feeling compelled to do this. Under questioning it was revealed that this behavior was particularly compulsive when he experienced most serious sexual frustration and with women who were sexually attractive to him.

He suffered continual sexual frustration. For weeks after each sexual experience he felt debilitated. He was unable to keep awake, and experienced pain in his genitals which he described as a "raging toothache down there." He believed that intercourse was so harmful that he typically set the alarm clock to ring five minutes after he began intercourse with his wife and when it rang would terminate the intercourse. His wife had been suffering this frustration with him for eighteen years. He also believed that any position but the common one of man astride woman was perverted and might lead to even more serious consequences. Because of the reference to "a toothache down there" I asked him whether he ever bit his wife during intercourse. This he vehemently denied. Before the TAT was administered the examiner hypothecated a fusion of aggression with the sexual wish—that he was in per-forming the sexual act venting aggression and that his pain and debility were punishment for what he had done. This was supported by many of his TAT stories, particularly by his interpretation of picture 13 depicting a naked woman in bed with a man standing over her.

> Husband has just killed or choked his wife—quarrel of some kind—bowed down with remorse—he is greatly worried and doesn't know what to do. She's lying half undressed on the bed. The result will be that he will be punished for his acts—act I mean.

This individual had a long history of unhappy relationships with women. His mother left him when their home was broken. His first wife left him during the depression when he lost his job and though he has lived for many years with his second wife there appears to be a great deal of residual aggression which he can express only in the act of sexual intercourse.

It was in this context that the therapist adopted strictly directive therapy, trying to relieve the sex act of some of its symbolic aggressive meaning. The results of the TAT were not discussed at all but reassurance was given that sex was not harmful, that he could indulge in it freely and that he might adopt any position which he and his wife found satisfying. He was so electrified by this revelation that he asked the therapist to repeat it over and over again for an hour and a half. It is not difficult to understand why he could not believe this. It was as though the therapist had given him permission to murder his wife. Previously he had attended a Y.M.C.A. course on sex in marriage and had left the course after hearing the lecturer advise that in marriage any position in sex was morally justifiable. Since this individual had a history of some 25 years of organic and psychiatric treatment we are certain that this was not the first time he had been reassured and that his acceptance of the therapist's suggestions might be short-lived. This we cannot say. He was never seen again.

5. LIMITATIONS

Useful as the TAT may be in diagnosis and therapy, there are many real limitations of its efficacy. In acutely disturbed individuals, the TAT may so intensify anxiety that it is contraindicated. In our experience, it may actually precipitate acute attacks of anxiety or depression. We do not yet know the conditions under which this will or will not happen.

Further, when the person is acutely disturbed we frequently find in the TAT stories nothing more than a reflection of this state with no indication whatever of the dynamics or origin of the state or even the content of anxiety. In certain cases, notably hysteria and anxiety, we find critical areas producing only shock reactions so that we can only say that there is anxiety but have no basis for further inference. Thus a typical hysteric reaction to a sex picture is that of the patient who says, "Gee, I don't know. . . . Kind of disgusting picture. . . . I don't know. I suppose everything will be okay."

Finally, it must not be supposed that one has only to read a patient his own phantasies and expect him to be capable of accepting and assimilating them.

In the next case the patient was asked to free-associate to his own story.

This girl has two books in her hands and she has just been turning in the opposite direction where she saw the woman leaning against the tree carrying a child—pregnant—and as she thought of the scene of domestic peace—the woman carrying the child and the man caring for the garden—she said to herself "that is not for me yet—I'll go back to my studies and later on I will give birth to a child—or I will have a child." What brought her up to the scene is that she is interested in gardening and loved horses. The outcome of it is that she goes back to school and continues her studies.

His associations to this story were as follows:

I have always loved understanding—which I have associated with my mother. I have always wanted to produce something. I have been ashamed of what I have produced—particularly my master's thesis—which was said to be the best one that had ever been done—but it didn't satisfy me. As a boy I used to read the classics, used to daydream—wondering whether I would be able to fulfil my ideals and aspirations. I set them very high—higher than I would ever attain. Since then I know that ideals have a lot of the content of illusion about them. Sometimes I feel as though it isn't worth trying because I can never really attain what I am aiming for. My flight into literature I think was an escape from reality.

When it was pointed out that his wish to produce something and his shame at his efforts might be related to the story of the girl whose aim it was to "give birth to a child" or "have" a child, this was considered too fantastic and bizarre a suggestion to be taken seriously. However, the frustration of his intense wish to create "something beautiful," a derivative of this earlier wish, was freely admitted. In this particular case therapy would have proceeded at a much more rapid pace had the origins of his wishes been left undisclosed. He was very excited by modern architecture and wished to do creative design in this field. Had the therapist been able to direct him into this without associating it with the identification with his mother, the suggestion would probably have been eagerly accepted. But the therapist's premature association of the present interest in creative design with the consciously unacceptable wish to create a child, provoked anxiety about an ambition which had previously been completely satisfying.

In this case the derivative of the original wish is freely admitted, the source denied. The reverse may also be true. The source is admitted, but the derivative is unacceptable. The following patient was also asked to free-associate to his own story.

> Here the impression gained is one of an old man who had early in his life done something which for the sake of a story say he had in some way "wronged" his wife. Possibly his wife had wanted children from the marriage and this man because of a dislike for children prevented him from carrying out his side of the marriage contract, that of having children. Then his wife in complete unhappiness had died. As the man advanced in years he, because of loneliness had become increasingly aware of just how cruel he had been to his wife and how through his cruelty to her had created his own state of unhappiness. Lonely and with sorrow in his heart he made his nightly pilgrimages to the grave of his wife where he prayed for forgiveness for what he had brought about. These pilgrimages he had maintained until his death.

His free associations to this story were the following:

> It's a funny thing—which I don't understand—the other day my mother asked me to change rooms with my younger brother and his wife, who had come to live with us till they can find a place of their own. She said my room was larger and that they ought to have it. For some reason I suddenly saw red, and became unreasonably enraged, and though I didn't say anything I felt as though I would lose control of myself. I don't understand it.

Further questioning revealed a long history of fighting with his younger brother and hatred of his mother for the preferential treatment accorded his brother. In early childhood, he had frequently accused her of being unfair. But these differences had been reconciled as he grew older. This was the first outburst of his former hostility, and the patient was able to understand the relationship when it was shown to him. But when I suggested the possible consequences of this hatred of the sibling for his marriage and his own future children, it created anxiety and he vehemently denied this. He then denied that he had ever felt hostile towards either his brother or mother. During the next few days he experienced acute anxiety as the result of this interpretation. Within a week he was able to admit the intensity of his feelings towards both mother and brother, but he was not able to assimilate the possibility that this same feeling might be transferred to his wife and children if he married. It was only some weeks later that he asked what to do if he should find himself reacting in this way in the marital situation.

In these two cases we find contrasting relationships between early and contemporary conflicts. In the first, the early wish is completely unacceptable, the derivative completely satisfying. In the second, the early hostility is known and admitted, the later consequences cannot be so easily tolerated.

But there are numerous cases in which neither the source nor present derivatives revealed in the TAT can be assimilated into consciousness. The same assessment of the readiness of an individual to accept anxiety-laden material must be employed in the use of the TAT as in any other type of therapeutic effort. As with any effective instrument its use is attended with equal potentialities of harm and benefit.

SUMMARY

We have examined briefly the usefulness of the TAT as a diagnostic instrument in clinical practice, how it may be employed as a method of exploration before therapy is undertaken and how it may supplement interview material.

As an adjunct of therapy the TAT may be helpful in eliciting memories long repressed. It may be used with more assurance in assessing the attitude of the patient toward psychotherapy. In the psychotherapy of children the TAT may be useful as a type of play therapy, although the conditions under which it may or may not serve such a function are still obscure. It has been found effective in stimulating catharsis of repressed feelings of grief, if interpretation is given, followed by reading to the patient those stories on which the interpretation is based. Whenever intensive psychotherapy is impossible or inadvisable, the TAT may be useful as a guide to directive therapy.

We have also examined some of the limitations in the use of this instrument in diagnosis and therapy. It may intensify or precipitate acute attacks of anxiety. Moreover, when the individual is acutely disturbed, the TAT stories may reflect no more than his anxiety state; the content of this anxiety, its dynamics and origins may be completely absent from the stories. Finally, there are many individuals who cannot or will not assimilate interpretations based on their TAT protocol. The readiness of the individual to assimilate such interpretation must be assessed with the caution essential in any type of psychotherapy.

REFERENCES

1. Amen, E. W.: Individual differences in apperceptive reaction: A study of the response of preschool children to pictures. Genet. Psychol. Monograph, 23: 319–385, 1941.
2. Balken, E. R., and Masserman, J. H.: The language of fantasy: III. The language of the fantasies of patients with conversion hysteria, anxiety state, and obsessive-compulsive neurosis. J. Psychol., 10: 75–86, 1940.
3. ——, and Van der Veer, A. H.: The clinical application of the Thematic Apperception Test to neurotic children. Psychol. Bull., 37: 517, 1940 (abstr.)
4. ——: Projective techniques for the study of personality: a critique. Psychol. Bull., 38: 596, 1941.
5. ——, and Van der Veer, A. H.: The clinical application of a test of imagination to neurotic children. Am. J. Orthopsychiat., 12: 68–80, 1942.
6. ——: A delineation of schizophrenic language and thought in a test of imagination. J. Psychol., 16: 239–271, 1943.
7. ——: Thematic Apperception. J. Psychol., 20: 189–197, 1945.
8. Bellak, L.: Analysis of the Thematic Apperception Test. Cambridge: Harvard Psychological Clinic (mimeographed).
9. ——: An experimental investigation of projection. Psychol Bull., 39: 489, 1942.
10. ——, and Jaques, E.: On the problem of dynamic conceptualization in case studies. Char. & Pers., 11: 20–39, 1942.
11. ——: The concept of projection: an experimental investigation and study of the concept. Psychiatry, 7: 353–370, 1944.
12. Bennett, G.: Some factors related to substitute value of activities in normal and schizophrenic persons: a technique for investigation of central areas of the personality. Char. & Pers., 10: 42–50, 1941.
13. ——: Some factors related to substitute value at the level of fantasy. Psychol. Bull., 39: 488, 1942.
14. Berman, P. M.: A method for diagnosing social relations from the Thematic Apperception Test. Radcliffe College (unpublished thesis), 1943.
15. Bishop, F., and Kelly, G. A.: A projective method of personality investigation. Psychol. Bull., 39: 599, 1942.
16. Brenman, M.: The recall of fairy tales in normal and hypnotic states. Psychol. Bull., 39: 488, 1942.
17. Brittain, H. L.: A study in imagination. Ped. Sem., 14: 137–207, 1907.
18. Cattell, R. B.: Projection and the design of projective tests of personality. Char. & Pers., 12: 177–194, 1944.
19. Christenson, J. A.: Clinical application of the Thematic Apperception Test. J. Abnorm. & Social Psychol., 38: 104–106, 1943.
20. Clark, L. P.: The phantasy method of analyzing narcissistic neurosis. Med. J. & Rec., 123: 154–158, 1926.
21. Clark, R.: A method of administering and evaluating the Thematic Apperception Test in group situations. Genet. Psychol. Monograph, 30: 1–55, 1944.
22. Combs, A. W.: A method of analysis for the Thematic Apperception Test and autobiography. J. Clin. Psychol., 2: 167–174, 1946.

23. ——: The validity and reliability of interpretation from autobiography and Thematic Apperception Test. J. Clin. Psychol., **2**: 240–247, 1946.

24. ——: The use of personal experience in Thematic Apperception Test story plots. J. Clin. Psychol., **2**: 357–363, 1946.

25. ——: A comparative study of motivations as revealed in Thematic Apperception stories and autobiography. J. Clin. Psychol., **3**: 65–74, 1947.

26. Deabler, H. L.: Use of Murray's "need psychology" in college personnel work. Psychol. Bull., **39**: 431, 1942.

27. Ebbinghaus, H.: Ueber eine neue Methode zur Prufung geistiger Fahigkeiten und ihre Anwendung bei Schulkindern. ZPs, **13**: 401–459, 1897.

28. Finkelstein, H.: Contributions of the thematic apperception test to the understanding of parent-son relationships. Radcliffe College (unpublished thesis), 1943.

29. Frank, L. K.: Projective methods for the study of personality. J. Psychol., **8**: 389–413, 1939.

30. Frenkel-Brunswik, E., and Sanford, R. N.: Some personality factors in anti-Semitism. J. Psychol., **20**: 271–291, 1945.

31. ——: Personality and prejudice in women. Am. Psychol., **1**: 239, 1946 (abstr.)

32. Freud, S.: General Introduction to Psychoanalysis. New York: Boni & Liveright, 1920.

33. Galton, F.: Brain, **2**: 149–162, 1880.

34. Garfield, S.: Clinical values of projective techniques in an army hospital. J. Clin. Psychol., **2**: 88–91, 1946.

35. Gerber, J. M.: Level of interpretation of children on the Thematic Apperception Test. Ohio State University (unpublished M.A. thesis), 1946.

36. Goodman, H.: The psychogenesis of conversion hysteria and anxiety states. Harvard University (unpublished thesis), 1944.

37. Harrison, R.: Studies in the use and validity of the Thematic Apperception Test with mentally disordered patients. II. A quantitative validity study. III. Validation by the method of "blind analysis." Char. & Pers., **9**: 122–133, 134–138, 1940.

38. ——: The Thematic Apperception and Rorschach methods of personality investigation in clinical practice. J. Psychol., **15**: 49–74, 1943.

39. ——, and Rotter, J. B.: A note on the reliability of the Thematic Apperception Test. J. Abnorm. & Social Psychol., **40**: 97–99, 1945.

40. Henry, W. E.: The Thematic Apperception technique in the study of culture-personality relations. Genet. Psychol. Monograph, **35**: 1–134, 1947.

41. Hood, J. A.: The selection of pictures for the exploration of personality by the projection method. University of Southern California (unpublished thesis), 1942.

42. Horn, D.: An experimental study of the diagnostic process in the clinical investigation of personality. Harvard University (unpublished Ph.D. thesis), 1943.

43. Horney, K.: Our Inner Conflicts. New York: W. W. Norton & Company, 1945.

44. Hutt, M. L.: The use of projective methods of personality measurement in army medical installations. J. Clin. Psychol., **1**: 134–140, 1945.

45. Jaques, E.: The clinical use of the Thematic Apperception Test with soldiers. J. Abnorm. & Social Psychol., **40**: 363–375, 1945.

46. Jung, C. G.: Studies in Word Association. (Translated by M. D. Eder.) New York: Moffatt Yard & Co., 1919

47. Kendig, I. V.: Projective techniques as a psychological tool in diagnosis. J. Clin. Psychopath. Psychother., **6**: 101–110, 1944.

48. Klein, G.: Scoring manual for the thematic apperception test—research form. Army Testing Program (mimeographed).

49. Kutash, S. B.: Performance of psychopathic defective criminals on the Thematic Apperception Test. J. Crim. Psychopathol., **5**: 319–340, 1943.

50. Lasaga y Travieso, J. I., and Martinez-Arango, C.: Some suggestions concerning the administration and interpretation of the TAT. J. Psychol., **22**: 117–163, 1946.

51. Lewin, K.: A Dynamic Theory of Personality. New York: McGraw-Hill, 1935.

52. Libby, W.: The imagination of adolescents. Am. J. Psychol., **19**: 249–252, 1908.

53. Loeblowitz-Lennard, H., and Riessman, F.: Recall in the Thematic Apperception Test: an experimental investigation into the meaning of recall of phantasy with reference to personality diagnosis. J. Pers., **14**: 41–46, 1945.

54. MacFarlane, J. W.: Critique of projective techniques. Psychol. Bull., **38**: 745, 1941.

55. Markmann, R.: Predictions of manifest personality trends by a thematic analysis of three pictures of the thematic apperception test. Radcliffe College (unpublished thesis), 1943.

56. Masserman, J. H., and Balken, E. R.: The clinical application of phantasy studies. J. Psychol., **6**: 81–88, 1938.

57. ——, and ——: The psychoanalytic and psychiatric significance of phantasy. Psychoanalyt. Rev., **26**: 343–379, 535–549, 1939.

58. Mayman, M., and Kutner, B.: Reliability of a procedure used in analyzing Thematic Apperception Test stories. (In preparation.)

59. Meadow, A.: An analysis of Japanese character structure. 73 pp.

60. Mill, J. S.: A System of Logic. London, 1843.

61. Mitchell, S.: The relationship between the TAT and overt behavior. Radcliffe College (unpublished thesis), 1943.

62. Morgan, C. D., and Murray, H. A.: A method for investigating phantasies: the Thematic Apperception Test. Arch. Neurol. & Psychiat., **34**: 289–306, 1935.

63. Murray, H. A.: Explorations in Personality. New York: Oxford University Press, 1938, 761 pp.

64. ——, and Bellak, L.: Thematic Apperception Test blank. Cambridge: Harvard Psychological Clinic, 1941 (mimeographed).

65. ——: Thematic Apperception Test direction. Cambridge: Harvard Psychological Clinic, 1942 (mimeographed), 9 pp.

66. ——: Thematic Apperception Test manual. Cambridge: Harvard University Press, 1943, 20 pp.

67. ——, and Stein, M.: Note on the selection of combat officers. Psychosom. Med., **5**: 386–391, 1943.

68. Oppenheimer, F.: Pamela: a case study in status symbols. J. Abnorm. & Social Psychol., **40**: 187–194, 1945.

69. Rapaport, D.: The Thematic Apperception Test: qualitative conclusions as to its interpretation. Psychol. Bull., **39**: 592, 1942.

70. ——: Principles underlying projective techniques. Char. & Pers., **10**: 213–219, 1942.

71. ——: The clinical application of the Thematic Apperception Test. Bull. Menninger Clin., **7**: 106–113, 1943.

72. ——: Diagnostic Psychological Testing. Chicago: The Year Book Publishers, 1946, vol. 2, 516 pp.

73. Rautman, A. L., and Brower, E.: War themes in children's stories. J. Psychol., **19**: 191–202, 1945.

74. Renaud, H.: Group differences in fantasies: head injuries, psychoneurotics, and brain diseases. J. Psychol., **21**: 327–346, 1946.

75. Richardson, L. H.: The personality of stutterers. Psychol. Monograph, **56**: 41 pp. 1944.

76. Rodnick, E. H., and Klebanoff, S. G.: Projective reactions to induced frustrations as a measure of social adjustment. Psychol. Bull., **39**: 489, 1942.

77. Rosenzweig, S., and Sarason, S.: An experimental study of the triadic hypothesis reaction to frustration, ego-defense and hypnotizability. I. Correlational approach. II. Thematic Apperception approach. Char. & Pers., **11**: 1–19, 150–165, 1942.

78. ——: Fantasy in personality and its study by test procedures. J. Abnorm. & Social Psychol., **37**: 1012, 1942.

79. Rotter, J. B.: Studies in the use and validity of the Thematic Apperception Test with mentally disordered patients. I. Method of analysis and clinical problems. Char. & Pers., **9**: 18–34, 1940.

80. ——: Thematic Apperception Test: Suggestions for administration and interpretation. J. Pers. **15**: 70–92, 1946.

81. Sanford, F. H.: Speech and personality: a comparative case study. Char. & Pers., **10**: 169–198, 1942.

82. Sanford, R. N.: Thematic Apperception Test—directions for administration and scoring. Cambridge: Harvard Psychological Clinic, 1939 (mimeographed), 48 pp.

83. ——: Some quantitative results from the analysis of children's stories. Psychol. Bull., **38**: 749, 1941.

84. —— et al.; Physique, personality and scholarship. Monographs of the Society for Research in Child Development, **8**: 705 pp., 1943.

85. Sarason, S. B., and Rosenzweig, S.: An experimental study of the triadic hypothesis· reaction to frustration, ego-defense, and hypnotizability. II. Thematic apperception approach. Char. & Pers., **11**: 150–165, 1942.

86. ——: The use of the Thematic Apperception Test with mentally deficient children. I. A study of high grade girls. Am. J. Ment. Deficiency, **47**: 414–421, 1943.

87. ——: Dreams and Thematic Apperception Test stories. J. Abnorm. & Social Psychol. **39**: 486–492, 1944.

88. ——: The use of the Thematic Apperception Test with mentally deficient children II. A study of high grade boys. Am. J. Ment. Deficiency, **48**: 169–173, 1944.

89. ——: Projective techniques in mental deficiency. Char. & Pers., **13**: 237–245, 1945

90. Sargent, H.: Projective methods: their origins, theory, and application in personality research. Psychol. Bull., **5**: 257–293, 1945.

91. Schwartz, L. A.: Social-situation pictures in the psychiatric interview. Paper presented at the meeting of the American Orthopsychiatric Association, 1931.

92. ——: Social situation pictures in the psychiatric interview. Am. J. Orthopsychiat., **2**: 124–132, 1932.

93. Shakow, D., Rodnick, E. H., and Lebeaux T.: A psychological study of a schizophrenic: exemplification of a method. J. Abnorm. & Social Psychol., **40**: 154–174, 1945.

94. Slutz, M.: The unique contributions of the Thematic Apperception Test to a developmental study. Psychol. Bull., **38**: 704, 1941.

95. Symonds, P. M.: Criteria for the selection of pictures for the investigation of adolescent phantasies. J. Abnorm. & Social Psychol., **34**: 271–274, 1939.

96. ——: Adolescent phantasy. Psychol. Bull., **38**: 596, 1941.

97. Temple, R., and Amen, E. W.: A study of anxiety reactions in young children by means of a projective technique. Genet. Psychol. Monograph, **30:** 59–114, 1944.

98. Tomkins, S. S.: Limits of material obtainable in the single case study by daily administration of the Thematic Apperception Test. Psychol. Bull., **39:** 490, 1942.

99. ——: Reliability of repeated TAT's as a function of the temporal interval between administrations. (unpublished study.)

100. Vernon, M. D.: The relation of cognition and phantasy in children. Brit. J. Psychol. Part I, **30:** 273–295, 1940; Part II, **31:** 1–22, 1940.

101. Wells, H.: Differences between delinquent and non-delinquent boys as indicated by the Thematic Apperception Test. Psychol. Bull., **42:** 534, 1945.

102. White, R. W.: Prediction of hypnotic suggestibility from a knowledge of subject's attitudes. J. Psychol., **3:** 265–277, 1937.

103. ——, and Sanford, R. N: Thematic Apperception Test. Cambridge: Harvard Psychological Clinic, 1941 (mimeographed), 15 pp.

104. ——: The personality of Joseph Kidd. Char. & Pers., **11:** 183–208, 318–360, 1943.

105. ——: Interpretation of imaginative productions. In Personality and Behavior Disorders, by J. McV. Hunt, pp. 235–239. New York: Ronald Press, 1944.

106. ——, Tomkins, S. S., and Alper T. G.: The realistic synthesis: a personality study. J. Abnorm. & Social Psychol., **40:** 228–248, 1945.

107. Wolfstein, M.: The reality principles in story preferences of neurotics and psychotics. Char. & Pers., **13:** 135–151, 1944.

108. Wyatt, F.: Formal aspects of the Thematic Apperception Test. Psychol. Bull., **39:** 491, 1942.

109. ——: Advances in the technique of the Thematic Apperception Test. Psychol. Bull., **42:** 532, 1945.

110. ——: Personality diagnosis in psychosomatic disturbances. Am. Psychol., **1:** 264, 1946 (abstr.)

INDEX

A

Active figures, identification with, 256, 265
Activity, 166
Administration, 21–24
  effectiveness, 25
  inquiry, 24
  instructions, 21ff
  rapport, 23
  recording, 24
  rejection, 22
  set-up, 21
Affect and intensity, 111, 255, 265
Age trends, 2
  in parent-child relationships, 132f
Aggression, 8, 10, 27, 83–87, 89f, 90–102, 148, 167ff, 236, 266
Agreement and difference, joint method of, 44f
Agreement, method of, 43f
Alper, T. G., 134
Ambiguous figures, interpretation of, 110, 256, 265
Ambivalence, 89ff
Antisocial behavior
  and overt behavior, 227–232
  dimensions of, 201–221
  direction, 205f, 232
  duration, 210, 232
  form, 201f, 232
  impact on other regions, 225ff, 233
  interpretation, 221–232, 233
  motivation, 202–205, 232
  role of hero, 206–210, 232
    sequelae, 211–221, 232
  temporal characteristics, 225, 233
Antisocial wishes, 266
Anxiety, 57, 64, 103, 104, 227, 236, 267, 284, 286
Applause, 237
Atonement, 221
Awareness, analysis of, 68–71, 105

B

Balken, E., 15
Barrier solution, 250f

Behavior, level of, 58, 63, 103, 248f
Bellak, L., 8, 12
Binet, Alfred, 1
Blank card, instruction, 23
Brain pathology, 10, 15, 27, 79
Brint, 148f
Brittain, H. L., 2

C

Cathesis, 279–282, 286
Cathexis of means, 249ff
Causes, two factors, both necessary and sufficient, 46ff
  either of two factors but not both, 48f
  either or both of two factors, 49f
Central value, 51, 190
Clark, L. P., 2
Clark, R., 5
Concomitant variation, method of, 45f
Condition abundance, 202
Condition lack, 203, 204
Conditions, definition, 31f
  objects, 34
Conflict, 74ff, 106, 111–114, 151, 154f, 214ff, 257
Coombs, A. W., 4, 10
Creativity, 237

D

Daydreams, level of (See Phantasy)
Dependence, 153, 236
Depression, 169
Diagnosis, 266–269
Difference, method of, 44
Differentiation
  of means and ends, 245f
  of older figures, 123
Dimensions
  of love and marital region, 153–170
  of sex region, 170–184
Dimensions of analysis, 26–29
  functional interrelations, 194–198, 200
  generality vs. specificity of concepts, 26ff
Direct reference, 109, 151, 176, 255, 265

Directive therapy (See Therapy)
Disruption of love relationship
    dimensions, 195, 196ff
    related to variation in other dimen-
        sions, 195, 196ff
    sequelae, 164–170
    source, 161f
Distance (See Remoteness)
Dominance, 115–118, 126, 140f, 154
Dreams (See Validity of TAT, 101)
Duration
    of love relationship, 158–161
    of reformation, 220f
    of sex relationship, 178

E

Early picture interpretation tests, 25
Ebbinghaus, H., 1
Effectiveness (See Administration)
Eggman, 134, 139
Ego Ideal, 118, 254, 265
Endogenous inhibition, 183f, 199
Endogenous punishment, 218
Endurance, 252ff, 265
Events, level of, 64
Exhibitionism, 172
Exogenous inhibition, 182f, 199
Exogenous punishment, 211–218
    attitude toward, 213–216
    nature and duration, 212f
    relatedness of crime and punish-
        ment, 217f
    success or failure of resistance, 216f
Experimentally-induced change (See
    Reliability)
Extensity, 73f, 81f, 106
Extraverts, 58, 63, 103, 104

F

Fame, 236, 237
Family
    conflict with other regions, 111–114,
        151
    direct reference to, 109, 151
    intensity of affect, 111, 151
    number and length of stories, 110,
        151
    parental impact within family, 114–
        123, 151
Feeling of inadequacy, 179, 183; (See
    also Inferiority)

Frank, 149f
Free association, 1, 72, 102
Freud, S., 72, 76, 101, 109
Future security, 240

G

Galton, F., 1
Gratuities, 63, 104
Grief, 64, 104, 279
Guilt, 64, 104, 179, 227

H

Harrison, F., 4, 12, 13, 14
Harvard Psychological Clinic, 3, 5
Helmler, 134–139
Help as work motive, 238
Henry, W. F., 12, 14, 25, 103
Hero, 124
    as instigator of antisocial behavior,
        206f
Heterosexual relationships, 170–172
History of TAT, 3f
Homosexual relationships, 172–175
Horn, D., 13
Horney, K., 29

I

Impact
    of family in other regions, 119–123
    of parents within family, 114–119
    of work on other regions, 258, 265
Impotence, 179, 183
Impulsivity, 63
Inferiority, 85–87, 204, 235
Inhibition, 63, 105
    of sexual behavior, 178–184
Inquiry (See Administration)
Intensity 73f, 81f, 106, 111, 255, 265
    of love need, 157
    of sex need, 176f
    related to variation in other dimen-
        sions, 194, 195, 196f
Introversion, 58, 103, 185
Invariance, 52
    of behavioral level, 58, 63, 103
    of level of feeling, thought, mood
        or memory, 58, 103, 191,
        200, 222

K

Karol, 142–147
Kidd, Joseph, 7, 71
Klebanoff, S. G., 8
Kutash, S. B., 59, 103, 227
Kutner, B., 4

L

Lans, 147f
Lasaga y Travieso, J. I., 22
Levels, definition of, 30f
    and work, 241–245
    cause and effect relations, 59ff, 103
    invariance of, 57ff, 103
    objects, 33f
    relative frequency of, 59, 103
    sequence analysis of, 61–68, 104f
Lewin, K., 29
Libby, W., 2
Love region, 124
    definition of situation, 153–156,
        194ff, 198
    dimensions of, 153–170
    disruption of, 155f, 161–170, 198f
    intensity, 157, 198
    reciprocity, 156f, 198
    temporal characteristics, 157–161,
        198

M

Maintenance of love relationship, 162ff
Marine, case of, 57
Markmann, R., 10, 138
Marna, 139–142
Masochism, 172
Masserman, J., 15
Masturbation, 175
Maturation
    of love relationship, 157f
    of sex relationship, 177f
Mayman, M., 4
Means, cathexis of, 249ff
Means-ends, 128
    cognizance, 246ff
    differentiation of, 245f
    elaboration, 247ff
Memory, 64
Mental defectives, 10
Mill, J. S., 43
Morgan, C. D., 3, 12

Motivation
    in work region, 234–241
    of antisocial behavior, 202–205
Multifactor analysis, 50ff
    invariance, 52
    necessary conditions, 52f, 184, 200
    threat, 51f
    values, 51
Murray, H. A., 3, 10, 12, 14, 21, 22, 23,
    24, 25, 26, 29, 56, 57, 103

N

Nancy, 184–190
Navaho, 12, 14, 25, 59, 103
Necessary conditions, 52f, 191
Need-press analysis, 26f, 55ff
Number and length of stories, 110, 255,
    265

O

Object description, level of, 103
Older figures, 110, 123, 151
Organization, 251
Overt and covert needs, 55ff, 102f

P

Parent-child relationships
    changes in, 132ff, 151f
    generalization of, 123–131, 151
Parental figures,
    impact on other regions, 114–123,
        151
    interpretation of ambiguous figures,
        110, 151
    interpretation of older figures, 110,
        151
    introduction of, 109f, 151
        omission of older figures, 110, 151
Passive figures, omission of, 256, 265
Passive pictures, restructuration, 256, 265
Passivity, 62f
    rejection of, 257, 265
Personality stability (See Reliability)
Phantasy, level of, 241ff, 248f, 264
Physical handicap, 236
Play therapy (See Therapy)
Poverty, 202, 203, 235
Power motive, 240
Prediction (See Validity of TAT)

Pressure, 73–76, 106
    estimate of pressure of repressed wish, 82
    estimate of pressure of repressing wish, 82
    estimate of ratio of conflicting pressures to total pressure, 80
    ratio of conflicting pressures, 74f, 107f
    ratio of conflicting pressures and ratio of combined pressures to total pressure, 75f
    relation of conflicting pressures to total pressure, 74, 107
Psychoanalysis, 12, 75f
Psychoneuroses, 10, 15, 27, 76
Psychopathic defective criminal, 59, 103, 227
Psychoses, 15, 76
Punishment, 211–219

Q

Qualifiers, 32f

R

Rapaport, D., 21, 22, 24, 25
Realism, 246
Reciprocity in love relationship, 156f
    as related to variation in other dimensions, 194, 195, 196
    in sexual relationship, 175f
Reconciliation, 163, 164
Recording (See Administration)
Reformation, 163, 219ff
Rejection, 183, 204, 235
Reliability, 4–9
    and elapsed interval, 6
    and experimentally induced change, 8f
    and personality stability, 7f
    interpreter reliability, 4f
    repeat reliability, 6–9
Remorse, 169f, 180
Remoteness, 27, 78ff, 107
    estimate of degree, 81
Renaud, H., 11, 15, 26, 79
Repayment, 239

Repression, 72–84, 105f
    eliciting repressed memories, 270ff
    history, 72
    identification of repressed wishes, 82
    measurement, 77–82, 101
    theory, 73–76, 106
Resistance, 72, 213f
Responsibility, acceptance of, 209f
Richardson, L. H., 15
Rivalry, 238
Rodnick, E. H., 8
Rorschach test, 12
Rotter, J. B., 4, 13, 21

S

Sadism, 172
Sanford, R. N., 4, 7, 26, 55, 56, 57, 102f
Sarason, S. B., 11
Schwartz, L. A., 3
Scoring sample, 34–41
Sequence analysis (See Levels)
Sex, 90–102, 266
Sex differences, 2
Sex region
    dimensions, 170–184
    hetrosexual relationships, 170–172
    homosexual relationships, 172–175, 199
    inhibition, 178–184, 199
    reciprocity, 175f, 199
    temporal characteristics, 177f, 199
    type of need, 170–175
Shame, 64, 104
Slutz, M., 4
Social context of antisocial behavior, 207ff
Social region, 124
Social Situation Picture Test, 3
Socio-economic status, 240
Special state, 31, 203
Spiritual fulfillment, 239
Stein, M. I., 14
Strivers, introduction of, 255f, 265
Stutterers, 15
Substitute satisfactions, 166f
Suicide, 169f, 185

Super-ego, 77, 222
Symonds, P. M., 11

T

Temporal characteristics, 157–161, 177f, 251–254
  related to variation in other dimensions, 195, 196, 197
Therapy, 270–286
  attitudes toward, 272–275, 286
  directive therapy, 282–284, 286
  instrument for catharsis, 279–282, 286
  limitations, 284ff
  play therapy, 275–279, 286
Thought, level of, 244f
Threat, 51, 190f
Time perspective, 251f, 265
Tomkins, S. S., 134

U

Unification, principle of, 28f

V

Validity of TAT, 9–19
  and case study, 13
  and dreams, 11f
  and groups of known difference, 13–16
  and past history, 10f
  and prediction, 16
  and psychoanalysis, 12
  and Rorschach test, 12
  increased validity in conjunction with other procedures, 16–19
Values, 51
Variability
  interpretation of, 192–194
  range of, 192, 200

Vector
  "against", 169, 172, 201, 203, 204
  "away from", 202
  "by", 154, 171
  "for", 154, 171, 202
  "from", 155, 172, 201, 202, 203, 204
  "on", 153, 170
  "over", 154, 171, 202
  "toward", 155, 171, 172
  "under", 203, 204
  "with", 155, 171
Vectors, definition of, 29f
  objects, 33
Voyeurism, 171

W

White, R. W., 7, 18, 71, 134
Wish
  instigators of, 64–68, 104f
  sequelae of, 61ff, 104
Work habits, 254
Work region, 124, 165
  cathexis of means, 249–251, 264
  complexity of organization, 251, 264
  conditions of, 258–263, 265
  differentiation of means-ends, 245f
  importance of, 254–258, 265
  level analysis, 241–245, 264
  means-end cognizance, 246–249, 264
  motivation of, 234–241, 264
  temporal characteristics, 251–254, 264f

X

"X", 83–87, 108

Y

"Y", 87–90, 108

Z

"Z", 7f, 11, 13, 90–102, 108, 224, 270ff, 273